AFFORDABLE HOME PLANS

430 HOME DESIGNS
FOR MODEST & MEDIUM BUDGETS

HOME PLANNERS, INC.
3275 W. INA ROAD, SUITE 110, TUCSON, ARIZONA 85741

CONTENTS

Published by Home Planners, Inc.
Editorial and Corporate Offices:
  3275 West Ina Road, Suite 110
  Tucson, Arizona 85741

Distribution Center:
  29333 Lorie Lane
  Wixom, Michigan 48393

9 8 7 6 5 4 3 2

The Affordable Home

In these times of inflated prices, the search for an affordable home can be a frustrating endeavor. A home that may meet all the necessary requirements of livability may not fall within budget considerations. And a home that meets price requirements may not serve livability needs or provide the quality extras that make a home special.

The 405 designs selected for this plan book are taken from our portfolio of designs of varying styles, sizes, types, and shapes. Our main objective was to publish a wide selection of houses and plans which, when constructed, fell into the medium cost range, yet still met the needs and wants of today's homeowners. While few of these designs are considered low-cost, none require an unlimited budget to build, and all are beautiful and functional.

Because construction costs vary to such a great degree throughout the country, it is impossible to quote a realistic cost figure for each design. A home with a $125,000 price tag in one part of the country, may be $85,000 elsewhere. For estimating purposes, it is possible to obtain a construction cost-per-square foot figure from a local builder or builders' association. Square footage costs must be regarded only as rough figures or estimates. Some houses with modest specifications may be built for $30 per square foot. Others may be as high as $60 or more per square foot. Garages, carports, porches, and basements are generally not included in the square footages quoted for each design. Cost figures for these need to be obtained separately.

A factor affecting the affordability of a new home is the degree to which the owner may become involved in its construction. If you and your family do all the painting, you have eliminated the expense of the painting subcontractor. If a family member is a tradesman and able to accomplish much of the finish work on the house, a cost-savings can be realized. Should you wish to act as your own general contractor, hiring, coordinating, and supervising the work of the many subcontractors, it may be possible to save additional sums of money. However, this is generally not recommended without some prior knowledge of, and/or experience in, residential building. And obviously, disastrous results may be the end-product of a family, without prior experience, undertaking the actual construction of a new home.

Individual specifications also impact the cost of building a home and should be carefully considered. To assure that the cost of your next house will stay within the affordable range, give much time and thought to the types of materials, fixtures, and equipment you will want to write into your specifications. There are many nonstructural areas where you, as owner, have the opportunity to select what satisfies your tastes, preferences, and requirements. Prudent selection will enhance your ability to build your affordable home. For instance, how much are you going to spend for bathroom and kitchen fixtures? How much for lighting fixtures? Is your paneling going to be the most expensive in the lumberyard or is an equally attractive but less costly type acceptable? And what about built-in furniture? Is the finish carpenter going to be on the job one week or four weeks?

Answers to these questions require that you make a distinction between your "needs" and "wants." The affordable home will be more easily attained if you remember that "needs" are just that. You must not allow their number to become unrealistically dominated by the "wants" of everyone in the family. Of course, "needs" and "wants" vary among families. Your family's "wants" may be somebody else's "needs." Nevertheless, too many "wants" can lead to the unaffordable home.

Because size is one of the prime considerations in the cost of building a house, and really the only one that can be identified on a nationwide basis, the designs in the book start at under 1,000 square feet. The One-Story Homes, beginning on page 13, range from 960 to 2,612 square feet. The 1½-Story Homes, page 103, begin at 1,200 square feet. The Two-Story Homes, page 155, start at 1,216 square feet. The smallest design in the Multi-Level Homes section, page 255, is 1,408 square feet.

When considering whether to make your next home a one-, 1½-, two-story, bi-level or tri-level, it is necessary to give a great deal of thought to how you, and the members of your family, want to function. While a two-story may be less expensive to build than a one-story with a similar number of square feet, selecting a two-story because it will be more affordable might be foolish. This would surely be the case if your family had a disdain for two-story living. But, neither would you want to house your family in a one-story if you felt the separation-of-functions feature of a tri-level design would fit its living patterns better.

Affordability may also hinge on the present size of your family and how you choose to finish-off your house. For instance, Design T162563, on pages 142-143, offers the possibility of two bedrooms on the first floor which could be supplemented by finishing off the second floor at a later date. Or, on page 286, there is Design T161974 which features a lower level whose development could easily be deferred to a later date. One-stories, like Design T162597 on page 82, will provide future informal living space when the basement is finished-off as a recreation room. Two-story designs have their expandable potential, too. Think of the expandable project potential of Design T162211, on pages 160-161, when the family room and extra bedroom are finished later.

As you review the designs in the book you will find that your affordable home can be a delightfully proportioned, eye-catching, neighborhood showplace. It need not be an unappealing, crackerbox. Its exterior can be Tudor, French, Early American, Spanish, or Contemporary. Its floor plan can be well planned with all the potential to assure years of convenient, family living patterns. With thoughtful, strategic planning, a determination of how you will participate in the construction procedure, a sorting out of your "needs" and "wants" and a decision on how many areas will be finished-off, you just may find your affordable home among the 405 designs in this plan book. You will surely discover that a study of these designs, and a review of the blueprints available for the design of your choice, is an exciting and rewarding family experience. Your first steps toward planning your affordable home can be fun and inexpensive.

How To Shop For Mortgage Money

Most people who are in the market for a new home spend months searching for the right house plan and building site. Ironically, these same people often invest very little time shopping for the money to finance their new home, though the majority will have to live with the terms of their mortgage for as long as they live in the home.

The fact is that not all lending institutions are alike, nor are the loans that they offer.

- Lending practices vary from one city and state to another. If you are a first-time builder or are new to an area, it is wise to hire a real estate (not divorce or general practice) attorney to help you unravel the maze of your area's laws and customs.
- Before talking with a lender, write down all your questions and take notes so you can make accurate comparisons.
- Do not be intimidated by financial officers. Do not hesitate to reveal what other institutions are offering; they may be challenged to meet or better the terms.

A GUIDE TO LENDERS

Where can you turn for home financing? Here is a list of sources for you to contact:

Savings and Loan Associations
Savings Banks/Mutual Savings Banks
Commercial Banks
Mortgage Banking Companies
Some Credit Unions

Each of the above institutions generally offers a variety of loan types, interest rates, and fees. It is recommended that you survey each type of institution in your area to determine exactly what type of financing is available so that you can make an intelligent and informed decision.

A GUIDE TO LOAN TYPES

Conventional Loans

These types of loans usually require a minimum down payment of 5% of the lower of the purchase price or appraised value of the property. However, in many cases, this down payment requirement has been increased to 10% depending on the type of loan and the requirements of the lending institution. Often, the minimum down payment requirement is applied to owner-occupied residences and is usually increased if the property is purchased as a vacation home or as an investment.

The most common type of conventional loan is the **fixed-rate loan** which has a fixed interest rate and fixed monthly payments. The term of the loan may vary, but such loans generally are available in fifteen- and thirty-year terms. The obvious advantage of a fifteen-year term is an earlier loan payoff as well as reduced interest charges.

Other types of conventional loans are called **adjustable rate mortgages (ARMS's)**. This type of loan usually has a lower initial interest rate than the fixed-rate loan, but the interest rate of payment may change depending on the loan terms and economic conditions. The frequency of these interest/payment adjustments depends on the individual loan, but they usually occur every twelve months.

Some key terms to understanding ARM loans are listed below:

Adjustment Period – The period between one rate change and the next. Therefore, a loan with an adjustment period of one year is known as a One Year ARM.

Index – The interest rate change is tied to an index rate. These indexes usually go up and down with the general movement of interest rates. If the index rate moves up, so does your monthly payment. If the index rate goes down, your monthly payment may also go down. There are a variety of indexes. Among the most common is the weekly average yield on U.S. Treasury securities adjusted to a constant maturity of one, three, or five years.

Margin – To determine the interest rate on an ARM, lenders add a few percentage points to the index rate. These percentage points are called the margin. The amount of the margin can differ from one lender to the next, but is usually constant through the life of the loan.

Caps – Most ARM loans limit the amount that the interest rate can increase. There are periodic caps which limit the increase from one adjustment period to the next and overall caps which limit the interest rate increase over the life of the loan.

Negative Amortization – Several ARM loans contain negative amortization which means that your mortgage balance can increase even though you are making regular monthly payments. This happens when the interest rate of the loan increases while your monthly payment remains the same.

Convertibility or Conversion Option – This is a clause in your agreement that allows you to convert the ARM to a fixed-rate mortgage at designated times. Not all ARM loans contain this option.

There are other types of less-common covential loans which are offered by many institutions: Graduated Payment Mortgages, Reverse Annuity Mortgages, and Bi-Weekly Mortgages. Consult with a financial officer of a lending institution for details on these other loan types.

Government Loans

FHA loans are government insured and have substantially lower down payments than conventional loans; however, there are maximum allowable loan amounts for these loans depending on the location of the property.

Another type of government loan is through the Veteran's Administration (VA). Like the FHA, the VA guarantees loans for eligible veterans and the spouses of those veterans who died while in the service. Down payment requirements are also extremely low on these types of loans.

There are a variety of loan types available under these government programs including fixed rate, ARM's and graduated payment mortgages. The financial officer of the lending institution will be able to explain these various loan types and the qualification standards.

How To Choose a Contractor

A contractor is part craftsman, part businessman, and part magician. Transforming your dreams and drawings into a finished house, they are responsible for the final cost of the structure, for the quality of the workmanship, and for the solving of all problems that occur quite naturally in the course of construction. Finding one suitable to build your house can take time, and even once you have found the right one, it may not be possible to contract services immediately. Those who are good are in demand and, where the season is short, they are often scheduling work up to a year in advance.

There are two types of residential contractors: the construction company and the carpenter-builder, often called a general contractor. Each of these has its advantages and disadvantages.

Carpenter-builders work directly on the job as field foremen. Because their background is that of a craftsman, their workmanship is probably good—but their paperwork may be slow or sloppy. Their overhead—which you pay for—is less than that of a large construction company. However, if the job drags on for any reason, their interest may flag because your project is overlapping their next job and eroding profits.

Construction companies that handle several projects concurrently have an office staff to keep the paperwork moving and an army of reliable subcontractors. Though you can be confident that they will meet deadlines, they may sacrifice workmanship in order to do so. Emphasizing efficiency, they are less personal to work with than a general contractor and many will not work with an individual unless there is representation by an architect.

To find a reliable contractor, start by asking friends who have built homes for recommendations. Check with local lumberyards and building supply outlets for names of possible candidates and call departments of consumer affairs. Keep in mind that these watchdog organizations can give only the number of complaints filed; they cannot tell you what percent of those claims were valid. Remember, too, that a large-volume operation is logically going to have more registered complaints against it than will an independent contractor.

Interview each of the potential candidates. Find out about specialties—custom houses, development houses, remodeling, or office buildings. Ask each to take you into—not just to the site of—current projects. Ask to see projects that are complete as well as work in progress, emphasizing that you are interested in projects comparable to yours. A $300,000 dentist's office will give you little insight into a contractor's craftsmanship.

Ask each contractor for bank references from both a commercial bank and any other appropriate lender. If in good financial standing, the contractor should have no qualms about giving you this information. Also ask about warranties. Most will give you a one-year warranty on the structure; some offer as much as a ten-year warranty.

Ask for references, even though no contractor will give you the name of a dissatisfied customer. Ask about follow-through. Was the building site cleaned up or did the owner have to dispose of the refuse? Ask about the organization of business. Did the paperwork go smoothly, or was there a delay in hooking up the sewer because of a failure to apply for a permit?

Talk to each of the candidates about fees. Most work on a "cost plus" basis; that is, the basic cost of the project—materials, subcontractors' services, wages of those working directly on the project, but not office help—plus a fee. Some have a fixed fee; others work on a percentage of the basic cost. A fixed fee is usually better for you if you can get one. If a contractor works on a percentage, ask for a cost breakdown of the best estimate and keep very careful track as the work progresses. A crafty contractor can always use a cost overrun to good advantage when working on a percentage.

Do not be overly suspicious of a contractor who won't work on a fixed fee. One who is very good and in great demand may not be willing to do so and may also be reluctant to submit a competitive bid.

Give the top two or three candidates each copies of the plans and your specifications for materials. If they are not each working from the same guidelines, the competitive bids will be of little value. Give each the same deadline for turning in a bid; two or three weeks is a reasonable period of time. Make an appointment with each of them and open the envelopes at this time.

If one bid is remarkably low, the contractor may have made an honest error in the estimate. Don't insist that the contractor hold to a bid if it is in error. Forcing a building price that is too low could be disastrous for both of you. You may want to review the bids with your architect, if you have one, or with your lender to discuss which to accept. They may not recommend the lowest. A low bid does not necessarily mean that you will get the best quality with economy.

If the bids are relatively close, the most important consideration may not be money at all. A bid from a contractor who is easy to talk to and inspires confidence may be the best choice. Any sign of a personality conflict between you and a contractor should be weighed when making a decision.

Once you have financing, you can sign a contract with the builder. Most have their own contract forms, but it is advisable to have a lawyer draw one up or, at the very least, review the standard contract. This usually costs a small flat fee.

A good contract should include the following:

- Plans and sketches of the work to be done, subject to your approval.
- A list of materials, including quantity, brand names, style or serial numbers. (Do not permit any "or equal" clause that will allow the contractor to make substitutions.)
- The terms—who (you or the lender) pays whom and when.
- A production schedule.
- The contractor's certification of insurance for workmen's compensation, damage, and liability.
- A rider stating that all changes, whether or not they increase the cost, must be submitted and approved in writing.

Of course, this list represents the least a contract should include. Once you have signed it, your plans are on the way to becoming a home.

How To Read Floor Plans and Blueprints

Selecting the most suitable house plan for your family is a matter of matching your needs, tastes, and life-style against the many designs we offer. When you study the floor plans in this issue, and the blueprints that you may subsequently order, remember that they are simply a two-dimensional representation of what will eventually be a three-dimensional reality.

Floor plans are easy to read. Rooms are clearly labeled, with dimensions given in feet and inches. Most symbols are logical and self-explanatory: The location of bathroom fixtures, planters, fireplaces, tile floors, cabinets and counters, sinks, appliances, closets, and sloped or beamed ceilings will be obvious.

A blueprint, although much more detailed, is also easy to read; all it demands is concentration. The blueprints that we offer come in many large sheets, each one of which contains a different kind of information. One sheet contains foundation and excavation drawings, another has a precise plot plan. An elevations sheet deals with the exterior walls of the house; section drawings show precise dimensions, fittings, doors, windows, and roof structures. This provides all the construction information needed by your contractor. And each set of blueprints contains a lengthy materials list with size and quantities of all necessary components. Using this list, your contractor and suppliers can make a start at calculating costs for you.

When you first study a floor plan or blueprint, imagine that you are walking through the house. By mentally visualizing each room in three dimensions, you can transform the technical data and symbols into something more real. Interior space should be organized in a logical way, based on the intended use of such space. Usually the space is divided into rooms which fall into one of three categories. The sleeping area includes bedrooms and bathrooms; the work area includes the kitchen, laundry, utility room, garage and other functional rooms; the living area includes the living and dining rooms, family room, and other gathering areas as well as entrance ways.

To begin a mental tour of the home, start at the front door. It's preferable to have a foyer or entrance hall in which to receive guests. A closet here is desirable; a powder room is a plus.

Look for good traffic circulation as you study the floor plan. You should not have to pass all the way through one main room to reach another. From the entrance area you should have direct access to the three principal areas of a house—the living, work, and sleeping zones. For example, a foyer might provide separate entrances to the living room, kitchen, patio, and a hallway or staircase leading to the bedrooms.

Study the layout of each zone. Most people expect the living room to be protected from cross traffic. The kitchen, on the other hand, should connect with the dining room—and perhaps also the utility room, basement, garage, patio or deck, or a secondary entrance. A homemaker whose workday centers in the kitchen may have special requirements: a window that faces the backyard; a

clear view of the family room where children play; a garage or driveway entrance that allows for a short trip with groceries; laundry facilities close at hand. Check for efficient placement of kitchen cabinets, counters, and appliances. Is there enough room in the kitchen for additional appliances, for eating in? Is there a dining nook?

Perhaps this part of the house contains a family room or a den/bedroom/office. It's advantageous to have a bathroom or powder room in this section.

As you study the plan, you may encounter a staircase, indicated by a group of parallel lines, the number of lines equaling the number of steps. Arrows labeled "up" mean that the staircase leads to a higher level, and those pointing down mean it leads to a lower one. Staircases in a split-level will have both up and down arrows on one staircase because two levels are depicted in one drawing and an extra level in another.

Notice the location of the stairways. Is too much floor space lost to them? Will you find yourself making too many trips?

Study the sleeping quarters. Are the bedrooms situated as you like? You may want the master bedroom near the kids, or you may want it as far away as possible. Is there at least one closet per person in each bedroom or a double one for a couple? Bathrooms should be convenient to each bedroom—if not adjoining, then with hallway access and on the same floor.

Once you are familiar with the relative positions of the rooms, look for such structural details as:

- Sufficient uninterrupted wall space for furniture arrangement.
- Adequate room dimensions.
- Potential heating or cooling problems—such as a room over a garage or next to the laundry.
- Window and door placement for good ventilation and natural light.
- Location of doorways—avoid having a basement staircase or a bathroom in view of the dining room.
- Adequate auxiliary space—closets, storage, bathrooms, countertops.
- Separation of activity areas. (Will noise from the recreation room disturb sleeping children or a parent at work?)

As you complete your mental walk through the house, bear in mind your family's long-range needs. A good house plan will allow for some adjustments now and additions in the future.

Take time to notice special amenities about the house. Look for through fireplaces and raised hearths, work islands in the kitchen, pass-through countertops between kitchen and breakfast nook, whirlpool baths, and convenient built-ins such as bookcases and wet bars. Note the placement of decks and balconies. Each member of your family may find the listing of favorite features a most helpful exercise. Why not try it?

A Checklist for Plan Selection

Developing an architectural plan from the various wants and needs of an individual or family that fits into lifestyle demands and design elegance is the most efficient way to assure a livable plan. It is not only possible but highly desirable to design a plan around such requirements as separate bedrooms for each member of the family, guest suites, a quiet study area, an oversized entertainment area, a two-car garage, a completely private master suite, and a living room fireplace. Incorporated into this can be such wants as Tudor styling, 1½-stories, a large entry hall, decks and balconies, and a basement.

In some cases, architectural style may seem to be the overwhelming consideration of a plan. However, it is important to remember that function will determine the overall livability of a home and should not be sacrificed to style. It should be a simple matter to make adjustments in style to accommodate needs without compromising any of the inherent flavor of the design.

While it is obviously best to begin with wants and needs and then design a home to fit these criteria, this is not always practical or even possible. A very effective way around this problem is to select a professionally prepared home plan which meets all needs and incorporates as many wants as possible. With careful selection, it will be possible to modify sizes and make other design adjustments to make the home as close to custom as can be. Care must be taken to choose just the right plan, however, for though some plans can be altered quite easily, some are more difficult, and some may be completely ruined by changes—a situation that could be avoided by selecting the appropriate plan. It is also important to remember that some wants may have to be compromised in the interest of meeting budgetary limitations. The important thing is to build the best possible home for the available money while satisfying all absolute needs.

Identifying wants and needs is a futile exercise without the careful consideration of costs involved. By realistically assessing costs and investigating a variety of cost-saving features that can be incorporated into wants and needs, a reasonably priced home can be had that serves livability requirements and retains style.

Following are some cost-controlling ideas that can make a big difference in the overall price of a home:

1. Square or rectangular homes are less expensive to build than irregularly shaped homes.
2. It is less expensive to build on a flat lot than on a sloping or hillside lot.
3. The use of locally manufactured or produced materials cuts costs greatly.
4. Using stock materials and stock sizes of components takes advantage of mass production cost reductions.
5. The use of materials that can be quickly installed cuts labor costs. Prefabricating large sections or panels eliminates much time on the site.
6. The use of prefinished materials saves significantly on labor costs.
7. The use of prehung doors cuts considerable time.
8. Designing the home with a minimum amount of hall space increases the usable square footage and provides more living space for the cost.
9. The use of prefabricated fireboxes for fireplaces cuts installation and foundation costs.
10. Investigating existing building codes before beginning construction eliminates unnecessary changes as construction proceeds.
11. Refraining from changing the design or any aspect of the plan after construction begins will help to hold down cost escalation.
12. Minimizing special jobs or custom-built items keeps costs from increasing.
13. Designing the house for short plumbing lines saves on piping and other materials.
14. Proper insulation saves heating and cooling costs.
15. Utilizing passive solar features, such as correct orientation, reduces future maintenance costs.

To help you consider all the important factors in evaluating a plan, the following checklist should be reviewed carefully. By comparing its various points to any plan and a wants and needs list, it will be possible to easily recognize the deficiencies of a plan or determine its appropriateness. Be sure to include family members in the decision-making process. Their ideas and desires will help in finding exactly the right plan.

CHECKLIST

The Neighborhood

1. _____ Reasonable weather conditions
2. No excess
   _____ a. wind
   _____ b. smog or fog
   _____ c. odors
   _____ d. soot or dust
3. _____ The area is residential
4. There are no
   _____ a. factories
   _____ b. dumps
   _____ c. highways
   _____ d. railroads
   _____ e. airports
   _____ f. apartments
   _____ g. commercial buildings
5. _____ City-maintained streets
6. No hazards in the area
   _____ a. quarries
   _____ b. storage tanks
   _____ c. power stations
   _____ d. unprotected swimming pools
7. Reasonably close to
   _____ a. work
   _____ b. schools
   _____ c. churches
   _____ d. hospital
   _____ e. shopping
   _____ f. recreation
   _____ g. public transportation
   _____ h. library
   _____ i. police protection
   _____ j. fire protection
   _____ k. parks
   _____ l. cultural activities
8. _____ Streets are curved
9. _____ Traffic is slow
10. _____ Intersections are at right angles
11. _____ Street lighting
12. _____ Light traffic
13. _____ Visitor parking
14. _____ Good design in street
15. _____ Paved streets and curbs
16. _____ Area is not deteriorating
17. _____ Desirable expansion
18. _____ Has some open spaces

19. _____ Numerous and healthy trees
20. _____ Pleasant-looking homes
21. _____ Space between homes
22. _____ Water drains off
23. _____ Near sewerage line
24. _____ Storm sewers nearby
25. _____ Mail delivery
26. _____ Garbage pickup
27. _____ Trash pickup
28. _____ No city assessments

The Lot

1. _____ Title is clear
2. _____ No judgments against the seller
3. _____ No restrictions as to the use of the land or the deed
4. _____ No unpaid taxes or assessments
5. _____ Minimum of 70 feet of frontage
6. _____ House does not crowd the lot
7. _____ Possible to build on
8. _____ Few future assessments (sewers, lights, and so forth)
9. _____ Good top soil and soil percolation
10. _____ Good view
11. _____ No low spots to hold water
12. _____ Water drains off land away from the house
13. _____ No fill
14. _____ No water runoff from high ground
15. _____ If cut or graded there is substantial retaining wall
16. _____ Permanent boundary markers
17. _____ Utilities available at property line
18. _____ Utility hookup is reasonable
19. _____ Utility rates are reasonable
20. _____ Taxes are reasonable
21. _____ Water supply is adequate
22. _____ Regular, simply shaped lot
23. _____ Trees
24. _____ Do not have to cut trees
25. _____ Privacy for outside activities
26. _____ Attractive front yard
27. _____ Front and rear yards are adequate
28. _____ Front yard is not divided up by walks and driveway
29. _____ Outdoor walks have stairs grouped

The Floor Plan

1. _____ Designed by licensed architect
2. _____ Supervised by reputable contractor
3. _____ Built by skilled builders
4. Orientation
    _____ *a.* sun
    _____ *b.* view
    _____ *c.* noise
    _____ *d.* breeze
    _____ *e.* contour of land
5. _____ Entry
6. _____ Planned for exterior expansion
7. Planned for interior expansion
    _____ *a.* attic
    _____ *b.* garage
    _____ *c.* basement
8. _____ Simple but functional plan
9. _____ Indoor recreation area
10. _____ Wall space for furniture in each room
11. Well-designed hall
    _____ *a.* leads to all areas
    _____ *b.* no congestions

    _____ *c.* no wasted space
    _____ *d.* 3' minimum widths
12. _____ Easy to clean
13. _____ Easy to keep orderly
14. _____ Plan meets family's needs
15. _____ All rooms have direct emergency escape
16. Doorways functional
    _____ *a.* no unnecessary doors
    _____ *b.* wide enough for moving furniture through
    _____ *c.* can see visitors through locked front door
    _____ *d.* do not swing out into halls
    _____ *e.* swing open against a blank wall
    _____ *f.* do not bump other subjects
    _____ *g.* exterior doors are solid
17. Windows are functional
    _____ *a.* not too small
    _____ *b.* enough but not too many
    _____ *c.* glare-free
    _____ *d.* roof overhang protection where needed
    _____ *e.* large ones have the best view
    _____ *f.* easy to clean
    _____ *g.* no interference with furniture placement
    _____ *h.* over kitchen sink
    _____ *i.* open easily
18. _____ No fancy gadgets
19. _____ Room sizes are adequate
20. _____ Well-designed stairs
    _____ *a.* treads are 9" minimum
    _____ *b.* risers are 8" maximum
    _____ *c.* 36" minimum width
    _____ *d.* 3' minimum landings
    _____ *e.* attractive
    _____ *f.* easily reached
21. _____ Overall plan "fits" family requirements
22. _____ Good traffic patterns
23. _____ Noisy areas separated from quiet areas
24. _____ Rooms have adequate wall space for furniture
25. _____ Halls are 3'6" minimum

The Living Area

1. _____ Minimum space 12' x 16'
2. _____ Front door traffic does not enter
3. _____ Not in a traffic pattern
4. _____ Windows on two sides
5. _____ Has a view
6. _____ Storage for books and music materials
7. _____ Decorative lighting
8. _____ Whole family plus guests can be seated
9. _____ Desk area
10. _____ Fireplace
11. _____ Wood storage
12. _____ No street noises
13. _____ Privacy from street
14. _____ Acoustical ceiling
15. _____ Cannot see or hear bathroom
16. _____ Powder room
17. _____ Comfortable for conversation
18. Dining room
    _____ *a.* used enough to justify
    _____ *b.* minimum of 3' clearance around table
    _____ *c.* can be opened or closed to kitchen and patio
    _____ *d.* can be opened or closed to living room
    _____ *e.* electrical outlets for table appliances

19. Family room
_____ *a.* minimum space 10' x 12'
_____ *b.* room for family activities
_____ *c.* room for noisy activities
_____ *d.* room for messy activities
_____ *e.* activities will not disturb sleeping area
_____ *f.* finish materials are easy to clean and durable
_____ *g.* room for expansion
_____ *h.* separate from living room
_____ *i.* near kitchen
_____ *j.* fireplace
_____ *k.* adequate storage
20. _____ Dead-end circulation
21. _____ Adequate furniture arrangements

The Entry

1. _____ The entry is a focal point
2. _____ The outside is inviting
3. _____ The landing has a minimum depth of 5'
4. _____ Protected from the weather
5. _____ Has an approach walk
6. _____ Well planted
7. _____ Coat closet
8. _____ Leads to living, sleeping, and service areas
9. _____ Floor material attractive and easy to clean
10. _____ Decorative lighting
11. _____ Space for table
12. _____ Space to hang mirror
13. _____ Does not have direct view into any room

The Bedrooms

1. _____ Adequate number of bedrooms
2. _____ Adequate size—10' x 12' minimum
3. _____ Open into a hall
4. _____ Living space
5. _____ Children's bedroom has study and play area
6. _____ Oriented to north side
7. _____ In quiet area
_____ *a.* soundproofing
_____ *b.* acoustical ceiling
_____ *c.* insulation in walls
_____ *d.* thermal glass
_____ *e.* double doors
_____ *f.* closet walls
8. _____ Privacy
9. _____ 4' minimum wardrobe rod space per person
10. _____ Master bedroom
_____ *a.* bath
_____ *b.* dressing area
_____ *c.* full-length mirror
_____ *d.* 12' x 12' minimum
11. Adequate windows
_____ *a.* natural light
_____ *b.* cross-ventilation
_____ *c.* windows on two walls
12. _____ Room for overnight guests
13. _____ Bathroom nearby
14. _____ Wall space for bed, nightstands, and dresser
15. _____ Quiet reading area

The Bathroom

1. _____ Well designed
2. _____ Plumbing lines are grouped
3. _____ Fixtures have space around them for proper use
4. _____ Doors do not interfere with fixtures
5. _____ Noises are insulated from other rooms
6. _____ Convenient to bedrooms
7. _____ Convenient to guests
8. _____ Ventilation
9. _____ Heating
10. _____ Attractive fixtures
11. _____ No windows over tub or shower
12. _____ Wall area around tub and shower
13. _____ Light fixtures are water tight
14. _____ Large medicine cabinet
15. _____ Children cannot open medicine cabinet
16. _____ No bathroom tie-ups
17. _____ Good lighting
18. _____ Accessible electrical outlets
19. _____ No electric appliance or switch near water supply
20. _____ Towel and linen storage
21. _____ Dirty clothes hamper
22. _____ Steamproof mirrors
23. _____ Wall and floor materials are waterproof
24. _____ All finishes are easy to maintain
25. _____ Curtain and towel rods securely fastened
26. _____ Grab bar by tub
27. _____ Mixing faucets
28. _____ Bath in service area
29. _____ No public view into open bathroom door
30. _____ Clean-up area for outdoor jobs and children's play

The Kitchen

1. _____ Centrally located
2. _____ The family can eat informally in the kitchen
3. _____ At least 20' of cabinet space
_____ *a.* counter space on each side of major appliances
_____ *b.* minimum of 8' counter work area
_____ *c.* round storage in corners
_____ *d.* no shelf is higher than 72"
_____ *e.* floor cabinets 24" deep and 36" high
_____ *f.* wall cabinets 15" deep
_____ *g.* 15" clearance between wall and floor cabinets
4. _____ Work triangle is formed between appliances
_____ *a.* between 12' and 20'
_____ *b.* no traffic through the work triangle
_____ *c.* refrigerator opens into the work triangle
_____ *d.* at least six electric outlets in work triangle
_____ *e.* no door between appliances
5. _____ No space between appliances and counters
6. _____ Window over sink
7. _____ No wasted space in kitchen
8. _____ Can close off kitchen from dining area
9. _____ Snack bar in kitchen
10. _____ Kitchen drawers are divided
11. _____ Built-in chopping block
12. _____ Writing and telephone desk
13. _____ Indoor play area visible from kitchen
14. _____ Outdoor play area visible from kitchen
15. _____ Exhaust fan
16. _____ Natural light
17. _____ Good lighting for each work area
18. _____ Convenient access to service area and garage
19. _____ Durable surfaces
20. _____ Dishwasher
21. _____ Disposal
22. _____ Built-in appliances
23. _____ Bathroom nearby
24. _____ Room for freezer
25. _____ Pantry storage

The Utility Room

1. _____ Adequate laundry area
2. _____ Well-lighted work areas
3. _____ 240-volt outlet
4. _____ Gas outlet
5. _____ Sorting area
6. _____ Ironing area
7. _____ Drip-drying area
8. _____ Sewing and mending area
9. _____ On least desirable side of lot
10. _____ Exit to outdoor service area
11. _____ Exit near garage
12. _____ Sufficient cabinet space
13. _____ Bathroom in area
14. _____ Accessible from kitchen
15. _____ Adequate space for washer and dryer
16. _____ Laundry tray
17. _____ Outdoor exit is protected from the weather
18. _____ Window

Working Areas

1. _____ Home repair area
2. _____ Work area for hobbies
3. _____ Storage for paints and tools
4. _____ Garage storage and collection
5. _____ Incinerator area
6. _____ Refuse area
7. _____ Delivery area
8. _____ Near parking
9. _____ 240-volt outlet for power tools

Storage

1. _____ General storage space for each person
2. _____ 4' of rod space for each person
3. _____ Closet doors are sealed to keep out dust
4. _____ Minimum wardrobe closet size is 40" x 22"
5. _____ Cedar closet storage for seasonal clothing
6. _____ Bulk storage area for seasonal paraphernalia
7. _____ Closets are lighted
8. _____ Walk-in closets have adequate turnaround area
9. Storage for:
   _____ a. linen and towels
   _____ b. cleaning materials
   _____ c. foods
   _____ d. bedding
   _____ e. outdoor furniture
   _____ f. sports equipment
   _____ g. toys—indoor
   _____ h. toys—outdoor
   _____ i. bicycles
   _____ j. luggage
   _____ k. out-of-season clothes
   _____ l. storm windows and doors
   _____ m. garden tools
   _____ n. tools and paints
   _____ o. hats
   _____ p. shoes
   _____ q. belts
   _____ r. ties
   _____ s. bridge tables and chairs
   _____ t. camping equipment
   _____ u. china
   _____ v. silver
   _____ w. minor appliances
   _____ x. books
10. _____ Closets are ventilated
11. _____ Closets do not project into room

12. _____ Toothbrush holders in bathrooms
13. _____ Soap holders in bathrooms
14. _____ Adequate built-in storage
15. _____ Drawers cannot pull out of cabinet
16. _____ Drawers slide easily
17. _____ Drawers have divided partitions
18. _____ Adult storage areas easy to reach
19. _____ Children storage areas easy to reach
20. _____ Guest storage near entry
21. _____ Heavy storage areas have reinforced floors
22. _____ Sides of closets easy to reach
23. _____ Tops of closets easy to reach
24. _____ No wasted spaces around stored articles
25. _____ Sloping roof or stairs do not render closet useless
26. _____ Entry closet

The Exterior

1. _____ The design looks "right" for the lot
2. _____ Design varies from other homes nearby
3. _____ Design fits with unity on its site
4. _____ Definite style architecture—not mixed
5. _____ Simple, honest design
6. _____ Garage design goes with the house
7. _____ Attractive on all four sides
8. _____ Colors in good taste
9. _____ Finish materials in good taste
10. _____ Has charm and warmth
11. _____ Materials are consistent on all sides
12. _____ No false building effects
13. _____ Well-designed roof lines—not chopped up
14. _____ Window tops line up
15. _____ Bathroom windows are not obvious
16. _____ Does not look like a box
17. _____ Easy maintenance of finish materials
18. _____ Windows are protected from pedestrian view
19. _____ Attractive roof covering
20. _____ Gutters on roof
21. _____ Downspouts that drain into storm sewer
22. _____ Glass area protected with overhang or trees
23. _____ Dry around the house
24. _____ Several waterproof electric outlets
25. _____ Hose bib on each side
26. _____ Style will look good in the future

Outdoor Service Area

1. _____ Clothes hanging area
2. _____ Garbage storage
3. _____ Can storage
4. _____ On least desirable side of site
5. _____ Next to indoor service area
6. _____ Near garage
7. _____ Delivery area for trucks
8. _____ Fenced off from rest of site

Outdoor Living Area

1. _____ Area for dining
2. _____ Area for games
3. _____ Area for lounging
4. _____ Area for gardening
5. _____ Fenced for privacy
6. _____ Partly shaded
7. _____ Concrete deck at convenient places
8. _____ Garden walks
9. _____ Easy access to house
10. _____ Paved area for bikes and wagons
11. _____ Easy maintenance

Landscaping

1. _____ Planting at foundation ties
2. _____ Garden area
3. _____ Well-located trees
4. _____ Healthy trees
5. _____ Plants of slow-growing variety
6. _____ Landscaping professionally advised
7. _____ Garden walks
8. _____ Easy maintenance
9. _____ Extras as trellis or gazebo

Construction

1. _____ Sound construction
2. _____ All work complies to code
3. _____ Efficient contractor and supervision
4. _____ Honest builders
5. _____ Skilled builders
6. _____ Constructed to plans
7. Floors are well constructed
   - _____ *a.* resilient
   - _____ *b.* subfloor diagonal to joints
   - _____ *c.* flat and even
   - _____ *d.* slab is not cold
   - _____ *e.* floor joists rest on 2" of sill—minimum
   - _____ *f.* girder lengths are joined under points of support
8. Foundation is well constructed
   - _____ *a.* level
   - _____ *b.* sill protected from termites
   - _____ *c.* vapor barrier
   - _____ *d.* no cracks
   - _____ *e.* no water seepage
   - _____ *f.* no dryrot in sills
   - _____ *g.* garage slab drains
   - _____ *h.* waterproofed
   - _____ *i.* walls are 8" thick
   - _____ *j.* basement height 7'6" minimum
   - _____ *k.* sills bolted to foundation
   - _____ *l.* adequate vents
9. Walls are well constructed
   - _____ *a.* plumb
   - _____ *b.* no waves
   - _____ *c.* insulation
   - _____ *d.* flashing at all exterior joints
   - _____ *e.* solid sheathing
   - _____ *f.* siding is neat and tight
   - _____ *g.* drywall joints are invisible
10. Windows are properly installed
    - _____ *a.* move freely
    - _____ *b.* weatherstripped
    - _____ *c.* caulked and sealed
    - _____ *d.* good-quality glass
11. Doors properly hung
    - _____ *a.* move freely
    - _____ *b.* exterior doors weatherstripped
    - _____ *c.* exterior doors are solid-core
    - _____ *d.* interior doors are hollow-core
12. Roof is well constructed
    - _____ *a.* rafters are straight
    - _____ *b.* all corners are flashed
    - _____ *c.* adequate vents in attic
    - _____ *d.* no leaks
    - _____ *e.* building paper under shingles
13. _____ Tile work is tight
14. _____ Hot water lines are insulated
15. _____ Mortar joints are neat
16. _____ Mortar joints do not form shelf to hold water
17. _____ Ceiling is 8'0" minimum
18. _____ No exposed pipes
19. _____ No exposed wires
20. _____ Tight joints at cabinets and appliances
21. _____ Stairs have railings
22. _____ Neat trim application
23. _____ Builder responsible for new home flaws

The Fireplace

1. _____ There is a fireplace
2. _____ Wood storage near the fireplace
3. _____ Draws smoke
4. _____ Hearth in front (minimum 10" on sides; 20" in front)
5. _____ Does not project out into the room
6. _____ Has a clean-out
7. _____ Chimney top 2' higher than roof ridge
8. _____ No leaks around chimney in roof
9. _____ No wood touches the chimney
10. _____ 2" minimum air space between framing members and masonry
11. _____ No loose mortar
12. _____ Has a damper
13. _____ Space for furniture opposite fireplace
14. _____ Doors minimum of 6' from fireplace
15. _____ Windows minimum of 3' from fireplace
16. _____ On a long wall
17. _____ Install "heatilator"
18. _____ Install glass doors to minimize heat loss

Equipment

1. _____ All equipment listed in specifications and plans
2. _____ All new equipment has warranty
3. _____ All equipment is up to code standards
4. _____ All equipment is functional and not a fad
5. _____ Owner's choice of equipment meets builder's allowance
6. _____ Public system for utilities
7. _____ Private well is deep; adequate and healthy water
8. Electrical equipment is adequate
   - _____ *a.* inspected and guaranteed
   - _____ *b.* 240 voltage
   - _____ *c.* 120 voltage
   - _____ *d.* sufficient electric outlets
   - _____ *e.* sufficient electric circuits—minimum of six
   - _____ *f.* circuit breakers
   - _____ *g.* television aerial outlet
   - _____ *h.* telephone outlets
   - _____ *i.* outlets in convenient places
9. Adequate lighting
   - _____ *a.* all rooms have general lighting
   - _____ *b.* all rooms have specific lighting for specific tasks
   - _____ *c.* silent switches
   - _____ *d.* some decorative lighting
   - _____ *e.* light at front door
   - _____ *f.* outdoor lighting
10. _____ Plumbing equipment is adequate
    - _____ *a.* inspected and guaranteed
    - _____ *b.* adequate water pressure
    - _____ *c.* hot water heater—50-gallon minimum
    - _____ *d.* shut-off valves at fixtures
    - _____ *e.* satisfactory city sewer or septic tank
    - _____ *f.* septic tank disposal field is adequate

_____ g. septic tank is large enough for house (1000 gallons for three-bedroom house, plus 250 gallons for each additional bedroom)

_____ h. water softener for hard water

_____ i. siphon vertex or siphon reverse-trap water closet

_____ j. clean-out plugs at all corners of waste lines

_____ k. water lines will not rust

_____ l. water pipes do not hammer

_____ m. waste lines drain freely

_____ n. cast iron with vitreous enamel bathtub

11. _____ Good ventilation through house and attic

12. Heating and cooling systems are adequate

_____ a. insulation in roof, ceiling, walls

_____ b. air conditioning system

_____ c. heating and cooling outlets under windows

_____ d. air purifier

_____ e. thermostatic control

_____ f. walls are clean over heat outlets

_____ g. comfortable in hot or cold weather

_____ h. automatic humidifier

_____ i. furnace blower is belt-driven

_____ j. quiet-heating plant

_____ k. ducts are tight

13. _____ Windows are of good quality

_____ a. storm windows

_____ b. secure locks

_____ c. screened

_____ d. double glazed in extreme weather (thermal)

_____ e. glass is ripple-free

_____ f. safety or safe thickness of glass

_____ g. moisture-free

_____ h. frost-free

14. Doors are of good quality

_____ a. secure locks on exterior doors

_____ b. attractive hardware

_____ c. hardware is solid brass or bronze

15. _____ All meters easily accessible to meter readers

16. _____ Fire extinguisher in house and garage

17. _____ Acoustical ceiling

18. _____ Facilities to lock mail box

19. _____ Facilities to receive large packages

20. _____ Gas or electric incinerator

21. Adequate small hardware

_____ a. soap dishes

_____ b. toilet-paper holders

_____ c. toothbrush holders

_____ d. towel holders

_____ e. bathtub grab bars

_____ f. door and drawer pulls

The Garage

1. _____ Same style as the house

2. _____ Fits with house

3. _____ Single garage 12' x 22' minimum

4. _____ Double garage 22' x 22' minimum

5. _____ Larger than minimum size if used for storage or workshop

6. _____ Protected passage to house

7. _____ Doors are safe

8. _____ Access to overhead storage

Financial Checklist

1. _____ Do you understand conveyancing fees (closing costs)?

2. _____ Is the house a good investment?

3. _____ Is the total cost approximately three times your annual income?

4. _____ Have you shopped for the best loan?

5. _____ Do you have a constant payment plan (sliding principal and interest)?

6. _____ Is there a prepayment penalty?

7. _____ Will a week's salary cover the total housing expense for one month?

8. _____ Are all the costs itemized in the contract?

9. Do you understand the following closing costs?

_____ a. title search

_____ b. lawyer

_____ c. plot survey

_____ d. insurance, fire, and public liability

_____ e. mortgage tax

_____ f. recording mortgage

_____ g. recording deed

_____ h. bank's commitment fee

_____ i. state and county taxes

_____ j. state and government revenue stamps

_____ k. title insurance (protects lender)

_____ l. homeowner's policy (protects owner)

_____ m. transferring ownership

_____ n. mortgage service charge

_____ o. appraisal

_____ p. notarizing documents

_____ q. attendant fee (paying off previous mortgage)

_____ r. personal credit check

10. _____ Do you have extra cash to cover unforeseen expenses?

11. Can you afford to pay the following?

_____ a. closing costs

_____ b. old assessments or bonds

_____ c. new assessments or bonds

_____ d. downpayment

_____ e. immediate repairs

_____ f. immediate purchases (furniture, appliances, landscape, tools, fences, carpets, drapes, patio)

_____ g. adequate insurance

_____ h. mortgage payments

_____ i. general maintenance

_____ j. utilities (water, heat, electricity, phone, gas, trash pickup)

_____ k. special design features wanted

_____ l. extras not covered in plans and contract

_____ m. prepayment of interest and taxes for first month of transition

_____ n. moving

_____ o. gardener

_____ p. travel to work

_____ q. interest on construction loan

_____ r. advances to contractors

12. _____ Who will pay for the following?

_____ a. supervision costs of architect or contractor

_____ b. inspection fees

_____ c. increased costs during building

_____ d. building permits

_____ e. difficulties in excavation

_____ f. dry wells

_____ g. extra features the building inspector insists upon

The above Checklist is used with permission. It is taken from Home Planners' Guide to Residential Design *by Charles Talcott, Don Hepler, and Paul Wallach; 1986; McGraw-Hill, Inc.*

THE ONE-STORY HOUSE:
Level-Headed Thinking for Low-Cost Living

PLAN T162878

A traditional favorite, the one-story home remains a popular choice because of its low-slung, ground-hugging profile, and its easy adaptability and livability.

Because of the simplicity of its single floor plan, the one-story takes on a variety of shapes — the most cost-efficient being the simple rectangle. With no projecting wings, bays, or other protrusions — all under a straight, in-line roof — this configuration assures the most prudent use of building materials. And the facility of its construction makes it less labor intensive — a penny-wise plus at the building stage.

Of course, low-cost construction is not the only consideration of affordability. While the simple rectangle may be the most reasonable to build, an overly wide house may not be appropriate for some sites. For instance, a 100-foot wide house may require the purchase of a large and costly lot. An equally livable arrangement with a 65-foot L-shaped house, or a 50-foot U-shaped house, will probably result in a smaller and less expensive building site.

Consider also the energy efficiency of a square one-story over the same size rectangle. A 20' by 80' rectangular home yields a 1,600 square foot area with 200 linear feet of wall space, while a 40' by 40' home has an equal amount of square footage with only 160 feet of wall space. This results in an obvious heating and cooling savings.

For the elderly or those who are handicapped and
continued on next page.

Design T162878
1,521 Sq. Ft.; 34,760 Cu. Ft.

● There is a great deal of livability in this one-story design. The efficient floor plan makes optimum use of limited floor space. Ideally located, the gathering room is warmed by a fireplace. Its sloped-ceiling gives it a spacious appeal. Adjacent is the dining room which opens up to the rear terrace via sliding glass doors for dining alfresco. Ready to serve the breakfast room and dining room, there is the interior kitchen. The laundry, basement stairs, and garage door are nearby. Two with an optional third bedroom are tucked away from the more active areas of the house. The master bedroom has sliding glass doors to the terrace for outdoor enjoyment. Study this cozy, clapboard cottage and imagine it as your next home.

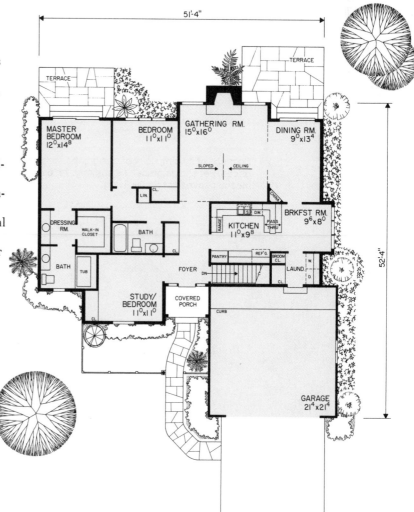

unable to climb stairs, the one-story is the clear-cut choice. Accessibility to all areas of the house and the freely adaptable floor plan mean that few if any accommodations need to be made for adjusted living.

Remember, too, that the one-story need not be plain-Jane in its style. While added features such as bump-outs and protrusions are expensive, the amount of convenience and charm they provide and the quality of living they deliver may prove cost effective in the long run. A front-facing bay window or a kitchen greenhouse could make all the difference in an otherwise boxy design.

Basements and attics are a great investment and a provident addition to the simple one-story house. Providing square footage at a relatively low cost, these bonus areas allow for increased space with less expenditure. In many areas, building codes do not permit the location of bedrooms in typical basements. However, full or partial basements are ideal for developing recreational space, hobby areas, laundries, and storage facilities. Such inexpensive space can make a small or modest-sized one-story house significantly more livable, incorporating economy and effectual use of area. In areas of the country where basements are not practical or even possible, storage space can be allocated to garages, attics, closets, and sheds.

The one-story enjoys an advantage over multi-storied houses in providing for today's indoor-outdoor lifestyles. The one-story house allows all zones — from living and sleeping areas to work spaces — direct access to patios, terraces, and gardens without the expense encountered in second-floor balconies and decks. Simple amenities such as sloping ceilings, glass gable ends, skylights, and sun rooms also help to open up interiors. Similarly, the U-shaped or L-shaped one-story often can enclose a pool or "outdoor room," further enhancing the economizing use of space and allowing added privacy.

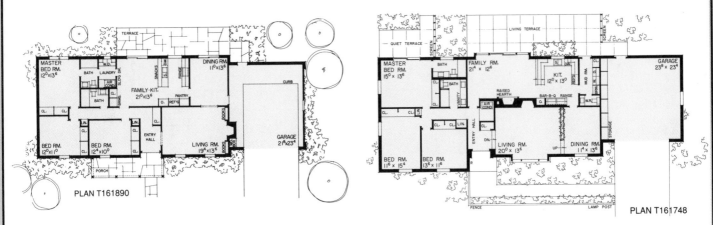

PLAN T161890

PLAN T161748

Because of its simplicity of design, the rectangle is modestly priced, yet shows graceful symmetry. An easy flow of traffic means convenient family living.

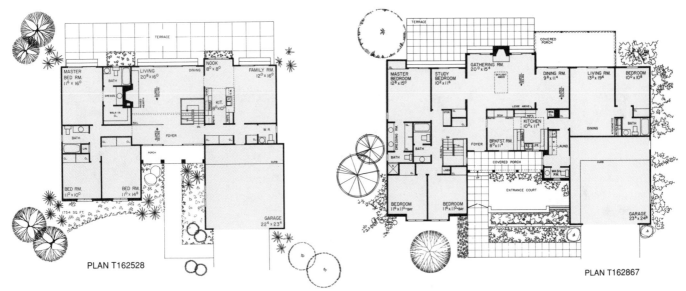

PLAN T162528

PLAN T162867

An elaborate entrance court and central foyer are hallmarks of the U-shaped house. Front-facing bedrooms are accented by special treatment of windows.

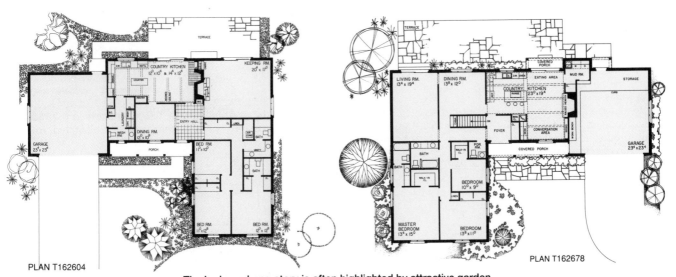

PLAN T162604

PLAN T162678

The L-shaped one-story is often highlighted by attractive garden walkways. With bedrooms in one arm of the L, a more defined delineation of living space is attained.

Design T162605
1,775 Sq. Ft.; 34,738 Cu. Ft.

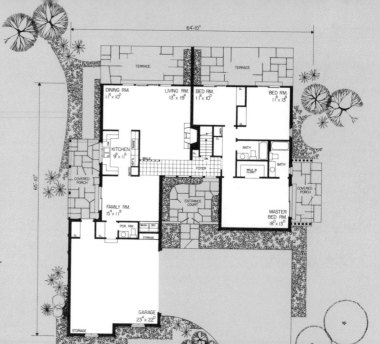

● Here are three modified L-shaped Tudor designs with tremendous exterior appeal and efficient floor plans. While each plan features three bedrooms and 2½ baths, the square footage differences are interesting. Note that each design may be built with or without a basement. This appealing exterior is highlighted by a variety of roof planes, patterned brick, wavy-edged siding and a massive chimney. The garage is oversized and has good storage potential. In addition to the entrance court, there are two covered porches and two terraces for outdoor living. Most definitely a home to be enjoyed by all family members.

Design T162206
1,769 Sq. Ft.; 25,363 Cu. Ft.

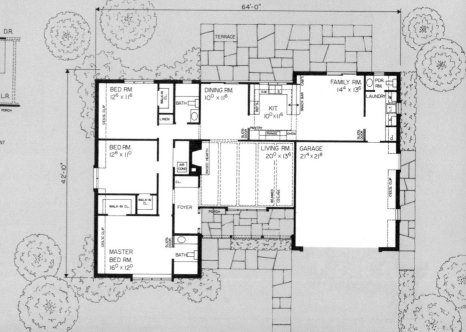

● The charm of Tudor adaptations has become increasingly popular in recent years. And little wonder. Its freshness of character adds a unique touch to any neighborhood. This interesting one-story home will be a standout wherever you choose to have it built. The covered front porch leads to the formal front entry-the foyer. From this point traffic flows freely to the living and sleeping areas. The outstanding plan features a separate dining room, a beamed ceiling living room, an efficient kitchen and an informal family room.

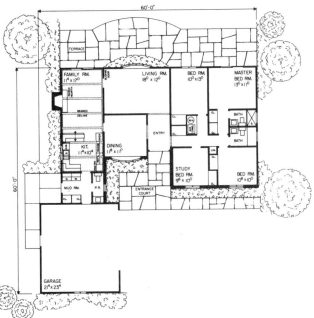

Design T162170
1,646 Sq. Ft.; 22,034 Cu. Ft.

● An L-shaped home with an enchanting Olde English styling. The wavy-edged siding, the simulated beams, the diamond lite windows, the unusual brick pattern and the interesting roof lines all are elements which set the character of authenticity. The center entry routes traffic directly to the formal living and sleeping zones of the house. The family room is highlighted by the beamed ceilings, the raised hearth fireplace and sliding glass doors to the rear terrace. The work center with its abundance of cupboard space will be fun in which to function. Four bedrooms, two full baths and good closet space are features of the sleeping area.

Design T161337
1,606 Sq. Ft.; 31,478 Cu. Ft.

● A pleasantly traditional facade
which captures a full measure of
warmth. Its exterior appeal results
from a symphony of such features
as: the attractive window detailing;
the raised planter; the paneled
door, carriage light and cupola of
the garage; the use of both horizontal siding and brick. The floor
plan has much to recommend this
design to the family whose requirements include formal and informal living areas. There is an
exceptional amount of livability in
this modest-sized design.

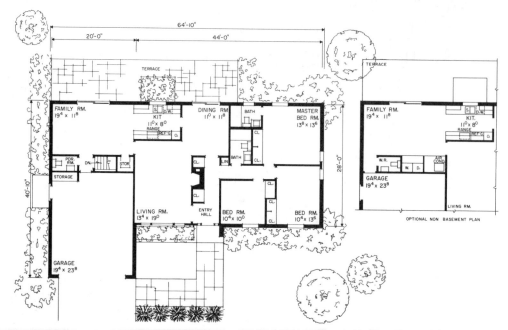

Design T161890
1,628 Sq. Ft.; 20,350 Cu. Ft.

● The pediment gable and columns help set the charm of this
modestly sized home. Here is gra-
ciousness normally associated with
homes twice its size. The pleasant
symmetry of the windows and the
double front doors complete the
picture. Inside, each square foot is
wisely planned to assure years of
convenient living. There are three
bedrooms, each with twin wardrobe closets. There are two full
baths economically grouped with
the laundry and heating equipment. A fine feature.

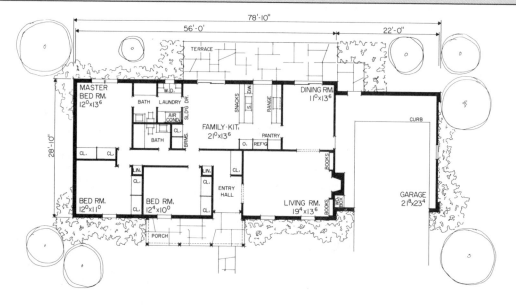

18

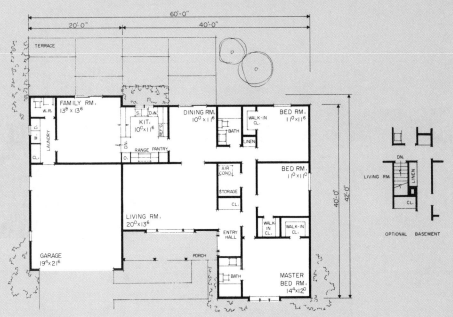

Design T161920
1,600 Sq. Ft.; 18,966 Cu. Ft.

● A charming exterior with a truly great floor plan. The front entrance with its covered porch seems to herald all the outstanding features to be found inside. Study the sleeping zone with its three bedrooms and two full baths. Each of the bedrooms has its own walk-in closet. Note the efficient U-shaped kitchen with the family and dining rooms to each side. Observe the laundry and the extra wash room. Blueprints for this design include details for both basement and non-basement construction.

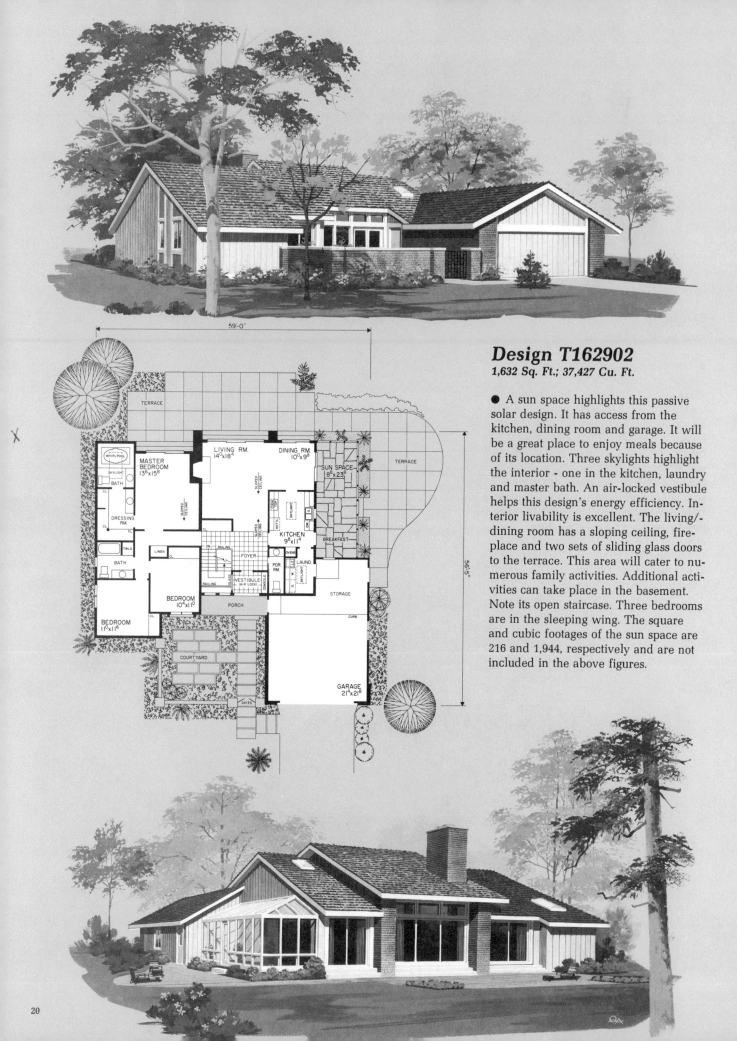

Design T162902
1,632 Sq. Ft.; 37,427 Cu. Ft.

● A sun space highlights this passive solar design. It has access from the kitchen, dining room and garage. It will be a great place to enjoy meals because of its location. Three skylights highlight the interior - one in the kitchen, laundry and master bath. An air-locked vestibule helps this design's energy efficiency. Interior livability is excellent. The living/dining room has a sloping ceiling, fireplace and two sets of sliding glass doors to the terrace. This area will cater to numerous family activities. Additional activities can take place in the basement. Note its open staircase. Three bedrooms are in the sleeping wing. The square and cubic footages of the sun space are 216 and 1,944, respectively and are not included in the above figures.

Design T162824
1,550 Sq. Ft.; 34,560 Cu. Ft.

● Low-maintenance and economy in building are the outstanding exterior features of this sharp one-story design. It is sheathed in long-lasting cedar siding and trimmed with stone for an eye-appealing facade. Entrance to this home takes you through a charming garden courtyard then a covered walk to the front porch. The garage extending from the front of the house serves two purposes; to reduce lot size and to buffer the interior of the house from street noise. Sliding glass doors are featured in each of the main rooms for easy access to the outdoors. A sun porch is tucked between the study and gathering rooms. Optional non-basement details are included with the purchase of this design.

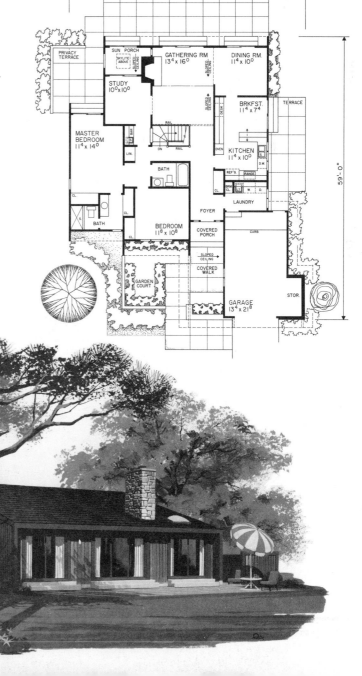

51'-4"

59'-0"

TERRACE

PRIVACY TERRACE

SUN PORCH
SKYLITE ABOVE

GATHERING RM.
13⁴ x 16⁰

DINING RM.
11⁴ x 10⁰

STUDY
10⁰ x 10⁰

BRKFST.
11⁴ x 7⁴

TERRACE

MASTER BEDROOM
11⁴ x 14⁰

KITCHEN
11⁴ x 10⁰

BATH

BEDROOM
11⁸ x 10⁸

FOYER

LAUNDRY

COVERED PORCH

CURB

BATH

COVERED WALK

SLOPED CEILING

GARDEN COURT

STOR.

GARAGE
13⁴ x 21⁸

OPTIONAL NON-BASEMENT

STUDY   GATHERING RM.   BRK.
M.B.R.   AIR COND.
          BATH   KIT.

Design T162741
1,842 Sq. Ft.; 37,045 Cu. Ft.

● Here is another example of what 1,800 square feet can deliver in comfort and convenience. The setting reminds one of the sun country of Arizona. However, this design would surely be an attractive and refreshing addition to any region. The covered front porch with its adjacent open trellis area shelters the center entry. From here traffic flows efficiently to the sleeping, living and kitchen zones. There is much to recommend each area. The sleeping with its fine bath and closet facilities; the living with its spaciousness, fireplace and adjacent dining room; the kitchen with its handy nook, excellent storage, nearby laundry and extra wash room.

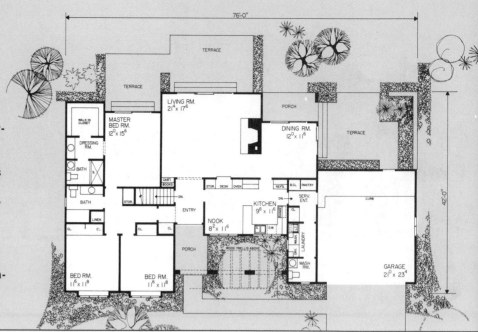

Design T162386
1,994 Sq. Ft.; 22,160 Cu. Ft.

● This distinctive home may look like the Far West, but don't let that inhibit you from enjoying the great livability it has to offer. Wherever built, you will surely experience a satisfying pride of ownership. Imagine, an entrance court in addition to a large side courtyard! A central core is made up of the living, dining and family rooms, plus the kitchen. Each functions with an outdoor living area. The younger generation has its sleeping zone divorced from the master bedroom. The location of the attractive attached garage provides direct access to the front entry. Don't miss the vanity, the utility room with laundry equipment, the snack bar and the raised hearth fireplace. Note three pass-thrus from the kitchen. Observe the beamed and sloping ceilings of the living areas.

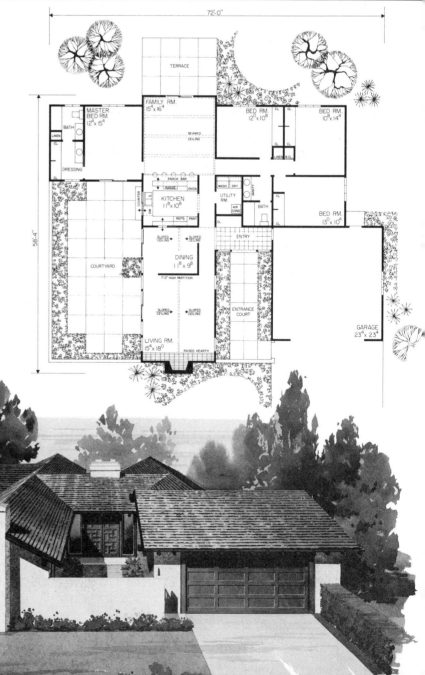

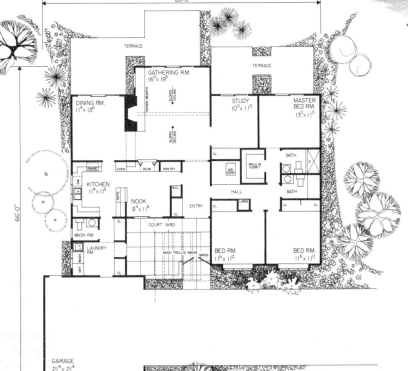

Floor plan labels:

60'-0"
66'-0"

TERRACE
TERRACE
GATHERING RM.
16'⁰ x 19'⁶
DINING RM.
11'⁴ x 13'⁶
STUDY
10'⁰ x 11'⁰
MASTER BED RM.
13'⁰ x 11'⁰
RAISED HEARTH
SLOPED CEILING
SLOPED CEILING
RANGE
OVEN
DESK
PANTRY
AIR COND.
WALK IN CLOSET
BATH
KITCHEN
11'⁴ x 11'⁶
HALL
BATH
NOOK
9'⁴ x 11'⁶
ENTRY
LINEN
WASH RM.
CL
LAUNDRY RM.
DRY
WASH
WOOD TRELLIS ABOVE
GATES
COURT YARD
BED RM.
11'⁶ x 11'⁰
BED RM.
11'⁶ x 11'⁰
GARAGE
21'⁴ x 21'⁴

Design T162743
1,892 Sq. Ft.; 23,300 Cu. Ft.

● For those who feel they really don't require both a living and a family room, this
refreshing contemporary will serve its occupants well, indeed. Ponder deeply its space
and livability; for this design makes a lot of
economic sense, too. First of all, placing the
attached garage at the front cuts down on
the size of a site required. It also represents
an appealing design factor. The privacy wall
and overhead trellis provide a pleasant front
courtyard. Inside, the gathering room satisfies the family's more gregarious instincts,
while there is always the study nearby to
serve as a more peaceful haven. The separate dining room and the nook offer dining
flexibility. The two full baths highlight the
economical back-to-back plumbing feature.
Note the rear terraces.

Design T162859
1,599 Sq. Ft.; 37,497 Cu. Ft.

● Incorporated into the extremely popular basic one-story floor plan is a super-insulated structure. This means that it has double exterior walls separated by R-33 insulation and a raised roof truss that insures ceiling insulation will extend to the outer wall. More popularity is shown in the always popular Tudor facade. Enter the home through the air-locked vestibule to the foyer. To the left is the sleeping area. To the right of the foyer is the breakfast room, kitchen and stairs to the basement. Viewing the rear yard are the gathering and dining rooms. Study the technical details described in the blueprints of the wall section so you can better understand this super-insulated house.

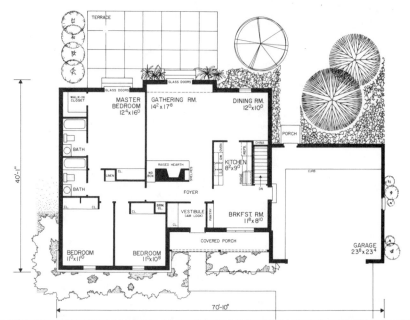

Design T162210
1,658 Sq. Ft.; 22,804 Cu. Ft.

● Certainly a unique adaptation of an Early American farm. Projecting from the main portion of the house are the living and garage wings. Anyone wishing to build an expansible house would find this design of interest. The main section of the house comprised of the bedroom, kitchen and family room areas would function ideally as the initial basic unit. Later, as the need arose, the spacious living-dining wing could be added. Then the two-car garage could be built.

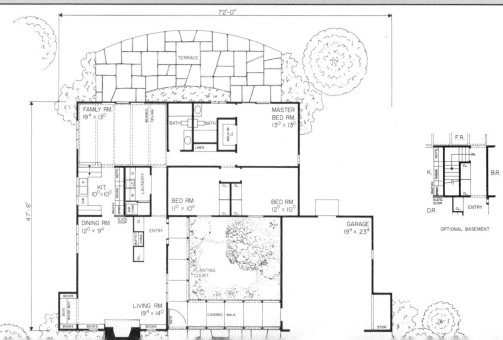

24

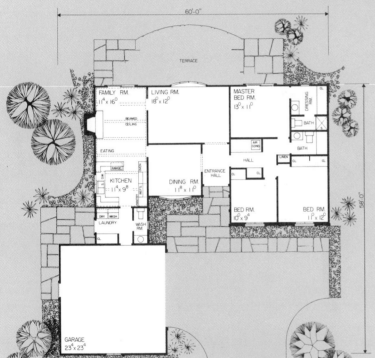

Design T162606
1,499 Sq. Ft.; 19,716 Cu. Ft.

Custom Alterations? See page 320 for customizing this plan to your specifications.

● This modest sized house with its 1,499 square feet could hardly offer more in the way of exterior charm and interior livabiltiy. Measuring only 60 feet in width means it will not require a huge, expensive piece of property. The orientation of the garage and the front drive court are features which promote an economical use of property. In addition to the formal, separate living and dining rooms, there is the informal kitchen/family room area. Note the beamed ceiling, the fireplace, the sliding glass doors and the eating area of the family room.

OPTIONAL BASEMENT

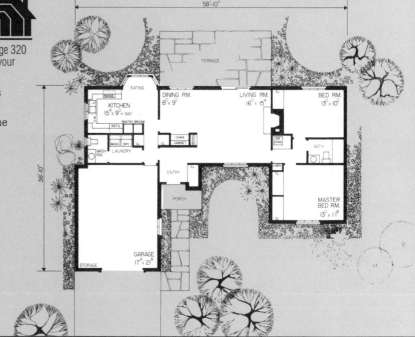

CUSTOMIZABLE

Design T162607
1,208 Sq. Ft.; 15,183 Cu. Ft.

Custom Alterations? See page 320 for customizing this plan to your specifications.

● Here is an English Tudor retirement cottage. Its byword is "convenience". There are two sizable bedrooms, a full bath, plus an extra wash room. The living and dining areas are spacious and overlook both front and rear yards. Sliding glass doors in both these areas lead to the outdoor terrace. Note the fireplace in the living room. In addition to the formal dining area with its built-in china cabinet, there is a delightful breakfast eating alcove in the kitchen. The U-shaped work area is wonderfully efficient. The laundry is around the corner. Blueprints include optional basement details.

OPTIONAL BASEMENT

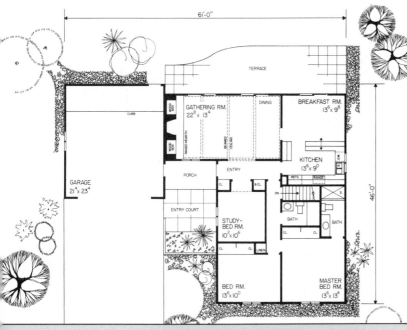

Design T162593 *1,391 Sq. Ft.; 28,781 Cu. Ft.*

● A fireplace wall! Including a raised hearth and two built-in wood boxes. A beamed ceiling, too. Inviting warmth in a spacious gathering room . . . more than 22' x 13' with ample space for a dining area. There's a sunny breakfast room, too, with sliding glass doors onto the terrace. And a pass-through from the kitchen. For efficiency, a U-shaped work area in the kitchen and lots of counter space. Two full baths. Three bedrooms! Including one with a private bath . . . and one suitable for use as a study, if that's your desire. This home is ideal for young families . . . equally perfect for those whose children are grown! It offers many of the attractive extras usually reserved for larger and more expensive designs. The appealing exterior will be appreciated.

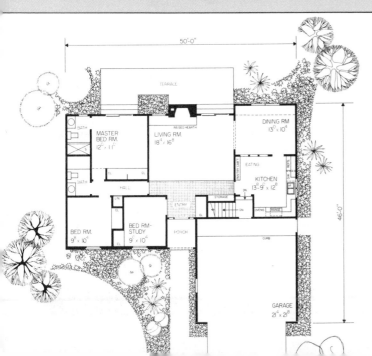

Design T162707 *1,267 Sq. Ft.; 27,125 Cu. Ft.*

● Here is a charming Early American adaptation that will serve as a picturesque and practical retirement home. Also, it will serve admirable those with a small family in search of an efficient, economically built home. The living area, highlighted by the raised hearth fireplace, is spacious. The kitchen features eating space and easy access to the garage and basement. The dining room is adjacent to the kitchen and views the rear yard. Then, there is the basement for recreation and hobby pursuits. The bedroom wing offers three bedrooms and two full baths. Don't miss the sliding doors to the terrace from the living room and the master bedroom. The storage units are plentiful including a pantry cabinet in the eating area of the kitchen.

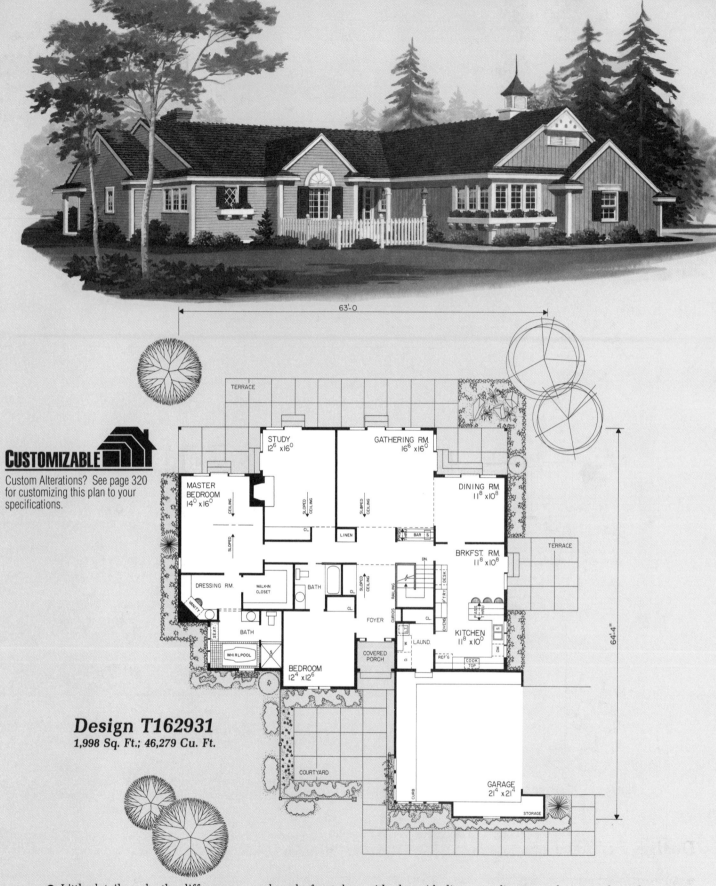

CUSTOMIZABLE

Custom Alterations? See page 320 for customizing this plan to your specifications.

63'-0

TERRACE

STUDY
12⁶ x16⁰

GATHERING RM.
16⁶ x16⁰

MASTER
BEDROOM
14⁰ x16⁰

SLOPED CEILING

SLOPED CEILING

DINING RM.
11⁸ x10⁸

CL

LINEN

BAR

S.

TERRACE

DRESSING RM.

WALK-IN
CLOSET

BATH

CL

SLOPED CEILING

BRKFST. RM.
11⁸ x10⁸

VANITY

BATH

CL

RAILING

DN.

DESK

PANTRY

OVENS

CURIOS

FOYER

CL

PASS-THRU

KITCHEN
11⁸ x10⁰

SEAT

WHIRLPOOL

S.

COVERED
PORCH

W

LAUND.

D

REF'G

COOK
TOP

DW

BEDROOM
12⁴ x12⁶

Design T162931
1,998 Sq. Ft.; 46,279 Cu. Ft.

COURTYARD

CURB

GARAGE
21⁴ x21⁴

STORAGE

64'-4"

● Little details make the difference. Consider these that make this such a charming showplace: Picket fenced courtyard, carriage lamp, window boxes, shutters, muntined windows, multi-gabled roof, cornice returns, vertical and horizontal siding with corner

boards, front door with glass side lites, etc. Inside this appealing exterior there is a truly outstanding floor plan for the small family or empty-nesters. The master bedroom suite is long on luxury, with a separate dressing room, private vanities, and whirlpool bath. An

adjacent study is just the right retreat. There's room to move and - what a warm touch! - it has its own fireplace. Other attractions: roomy kitchen and breakfast area, spacious gathering room, rear and side terraces, and an attached two-car garage with storage.

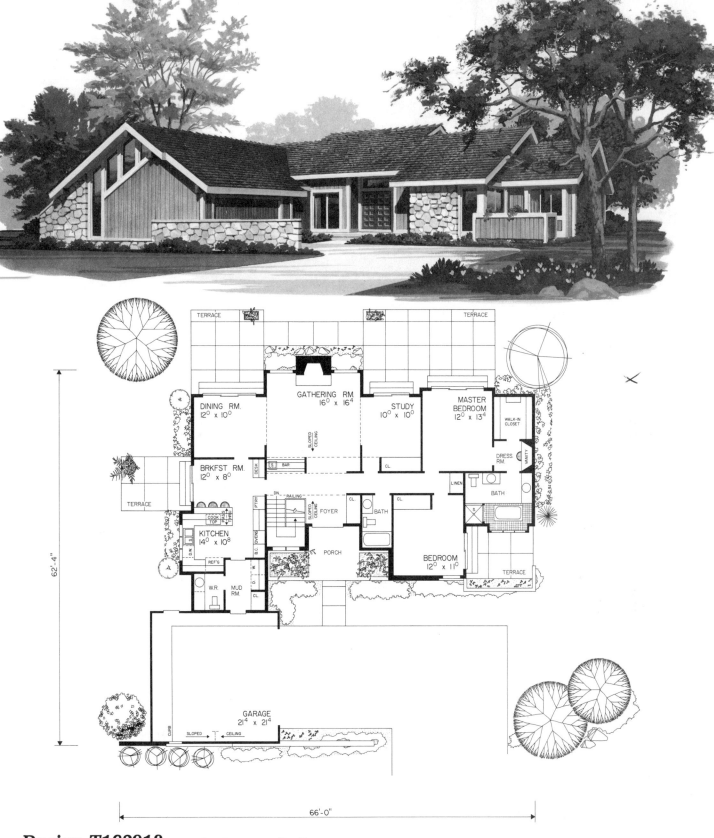

Design T162918 *1,693 Sq. Ft.; 41,325 Cu. Ft.*

● An exciting contemporary facade with fieldstone, vertical siding and interesting roof lines. The projecting garage creates a pleasing drive court as the impressive approach to this moderately-sized home. Double front doors open into a spacious foyer. Traffic is efficiently routed to all areas of the interior. Of particular interest is the open staircase to the lower level basement. Sloped ceilings in this area and the gathering room, along with the open planning reinforce the delightful feeling of spaciousness. The U-shaped kitchen is handy to the utility area and works well with the formal and informal dining areas. Like the dining room, the study flanks the gathering room. Open planning makes this 38 foot wide area a cheerful one, indeed. The master bedroom suite features a big walk-in closet, a dressing area with vanity and an outstanding bath. Note the terraces.

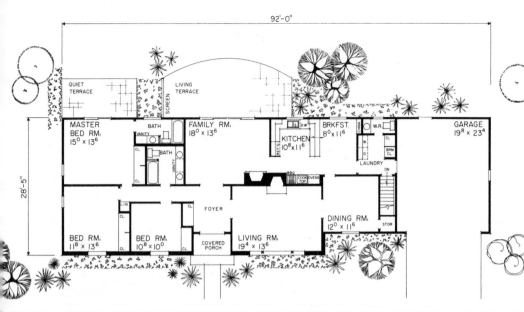

Design T161325
1,942 Sq. Ft.; 35,384 Cu. Ft.

● The large front entry hall permits direct access to the formal living room, the sleeping area and the informal family room. Both of the living areas have a fireplace. When formal dining is the occasion of the evening the separate dining room is but a step from the living room. The U-shaped kitchen is strategically flanked by the family room and the breakfast areas.

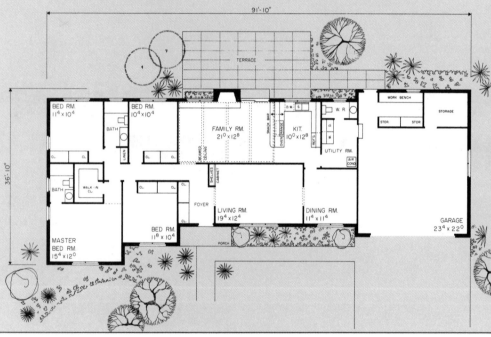

Design T162316
2,000 Sq. Ft.; 25,242 Cu. Ft.

● If you are looking for a four bedroom version of the two other designs on this page, look no further. Here, in essentially the same number of square feet, is a Colonial adaptation for a larger family. The floor planning of this basic design results in excellent zoning. The four bedroom, two-bath sleeping zone comprises a wing of its own directly accessible from the main foyer.

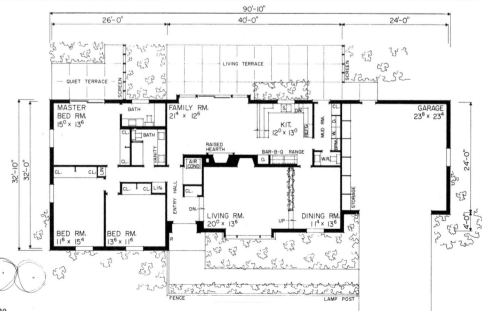

Design T161748
1,986 Sq. Ft.; 23,311 Cu. Ft.

● A sunken living room, two fireplaces, 2½ baths, a rear family room, a formal dining room, a mud room and plenty of storage facilities are among the features of this popular design. Blueprints include optional basement details.

OPTIONAL BASEMENT

Design T161989
2,282 Sq. Ft.; 41,831 Cu. Ft.

● High style with a plan as contemporary as today and tomorrow. There is, indeed, a feeling of coziness that emanates from the ground-hugging qualities of this picturesque home. Inside, there is livability galore. There's the sunken living room and the separate dining room to function as the family's formal living area. Then, overlooking the rear yard, there's the informal living area with its beamed ceiling family room, kitchen and adjacent breakfast room.

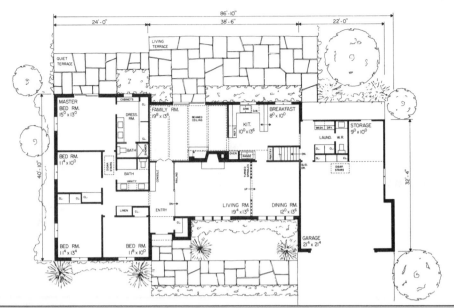

Design T162318
2,029 Sq. Ft.; 31,021 Cu. Ft.

● Warmth and charm are characteristics of Tudor adaptations. This modest sized home with its twin front-facing gabled roofs represents a great investment. While it will be an exciting and refreshing addition to any neighborhood, its appeal will never grow old. The covered, front entrance opens to the center foyer. Traffic patterns flow in an orderly and efficient manner to the three main zones — the formal dining zone, the sleeping zone and the informal living zone.

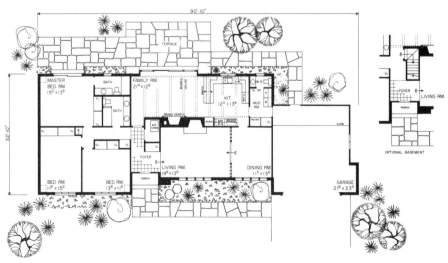

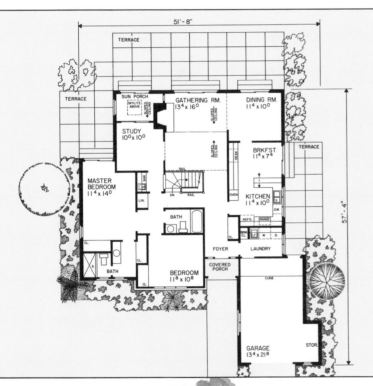

Design T162825
1,584 Sq. Ft.; 37,215 Cu. Ft.

● With today's tight economy, this house will be a real bargain. It has all of the necessary features to insure gracious living yet keep costs down - generous living space, packed with amenities and constructed with durable materials. Locating the garage to the front of this design is practical because it makes the overall width only 51' so it will fit on a narrow lot and it will act as a buffer against street noise. The interior of this home will be interesting. Three sets of sliding glass doors at the rear of the plan will flood the interior with natural light. Since it is a modified open plan it will allow the sunlight to penetrate deep into the interior. The gathering room which seems expanded by the cathedral ceiling has a fireplace.

Design T162672
1,717 Sq. Ft.; 37,167 Cu. Ft.

● The traditional appearance of this one-story is emphasized by its covered porch, multi-paned windows, narrow clapboard and vertical wood siding. Not only is the exterior eye-appealing but the interior has an efficient plan and is very livable. The front U-shaped kitchen will work with the breakfast room and mud room, which houses the laundry facilities. An access to the garage is here. Outdoor dining can be enjoyed on the covered porch adjacent to the dining room. Both of these areas, the porch and dining room, are convenient to the kitchen. Sleeping facilities consist of three bedrooms and two full baths. Note the three sets of sliding glass doors leading to the terrace.

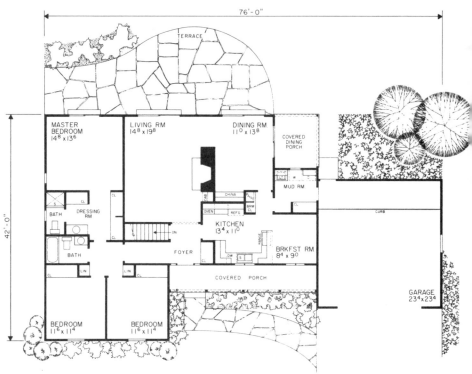

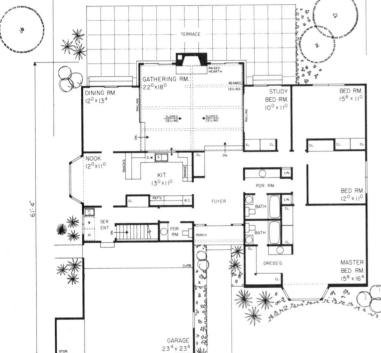

Design T162527
2,392 Sq. Ft.; 42,579 Cu. Ft.

● Vertical boards and battens, field-stone, bay window, a dovecote, a gas lamp and a recessed front entrance are among the appealing exterior features of this U-shaped design. Through the double front doors, flanked by glass side lites, one enters the spacious foyer. Straight ahead is the cozy sunken gathering room with its sloping, beamed ceiling, raised hearth fireplace and two sets of sliding glass doors to the rear terrace. To the right of the foyer is the sleeping wing with its three bedrooms, study (make it the fourth bedroom if you wish) and two baths. To the left is the strategically located powder room and large kitchen with its nook and bay window.

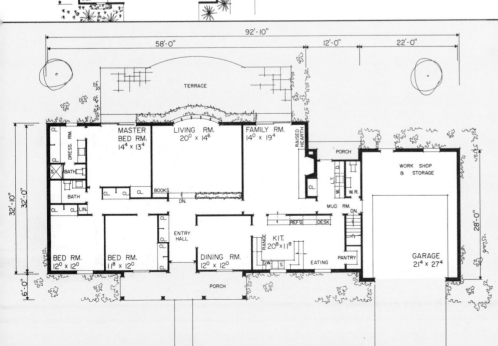

Design T161788
2,218 Sq. Ft.; 36,002 Cu. Ft.

● "Charm" is one of the many words which may be used to correctly describe this fine design. In addition to its eye-appeal, it has a practical and smoothly functioning floor plan. The detail of the front entrance, highlighted by columns supporting the projecting pediment gable, is outstanding. Observe the window treatment and the double, front doors. Perhaps the focal point of the interior will be the formal living room. It is, indeed, dramatic with its bay window overlooking the backyard. Three bedrooms and two baths are in the private area.

Design T162795
1,952 Sq. Ft.; 43,500 Cu. Ft.

● This three-bedroom design leaves
no room for improvement. Any size
family will find it difficult to sur-
pass the fine qualities that this
home offers. Begin with the exteri-
or. This fine contemporary design
has open trellis work above the
front, covered private court. This
area is sheltered by a privacy wall
extending from the projecting garage. Inside, the floor plan will be
just as breathtaking. Begin at the
foyer and choose a direction. To the
right is the sleeping wing equipped
with three bedrooms and two baths.
Straight ahead from the foyer is the
gathering room with thru-fireplace
to the dining room. To the right is
the work center. This area includes
a breakfast room, a U-shaped kitch-
en and laundry.

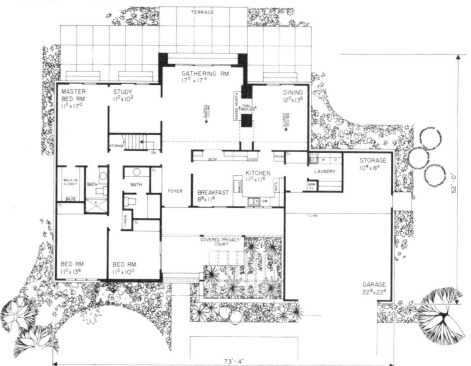

Design T162754
1,844 Sq. Ft.; 26,615 Cu. Ft.

● This really is a most dramatic and re-freshing contemporary home. The slope of its wide overhanging roofs is carried right indoors to provide an extra measure of spaciousness. The U-shaped privacy wall of the front entrance area provides an ap-pealing outdoor living spot accessible from the front bedroom. The rectangular floor plan will be economical to build. Notice the efficient use of space and how it all makes its contribution to outstanding livability. The small family will find its living patterns delightful, indeed. Two bedrooms and two full baths comprise the sleeping zone. The open planning of the L-shaped living and dining rooms is most desirable. The thru-fireplace is just a great room divider. The kitchen and breakfast nook function well together. There is laundry and mechanical room nearby.

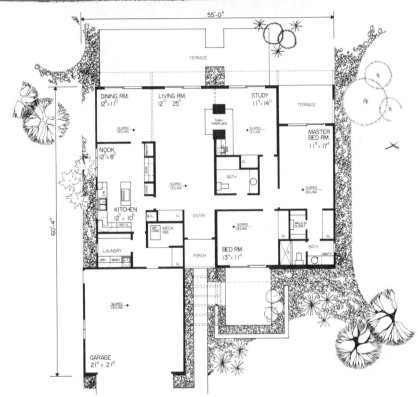

Design T162796
1,828 Sq. Ft.; 39,990 Cu. Ft.

● This home features a front living room with sloped ceil-ing and sliding glass doors which lead to a front private court. What a delightful way to introduce this design. This bi-nuclear design has a great deal to offer. First - the children's and parent's sleeping quarters are on opposite ends of this house to assure the utmost in privacy. Each area has its own full bath. The interior kitchen is a great idea. It frees up valuable wall space for the living areas ex-clusive use. There is a snack bar in the kitchen/family room for those very informal meals. Also, a planning desk is in the family room. The dining room is conveniently lo-cated near the kitchen plus it has a built-in china cabinet. The laundry area has plenty of storage closets plus the stairs to the basement. This home will surely be a welcome addition to any setting.

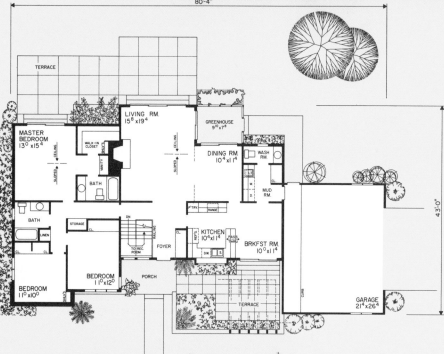

Design T162871
1,824 Sq. Ft. - Living Area
81 Sq. Ft. - Greenhouse Area
44,590 Cu. Ft.

● A greenhouse area off the dining room and living room provides a cheerful focal point for this comfortable three-bedroom Trend home. The spacious living room features a cozy fireplace and sloped ceiling. In addition to the dining room, there's a less formal breakfast room just off the modern kitchen. Both kitchen and breakfast areas look out into a front terrace. Stairs just off the foyer lead down to a recreation room. Master bedroom suite opens to a terrace. A mud room and washroom off the garage allow rear entry to the house during inclement weather.

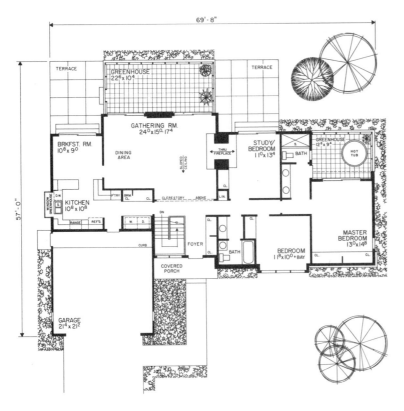

Design T162886
1,733 Sq. Ft.; 34,986 Cu. Ft.

● This one-story house is attractive with its contemporary exterior. It has many excellent features to keep you and your family happy for many years. For example, notice the spacious gathering room with sliding glass doors that allow easy access to the greenhouse. Another exciting feature of this room is that you will receive an abundance of sunshine through the clerestory windows. Also, this plan offers you two nice-sized bedrooms. The master suite is not only roomy but also unique because through both the bedroom and the bath you can enter a greenhouse with a hot tub. The hot tub will be greatly appreciated after a long, hard day at work. Don't forget to note the breakfast room with access to the terrace. You will enjoy the efficient kitchen that will make preparing meals a breeze. A greenhouse window here is charming. An appealing, open staircase leads to the basement. The square and cubic footages of the greenhouses are 394 and 4,070 respectively and are not included in the above figures.

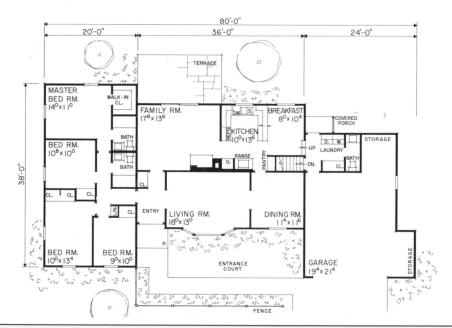

Design T161829
1,800 Sq. Ft.; 32,236 Cu. Ft.

● All the charm of a traditional heritage is wrapped up in this U-shaped home with its narrow, horizontal siding, delightful window treatment and high-pitched roof. The massive center chimney, the bay window and the double front doors are plus features. Inside, the living potential is outstanding. The sleeping wing is self-contained and has four bedrooms and two baths. The large family and living rooms cater to the divergent age groups.

Design T162603
1,949 Sq. Ft.; 41,128 Cu. Ft.

● Surely it would be difficult to beat the appeal of this traditional one-story home. Its slightly modified U-shape with the two front facing gables, the bay window, the covered front porch and the interesting use of exterior materials all add to the exterior charm. Besides, there are three large bedrooms serviced by two full baths and three walk-in closets. The excellent kitchen is flanked by the formal dining room and the informal family room. Don't miss the pantry, the built-in oven and the pass-thru to the snack bar. The handy first floor laundry is strategically located to act as a mud room. The extra wash room is but a few steps away. The sizable living room highlights a fireplace and a picture window. Note the location of the basement stairs.

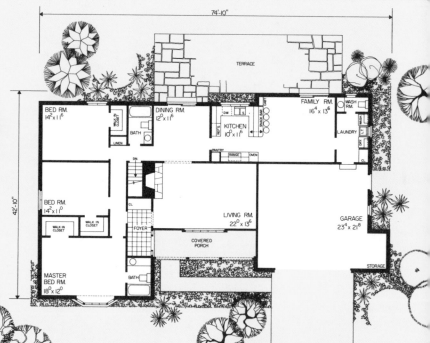

Design T161980
1,901 Sq. Ft.; 36,240 Cu. Ft.

● Planned for easy living, the daily living patterns of the active family will be pleasant ones, indeed. All the elements are present to assure a wonderful family life. The impressive exterior is enhanced by the recessed front entrance area with its covered porch. The center entry results in a convenient and efficient flow of traffic. A secondary entrance leads from the covered side porch, or the garage, into the first floor laundry. Note the powder room nearby.

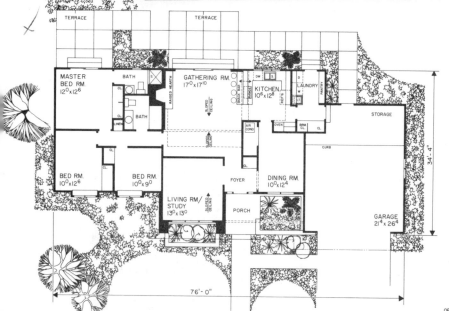

Floor plan labels:
TERRACE · TERRACE · MASTER BED RM. 12⁰x12⁶ · BATH · GATHERING RM. 17⁰x17¹⁰ · KITCHEN 10⁶x12⁸ · LAUNDRY · PANTRY · RAISED HEARTH · SL-OPED CEILING · BATH · LINEN · STORAGE · AIR COND · OVEN · BRM CL · CL · CURB · BED RM. 10⁰x12⁶ · BED RM. 10⁰x9⁰ · FOYER · DINING RM. 10⁰x12⁴ · LIVING RM./ STUDY 13⁰x13⁰ · PORCH · GARAGE 21⁴x26⁴ · 34'-4" · 76'-0"

Design T162818
1,566 Sq. Ft.; 20,030 Cu. Ft.

● This is most certainly an outstanding contemporary design. Study the exterior carefully before your journey to inspect the floor plan. The vertical lines are carried from the siding to the paned windows to the garage door. An overhanging hip-roof protects the interior. The front entry is recessed so the overhanging roof creates a covered porch. Note the planter court with privacy wall. The floor plan is just as outstanding. The rear gathering room has a sloped ceiling, raised hearth fireplace, sliding glass doors to the terrace and a snack bar with pass-thru to the kitchen.

FOYER · DINING RM. 10⁰x12⁴

OPTIONAL BASEMENT PLAN

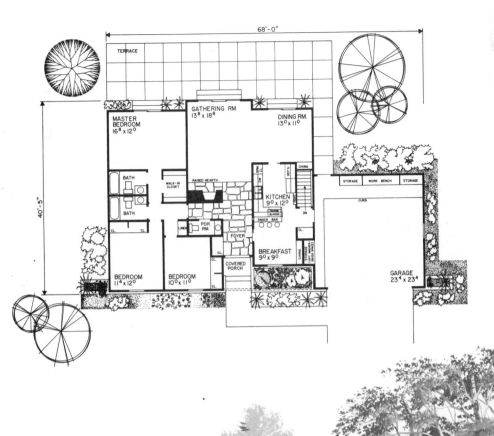

Design T162671
1,589 Sq. Ft.; 36,210 Cu. Ft.

● The rustic exterior of this one-story home features vertical wood siding. The entry foyer is floored with flagstone and leads to the three areas of the plan: sleeping, living and work center. The sleeping area has three bedrooms, the master bedroom has sliding glass doors to the rear terrace. The living area, consisting of gathering and dining rooms, also has access to the terrace. The work center is efficiently planned. It houses the kitchen with snack bar, breakfast room with built-in china cabinet and stairs to the basement. This is a very livable plan.

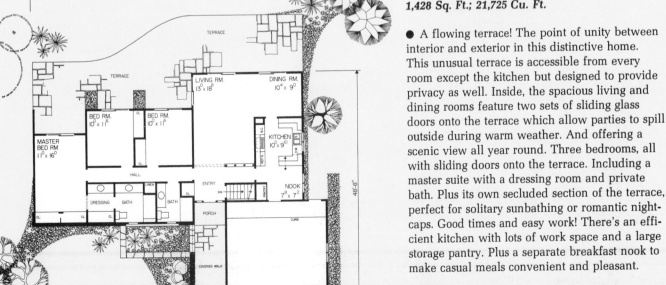

Design T162591
1,428 Sq. Ft.; 21,725 Cu. Ft.

● A flowing terrace! The point of unity between interior and exterior in this distinctive home. This unusual terrace is accessible from every room except the kitchen but designed to provide privacy as well. Inside, the spacious living and dining rooms feature two sets of sliding glass doors onto the terrace which allow parties to spill outside during warm weather. And offering a scenic view all year round. Three bedrooms, all with sliding doors onto the terrace. Including a master suite with a dressing room and private bath. Plus its own secluded section of the terrace, perfect for solitary sunbathing or romantic nightcaps. Good times and easy work! There's an efficient kitchen with lots of work space and a large storage pantry. Plus a separate breakfast nook to make casual meals convenient and pleasant.

Design T162232
1,776 Sq. Ft.; 17,966 Cu. Ft.

● This appealing, flat roof design has its roots in the Spanish Southwest. The arched, covered porch with its heavy beamed ceiling sets the note of distinction. The center foyer routes traffic effectively to the main zones of the house. Down a step is the sunken living room. Privacy will be the byword here. The cluster of three bedrooms features two full baths and good storage facilities.

Design T162557
1,955 Sq. Ft.; 43,509 Cu. Ft.

● This eye-catching design with a flavor of the Spanish Southwest will be as interesting to live in as it will be to look at. The character of the exterior is set by the wide overhanging roof with its exposed beams; the massive arched pillars; the arching of the brick over the windows; the panelled door and the horizontal siding that contrasts with the brick. The elegantly large master bedroom/study suite is a focal point of the interior. However, if necessary, the study could become the fourth bedroom. The living and dining rooms are large and are separated by a massive raised hearth fireplace.

Design T162528
1,754 Sq. Ft.; 37,832 Cu. Ft.

● This inviting U-shaped western ranch adaptation offers outstanding living potential behind its double front doors and flanking glass panels. In but 1,754 square feet there are three bedrooms, 2½ baths, a formal living room and an informal family room, an excellently functioning interior kitchen, an adjacent breakfast nook and good storage facilities. The open stairwell to the lower level basement can be an interesting, interior feature. Note raised hearth fireplace and sloped ceiling.

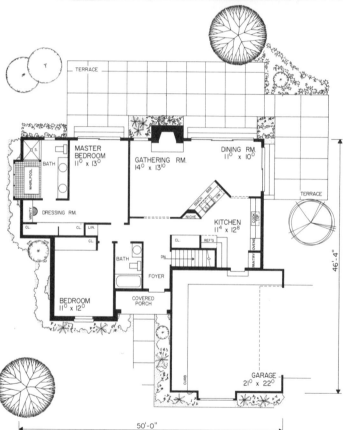

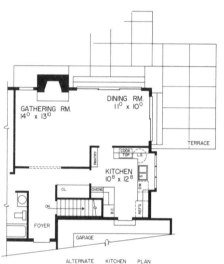

ALTERNATE KITCHEN PLAN

Design T162911 1,233 Sq. Ft.; 27,997 Cu. Ft.

● A low budget retirement house can be a neighborhood showplace, too. Exquisite proportion, fine detailing, projecting wings, and interesting roof lines help provide the appeal of this modest one-story. Each of the bedrooms has excellent wall space and wardrobe storage potential. The master bath features a vanity, twin lavatories, stall shower, plus a whirlpool. Another full bath is strategically located to service the second bedroom as well as other areas of the house. Open planning results in a spacious living-dining area with fireplace and access to the outdoor terraces. This design offers a choice between two kitchen layouts. Which do you prefer? The one which functions informally with the gathering room, or its more formal counterpart? Each layout has all the amenities to assure a pleasant and efficient workday. Don't miss the basement for additional livability.

CONSTRUCTION COSTS

Lumber, building materials and labor account for about 70% of a new home's cost. To construct a $140,000 house, smart budgeters allocate just over $96,000 for labor and materials. Here, on average, are the most expensive items:

- Heating, ventilating, and air conditioning $8,000
- Structural framing ... $25,500
- Electrical work $4,500
- Plumbing $6,100
- Foundation $8,600

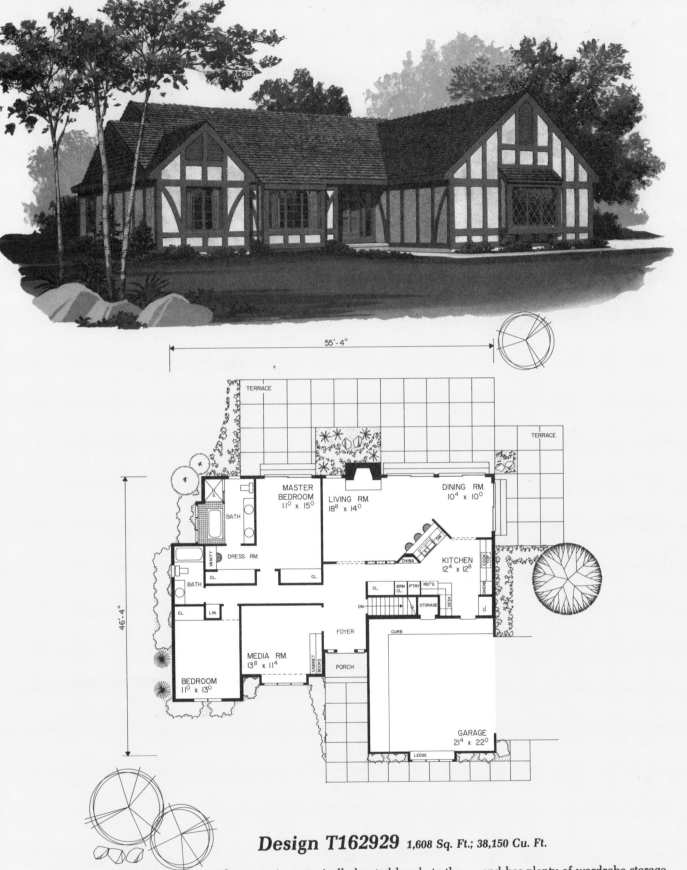

TERRACE

TERRACE

MASTER BEDROOM
11⁰ x 15⁰

LIVING RM.
18⁸ x 14⁰

DINING RM.
10⁴ x 10⁰

BATH

S

DRESS. RM.

VANITY

CL.

CL.

KITCHEN
12⁴ x 12⁸

CHINA

BATH

CL.

LIN.

CL.

BRM CL.

PTRY

REF'G

DESK

STORAGE

CL.

OVEN

COOK TOP

FOYER

CURB

DN-

BEDROOM
11⁰ x 13⁰

MEDIA RM.
13⁸ x 11⁴

CABINET BOOKS

PORCH

GARAGE
21⁴ x 22⁰

LEDGE

55'-4"

46'-4"

Design T162929 *1,608 Sq. Ft.; 38,150 Cu. Ft.*

● Here is a cozy Tudor exterior with a contemporary interior for those who prefer the charm of yesteryear combined with the convenience and practicality of today. This efficient floor plan will cater nicely to the living patterns of the small family; be it a retired couple or newlyweds. The efficient kitchen is strategically located handy to the garage, dining room, dining terrace and the front door. The spacious living area has a dramatic fireplace that functions with the rear terrace. A favorite spot will be the media room. Just the place for the TV, VCR and stereo systems. The master bedroom is large and has plenty of wardrobe storage along with a master bath featuring twin lavatories and a tub plus stall shower. Don't miss the extra guest room (or nursery). This affordable home has a basement for the development of additional recreational facilities.

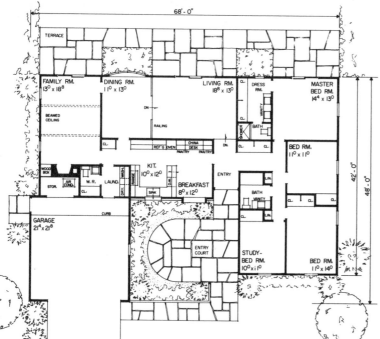

Floor plan labels:

- TERRACE
- FAMILY RM. 13⁰ x 18⁸
- DINING RM. 11⁰ x 13⁰
- LIVING RM. 18⁸ x 13⁰
- DRESS RM.
- MASTER BED RM. 14⁴ x 13⁰
- BEAMED CEILING
- BATH
- BED RM. 11⁰ x 11⁰
- KIT. 10⁰ x 12⁰
- BREAKFAST 8⁰ x 12⁰
- ENTRY
- BATH
- WOOD BOX
- AIR COND.
- W.R.
- LAUND.
- STOR.
- GARAGE 21⁴ x 21⁸
- CURB
- ENTRY COURT
- STUDY-BED RM. 10⁰ x 11⁰
- BED RM. 11⁰ x 14⁰
- 68'-0"
- 42'-0"
- 48'-0"

Design T161950
2,076 Sq. Ft.; 27,520 Cu. Ft.

● If you were to count the various reasons that will surely cause excitement over the prospect of moving into this home, you would certainly be able to compile a long list. You might head your list with the grace and charm of the front exterior. You'd certainly have to comment on the delightful entry court, the picket fence and lamp post, and the recessed front entrance. Comments about the interior obviously would begin with the listing of such features as: spaciousness galore; sunken living room; separate dining room; beamed ceiling family room; excellent kitchen with pass-thru to breakfast room; two full baths, plus wash room, etc.

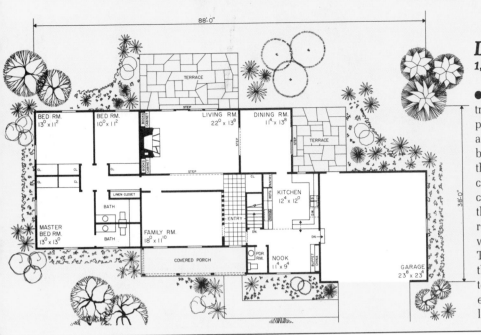

Design T162360
1,936 Sq. Ft.; 37,026 Cu. Ft.

● The charming characteristics of this traditional one-story are many. Fine proportion and pleasing lines assure a long and rewarding study. A list of them may begin with the fine window treatment, the covered front porch with its stolid columns, the raised panelled door, the carriage lamp, the horizontal siding, and the cupola. Inside, the family's everyday routine will enjoy all the facilities which will surely guarantee pleasurable living. The formal rear sunken living room and the dining room function with their own terraces. A 3½ foot high wall with turned wood posts on top separate the excellent family room from the entry hall.

Design T162867
2,388 Sq. Ft.; 49,535 Cu. Ft.

● A live-in relative would be very comfortable in this home. This design features a self-contained suite (473 sq. ft.) consisting of a bedroom, bath, living room and kitchenette with dining area. This suite is nestled behind the garage away from the main areas of the house. The rest of this traditional one-story house faced with fieldstone and vertical wood siding is also very livable. One whole wing houses the four family bedrooms and bath facilities. The center of the plan has a front U-shaped kitchen and breakfast room. Formal dining room and large gathering room will enjoy the view of the backyard. The large rear covered porch will receive much use.

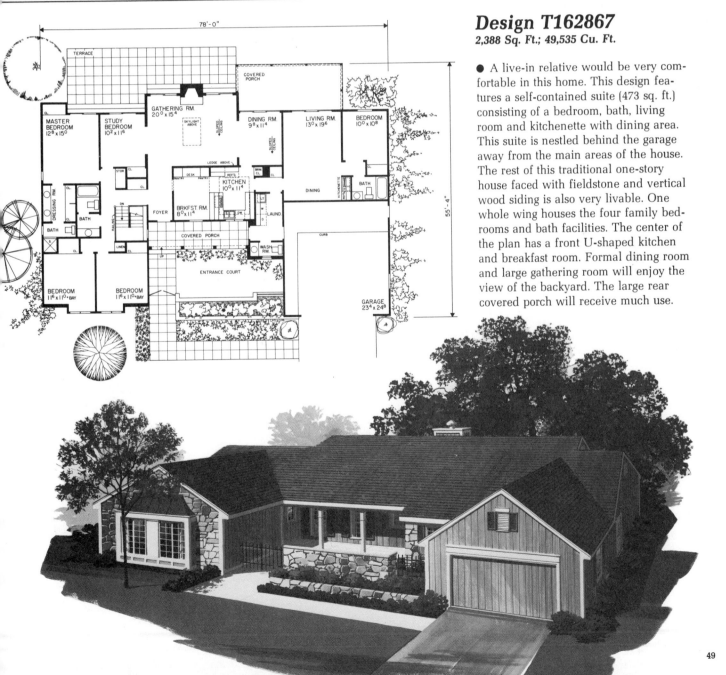

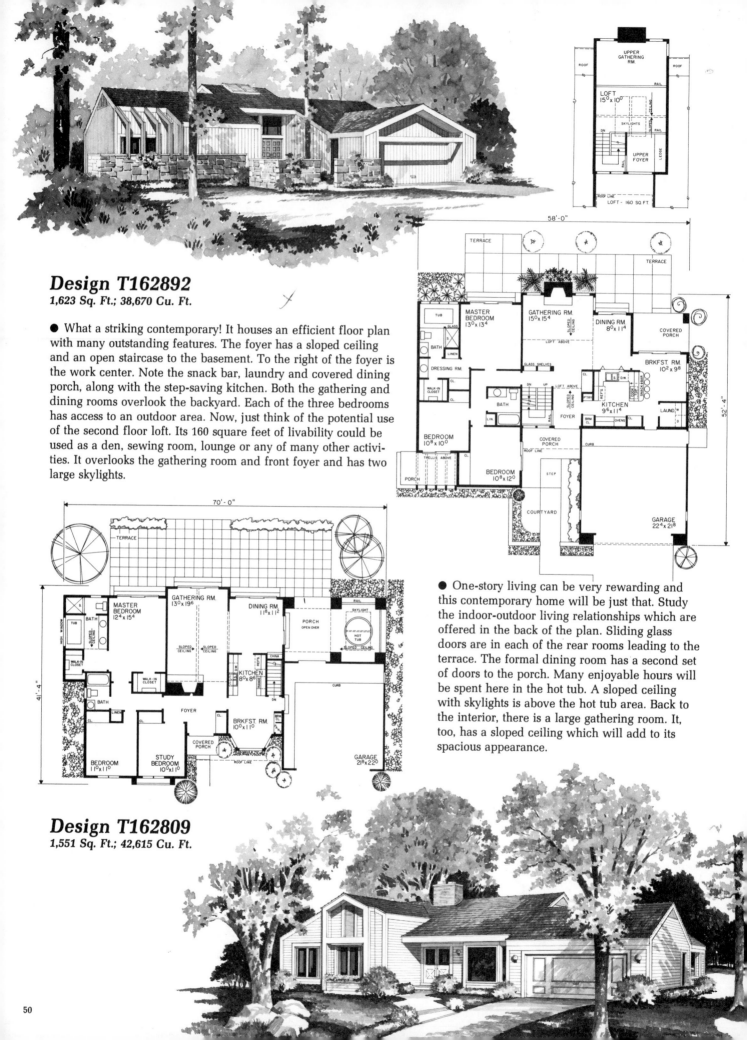

Design T162892
1,623 Sq. Ft.; 38,670 Cu. Ft.

● What a striking contemporary! It houses an efficient floor plan with many outstanding features. The foyer has a sloped ceiling and an open staircase to the basement. To the right of the foyer is the work center. Note the snack bar, laundry and covered dining porch, along with the step-saving kitchen. Both the gathering and dining rooms overlook the backyard. Each of the three bedrooms has access to an outdoor area. Now, just think of the potential use of the second floor loft. Its 160 square feet of livability could be used as a den, sewing room, lounge or any of many other activities. It overlooks the gathering room and front foyer and has two large skylights.

Design T162809
1,551 Sq. Ft.; 42,615 Cu. Ft.

● One-story living can be very rewarding and this contemporary home will be just that. Study the indoor-outdoor living relationships which are offered in the back of the plan. Sliding glass doors are in each of the rear rooms leading to the terrace. The formal dining room has a second set of doors to the porch. Many enjoyable hours will be spent here in the hot tub. A sloped ceiling with skylights is above the hot tub area. Back to the interior, there is a large gathering room. It, too, has a sloped ceiling which will add to its spacious appearance.

OPTIONAL BASEMENT PLAN

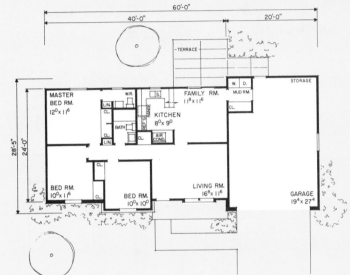

Design T161311
1,050 Sq. Ft.; 11,370 Cu. Ft.

● Delightful design and effective, flexible planning come in little packages, too. This fine traditional exterior with its covered front entrance features an alternate basement plan. Note how the non-basement layout provides a family room and mud room, while the basement option shows kitchen eating and dining room. Sensible planning.

Design T161309
1,100 Sq. Ft.; 15,600 Cu. Ft.

● Here is a real low-cost charmer. Delightful proportion and an effective use of materials characterize this Colonial version. Vertical boards and battens, a touch of stone and pleasing window treatment catch the eye. The compact, economical plan offers spacious formal living and dining areas plus a family room. The kitchen is strategically located—it overlooks the rear yard and is but a few steps from the outdoor terrace. The attached garage has a large storage and utility area to the side.

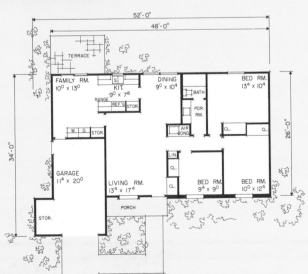

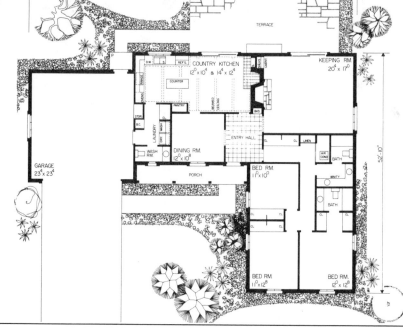

OPTIONAL BASEMENT

Design T162604
1,956 Sq. Ft.; 28,212 Cu. Ft.

● A feature that will set the whole wonderful pattern of true family living will be the 26 foot wide country kitchen. The spacious, L-shaped kitchen has its efficiency enhanced by the island counter work surface. Beamed ceilings, fireplace and sliding glass doors add to the cozy atmosphere of this area. The laundry, dining room and entry hall are but a step or two away. The big keeping room also has a fireplace and can function with the terrace. There are built-in bookshelves and cabinets in the keeping room and more bookshelves in the entry hall. Observe the two baths and three bedrooms in the sleeping wing. Blueprints include details for both basement and non-basement.

Design T162142
2,450 Sq. Ft.; 43,418 Cu. Ft.

● Adaptations of Old England have become increasingly popular in today's building scene. And little wonder; for many of these homes when well-designed have a very distinctive charm. Here is certainly a home which will be like no other in its neighborhood. Its very shape adds an extra measure of uniqueness. And inside, there is all the livability the exterior seems to foretell. The sleeping wing has four bedrooms, two full baths and the laundry room - just where the soiled linen originates. Both formal and informal living areas are ready to serve the active family.

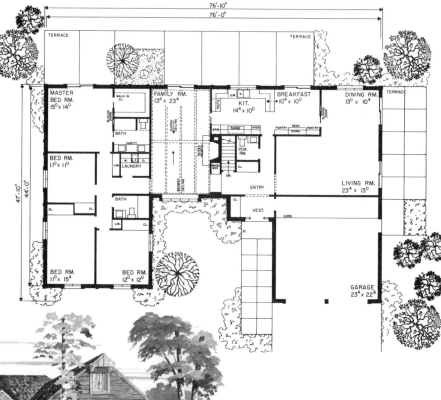

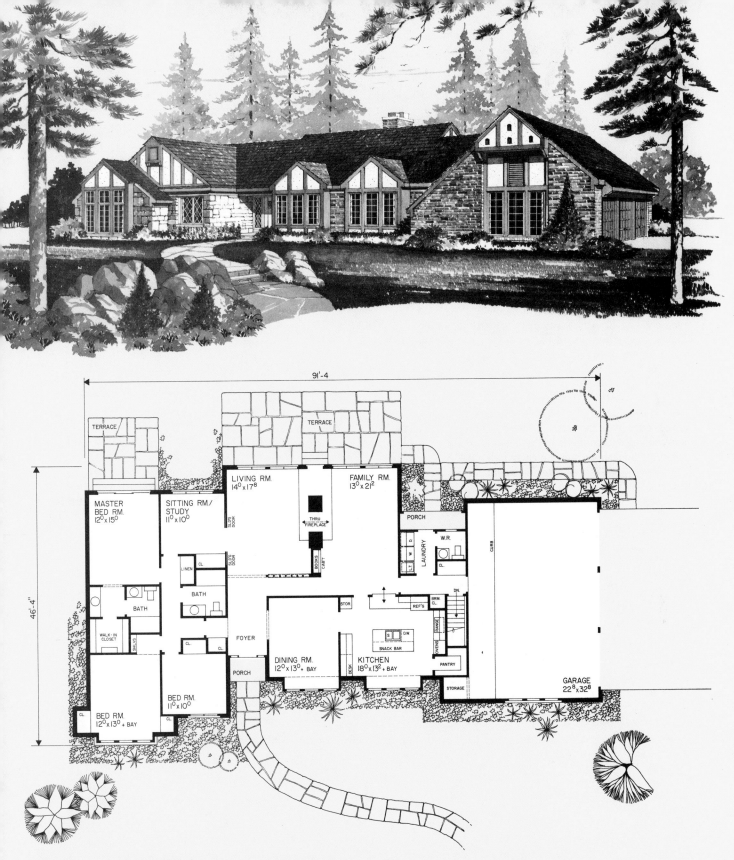

Design T162785 *2,375 Sq. Ft.; 47,805 Cu. Ft.*

● Exceptional Tudor design! Passersby will surely take a second glance at this fine home wherever it may be located. And the interior is just as pleasing. As one enters the foyer and looks around, the plan will speak for itself in the areas of convenience and efficiency. Cross room traffic will be avoided. There is a hall leading to each of the three bedrooms and study of the sleeping wing and another leading to the living room, family room, kitchen and laundry with wash room. The formal dining room can be entered from both the foyer and the kitchen. Efficiency will surely be the by-word when describing the kitchen. Note the fine features: a built-in desk, pantry, island snack bar with sink and pass-thru to the family room. The fireplace will be enjoyed in the living and family rooms.

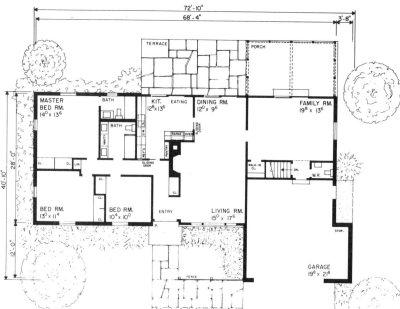

Design T161100
1,752 Sq. Ft.; 34,304 Cu. Ft.

● This modest sized, brick veneer home has a long list of things in its favor—from its appealing exterior to its feature-packed interior. All of the elements of its exterior complement each other to result in a symphony of attractive design features. The floor plan features three bedrooms, two full baths, an extra wash room, a family room, kitchen eating space, a formal dining area, two sets of sliding glass doors to the terrace and one set to the covered porch, built-in cooking equipment, a pantry and vanity with twin lavatories. Further, there is the living room fireplace, attached two-car garage with a bulk storage unit and a basement for extra storage and miscellaneous recreational activities. A fine investment.

Design T161343
1,620 Sq. Ft.; 18,306 Cu. Ft.

● This is truly a prize-winner! The traditional, L-shaped exterior with its flower court and covered front porch is picturesque, indeed. The formal front entry routes traffic directly to the three distinctly zoned areas—the quiet sleeping area; the spacious; formal living and dining area; the efficient, informal family-kitchen. A closer look at the floor plan reveals four bedrooms, two full baths, good storage facilities, a fine snack bar and sliding glass doors to the rear terrace. The family-kitchen is ideally located. In addition to being but a few steps from both front and rear entrances, one will enjoy the view of both yards. Blueprints include basement and non-basement details.

Design T161896
1,690 Sq. Ft.; 19,435 Cu. Ft.

● Complete family livability is provided by this exceptional floor plan. Further, this design has a truly delightful traditional exterior. The fine layout features a center entrance hall with storage closet in addition to the wardrobe closet. Then, there is the formal, front living room and the adjacent, separate dining room. The U-shaped kitchen has plenty of counter and cupboard space. There is even a pantry. The family room functions with the kitchen and is but a step from the outdoor terrace. The mud room has space for storage and laundry equipment. The extra wash room is nearby. The large family will find those four bedrooms and two full baths just the answer to sleeping and bath accommodations.

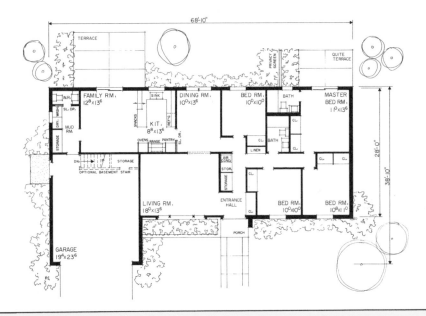

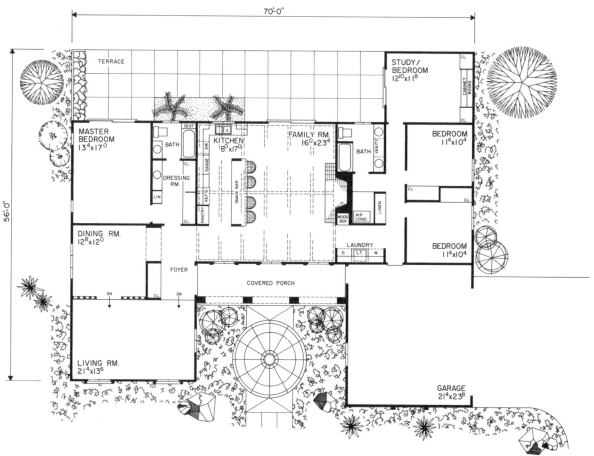

Design T162236 2,307 Sq. Ft.; 28,800 Cu. Ft.

● Living in this Spanish adaptation will truly be fun for the whole family. It will matter very little whether the backdrop matches the mountains above, becomes the endless prairie, turns out to be the rolling farmland, or is the backdrop of a suburban area. A family's flair for distinction will be satisfied by this picturesque exterior, while its requirements for everyday living will be gloriously catered to. The hub of the plan will be the kitchen-family room area. The beamed ceiling and raised hearth fireplace will contribute to the cozy, informal atmosphere. The separate dining room and the sunken living room function together formally. The master bedroom will enjoy its privacy from the three children's rooms located at the opposite end of the plan.

Design T162820 2,261 Sq. Ft.; 46,830 Cu. Ft.

● A privacy wall around the courtyard with pool and trellised planter area is a gracious area by which to enter this one-story design. The Spanish flavor is accented by the grillework and the tiled roof. Interior livability has a great deal to offer. The front living room has slid-ing glass doors which open to the entrance court; the adjacent dining room features a bay window. Informal activities will be enjoyed in the rear family room. Its many features include a sloped, beamed ceiling, raised hearth fireplace, sliding glass doors to the terrace and a snack bar for those very informal meals. A laundry and powder room are adjacent to the U-shaped kitchen. The sleeping wing can remain quiet away from the plan's activity centers. Notice the three-car garage with an extra storage area.

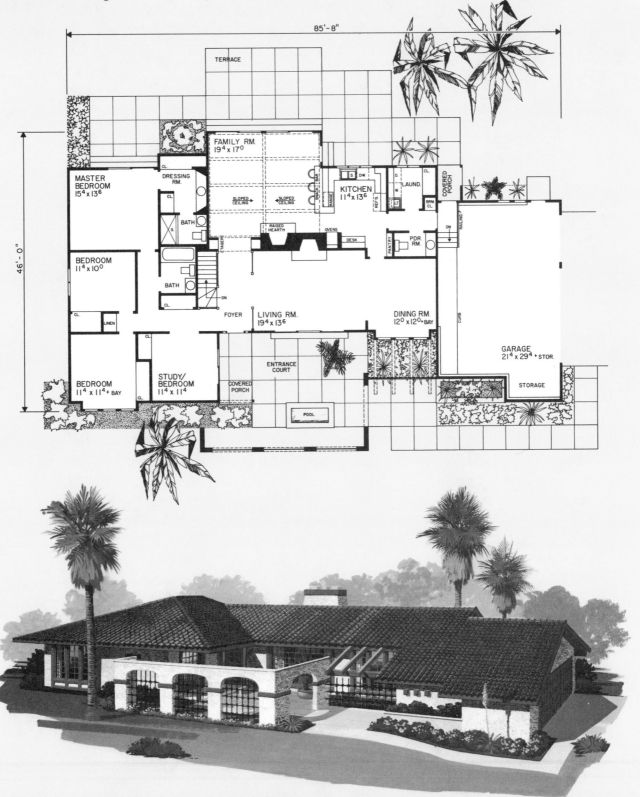

Design T162755
1,200 Sq. Ft.; 23,925 Cu. Ft.

● Here is truly an outstanding, low-cost design created to return all the pride of ownership and livability a small family or retired couple would ask of a new home. The living/dining area measures a spacious 23 feet. It has a fireplace and two sets of sliding glass doors leading to the large rear terrace. The two bedrooms also have access to this terrace. The kitchen is a real step-saver and has a pantry nearby. The study, which has sliding glass doors to the front porch, will function as that extra all-purpose room. Use it for sewing, guests, writing or reading or just plain napping. The basement offers the possibility for the development of additional recreation space. Note the storage area at the side of the garage. Many years of enjoyable living will surely be obtained in this home designed in the contemporary fashion.

Design T162744
1,381 Sq. Ft.; 17,530 Cu. Ft.

● Here is a practical and an attractive contemporary home for that narrow building site. It is designed for efficiency with the small family or retired couple in mind. Sloping ceilings foster an extra measure of spaciousness. In addition to the master bedroom, there is the study that can also serve as the second bedroom or as an occasional guest room. The single bath is compartmented and its dual access allows it to serve living and sleeping areas more than adequately. Note raised hearth fireplace, snack bar, U-shaped kitchen, laundry, two terraces, etc.

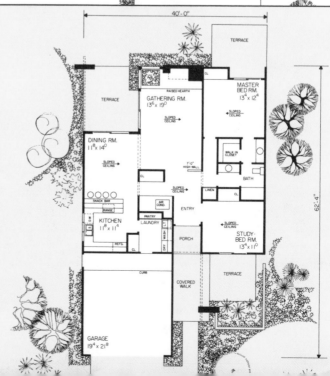

Design T161357
1,258 Sq. Ft.; 13,606 Cu. Ft.

● Here is a relatively low-cost home with a majority of the features found in today's high-priced homes. The three-bedroom sleeping area highlights two full baths. The living area is a huge room of approximately 25 feet in depth zoned for both formal living and dining. The kitchen is extremely well-planned with even a built-in desk and pantry. The family room has a snack bar and sliding glass doors to the terrace. Blueprints include optional basement details.

OPTIONAL
BASEMENT PLAN

Design T161191
1,232 Sq. Ft.; 15,400 Cu. Ft.

● A careful study of the floor plan for this cozy appearing traditional home reveals a fine combination of features which add tremendously to convenient living. For instance, observe the wardrobe and storage facilities of the bedroom area. A built-in chest in the one bedroom and also one in the family room. Then, notice the economical plumbing of the two full back-to-back baths. Postively a money saving feature for today and in the future.

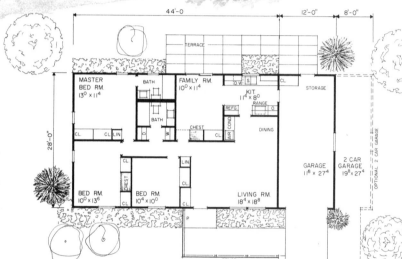

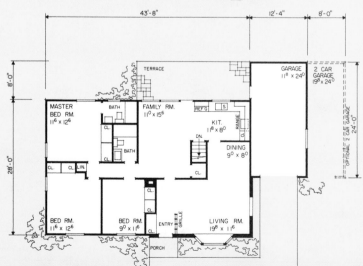

Design T161075
1,232 Sq. Ft.; 24,123 Cu. Ft.

● This picturesque traditional one-story home has much to offer the young family. Because of its rectangular shape and its predominantly frame exterior, construction costs will be economical. Passing through the front entrance, visitors will be surprised to find so much livability in only 1,232 square feet. The attached garage is extra long to accommodate the storage of garden equipment, lawn furniture, bicycles, etc.

Design T161939
1,387 Sq. Ft.; 28,000 Cu. Ft.

● A finely proportioned house with more than its full share of charm. The brick veneer exterior contrasts pleasingly with the narrow horizontal siding of the oversized attached two-car garage. Perhaps the focal point of the exterior is the recessed front entrance with its double Colonial styled doors. The secondary service entrance through the garage to the kitchen area is a handy feature. Study the plan.

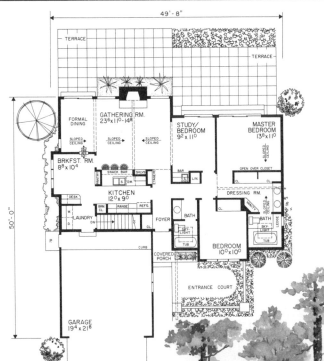

Design T162864
1,387 Sq. Ft.; 29,160 Cu. Ft.

● Projecting the garage to the front of a house is very economical in two ways. One, it reduces the required lot size for building (in this case the overall width is under 50 feet). And, two, it will protect the interior from street noise and unfavorable winds. Many other characteristics about this design deserve mention, too. The entrance court and covered porch are a delightful way to enter this home. Upon entering, the foyer will take you to the various areas. The interior kitchen has an adjacent breakfast room and a snack bar on the gathering room side. Here, one will enjoy a sloped ceiling and a fireplace. A study with a wet bar is adjacent. If need be, adjust the plan and make the study the third bedroom. Sliding glass doors in the study and master bedroom open to the terrace.

CUSTOMIZABLE
Custom Alterations? See page 320 for customizing this plan to your specifications.

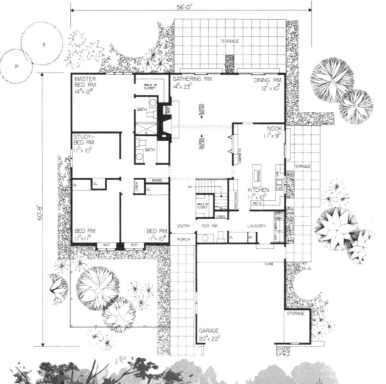

Design T162550
1,892 Sq. Ft.; 39,590 Cu. Ft.

● An enchanting low-slung traditional ranch with exceptional appeal. The low-pitched roof has a wide overhang and exposed beams. Stone and vertical siding offer a pleasing contrast. However, you may wish to substitute other materials of your choice. The diamond lite windows, the fence with its lamp post, the double front doors and the dovecote above the carriage lamp of the garage are among the interesting exterior features. Inside, there are four bedrooms and two full baths in the sleeping wing. The L-shaped living area is spacious and features a sloping ceiling for the gathering and dining rooms. The open stairwell to the basement recreation area is attractive. The pleasant kitchen is flanked by the nook and laundry.

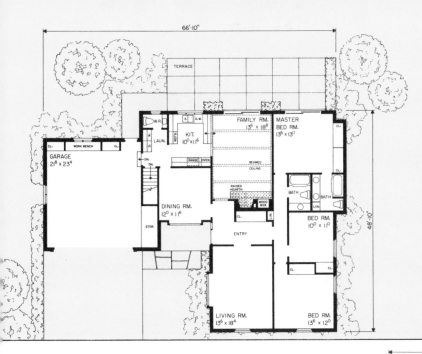

Design T162261
1,825 Sq. Ft.; 33,814 Cu. Ft.

● This distinctive L-shaped home virtually exudes traditional warmth and charm. And little wonder, for the architectural detailing is, indeed, exquiste. Notice the fine window detailing, the appealing cornice work, the attractiveness of the garage door and the massive chimney. The dove-cote and the weathervane add to the design impact. The covered front porch shelters the entry which is strategically located to provide excellent traffic patterns. A service entry from the garage is conveniently located handy to the laundry, wash room, kitchen and stairs to the basement. The beamed ceilinged family room will naturally be everyone's favorite spot for family living.

Design T162777
2,006 Sq. Ft.; 44,580 Cu. Ft.

● Many years of delightful living will be enjoyed in this one-story traditional home. The covered, front porch adds a charm to the exterior as do the paned windows and winding drive. Inside, there is livability galore. An efficient kitchen with island range and adjacent laundry make this work area very pleasing. A breakfast nook with bay window and built-in desk will serve the family when informal dining is called upon. A formal dining room with sliding glass doors leads to the rear terrace. The large gathering room with raised hearth fireplace can serve the family on any occasion gracefully. The sleeping wing consists of two bedrooms and a study (or make it three bedrooms). The master bedroom includes all of the fine features one would expect: a huge walk-in closet, a vanity, a bath and sliding glass doors to a private terrace.

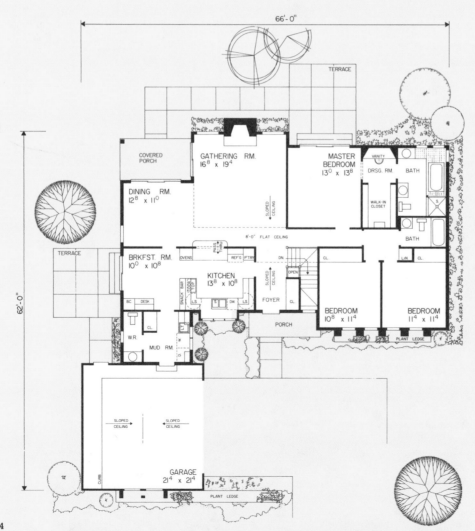

Design T162912
1,864 Sq. Ft.; 45,343 Cu. Ft.

● This modern design with smart Spanish styling incorporates careful zoning by room functions with lifestyle comfort. All three bedrooms, including a master bedroom suite, are isolated at one end of the one-story home for privacy and out of traffic patterns. Entry to a breakfast room and kitchen is possible through a mud room off the garage. That's good news for people carrying groceries from car to kitchen or people with muddy shoes during inclement weather. The modern kitchen includes a snack bar and cook top with multiple access to breakfast room, side foyer, and pass-thru to hallway. There's also a nearby formal dining room. A large rear gathering room features sloped ceiling and its own fireplace. Note the two-car garage and built-in plant ledge in front. Gabled end window treatment plus varied roof lines further enhance the striking appearance of this efficient design.

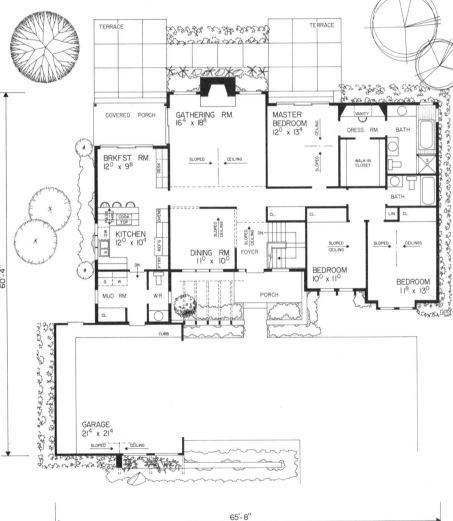

Design T162917
1,813 Sq. Ft.; 39,765 Cu. Ft.

CAN YOU BE YOUR OWN CONTRACTOR?

Many answer yes, but most should answer no. Don't let overconfidence bust your budget and ruin your schedule. Consider these questions:

- Do you have both the time and the patience to schedule and supervise a series of complex operations?
- Are you knowledgeable about construction? If not, are you willing to study and learn?
- Will you save more money than you could earn (after taxes) by applying the same effort to your regular work?
- Do you have the assertiveness to oversee workers?
- Can you stay cool in the heat of inevitable emergencies?
- Are you a reasonably skilled do-it-yourselfer?

● Here's an attractive design with many of today's most-asked-for features: gathering room with fireplace, separate formal dining room, roomy kitchen with equally spacious breakfast area, and three bedrooms, including a master suite with huge walk-in closet and two private vanities. One other plus: a great-to-stretch-out-on terrace leading to the backyard.

Source: *"Adding On,"* Better Homes and Gardens Books, Meredith Corp.

Design T161346
1,644 Sq. Ft.; 19,070 Cu. Ft.

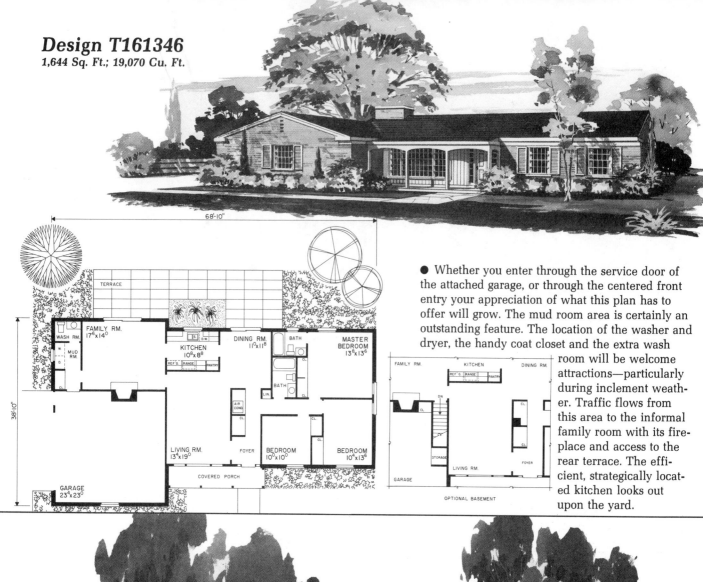

- Whether you enter through the service door of the attached garage, or through the centered front entry your appreciation of what this plan has to offer will grow. The mud room area is certainly an outstanding feature. The location of the washer and dryer, the handy coat closet and the extra wash room will be welcome attractions—particularly during inclement weather. Traffic flows from this area to the informal family room with its fireplace and access to the rear terrace. The efficient, strategically located kitchen looks out upon the yard.

Design T161091
1,666 Sq. Ft.; 28,853 Cu. Ft.

- What could be finer than to live in a delightfully designed home with all the charm of the exterior carried right inside. The interior points of interest are many. However, the focal point will surely be the family-kitchen. The work center is U-shaped and most efficient. The family activity portion of the kitchen features an attractive fireplace which will contribute to a feeling of warmth and fellowship.

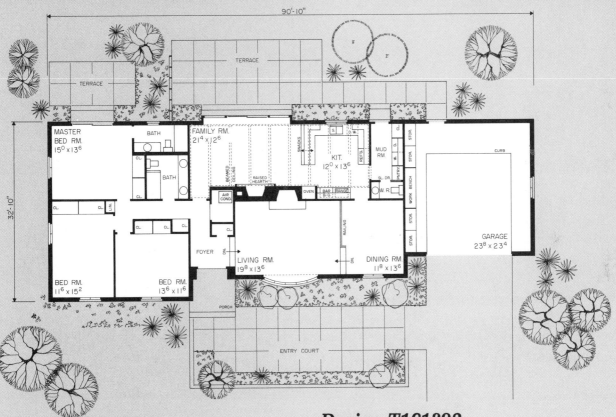

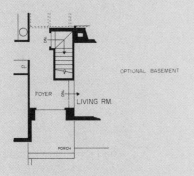

OPTIONAL BASEMENT

Design T161892
2,036 Sq. Ft.; 26,575 Cu. Ft.

● The romance of French Provincial is captured here by the hip-roof masses, the charm of the window detailing, the brick quoins at the corners, the delicate dentil work at the cornices, the massive centered chimney, and the recessed double front doors. The slightly raised entry court completes the picture. The basic floor plan is a favorite of many. And little wonder, for all areas work well together, while still maintaining a fine degree of separation of functions. The highlight of the interior, perhaps, will be the sunken living room. The family room, with its beamed ceiling, will not be far behind in its popularity. The separate dining room, mud room, efficient kitchen, complete the livability.

Design T162678
1,971 Sq. Ft.; 42,896 Cu. Ft.

● This impressive L-shaped Tudor is wonderfully zoned. The focal point, of course, is the country kitchen. It has a beamed ceiling, island counter with snack bar and large informal living space. The raised hearth fireplace is flanked by eating and conversation areas. The formal living and dining rooms are free of unnecessary traffic. The bed rooms occupy a wing of their own. Don't miss powder and mud rooms.

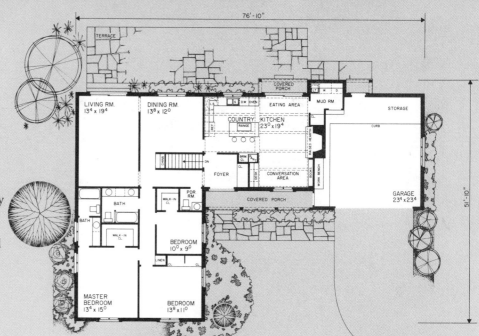

Design T162728
1,825 Sq. Ft.; 38,770 Cu. Ft.

● Your family's new lifestyle will surely flourish in this charming, L-shaped English adaptation. The curving front driveway produces an impressive approach. A covered front porch shelters the centered entry hall which effectively routes traffic to all areas. The fireplace is the focal point of the spacious, formal living and dining area. The kitchen is strategically placed to service the dining room and any informal eating space developed in the family room. In addition to the two full baths of the sleeping area, there is a handy wash room at the entrance from the garage. A complete, first floor laundry is nearby and has direct access to the yard. Sliding glass doors permit easy movement to the outdoor terrace and side porch. Don't overlook the basement and its potential for the development of additional livability and/or storage.

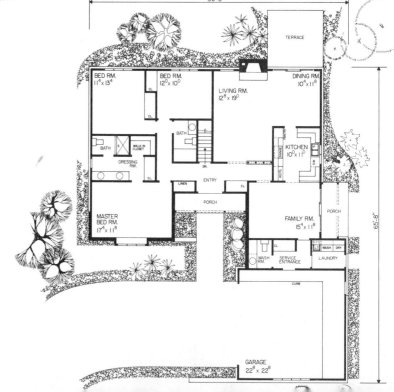

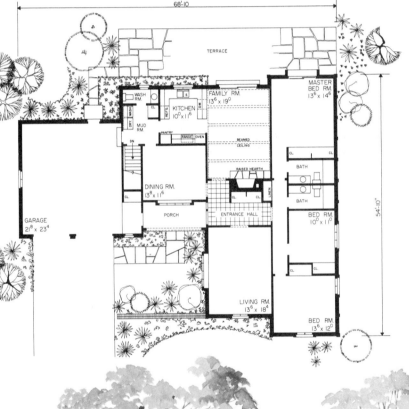

Design T162374
1,919 Sq. Ft.; 39,542 Cu. Ft.

● This English adaptation will never grow old. There is, indeed, much here to please the eye for many a year to come. The wavy-edged siding contrasts pleasingly with the diagonal pattern of brick below. The diamond lites of the windows create their own special effect. The projecting brick wall creates a pleasant court outside the covered front porch. The floor plan is well-zoned with the three bedrooms and two baths comprising a distinct sleeping wing. Flanking the entrance hall is the formal living room and the informal, multi-purpose family room. The large dining room is strategically located. The mud room area is adjacent to the extra wash room and the stairs to the basement.

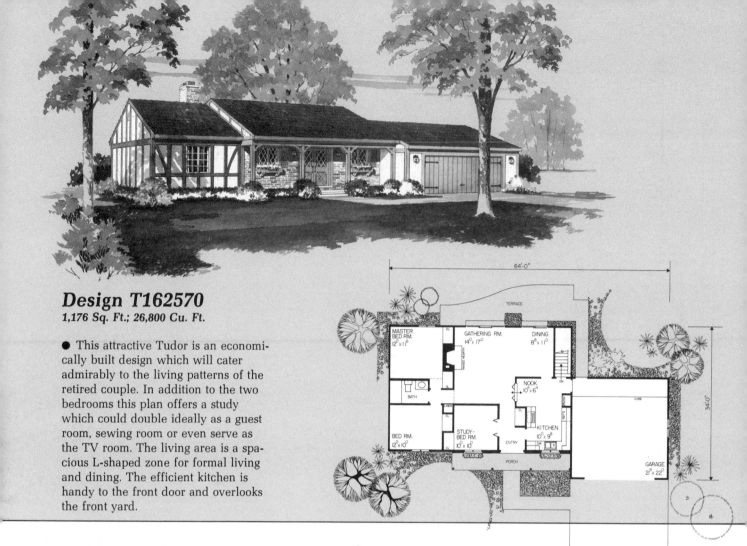

Design T162570
1,176 Sq. Ft.; 26,800 Cu. Ft.

● This attractive Tudor is an economically built design which will cater
admirably to the living patterns of the
retired couple. In addition to the two
bedrooms this plan offers a study
which could double ideally as a guest
room, sewing room or even serve as
the TV room. The living area is a spacious L-shaped zone for formal living
and dining. The efficient kitchen is
handy to the front door and overlooks
the front yard.

Design T161522
960 Sq. Ft.; 18,077 Cu. Ft.

● Certainly a home to make its occupants
proud. The front exterior is all brick veneer,
while the remainder of the house and garage
is horizontal siding. The slightly overhanging
roof, the wood shutters and the carriage lights
flanking the front door are among the features
that surely will catch the eyes of the passer-
by. The living room has excellent wall space
for furniture placement. The family room, the
full basement and the attached garage are
other features.

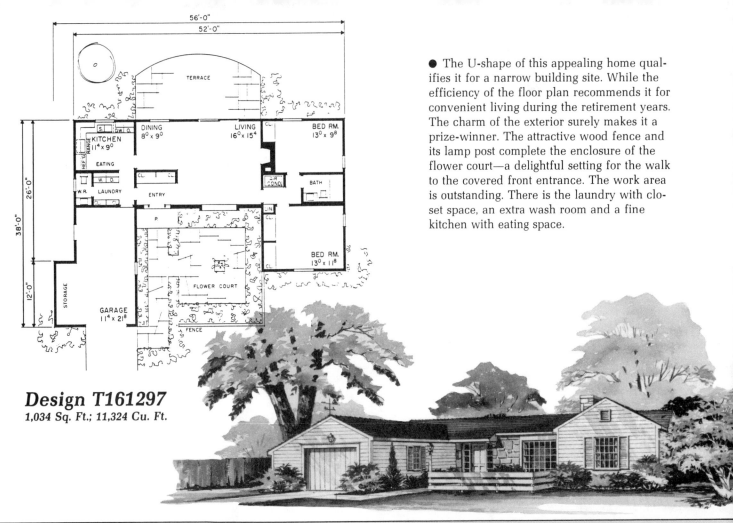

Design T161297
1,034 Sq. Ft.; 11,324 Cu. Ft.

● The U-shape of this appealing home qualifies it for a narrow building site. While the efficiency of the floor plan recommends it for convenient living during the retirement years. The charm of the exterior surely makes it a prize-winner. The attractive wood fence and its lamp post complete the enclosure of the flower court—a delightful setting for the walk to the covered front entrance. The work area is outstanding. There is the laundry with closet space, an extra wash room and a fine kitchen with eating space.

Design T161113
1,008 Sq. Ft.; 19,737 Cu. Ft.

● If yours is a restricted building budget and you are looking for plenty of good old fashioned livability, this design is worth much study. The three bedrooms easily will serve all of the family members. Note the convenience of the full bath accessible from both the master bedroom and the kitchen.

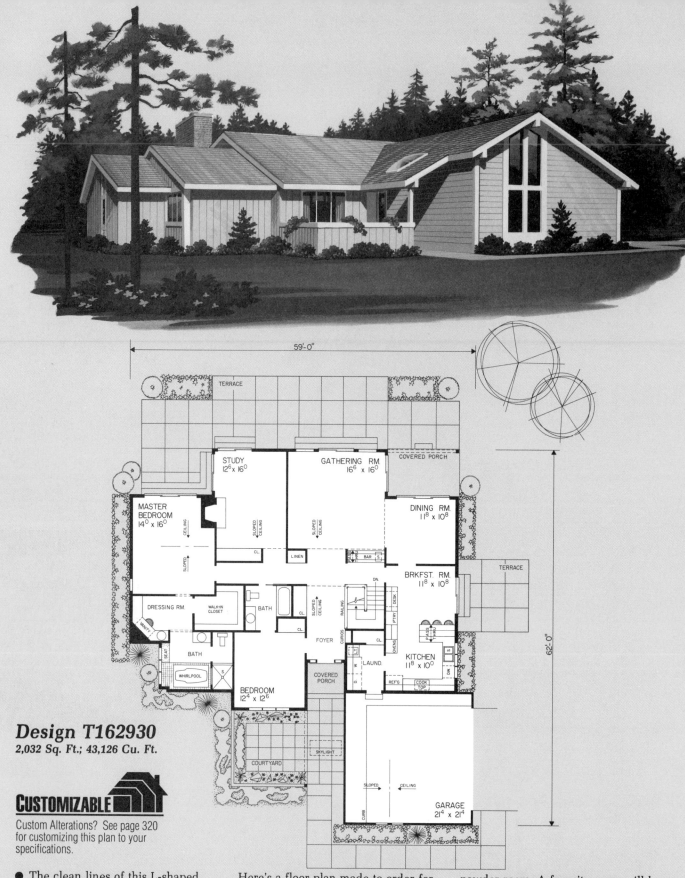

Design T162930
2,032 Sq. Ft.; 43,126 Cu. Ft.

CUSTOMIZABLE

Custom Alterations? See page 320 for customizing this plan to your specifications.

● The clean lines of this L-shaped contemporary are enhanced by the interesting, wide overhanging roof planes. Horizontal and vertical siding compliment one another. The low privacy fence adds interest as it forms a delightful front courtyard adjacent to the covered walkway to the front door.

Here's a floor plan made to order for the active small family or empty-nesters. Sloping ceilings and fine glass areas foster a spacious interior. The master bedroom has an outstanding dressing room and bath layout. The guest room has its own full bath. Note how this bath can function as a handy

powder room. A favorite room will be the study with its fireplace and two sets of sliding glass doors. Don't miss the open-planned gathering and dining rooms, or the kitchen/laundry area. The breakfast room has its own terrace. Notice the rear covered porch. Fine indoor-outdoor relationships.

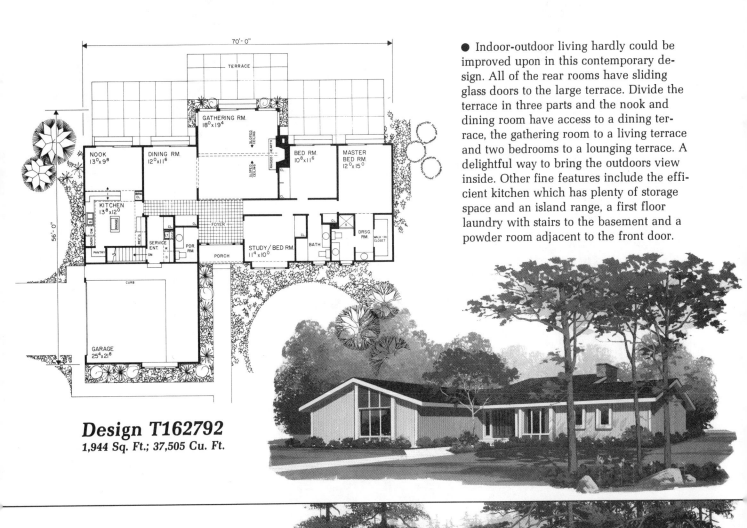

Design T162792
1,944 Sq. Ft.; 37,505 Cu. Ft.

● Indoor-outdoor living hardly could be improved upon in this contemporary design. All of the rear rooms have sliding glass doors to the large terrace. Divide the terrace in three parts and the nook and dining room have access to a dining terrace, the gathering room to a living terrace and two bedrooms to a lounging terrace. A delightful way to bring the outdoors view inside. Other fine features include the efficient kitchen which has plenty of storage space and an island range, a first floor laundry with stairs to the basement and a powder room adjacent to the front door.

Design T162790
2,075 Sq. Ft.; 45,630 Cu. Ft.

● Enter this contemporary home through the double front doors and immediately view the sloped ceiling in the living room. This room will be a sheer delight when it comes to formal entertaining. It has easy access to the kitchen and also a powder room is nearby. The work area will be convenient. An island work center with snack bar is in the kitchen. The laundry is adjacent to the service entrance and stairs leading to the basement. This area is planned to be a real "step saver". The sleeping wing consists of two family bedrooms, bath and master bedroom suite. Maybe the most attractive feature of this design is the rear, covered porch with skylights above. It is accessible by way of sliding glass doors in the family/dining area, living room and master bedroom. This design will prove to be efficient and livable.

Design T162737
1,796 Sq. Ft.; 43,240 Cu. Ft.

● You will be able to build this distinctive, modified U-shaped one-story home on a relatively narrow site. But, then, if you so wished, with the help of your architect and builder you may want to locate the garage to the side of the house. Inside, the living potential is just great. The interior U-shaped kitchen handily services the dining and family rooms and nook. A rear covered porch functions ideally with the family room while the formal living room has its own terrace. Three bedrooms and two baths highlight the sleeping zone (or make it two bedrooms and a study). Notice the strategic location of the wash room, laundry, two storage closets and the basement stairs.

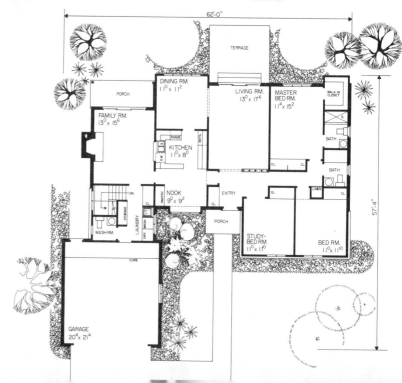

Design T162742
1,907 Sq. Ft.; 38,950 Cu. Ft.

● Colonial charm is expressed in this one-story design by the vertical siding, the post pillars, the cross fence, paned glass windows and the use of stone. A 19' wide living room, a sloped ceilinged family room with a raised hearth fireplace and its own terrace, a kitchen with many built-ins and a dining room with built-in china cabinets are just some of the highlights. The living terrace is accessible from the dining room and master bedroom. There are two more bedrooms and a full bath in addition to the master bedroom.

Design T162738
1,898 Sq. Ft.; 36,140 Cu. Ft.

● Impressive architectural work is indeed apparent in this three bedroom home. The three foot high entrance court wall, the high pitched roof and the paned glass windows all add to this home's appeal. It is also apparent that the floor plan is very efficient with the side U-shaped kitchen and nook with two pantry closets, the rear dining and gathering rooms and the three (or make it two with a study) bedrooms and two baths of the sleeping wing. Indoor-outdoor living also will be enjoyed in this home with a dining terrace off the nook and a living terrace off the gathering room and master bedroom. Note the fireplace in the gathering room and bay window in dining room.

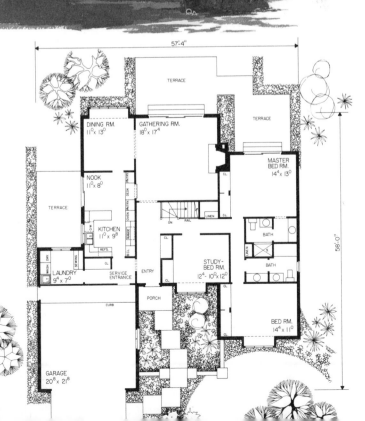

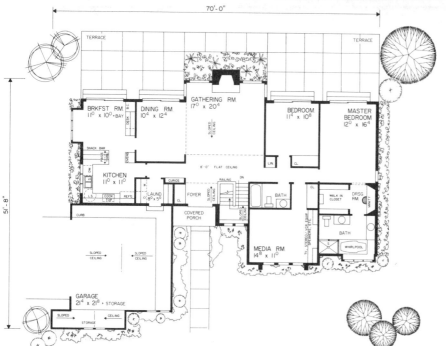

Design T162913
1,835 Sq. Ft.; 42,988 Cu. Ft.

● This smart design features multi-gabled ends, varied roof lines, and vertical windows. It also offers efficient zoning by room functions and plenty of modern comforts for Contemporary family lifestyle. A covered porch leads through a foyer to a large central gathering room with fireplace, sloped ceiling, and its own special view of a rear terrace. A modern kitchen with snack bar has a pass-thru to a breakfast room with view of the terrace. There's also an adjacent dining room. A media room isolated along with bedrooms from rest of the house offers a quiet private area for listening to stereos or VCRs. A master bedroom suite includes its own whirlpool. A large two-car garage includes extra storage.

Design T162875
1,913 Sq. Ft.; 36,271 Cu. Ft.

● This elegant Spanish design incorporates excellent indoor-outdoor living relationships for modern families who enjoy the sun and comforts of a well planned new home. Note the overhead openings for rain and sun to fall upon a front garden, while a twin arched entry leads to the front porch and foyer. Inside the floor plan features a modern kitchen with pass-thru to a large gathering room with fireplace. Other features include a dining room, laundry room, a study off the foyer, plus three bedrooms including master bedroom with its own whirlpool.

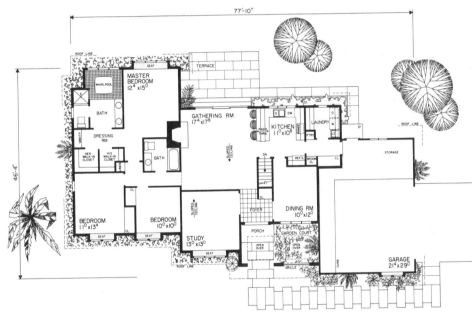

Design T162351 *1,862 Sq. Ft.; 22,200 Cu. Ft.*

● The extension of the wide overhanging roof of this distinctive home provides shelter for the walkway to the front door. A raised brick planter adds appeal to the outstanding exterior design. The living patterns offered by this plan are delightfully different, yet extremely practical. Notice the separation of the master bedroom from the other two bedrooms. While assuring an extra measure of quiet privacy for the parents, this master bedroom location may be ideal for a live-in-relative. Locating the kitchen in the middle of the plan frees up valuable outside wall space and leads to interesting planning. The front living room is sunken for dramatic appeal and need not have any crossroom traffic. The utility room houses the laundry and heating and cooling equipment.

Design T161057 1,320 Sq. Ft.; 13,741 Cu. Ft.

● Here is a relatively small contemporary with 1,320 square feet that is just loaded with livability. Its overall dimension of 56 feet means that it won't require a big, expensive piece of property either. The flexibility of the floor planning is great, too. Notice the room locations. The three bedrooms and compartmented bath occupy the far end of the house. The living room is by itself and will have privacy. The dining room is next to the kitchen and enjoys a view of the front court area.

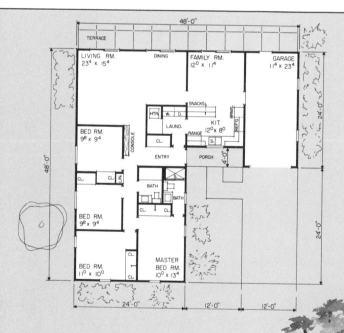

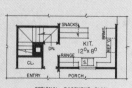

OPTIONAL BASEMENT PLAN

Design T161327
1,392 Sq. Ft.; 18,480 Cu. Ft.

● A design to overcome the restrictions of a relatively narrow building site. This home has one of the best one-story plans you'll ever see. Its four bedrooms and two baths form what amounts to a separate wing. The fourth bedroom is located next to the living room so it may serve as a study, if needed. The traffic plan pivoting in the front entry, is excellent. And the kitchen is in just the right place - next to the dining and family rooms, close to the front and side doors and near the laundry.

Design T161058
1,200 Sq. Ft.; 13,392 Cu. Ft.

● When you build this charming L-shaped traditionally designed home don't leave out the
wood fence and lamp post. These are just the
features needed to complete the picture. A
porch shelters the front door which leads to the
centered entry flanked by the formal living
room and the informal family room. The kitch-
en is but a step from the separate dining room.
The laundry equipment, the extra wash room
and heater location are all grouped together.

Design T161193
1,396 Sq. Ft.; 17,213 Cu. Ft.

● This L-shaped, one-story with its attached
two-car garage incorporates many of the time-
tested features of older New England. The attractive cut-up windows, the shutters, the
panelled door, the fence and the wood siding
contribute to the charm of the exterior. The
floor plan is outstanding by virtue of such prov-
en features as the separate dining room, the
family-kitchen, the quiet living room with its
bay window and the privacy of the bedroom
area. The U-shaped work center will be easy to
work in and very efficient.

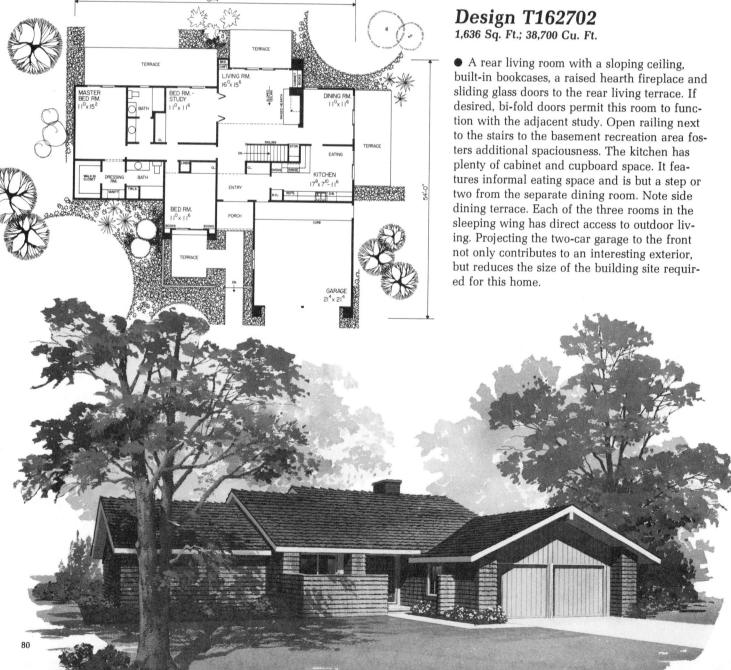

Design T162702
1,636 Sq. Ft.; 38,700 Cu. Ft.

● A rear living room with a sloping ceiling, built-in bookcases, a raised hearth fireplace and sliding glass doors to the rear living terrace. If desired, bi-fold doors permit this room to function with the adjacent study. Open railing next to the stairs to the basement recreation area fosters additional spaciousness. The kitchen has plenty of cabinet and cupboard space. It features informal eating space and is but a step or two from the separate dining room. Note side dining terrace. Each of the three rooms in the sleeping wing has direct access to outdoor living. Projecting the two-car garage to the front not only contributes to an interesting exterior, but reduces the size of the building site required for this home.

Design T162703
1,445 Sq. Ft.; 30,300 Cu. Ft.

● This modified, hip-roofed contemporary design will be the answer for those who want something both practical, yet different, inside and out. The covered front walk sets the stage for entering a modest sized home with tremendous livability. The focal point will be the pleasant conversation lounge. It is sunken, partially open to the other living areas and shares the enjoyment of the thru-fireplace with the living room. There are two bedrooms, two full baths and a study. The kitchen is outstanding.

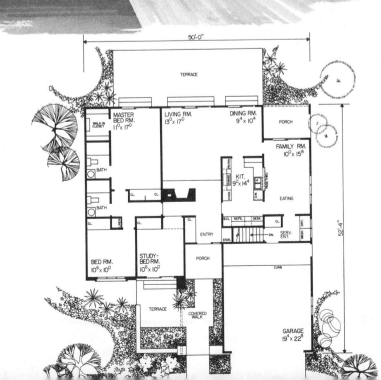

Design T162753
1,539 Sq. Ft.; 31,910 Cu. Ft.

● In this day and age of expensive building sites, projecting the attached garage from the front line of the house makes a lot of economic sense. It also lends itself to interesting roof lines and plan configurations. Here, a pleasing covered walkway to the front door results. A privacy wall adds an extra measure of design appeal and provides a sheltered terrace for the study/bedroom. You'll seldom find more livability in 1,539 square feet. Imagine, three bedrooms, two baths, a spacious living/dining area and a family room.

Design T162597
1,515 Sq. Ft.; 32,000 Cu. Ft.

● Whether it be a starter house you are after, or one in which to spend your retirement years, this pleasing frame home will provide a full measure of pride of ownership. The contrast of vertical and horizontal lines, the double front doors . . . . .

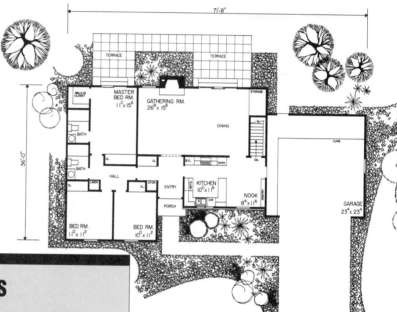

. . . . . and the coach lamp at the garage create an inviting exterior. The floor plan functions in an orderly and efficient manner. The 26 foot gathering room has a delightful view of the rear yard and will take care of those formal dining occasions. There are two full baths serving the three bedrooms. There are plenty of storage facilities, two sets of glass doors to the terraces, a fireplace in the gathering room, a basement and an attached two-car garage to act as a buffer against the wind. A delightful home, indeed.

Plans With Optional Exteriors

Design T162505
1,366 Sq. Ft.; 29,329 Cu. Ft.

● This design offers you a choice of three distinctively different exteriors. Which is your favorite? Blueprints show details for all three optional elevations.

A study of the floor plan reveals a fine measure of livability. In less than 1,400 square feet there are features galore. An excellent return on your construction dollar. In addition to the two eating areas and the open planning of the gathering room, the indoor-outdoor relationships are of great interest. The basement may be developed for recreational activities.

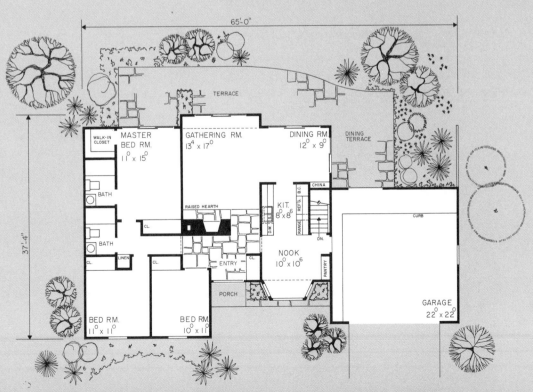

Three Distinctively Styled Exteriors . . .

Design T162705 1,746 Sq. Ft.; 37,000 Cu. Ft.

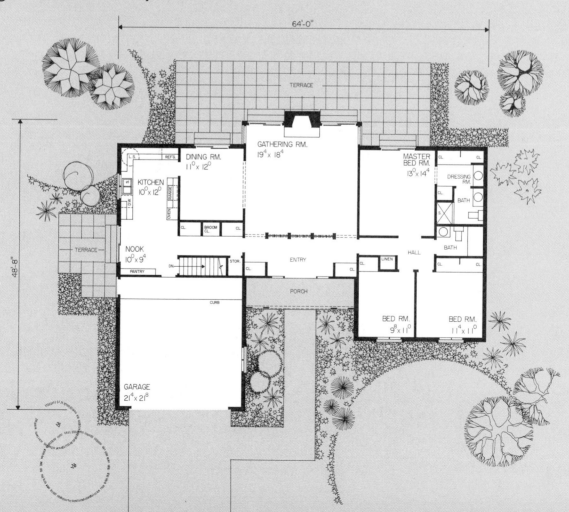

Design T162706 1,746 Sq. Ft.; 36,800 Cu. Ft.

. . . One Practical, Efficient Floor Plan

● Three different exteriors! But inside it's all the same livable house. Begin with the impressive entry hall . . . more than 19' long and offering double entry to the gathering room. Now the gathering room which is notable for its size and design. Notice how the fireplace is flanked by sliding glass doors leading to the terrace! That's unusual.

There's a formal dining room, too! The right spot for special birthday dinners as well as supper parties for friends. And an efficient kitchen that makes meal preparation easy whatever the occasion. Look for a built-in range and oven here . . . plus a bright dining nook with sliding doors to a second terrace. Three large bedrooms! All

located to give family members the utmost privacy. Including a master suite with a private dressing room, bath and a sliding glass door opening onto the main terrace. For blueprints of the hip-roof French adaptation on the opposite page order T162705. For the Contemporary version order T162706. For the Colonial order T162704.

Design T162704 1,746 Sq. Ft.; 38,000 Cu. Ft.

Design T161305 1,382 Sq. Ft.; 16,584 Cu. Ft.

● Order blueprints for any one of the three exteriors shown on this page and you will receive details for building this outstanding floor plan. You'll find the appeal of these exteriors difficult to beat. As for the plan, in less than 1,400 square feet there are three bedrooms, two full baths, a separate dining room, a formal living room, a fine kitchen overlooking the rear yard and an informal family room. In addition, there is the attached two-car garage. Note the location of the stairs when this plan is built with a basement. Each of the exteriors is predominantly brick - the front of Design T161305 (above) features both stone and vertical boards and battens with brick on the other three sides. Observe the double front doors of the French design, T161382 (below) and the Contemporary design, T161383 (bottom). Study the window treatment.

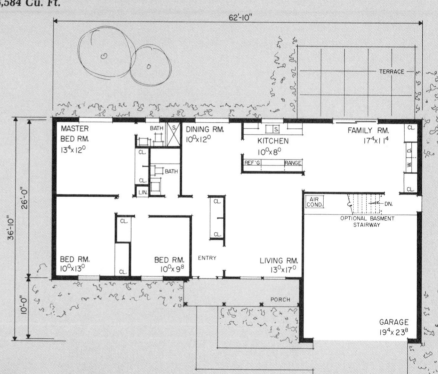

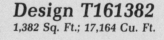

Design T161382
1,382 Sq. Ft.; 17,164 Cu. Ft.

Design T161383
1,382 Sq. Ft.; 15,448 Cu. Ft.

Design T161307 1,357 Sq. Ft.; 14,476 Cu. Ft.

● These three stylish exteriors have the same practical, L-shaped floor plan. Design T161307 (above) features a low-pitched, wide-overhanging roof, a pleasing use of horizontal siding and brick and an enclosed front flower court. Design T161380 (below) has its charm characterized by the pediment gables, the effective window treatment and the masses of brick. Design T161381 (bottom) is captivating because of its hip-roof, its dentils, panelled shutters and lamp post. Each of these three designs has a covered front porch. Inside, there is an abundance of livability. The formal living and dining area is spacious, and the U-shaped kitchen is efficient. There is informal eating space, a separate laundry and a fine family room. Note the sliding glass doors to the terrace. The blueprints include details for building either with or without a basement. Observe the pantry of the non-basement plan.

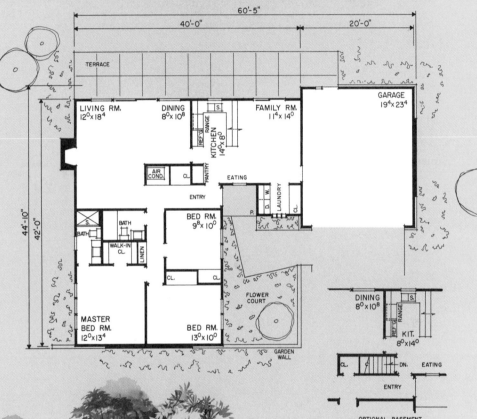

Design T161380
1,399 Sq. Ft.; 17,709 Cu. Ft.

Design T161381
1,399 Sq. Ft.; 17,937 Cu. Ft.

Design T162810
3-Bedroom Plan

Design T162814
4-Bedroom Plan

1,536 Sq. Ft.; 34,560 Cu. Ft.

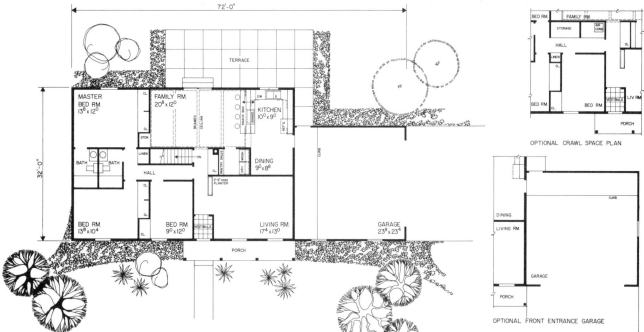

OPTIONAL CRAWL SPACE PLAN

OPTIONAL FRONT ENTRANCE GARAGE

● 2 x 6 stud wall construction front and center! The designs on these two pages are particularly energy-efficient minded. All exterior walls employ the use of the larger size stud (in preference to the traditional 2 x 4 stud) to permit the installation of extra thick insulation. The high cornice design also allows for more ceiling insulation. In addition to the insulation factor, 2 x 6 studs are practical from an economic standpoint. According to many experts, the use of 2 x 6's spaced 24 inches O.C. results in the need for less lumber and saves construction time. However, the energy-efficient features of this series do not end with the basic framing members. Efficiency begins right at the front door where the vestibule acts as an airlock restricting the flow of cold air to the interior. The basic rectangular shape of the house spells efficiency. No complicated and costly construction here. Yet, there has been no sacrifice of delightful exterior appeal. Efficiency and economy are also embodied in such features as back-to-back plumbing, centrally located furnace, minimal window and door openings and, most important of all - size.

Design T162811
3-Bedroom Plan

Design T162815
4-Bedroom Plan

1,581 Sq. Ft.; 36,694 Cu. Ft.

Design T162812
3-Bedroom Plan

Design T162816
4-Bedroom Plan

1,581 Sq. Ft.; 35,040 Cu. Ft.

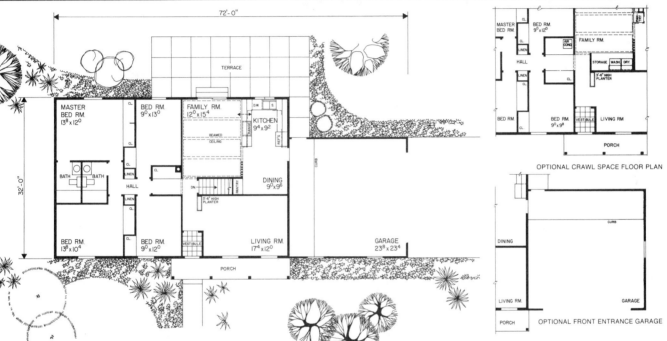

OPTIONAL CRAWL SPACE FLOOR PLAN

OPTIONAL FRONT ENTRANCE GARAGE

Within 1,536 square feet there is outstanding livability and a huge variety of options from which to choose. For instance, of the four stylish exteriors, which is your favorite? The cozy, front porch Farmhouse adaptation; the pleasing Southern Colonial version, the French creation, or the rugged Western facade? Further, do you prefer a three or a four bedroom floor plan? With or without a basement? Front or side-opening garage? If you wish to order blueprints for the hip-roofed design with three bedrooms, specify Design T162812; for the four bedroom option specify T162816. To order blueprints for the three bedroom Southern Colonial, request Design T162811; for the four bedroom model, ask for Design T162815, etc. All blueprints include the optional non-basement and front opening garage details. Whatever the version you select, you and your family will enjoy the beamed ceiling of the family room, the efficient, U-shaped kitchen, the dining area, the traffic-free living room and the fine storage facilities. Truly, a fine design series created to give each home buyer the maximum amount of choice and flexibility.

Design T162813
3-Bedroom Plan

Design T162817
4-Bedroom Plan

1,536 Sq. Ft.; 33,334 Cu. Ft.

Design T162802
1,729 Sq. Ft.; 42,640 Cu. Ft.

● The three exteriors shown at the left house the same, efficiently planned one-story floor plan shown below. Be sure to notice the design variations in the window placement and roof pitch. The Tudor design to the left is delightful. Half-timbered stucco and brick comprise the facade of this English Tudor variation of the plan. Note authentic bay window in the front bedroom.

Design T162803
1,679 Sq. Ft.; 36,755 Cu. Ft.

● Housed in varying facades, this floor plan is very efficient. The front foyer leads to each of the living areas. The sleeping area of two, or optional three, bedrooms is ready to serve the family. Then there is the gathering room. This room is highlighted by its size, 16 x 20 feet. A contemporary mix of fieldstone and vertical wood siding characterizes this exterior. The absence of columns or posts gives a modern look to the covered porch.

Design T162804
1,674 Sq. Ft.; 35,465 Cu. Ft.

● Stuccoed arches, multi-paned windows and a gracefully sloped roof accent the exterior of this Spanish-inspired design. Like the other two designs, the interior kitchen will efficiently serve the dining room, covered dining porch and breakfast room with great ease. Blueprints for all three designs include details for an optional non-basement plan.

CUSTOMIZABLE

Custom Alterations? See page 320 for customizing this plan to your specifications.

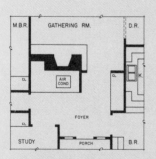

OPTIONAL NON-BASEMENT

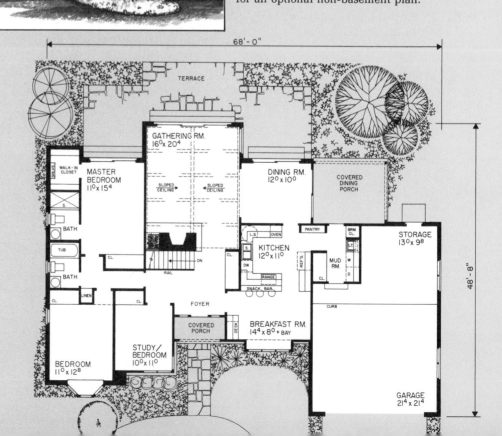

Design T162805
1,547 Sq. Ft.; 40,880 Cu. Ft.

● Three completely different exterior facades share one compact, practical and economical floor plan. The major design variations are roof pitch, window placement and garage openings. Each design will hold its own when comparing the three exteriors. The design to the right is a romantic stone-and-shingle cottage design. This design, along with the other two designs presented here, is outstanding.

Design T162806
1,584 Sq. Ft.; 41,880 Cu. Ft.

● Even though these exteriors are extremely different in their styling and also have a few design variations, their floor plans are identical. Each will provide the family with a livable plan. In this brick and half-timbered stucco Tudor version, like the other two, the living-dining room expands across the rear of the plan and has direct access to the covered porch. Notice the built-in planter adjacent to the open staircase leading to the basement.

Design T162807
1,576 Sq. Ft.; 35,355 Cu. Ft.

● Along with the living-dining areas of the other two plans, this sleek contemporary styled home's breakfast room also will have a view of the covered porch. A desk, snack bar and mud room housing the laundry facilities are near the U-shaped kitchen. Clustering these work areas together is very convenient. The master bedroom has a private bath.

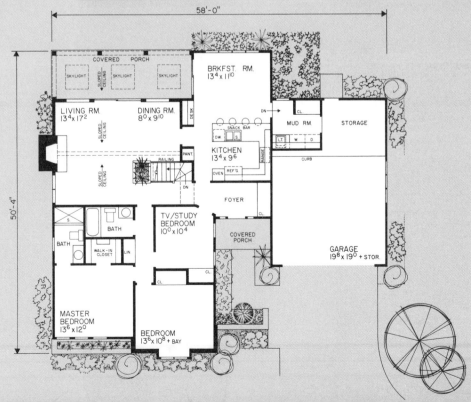

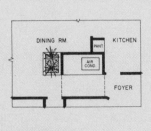

OPTIONAL NON-BASEMENT

91

Design T162941
1,842 Sq. Ft.; 42,688 Cu. Ft.

● Here is a basic floor plan which goes with each of the differently styled exteriors. The Early American version above is charming, indeed. Horizontal siding, stone, window boxes, a dovecote, a picket fence and a garden court enhance its appeal. Note the covered entrance.

Design T162942
1,834 Sq. Ft.; 42,516 Cu. Ft.

● The Tudor exterior above will be the favorite of many. Stucco, simulated timber work and diamond-lite windows set its unique character. Each of the delightful exteriors features eye-catching roof lines. Inside, there is an outstanding plan to cater to the living patterns of the small family, empty nesters, or retirees.

Design T162943
1,834 Sq. Ft.; 41,965 Cu. Ft.

● The Contemporary optional exterior above features vertical siding and a wide-overhanging roof with exposed rafter ends. The foyer is spacious with sloped ceiling and a dramatic open staircase to the basement recreation area. Other ceilings in the house are also sloped. The breakfast, dining and media rooms are highlights, along with the laundry, the efficient kitchen, the snack bar and the master bath.

● Here is a unique series of designs with three charming exterior adaptations-Southern Colonial, Western Ranch, French Provincial - and two distinctive floor plans. Each plan has a different design number and is less than 1,600 square feet.

If yours is a preference for the floor plan featuring the 26 foot keeping room, you should order blueprints for Design T162611. Of course, the details for each of the three delightful exteriors will be included. On the other hand, should the plan with the living, dining and family rooms be your favorite, order blueprints for Design T162612 and get details for all three exteriors.

There are many points of similarity in the two designs. Each has a fireplace, 2½ baths, sliding glass doors to the rear terrace, master bedroom with walk-in closet and private bath with stall shower and a basement. It is interesting to note that two of the exteriors have covered porches. Don't miss the beamed ceilings, the various storage facilities and the stall showers.

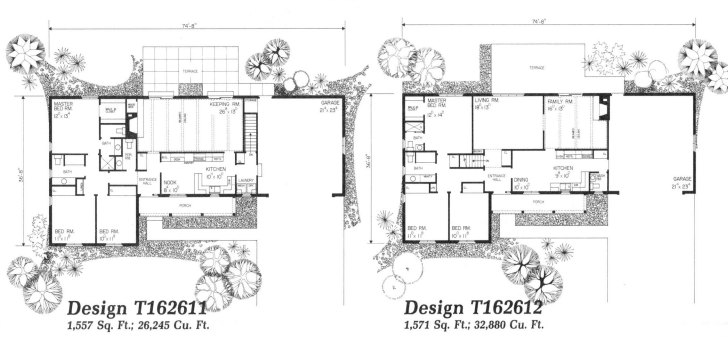

Design T162611
1,557 Sq. Ft.; 26,245 Cu. Ft.

Design T162612
1,571 Sq. Ft.; 32,880 Cu. Ft.

Design T161387
1,488 Sq. Ft.; 16,175 Cu. Ft.

Design T161388
1,488 Sq. Ft.; 18,600 Cu. Ft.

Design T161389
1,488 Sq. Ft.; 18,600 Cu. Ft.

French Colonial, Contemporary . . .
. . . All With Same Floor Plan

● Your choice of exterior goes with the outstanding floor plan on the opposing page. If your tastes include a liking for French Provincial, Design T161389 will provide a lifetime of satisfaction. On the other hand, should you prefer the simple straightforward lines of comtemporary design, the exterior for Design T161387 will be your favorite. For those who enjoy the warmth of Colonial adaptations, the charming exterior for Design T161388 will be perfect. Of interest, is a comparison of these three exteriors. Observe the varying design treatment of the windows, the double front doors, the garage doors and the roof lines. Don't miss other architectural details. Study each exterior and the floor plan carefully. Three charming designs you won't want to miss.

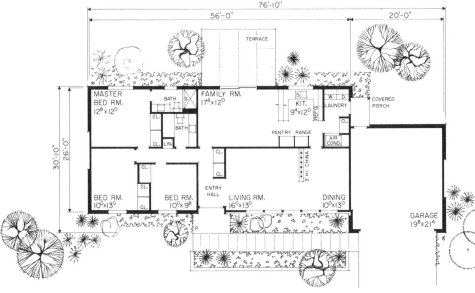

Design T161865
1,598 Sq. Ft.; 25,626 Cu. Ft.

Design T161864
1,598 Sq. Ft.; 27,611 Cu. Ft.

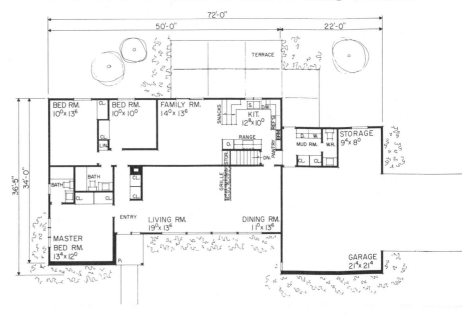

Design T161866
1,598 Sq. Ft.; 27,248 Cu. Ft.

Your Choice Of Exterior . . .
. . . Goes With This Fine Plan

● What's your favorite exterior? The one above which has a distinctive colonial appearance, or that with its sleek contemporary look? Maybe you prefer the more formal hip-roof exterior with its French feeling. Whatever your choice, you'll know your next home will be one that is delightfully proportioned and is sure to be among the most attractive in the neighborhood. It is interesting to note that each exterior highlights an effective use of wood siding and stone (or brick, as in the case of Design T161866). The floor plan features three bedrooms, 2½ baths, a formal living and dining room, a snack bar and a mud room. The master bedroom of the contemporary design has its window located in the left side elevation wall. Don't miss storage.

Design T162821
1,363 Sq. Ft. - First Floor
357 Sq. Ft. - Second Floor
37,145 Cu. Ft.

Mansard Roof Adaptation

A Trend House . . .

● Here is a truly unique house whose interior was designed with the current decade's economies, lifestyles and demographics in mind. While functioning as a one-story home, the second floor provides an extra measure of livability when required. In addition, this two-story section adds to the dramatic appeal of both the exterior and the interior. Within only 1,363 square feet, this contemporary delivers refreshing and outstanding living patterns for those who are buying their first home, those who have raised their family and are looking for a smaller home and those in search of a retirement home. The center entrance routes traffic effectively to each area. The great room with its raised hearth fireplace, two-story arching and delightful glass areas is most distinctive. The kitchen is efficient and but a step from the dining room. The covered porch will provide an ideal spot for warm-weather, outdoor dining. The separate laundry room is strategically located. The sleeping area may consist of one bedroom and a study, or two bedrooms. Each room functions with the sheltered wood deck - a perfect location for a hot tub.

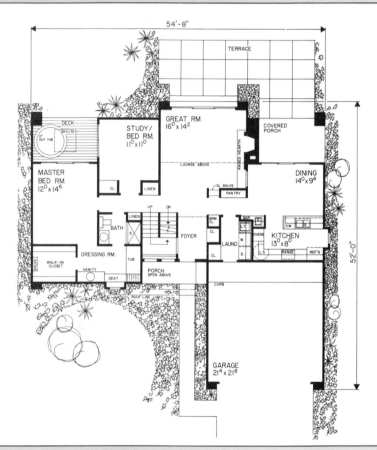

Design T162822
1,363 Sq. Ft. - First Floor
351 Sq. Ft. - Second Floor
36,704 Cu. Ft.

Gable Roof Version

UPPER GREAT RM.

RAILING

CL.

LOUNGE / HOBBIES
16⁰ x 9²

SKYLITE

CL.

DN

RAILING

UPPER
FOYER

STOR./
BATH

RAILING

BALCONY

LOUNGE / GUEST RM. /
GRANDCHILDREN'S RM.
16⁰ x 19²

CL.

CL.

DN

RAILING

UPPER
FOYER

BATH

RAILING

ALTERNATE SECOND FLOOR

...For the 90's and Decades to Come

● The full bath is planned to have easy access to the master bedroom and living areas. Note the stall shower, tub, seat and vanity. The second floor offers two optional layouts. It may serve as a lounge, studio or hobby area overlooking the great room. Or, it may be built to function as a complete private guest room. It would be a great place for the visiting grandchildren. Don't miss the outdoor balcony. Additional livability and storage facilities may be developed in the basement. Then, of course, there are two exteriors to choose from. Design T162821, with its horizontal frame siding and deep, attractive cornice detail, is an eye-catcher. For those with a preference for a contemporary fashioned gable roof and vertical siding, there is Design T162822. With the living areas facing the south, these designs will enjoy benefits of passive solar exposure. The overhanging roofs will help provide relief from the high summer sun. This is surely a modest-sized floor plan which will deliver new dimensions in small-family livability.

Design T162155 1,152 Sq. Ft.; 12,846 Cu. Ft.

● Four bedrooms, 1½ baths, an efficient kitchen, an L-shaped living/dining area, plenty of storage facilities and an attached carport are among the highlights of this modest home. All three exteriors are included.

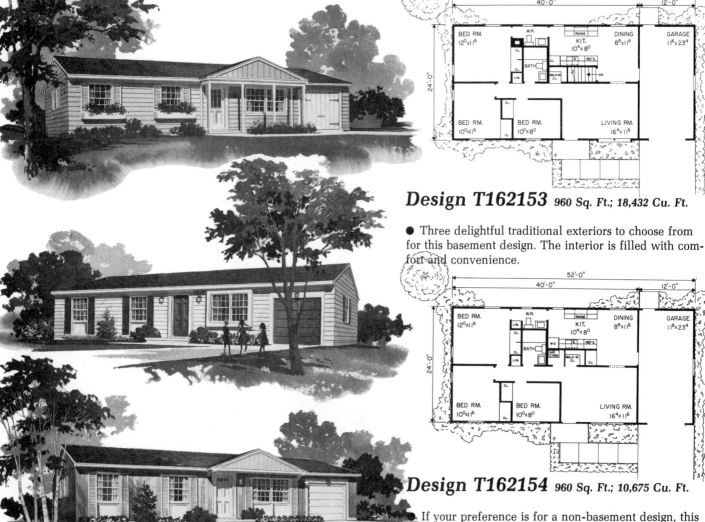

Design T162153 960 Sq. Ft.; 18,432 Cu. Ft.

● Three delightful traditional exteriors to choose from for this basement design. The interior is filled with comfort and convenience.

Design T162154 960 Sq. Ft.; 10,675 Cu. Ft.

● If your preference is for a non-basement design, this plan is available. It still houses four bedrooms and 1½ baths. Single car garage is attached.

Design T161323 1,344 Sq. Ft.; 17,472 Cu. Ft.

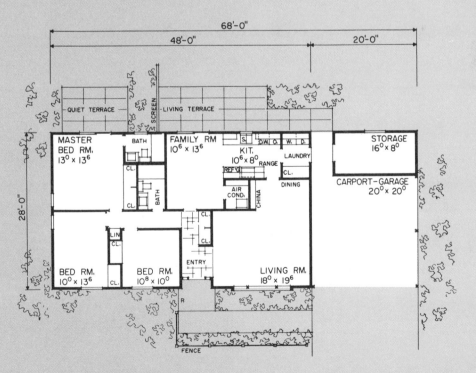

MASTER BED RM. 13⁰ x 13⁶

BATH

FAMILY RM. 10⁶ x 13⁶

STORAGE 16⁰ x 8⁰

KIT. 10⁶ x 8⁰

LAUNDRY

RANGE

REF'G

AIR COND.

DINING

CHINA

CARPORT–GARAGE 20⁰ x 20⁰

BED RM. 10⁰ x 13⁶

BED RM. 10⁸ x 10⁰

ENTRY

LIVING RM. 18⁰ x 19⁶

QUIET TERRACE

SCREEN

LIVING TERRACE

FENCE

68'-0"

48'-0"

20'-0"

28'-0"

● Incorporated in the set of blueprints for this design are details for building each of the three charming, traditional exteriors. Each of the three alternate exteriors has a distinction all its own. A study of the floor plan reveals fine livability. There are two full baths, a fine family room, an efficient work center, a formal dining area, bulk storage facilities and sliding glass doors to the quiet and living terraces. Laundry is strategically located near the kitchen.

Design T162200

1,695 Sq. Ft.; 18,916 Cu. Ft.

● The two plans featured here are both housed in this L-shaped ranch home. Its exterior shows a Spanish influence by utilizing a stucco exterior finish, grilled windows and an arched entryway. Beyond the arched entryway is the private front court which leads to the tiled foyer. Interior livability has been well planned in both designs.

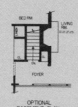

OPTIONAL BASEMENT PLAN

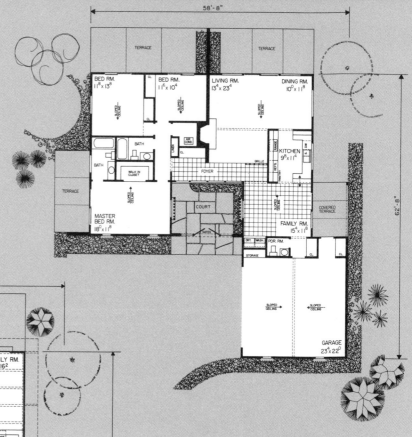

Design T162677

1,634 Sq. Ft.; 26,770 Cu. Ft.

● Notice the difference in these plan's livability. Design T162200 has a shared living dining room overlooking the backyard and a front master bedroom with a side terrace where Design T162677 has a separate front dining room, family room with access to the rear terrace and a rear master bedroom with an adjacent covered porch. Both designs have two additional bedrooms besides the master bedroom. Access to the basement varies in each plan.

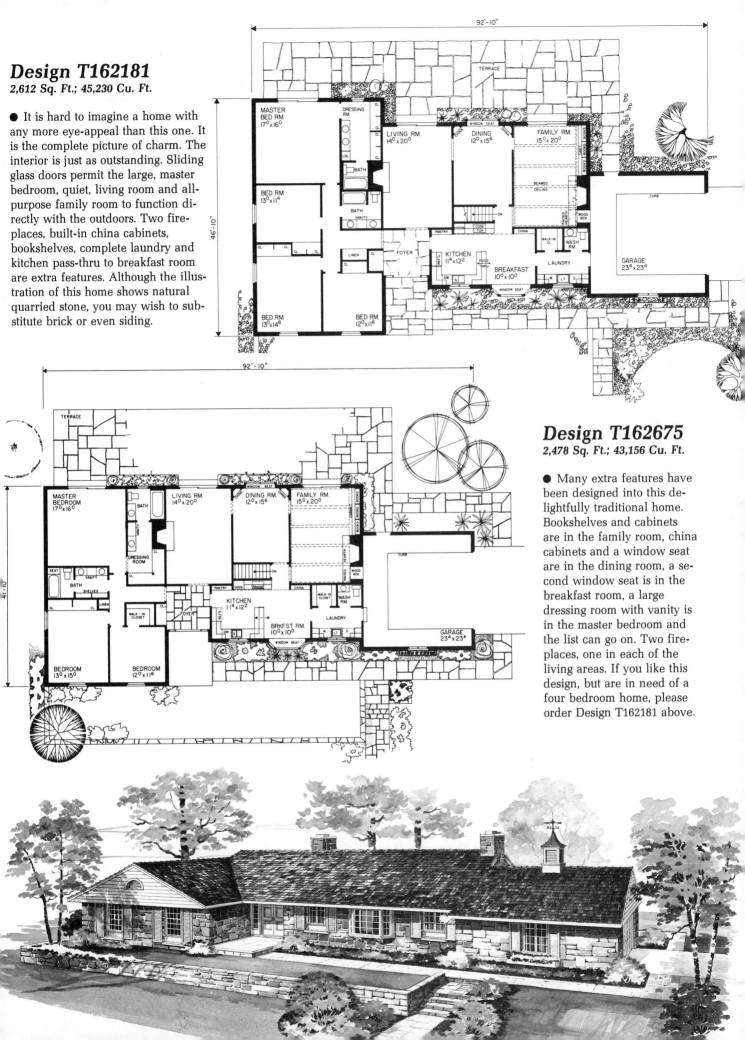

Design T162181
2,612 Sq. Ft.; 45,230 Cu. Ft.

● It is hard to imagine a home with any more eye-appeal than this one. It is the complete picture of charm. The interior is just as outstanding. Sliding glass doors permit the large, master bedroom, quiet, living room and all-purpose family room to function directly with the outdoors. Two fireplaces, built-in china cabinets, bookshelves, complete laundry and kitchen pass-thru to breakfast room are extra features. Although the illustration of this home shows natural quarried stone, you may wish to substitute brick or even siding.

Design T162675
2,478 Sq. Ft.; 43,156 Cu. Ft.

● Many extra features have been designed into this delightfully traditional home. Bookshelves and cabinets are in the family room, china cabinets and a window seat are in the dining room, a second window seat is in the breakfast room, a large dressing room with vanity is in the master bedroom and the list can go on. Two fireplaces, one in each of the living areas. If you like this design, but are in need of a four bedroom home, please order Design T162181 above.

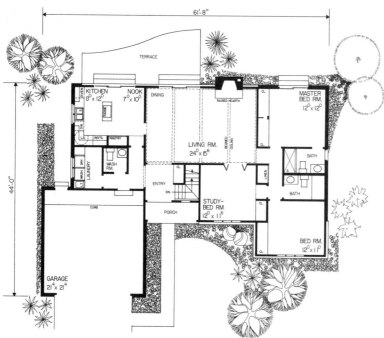

Design T162565
1,540 Sq. Ft.; 33,300 Cu. Ft.

● This modest sized floor plan has much to offer in the way of livability. It may function as either a two or three bedroom home. The living room is huge and features a fine, raised hearth fireplace. The open stairway to the basement is handy and will lead to what may be developed as the recreation area. In addition to the two full baths, there is an extra wash room. Adjacent is the laundry room and the service entrance from the garage. The blueprints you order for this design will show details for each of the three delightful elevations above. Which is your favorite? The Tudor, the Colonial or the Contemporary?

THE 1¹/₂-STORY HOUSE:
Expandable and Affordable

PLAN T162927

Historically, the American home has been associated with a one- or two-room structure which changed significantly in appearance and living area as the family grew. Sometimes the first addition was horizontal with the construction of a bedroom or keeping room. Frequently, the expansion was vertical for the development of upstairs sleeping rooms.

Present-day 1¹/₂-story houses are as divergent as they are functional and affordable. Some contain all sleeping areas on the second floor, providing a cozy separation from living areas; others have bedrooms on both floors, allowing for a more private first floor master bedroom suite or guest room. Frequently, such plans are essentially one-story houses with a bonus second floor bedroom space, providing perfect quarters for "empty-nesters" with visiting children and other guests. Because of the added half story, this design is more dramatic and spacious feeling, adding height to the typical one-story plan. Whatever the arrangement, the 1¹/₂-story house delivers expanded sleeping capabilities to meet growing needs with only a modest investment.

Perhaps the most affordable aspect of the 1¹/₂-story house is that it provides a completed first floor bedroom or two and an unfinished "attic" upon occupancy. Later, the second floor can be converted as needed and as the budget permits.

Examples abound of "starter" houses that began as somewhat minimal housing units then blossomed to accommodate increased needs. The popular and highly

continued on next page

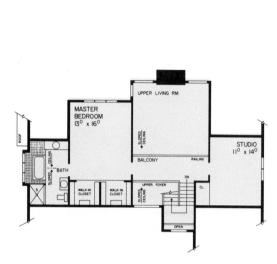

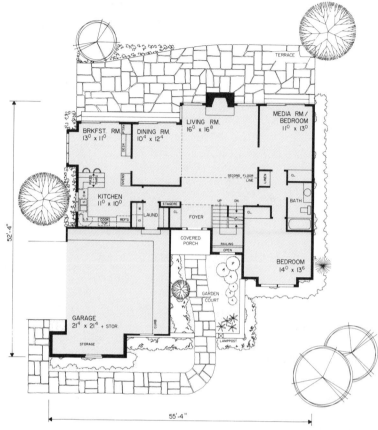

● This charming Early American design with stone and board exterior is just as warm on the inside. Features include a complete second-floor master bedroom suite with an upper living room, studio, upper foyer, and master bathroom. The upper living room and master bathroom feature sloped ceilings. The first floor features a convenience kitchen with pass-thru to a breakfast room. There's also a formal dining room just steps away in the rear of the house. An adjacent rear living room enjoys its own fireplace. Other features include a rear media room or optional third bedroom. This could be

a great place for VCR's, computers, stereos, and even TV's. A downstairs bedroom enjoys an excellent front view. Other highlights include a garden court, covered porch, and large garage with extra storage. This is one well-packaged house, indeed, with plenty to offer the entire family.

Design T162927
1,425 Sq. Ft. - First Floor
704 Sq. Ft. - Second Floor
39,650 Cu. Ft.

identifiable rambling Cape Cod house is a case in point. Its symmetrical styling and distinctive detailing (such as multi-paned windows and central entrance foyer) usually complement the half story bedrooms or a study/studio. This expandable capability of the 1½-story house recommends it for prime consideration as an affordable house type. Neither one-story, two-story, nor multi-level houses lend themselves to expansion as ideally as 1½-stories.

As you review the designs in this section, note the varying sizes, shapes, and styles. Observe, for example, how the eminently affordable houses on pages 124 and 125 grow to become four-bedroom, two-bath, big-family houses. Don't miss the "rambling" nature of T162563 on pages 142 and 143 or the expandable design on pages 106 and 107. And, of course, be aware of the Contemporary and Tudor adaptations and their special amenities.

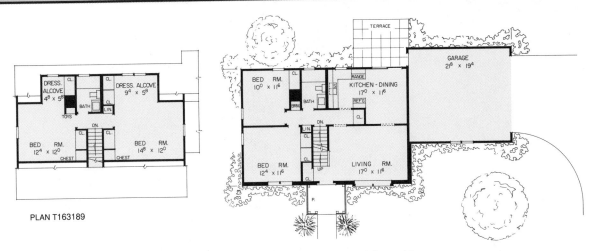

PLAN T163189

A comfortable alternative with two bedrooms upstairs and two downstairs. As a start-up home, the half story could remain unfinished until needed.

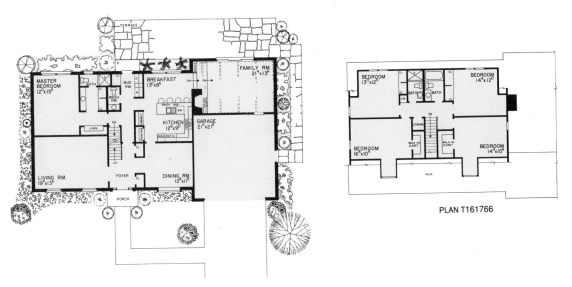

PLAN T161766

The master bedroom suite enjoys secluded privacy when located on the first floor away from four half-story bedrooms upstairs.

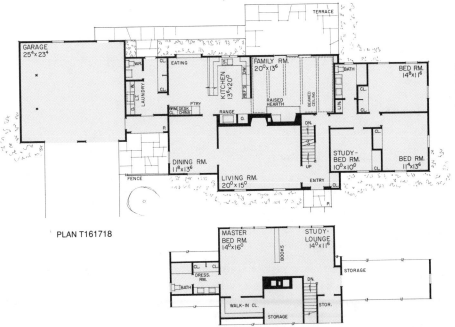

PLAN T161718

Using the half story for a master bedoom suite, complete with study or lounge, provides a special spot of quiet in a house of activity.

Expanding the Half-House

Design T162682 976 Sq. Ft. - First Floor (Basic Plan)
1,230 Sq. Ft. - First Floor (Expanded Plan); 744 Sq. Ft. - Second Floor (Both Plans)
29,355 Cu. Ft. Basic Plan; 35,084 Cu. Ft. Expanded Plan

32'-0"

TERRACE

DINING RM.
10^8 x 12^0

COUNTRY KITCHEN
20^0 x 13^0 - 15^8

30'-0"

PDR
RM.

FOYER

LIVING RM.
20^0 x 13^0

BOOKS

PORCH

BEDROOM
12^{10} x 9^8

BEDROOM
12^{10} x 9^8

LINEN

BATH

BATH

MASTER
BEDROOM
11^{10} x 14^0

ROOF

● Here is an expandable Colonial with a full measure of Cape Cod Charm. For those who wish to build the basic house, there is an abundance of low-budget livability. Twin fireplaces serve the formal living room and the informal country kitchen. Note the spaciousness of both areas. A dining room and powder room are also on the first floor of this basic plan. Upstairs three bedrooms and two full baths.

CUSTOMIZABLE

Custom Alterations? See page 320 for customizing this plan to your specifications.

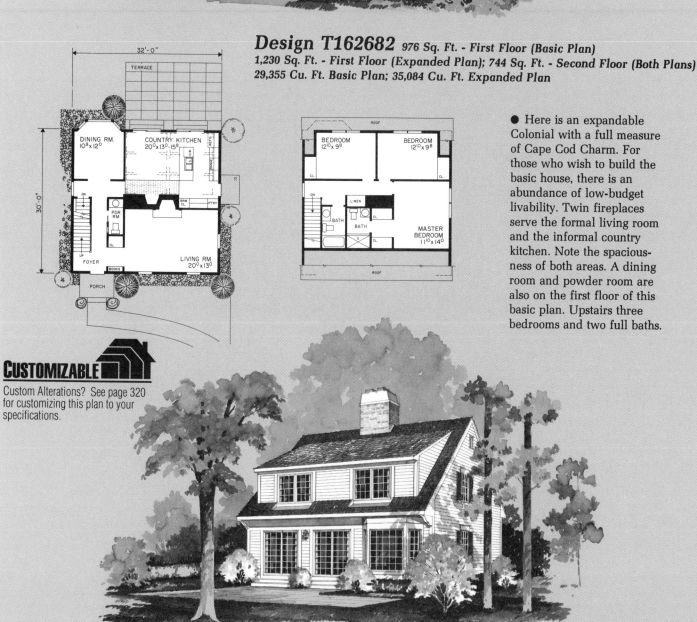

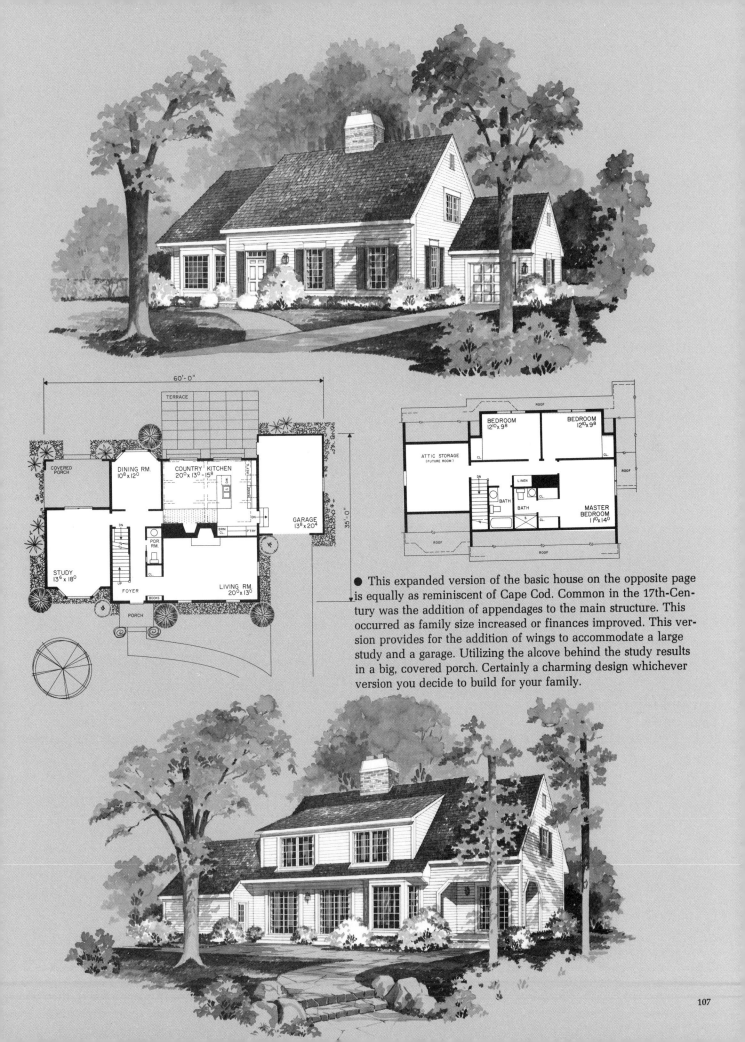

60'-0"

TERRACE

COVERED PORCH

DINING RM.
10⁸x12⁰

COUNTRY KITCHEN
20⁰x13⁰-15⁸

GARAGE
13⁸x20⁴

35'-0"

STUDY
13⁶x18⁰

PDR. RM.

BRM. CL.

P'TRY

DN

CL.

UP

FOYER

BOOKS

LIVING RM.
20⁰x13⁰

PORCH

ROOF

BEDROOM
12¹⁰x9⁸

BEDROOM
12¹⁰x9⁸

ATTIC STORAGE
(FUTURE ROOM)

ROOF

DN

LINEN

CL.

BATH

BATH

CL.

MASTER BEDROOM
11¹⁰x14⁰

CL.

ROOF

ROOF

● This expanded version of the basic house on the opposite page is equally as reminiscent of Cape Cod. Common in the 17th-Century was the addition of appendages to the main structure. This occurred as family size increased or finances improved. This version provides for the addition of wings to accommodate a large study and a garage. Utilizing the alcove behind the study results in a big, covered porch. Certainly a charming design whichever version you decide to build for your family.

Design T161791
1,157 Sq. Ft. - First Floor
875 Sq. Ft. - Second Floor
27,790 Cu. Ft.

● Wherever you build this cozy house, an aura of Cape Cod is sure to unfold. The symmetry is pleasing, indeed; the livability is exceptional.

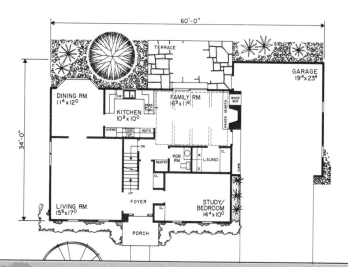

Design T161901
1,200 Sq. Ft. - First Floor
744 Sq. Ft. - Second Floor
27,822 Cu. Ft.

● Colonial charm hardly could be more appealingly captured than it is by this winsome design. The center entrance routes traffic most efficiently.

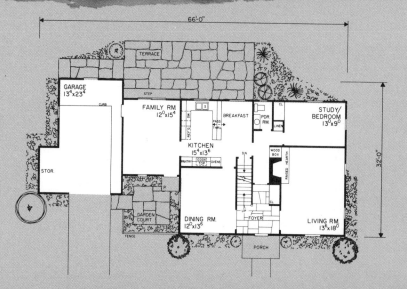

Design T161870

1,136 Sq. Ft. - First Floor
936 Sq. Ft. - Second Floor
26,312 Cu. Ft.

● Besides an enchanting exterior, this home has formal dining and living rooms, plus informal family and breakfast rooms. Note 2½ baths.

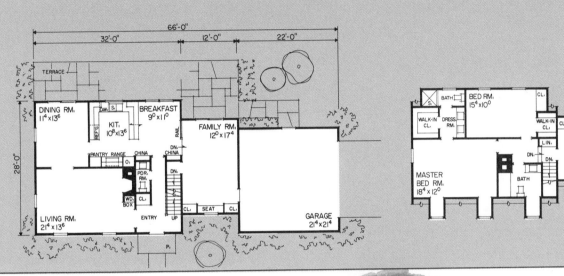

Design T163126

1,141 Sq. Ft. - First Floor
630 Sq. Ft. - Second Floor
25,533 Cu. Ft.

● Positively outstanding. From the delightful flower court to the upstairs storage room, this New England adaptation has much to talk about.

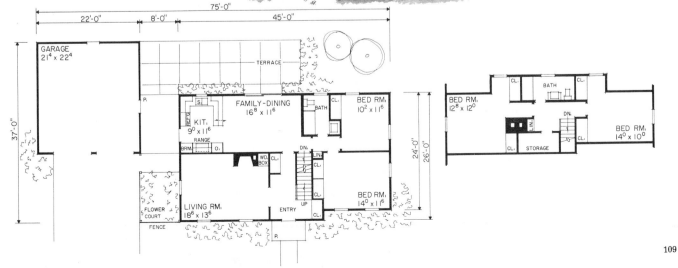

Design T162650

1,451 Sq. Ft. - First Floor
1,091 Sq. Ft. - Second Floor; 43,555 Cu. Ft.

● The rear view of this design is just as appealing as the front. The dormers and the covered porch with pillars is a charming way to introduce this house to the on-lookers. Inside, the appeal is also outstanding. Note the size (18 x 25) of the gathering room which is open to the dining room. Kitchen-nook area is very spacious and features an island range, built-in desk and more. It is a great convenience having the laundry in the service area which is close to the kitchen. Imagine, a fireplace in both the gathering room and the master bedroom! Make special note of the front and rear service entrances.

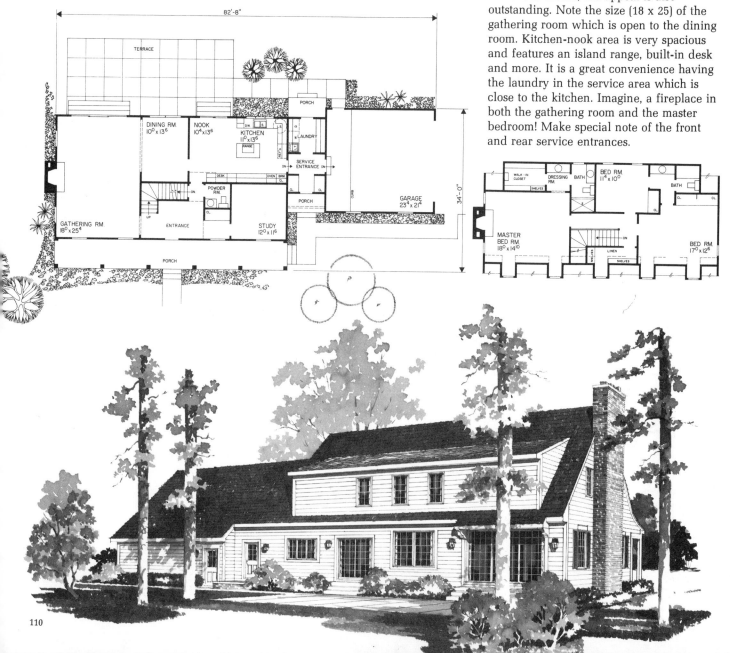

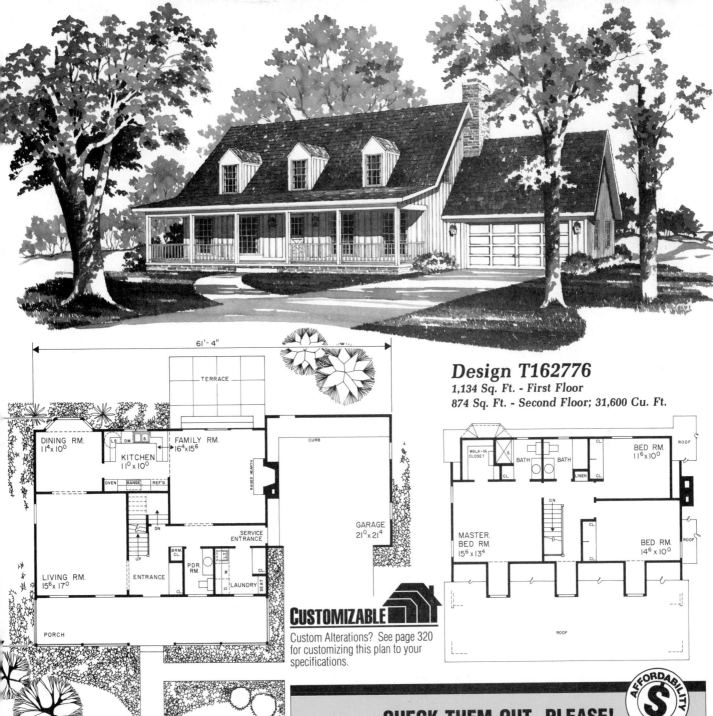

Design T162776

1,134 Sq. Ft. - First Floor
874 Sq. Ft. - Second Floor; 31,600 Cu. Ft.

CUSTOMIZABLE

Custom Alterations? See page 320 for customizing this plan to your specifications.

● This board-and-batten farmhouse design has all of the country charm of New England. The large front covered porch will be appreciated during the beautiful warm weather months. Immediately off the front entrance is the delightful corner living room. The dining room with bay windows will be easily served by the U-shaped kitchen. Informal family enjoyment will be obtained in the family room which features a raised hearth fireplace, sliding glass doors to the rear terrace and easy access to the work center of powder room, laundry and service entrance. The second floor houses all of the sleeping facilities. There is a master bedroom with a private bath and walk-in closet. Two other bedrooms share a bath. This is an excellent one-and-a-half story design.

CHECK THEM OUT, PLEASE!

AFFORDABILITY TIP

Generally, builders are reputable businesspeople and skilled artisans. Of course, you should know that *before* hiring one for the duration. Ask questions like these:

- Has the builder been established in business for some time?
- Does he have a record of building good houses? Will he show you several and give you the owners' names?
- Do local building material suppliers and subcontractors give the builder a good rating?
- Is the builder a member of the local home builder chapter of the National Association of Home Builders?
- Does the builder offer warranties covering workmanship, materials, and major household systems?
- Does the builder have a listed telephone number?

Source: "How to Avoid the 10 Biggest Home-Buying Traps," The Building Institute.

Design T162780
2,006 Sq. Ft. - First Floor
718 Sq. Ft. - Second Floor; 42,110 Cu. Ft.

● This 1½-story contemporary has more fine features than one can imagine. The livability is outstanding and can be appreciated by the whole family. Note the fine indoor-outdoor living relationships.

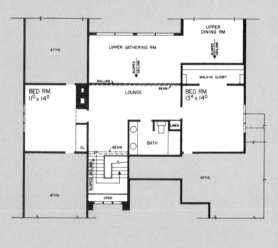

Design T162772
1,579 Sq. Ft. - First Floor
1,240 Sq. Ft. - Second Floor; 39,460 Cu. Ft.

● This four-bedroom two-story contemporary design is sure to suit your growing family needs. The rear U-shaped kitchen, flanked by the family and dining rooms, will be very efficient to the busy homemaker. Parents will enjoy all the convenience of the master bedroom suite.

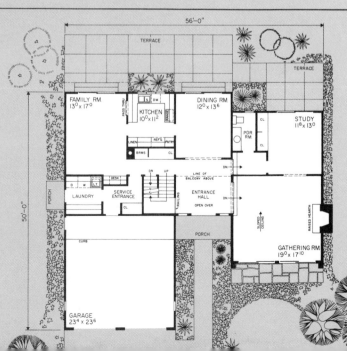

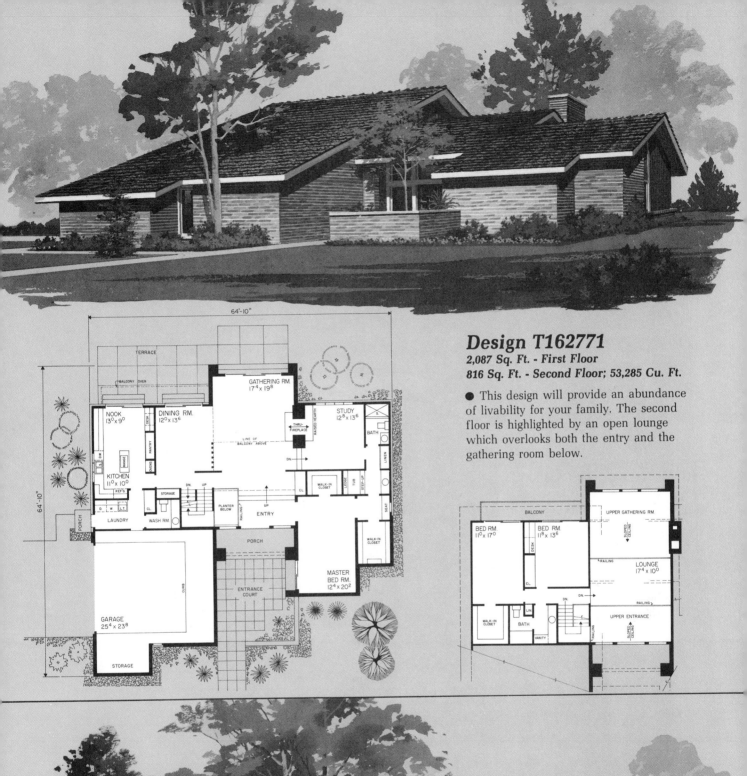

Design T162771
2,087 Sq. Ft. - First Floor
816 Sq. Ft. - Second Floor; 53,285 Cu. Ft.

● This design will provide an abundance of livability for your family. The second floor is highlighted by an open lounge which overlooks both the entry and the gathering room below.

First floor plan labels:
TERRACE
BALCONY OVER
GATHERING RM. 17⁴ x 19⁸
NOOK 13⁰ x 9⁰
DINING RM. 12⁰ x 13⁶
DESK
PANTRY
OVEN
THRU-FIREPLACE
RAISED HEARTH
STUDY 12⁸ x 13⁶
BATH
LINEN
LINE OF BALCONY ABOVE
KITCHEN 11⁰ x 10⁰
RANGE
REF'G
DN.
UP
STORAGE
WALK-IN CLOSET
LEDGE
TUB
STEP-UP
CL.
LAUNDRY
WASH RM.
PLANTER BELOW
RAILING
ENTRY
UP
PORCH
MASTER BED RM. 12⁴ x 20²
WALK-IN CLOSET
SEAT
GARAGE 25⁴ x 23⁸
CURB
ENTRANCE COURT
STORAGE
64'-10"
64'-10"

Second floor plan labels:
BALCONY
UPPER GATHERING RM.
BED RM. 11⁰ x 17⁰
BED RM. 11⁸ x 13⁶
DESK
CL.
SLOPED CEILING
LOUNGE 17⁴ x 10⁰
RAILING
WALK-IN CLOSET
BATH
LIN.
DN.
DN.
VANITY
RAILING
UPPER ENTRANCE
SLOPED CEILING

Design T161766 1,638 Sq. Ft. - First Floor; 1,006 Sq. Ft. - Second Floor; 35,352 Cu. Ft.

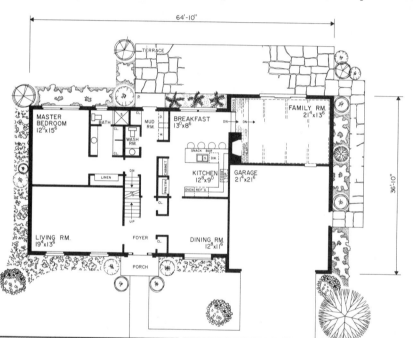

● This cozy home has over 2,600 square feet of livable floor area! And the manner in which this space to put to work to function conveniently for the large family is worth studying. Imagine five bedrooms, three full baths, living, dining and family rooms. Note large kitchen.

Design T161970
1,664 Sq. Ft. - First Floor
1,116 Sq. Ft. - Second Floor
41,912 Cu. Ft.

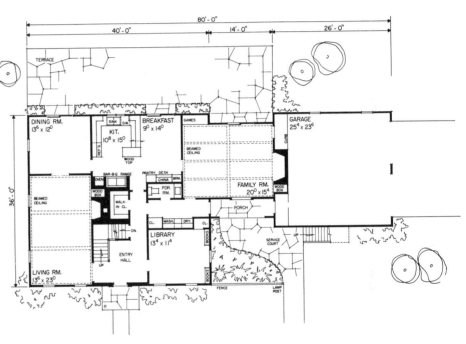

● The prototype of this Colonial house was an integral part of the 18th-Century New England landscape; the updated version is a welcome addition to any suburban scene.

Design T161747 1,690 Sq. Ft. - First Floor
1,060 Sq. Ft. - Second Floor; 38,424 Cu. Ft.

● This one-and-a-half story design has everything that any family could want, or need, in a new home. Two fireplaces! One in each of the front living areas. Note the efficient planning of the kitchen area. It is adjacent to the breakfast and dining rooms plus the mud room with wash room. Three bedrooms are on the second floor.

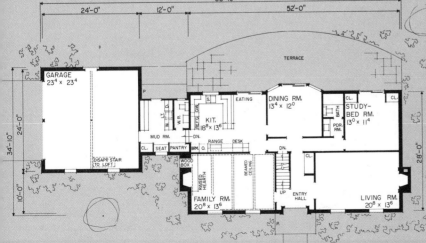

Design T162657 1,217 Sq. Ft. - First Floor
868 Sq. Ft. - Second Floor; 33,260 Cu. Ft.

● Deriving its design from the traditional Cape Cod style, this facade features clapboard siding, small-paned windows and a transom-lit entrance flanked by carriage lamps. A central chimney services two fireplaces, one in the country-kitchen and the other in the formal living room which is removed from the disturbing flow of traffic. The master suite is located to the left of the upstairs landing. A full bathroom services two additional bedrooms.

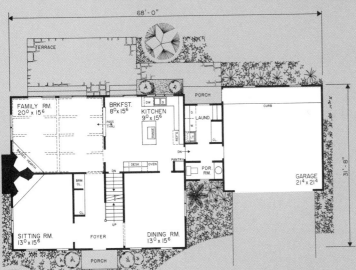

68'-0"

TERRACE

FAMILY RM.
20⁰ x 15⁶

BRKFST.
8⁰ x 15⁶

KITCHEN
9⁰ x 15⁶

PORCH

LAUND.

PASSED HEARTH

PASS THRU

BDRM CL

CL

DN

DESK OVEN

PANTRY

PDR. RM.

UP

SITTING RM.
13⁰ x 15⁶

FOYER

DINING RM.
13⁰ x 15⁶

PORCH

CURB

GARAGE
21⁴ x 21⁴

31'-8"

ROOF

BEDROOM
11⁰ x 10⁶

BATH

BATH

WALK-IN CLOSET

LINEN

SHELVES

DN

CL

BEDROOM
17⁸ x 10⁶

WALK-IN CLOSET

MASTER BEDROOM
13⁰ x 14⁸

ROOF

Design T162644

1,349 Sq. Ft. - First Floor
836 Sq. Ft. - Second Floor
36,510 Cu. Ft.

● What a delightful, compact two-story this is! This design has many fine features tucked within its framework. The bowed roofline of this house stems from late 17th-Century architecture.

Design T162278

1,804 Sq. Ft. - First Floor
939 Sq. Ft. - Second Floor
44,274 Cu. Ft.

● The Tudor charm is characterized in each of these three one-and-a-half story designs. Study each of them for its own special features.

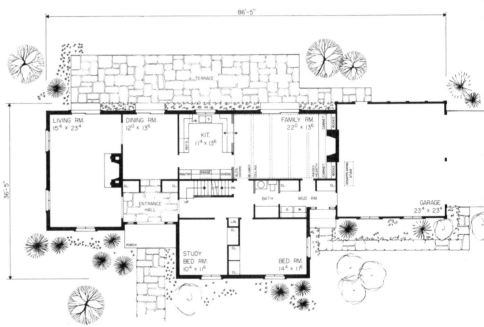

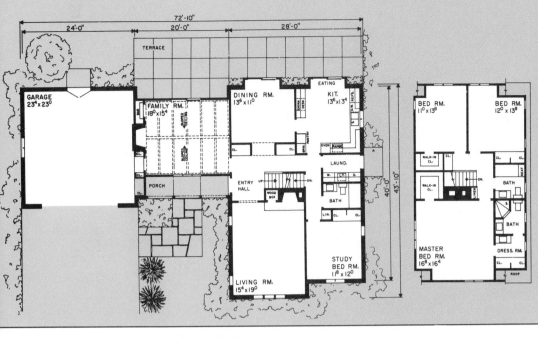

Design T162126
1,566 Sq. Ft. - First Floor
930 Sq. Ft. - Second Floor
38,122 Cu. Ft.

● The configuration of this home is interesting. Its L-shape allows for flexible placement on your lot which makes it ideal for a corner lot. Exterior Tudor detailing is outstanding. Interior living potential is also excellent. Large formal and informal rooms are on the first floor along with the kitchen, dining room, laundry and spare bedroom or study. Three more bedrooms are on the second floor. Closets are plentiful throughout.

● This is a most interesting home; both inside and out. Its L-shape with covered front porch and diamond lite windows is appealing. Its floor plan with extra bedroom, lounge and storage room is exceptional.

Design T162241
1,617 Sq. Ft. - First Floor
1,348 Sq. Ft. - Second Floor
43,225 Cu. Ft.

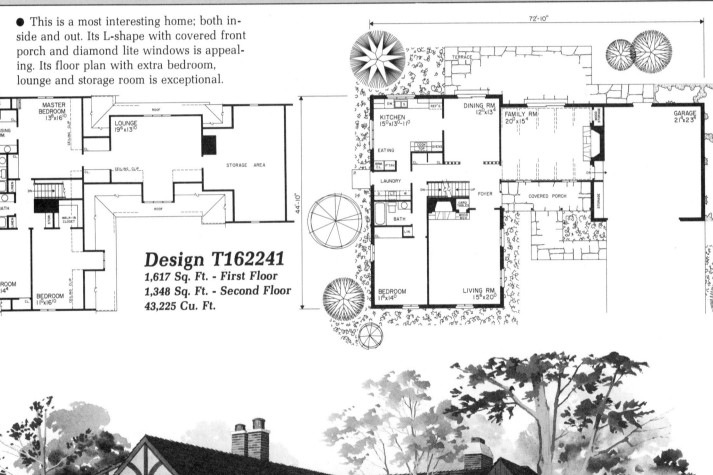

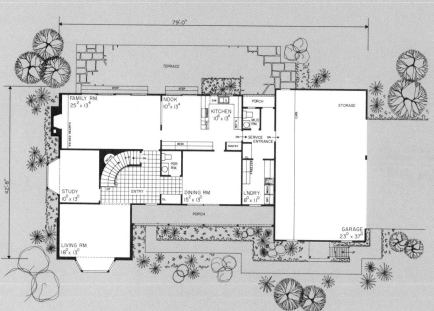

TERRACE

79'-0"

42'-8"

FAMILY RM. 25² x 13⁴

NOOK 10⁰ x 13⁴

KITCHEN 10⁶ x 13⁴

PORCH

STORAGE

DESK

MUD RM.

PANTRY

SERVICE ENTRANCE

FREEZER

STUDY 10⁰ x 13⁰

ENTRY

PDR. RM.

DINING RM. 15⁶ x 13⁰

LNDRY. 8⁰ x 11⁰

UP

RAISED HEARTH

PORCH

LIVING RM. 18⁰ x 13⁰

GARAGE 23⁰ x 37⁰

Design T162513
1,799 Sq. Ft. - First Floor
1,160 Sq. Ft. - Second Floor
47,461 Cu. Ft.

ROOF

WALK-IN CLOSET

MASTER BED RM. 17⁴ x 13⁴

BED RM. 12⁰ x 13⁴

BED RM. 12⁰ x 13⁴

DRESSING RM.

BATH

CL.

CL.

ROOF

ATTIC

ATTIC

DN

RAILING

UPPER ENTRY

STUDY 12⁰ x 8⁴

LINEN

SEAT

BATH

ATTIC

CEIL GLG.

ROOF

ROOF

● What an appealing story-and-a-half de-sign. Delightful, indeed, is the colonial de-tailing of the garage. The large entry hall with its open curving staircase is dramatic.

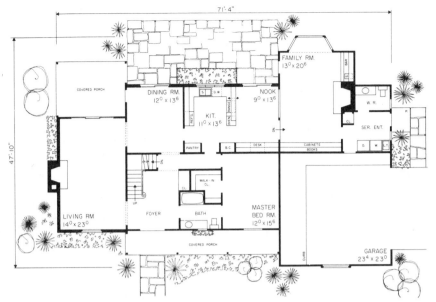

● The large family will enjoy the wonderful living patterns offered by this charming home. Don't miss the covered rear porch and the many features of the family room.

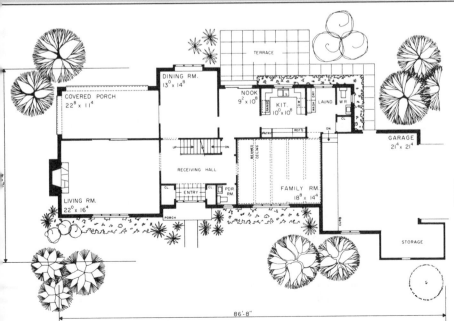

Design T162338

1,505 Sq. Ft. - First Floor
1,219 Sq. Ft. - Second Floor
38,878 Cu. Ft.

● A spacious receiving hall is a fine setting for the welcoming of guests. Here traffic flows effectively to all areas of the plan. Outstanding livability throughout the entire plan.

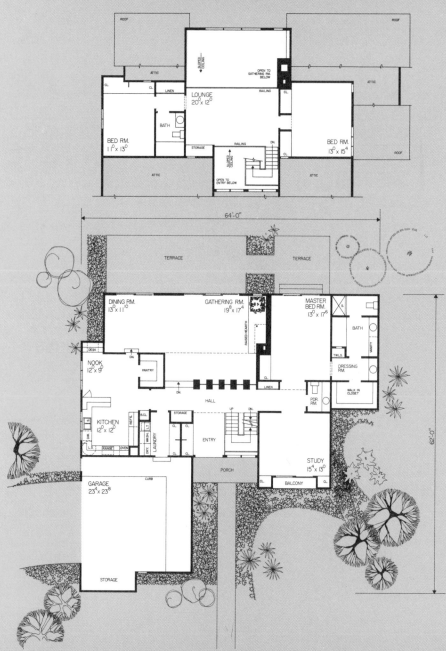

Design T162708

2,108 Sq. Ft. - First Floor
824 Sq. Ft. - Second Floor
52,170 Cu. Ft.

● Here is a one-and-a-half story home whose exterior is distinctive. It has a contemporary feeling, yet it retains some of the fine design features and proportions of traditional exteriors. Inside the appealing double front doors there is livability galore. The sunken rear living-dining area is delightfully spacious and is looked down into from the second floor lounge. The open end fireplace, with its raised hearth and planter, is another focal point. The master bedroom features a fine compartmented bath with both shower and tub. The study is just a couple steps away. The U-shaped kitchen is outstanding. Notice the pantry and laundry. Upstairs provides children with their own sleeping, studying and TV quarters. Absolutely a great design! Study all the fine details closely with your family.

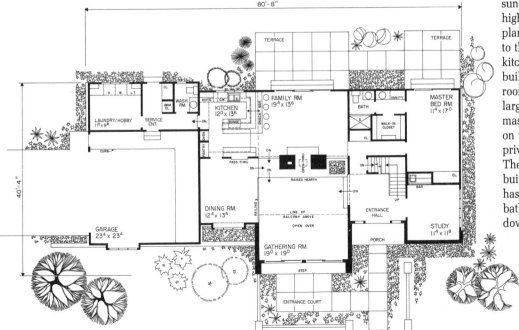

Design T162782

2,060 Sq. Ft. - First Floor
897 Sq. Ft. - Second Floor
47,750 Cu. Ft.

● What makes this such a distinctive four bedroom design? Let's list some of the features. This plan includes great formal and informal living for the family at home or when entertaining guests. The formal gathering room and informal family room share a dramatic raised hearth fireplace. Other features of the sunken gathering room include: high, sloped ceilings, built-in planter and sliding glass doors to the front entrance court. The kitchen has a snack bar, many built-ins, a pass-thru to dining room and easy access to the large laundry/washroom. The master bedroom suite is located on the main level for added privacy and convenience. There's even a study with a built-in bar. The upper level has three more bedrooms, a bath and a lounge looking down into the gathering room.

Design T161365
975 Sq. Ft. - First Floor
583 Sq. Ft. - Second Floor
20,922 Cu. Ft.

● This snug little story-and-a-half has three bedrooms, plus a study with built-in desk and book shelves! It also has two baths, formal and informal dining areas, a good-sized living room and two-car garage.

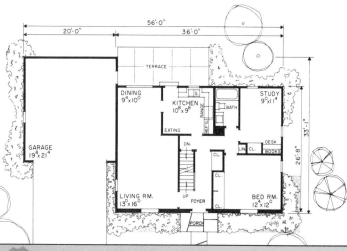

Design T161372
768 Sq. Ft. - First Floor
432 Sq. Ft. - Second Floor
17,280 Cu. Ft.

● Low cost livability could hardly ask for more. Here is an enchanting Colonial exterior and a four bedroom floor plan. Note stairs to basement and carport.

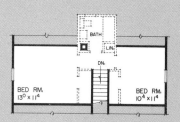

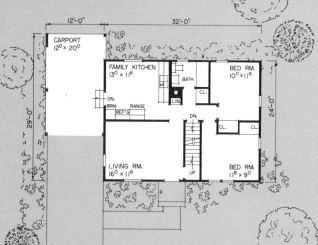

Design T163189

884 Sq. Ft. - First Floor
598 Sq. Ft. - Second Floor
18,746 Cu. Ft.

● Four bedrooms, two baths, a large kitchen/dining area, plenty of closets, a full basement and an attached two-car garage are among the highlights of this design. Note the uniqueness of the second floor.

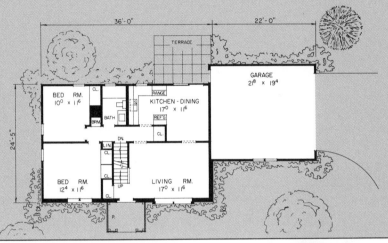

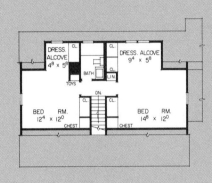

Design T161394

832 Sq. Ft. - First Floor
512 Sq. Ft. - Second Floor
19,385 Cu. Ft.

● The growing family with a restricted building budget will find this a great investment - a convenient living floor plan inside an attractively designed facade.

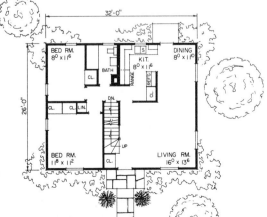

● Here is a home that truly fits the description of traditional charm. The symmetry is, indeed, delightful. A certain magnetic aura seems to reach out with a whisper of welcome. Observe the spacious family-kitchen area, the study, the separate dining room and the extra bath.

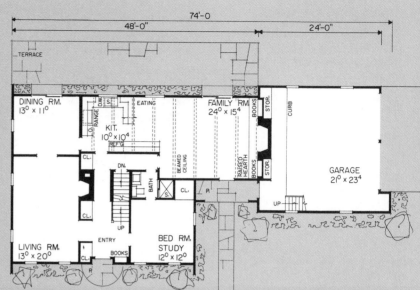

Design T161701
1,344 Sq. Ft. - First Floor
948 Sq. Ft. - Second Floor; 33,952 Cu. Ft.

Design T162395
1,481 Sq. Ft. - First Floor
861 Sq. Ft. - Second Floor
34,487 Cu. Ft.

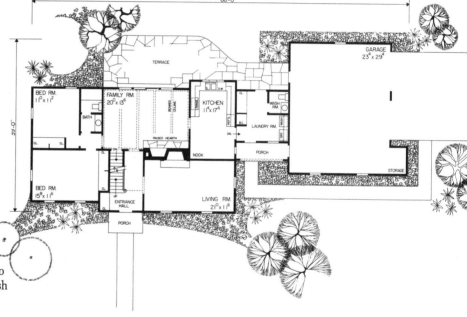

● New England revisited. The appeal of this type of home is ageless. As for its livability, it will serve its occupants admirably for generations to come. With two bedrooms downstairs, you may want to finish off the second floor at a later date.

Design T162520
1,419 Sq. Ft. - First Floor
1,040 Sq. Ft. - Second Floor; 39,370 Cu. Ft.

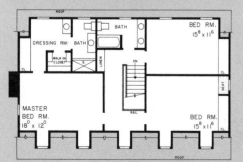

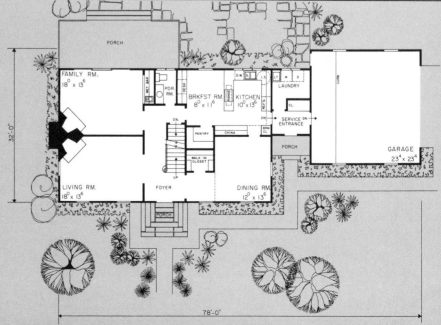

● From Tidewater Virginia comes this historic adaptation, a positive reminder of the charm of Early American architecture. Note how the center entrance gives birth to fine traffic circulation.

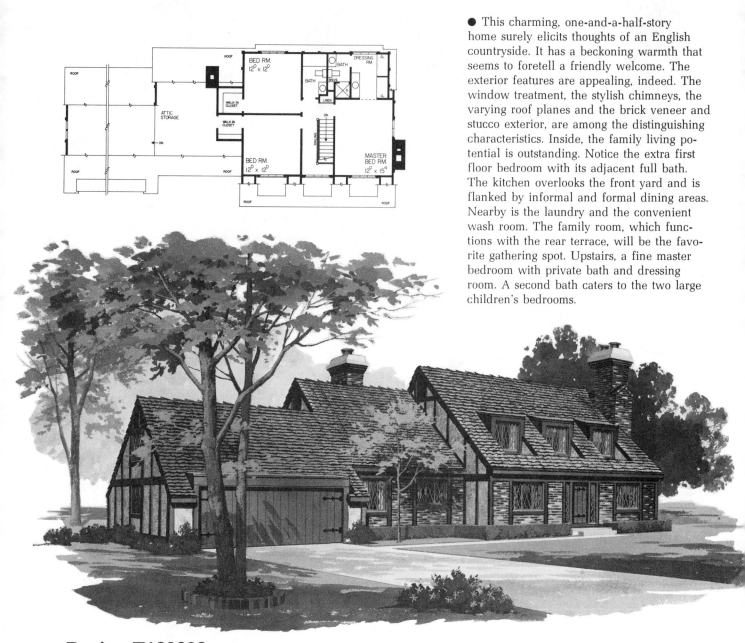

● This charming, one-and-a-half-story home surely elicits thoughts of an English countryside. It has a beckoning warmth that seems to foretell a friendly welcome. The exterior features are appealing, indeed. The window treatment, the stylish chimneys, the varying roof planes and the brick veneer and stucco exterior, are among the distinguishing characteristics. Inside, the family living potential is outstanding. Notice the extra first floor bedroom with its adjacent full bath. The kitchen overlooks the front yard and is flanked by informal and formal dining areas. Nearby is the laundry and the convenient wash room. The family room, which functions with the rear terrace, will be the favorite gathering spot. Upstairs, a fine master bedroom with private bath and dressing room. A second bath caters to the two large children's bedrooms.

Design T162626 1,420 Sq. Ft. - First Floor; 859 Sq. Ft. - Second Floor; 34,974 Cu. Ft.

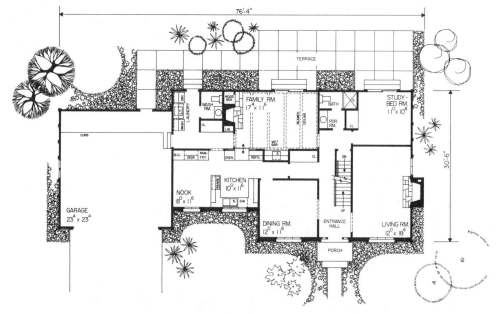

Design T162906 2,121 Sq. Ft. - First Floor
913 Sq. Ft. - Second Floor; 45,180 Cu. Ft.

● This striking Contemporary with Spanish good
looks offers outstanding living for lifestyles of
today. A three-car garage opens to a mudroom,
laundry, and washroom to keep the rest of the
house clean. An efficient, spacious kitchen opens
to a spacious dining room, with pass-thru also
leading to a family room. The family room and adjoining master bedroom suite overlook a backyard
terrace. Just off the master bedroom is a sizable
study that opens to a foyer. Steps just off the foyer
make upstairs access quick and easy. The center
point of this modern Contemporary is a living
room that faces a front courtyard and a lounge
above the living room. Three second-story bedrooms and an upper foyer join the upstairs lounge.

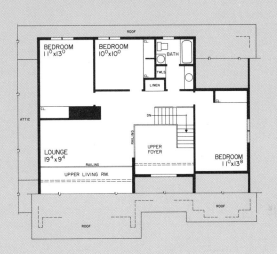

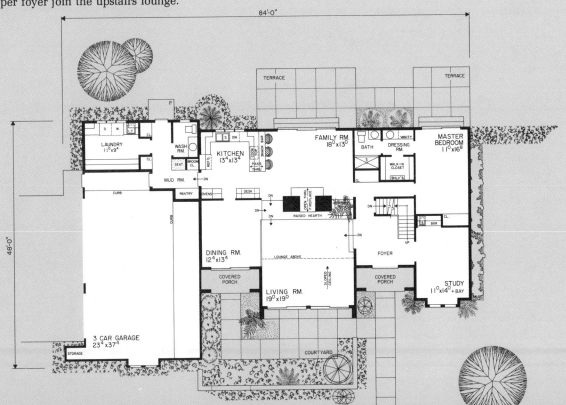

Design T162377
1,170 Sq. Ft. - First Floor
815 Sq. Ft. - Second Floor; 22,477 Cu. Ft.

● What an impressive up-to-date home this is. Its refreshing configuration will command a full measure of attention. Note that all of the back rooms on the first floor are a couple steps lower than the entry and living room area. Four bedrooms serviced by two full baths comprise the second floor which looks down into the formal, front living room.

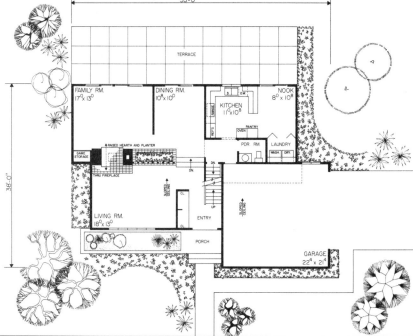

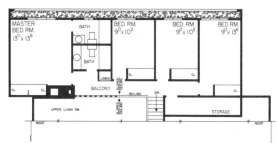

● This delightful Tudor design's configuration permits a flexible orientation on its site with either the garage doors or the front doors facing the street. One-and-a-half-story designs offer great flexibility in their livability. Complete livability is offered on the first floor then by utilizing the second floor another three bedrooms and bath are available. First floor features include a sunken family room with fireplace and built-in bookshelves, rear living room with sliding glass doors to the terrace, large formal dining room, laundry and two washrooms.

Design T161877 1,162 Sq. Ft. - First Floor
883 Sq. Ft. - Second Floor; 27,617 Cu. Ft.

● This simple, straightforward plan has much to offer in the way of livability and economical construction costs. Worthy of particular note are the excellent traffic patterns and the outstanding use of space. There is no wasted space here. Notice the cozy family room with its raised hearth fireplace, wood box and sliding glass doors to the sweeping outdoor deck. The efficient kitchen is flanked by the informal snack bar and the formal dining area. Open planning between the living and dining areas promotes a fine feeling of spaciousness.

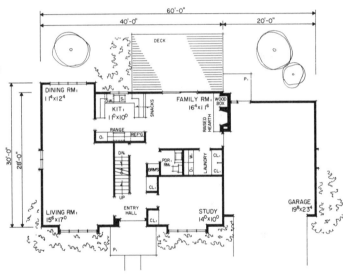

Design T162674 1,922 Sq. Ft. - First Floor; 890 Sq. Ft. - Second Floor; 37,411 Cu. Ft.

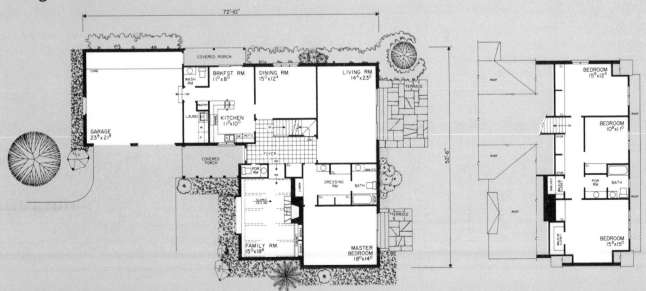

Design T162510 1,191 Sq. Ft. - First Floor
533 Sq. Ft. - Second Floor; 27,500 Cu. Ft.

● The pleasant in-line kitchen of this design is flanked by a separate dining room and a family room. The master bedroom is on the first floor with two more bedrooms on the second floor. Sliding glass doors across the rear allow for the greatest possible enjoyment of the terrace area. This house would be particularly effective if the rear of the house had a southern exposure. Note laundry area.

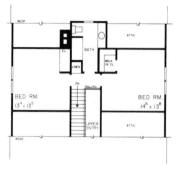

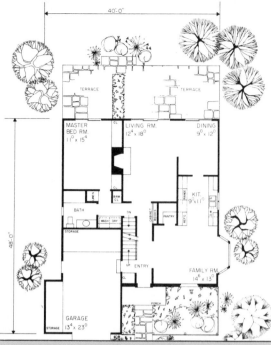

Design T162569 1,102 Sq. Ft. - First Floor
764 Sq. Ft. - Second Floor; 29,600 Cu. Ft.

● What an enchanting updated version of the popular Cape Cod cottage. There are facilities for both formal and informal living pursuits. Note the spacious family/nook area, the fine, formal dining room/living room relationship, the sliding glass doors to the rear terrace, the first floor laundry and the efficient kitchen. The second floor houses the three bedrooms and two economically located baths.

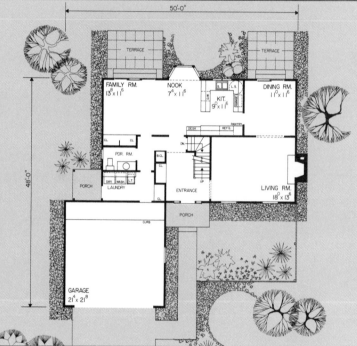

Design T162571 1,137 Sq. Ft. - First Floor
795 Sq. Ft. - Second Floor; 28,097 Cu. Ft.

● Cost efficient space! That's the bonus with this attractive Cape Cod. Start in the living room . . . spacious and inviting with full-length paned windows. In the formal dining room, a bay window adds the appropriate touch.

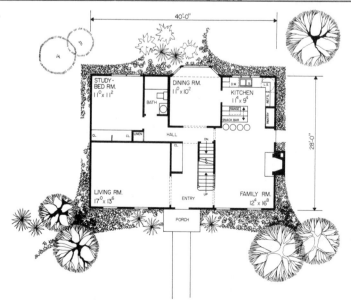

Design T162631

1,634 Sq. Ft. - First Floor
1,011 Sq. Ft. - Second Floor; 33,720 Cu. Ft.

● Two fireplaces and much more! Notice how all the rooms are accessible from the main hall. That keeps traffic in each room to a minimum, saving you work by preserving your furnishings. There's more. A large family room featuring a beamed ceiling, a fireplace with built-in wood box and double doors onto the terrace. An exceptional U-shaped kitchen is ready to serve you. It has an adjacent breakfast nook. Built-ins, too . . a desk, storage pantry, oven and range. Plus a first floor laundry close at hand.

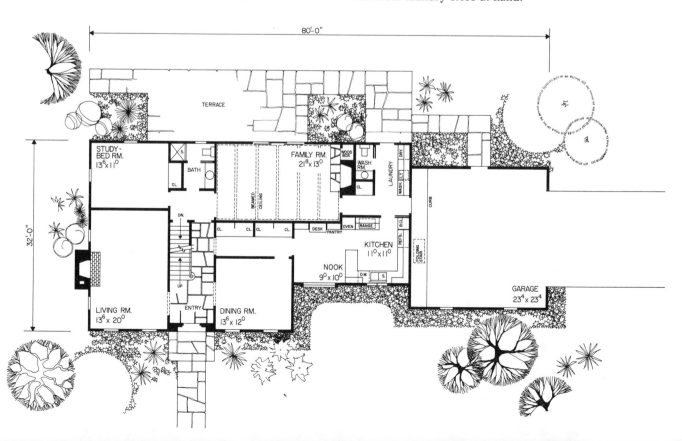

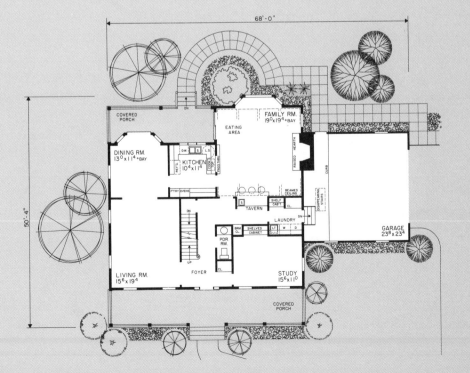

Design T162890

1,612 Sq. Ft. - First Floor
1,356 Sq. Ft. - Second Floor
47,010 Cu. Ft.

● An appealing Farmhouse that is complimented by an inviting front porch. Many memorable summer evenings will be spent here. Entering this house, you will notice a nice-sized study to your right and spacious living room to the left. The adjacent dining room is enriched by an attractive bay window. Just a step away, an efficient kitchen will be found. Many family activities will be enjoyed in the large family room. The tavern/snack bar will make entertaining guests a joy. A powder room and laundry are also on the first floor. Upstairs you'll find a master bedroom suite featuring a bath with an oversized tub and shower and a dressing room. Also on this floor; two bedrooms, full bath and a large attic.

Design T161718

2,012 Sq. Ft - First Floor
589 Sq. Ft - Second Floor
45,405 Cu. Ft.

Second Floor

MASTER BED RM. 14⁰×16⁰

STUDY-LOUNGE 14⁰×11⁶

BOOKS

CL. CL.

DRESS. RM.

BATH

DN.

STORAGE

WALK-IN CL.

STORAGE

STOR.

First Floor

100'-0"

26'-0" 52'-0" 22'-0"

GARAGE 25⁴×23⁴

TERRACE

W.R.

CL. EATING

LAUNDRY

D. L.W.

S.

DW.

REF'G.

FAMILY RM. 20⁰×13⁶

RAISED HEARTH

BEAMED CEILING

BATH

BED RM. 14⁸×11⁶

CL.

CL.

LIN.

32'-0" 26'-0"

BRM. DESK CL. CHINA

P'TRY

KITCHEN 13⁶×20⁰

RANGE

O.

DN.

UP

STUDY-BED RM. 10⁰×10⁰

CL.

CL.

BED RM. 11⁴×13⁶

P.

DINING RM. 11⁸×13⁶

FENCE

LIVING RM. 20⁰×15⁰

ENTRY

CL.

P.

● This house has everything - an extremely attractive exterior and a fine working, convenient floor plan. Don't miss upstairs suite.

Design T161794
2,122 Sq. Ft. - First Floor
802 Sq. Ft. - Second Floor
37,931 Cu. Ft.

● The inviting warmth of this delightful story-and-a-half home catches the eye of even the most casual observer. Imagine, four big bedrooms! Formal and informal living can be enjoyed throughout this charming plan. Two fireplaces. One has a raised hearth and an adjacent wood box. A very private, formal dining room for those very special occasions. A U-shaped kitchen with pass-thru to family room. Note the two distinct rear terraces.

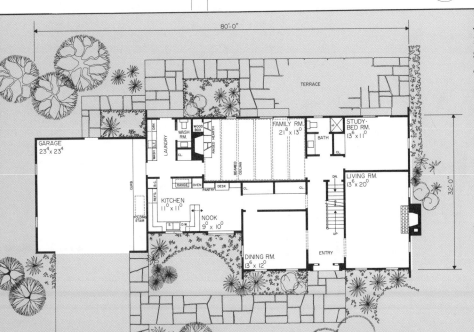

Design T161987
1,632 Sq. Ft. - First Floor
980 Sq. Ft. - Second Floor
35,712 Cu. Ft.

● The comforts of home will surely be endless and enduring when experienced and enjoyed in this Colonial adaptation. What's your favorite feature?

Design T162373 1,160 Sq. Ft. - First Floor
1,222 Sq. Ft. - Second Floor; 33,775 Cu. Ft.

● Finding more livability wrapped in such an attractive facade would be difficult, indeed. This charming Tudor adaptation will return big dividends per construction dollar.

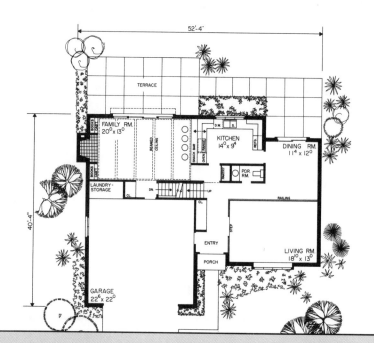

Design T161991
1,262 Sq. Ft. - First Floor
1,108 Sq. Ft. - Second Floor; 31,073 Cu. Ft.

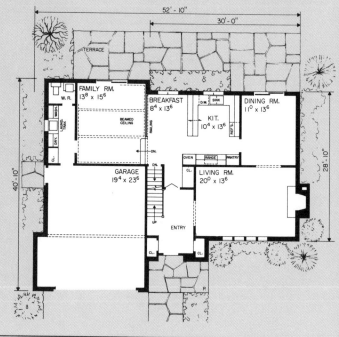

● Put yourself and your family in this English cottage adaptation and you'll all rejoice over your new home for many a year. The pride of owning and living in a home that is distinctive will be a constant source of satisfaction. Count the features that will serve your family well for years.

Design T162854 1,261 Sq. Ft. - First Floor
950 Sq. Ft. - Second Floor; 36,820 Cu. Ft.

● The charm of old England has been captured in this outstanding one-and-a-half story design. Interior livability will efficiently serve all family members.

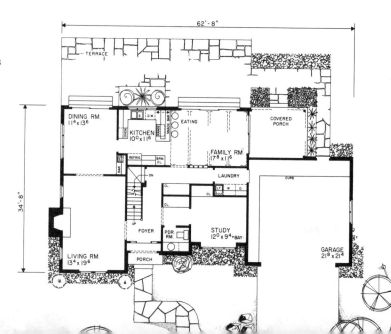

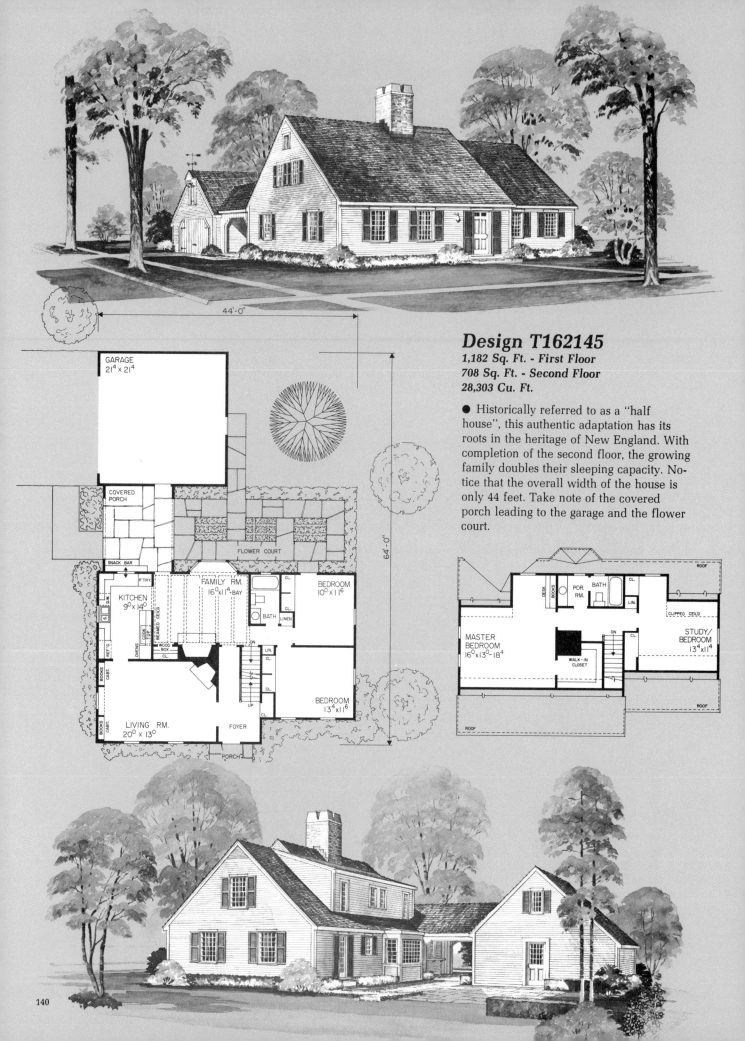

GARAGE
21⁴ x 21⁴

COVERED PORCH

FLOWER COURT

44'-0"

64'-0"

SNACK BAR

P'TRY.

KITCHEN
9⁰ x 14⁰

FAMILY RM.
16⁰ x 11⁴ BAY

BEDROOM
10⁰ x 11⁶

BEAMED CEIL'G

OVENS

COOK TOP

WOOD BOX

BATH

LINEN

CL.

CL.

CL.

CL.

REF'G.

BOOKS CABT.

LIN

UP

DN

CL.

BEDROOM
13⁴ x 11⁶

BOOKS CABT.

LIVING RM.
20⁰ x 13⁰

FOYER

PORCH

Design T162145

1,182 Sq. Ft. - First Floor
708 Sq. Ft. - Second Floor
28,303 Cu. Ft.

● Historically referred to as a "half house", this authentic adaptation has its roots in the heritage of New England. With completion of the second floor, the growing family doubles their sleeping capacity. Notice that the overall width of the house is only 44 feet. Take note of the covered porch leading to the garage and the flower court.

ROOF

DESK

BOOKS

PDR. RM.

BATH

CL.

LIN.

CLIPPED CEIL'G

MASTER BEDROOM
16⁰ x 13⁰-18⁴

WALK-IN CLOSET

DN

CL.

STUDY/ BEDROOM
13⁴ x 11⁴

ROOF

ROOF

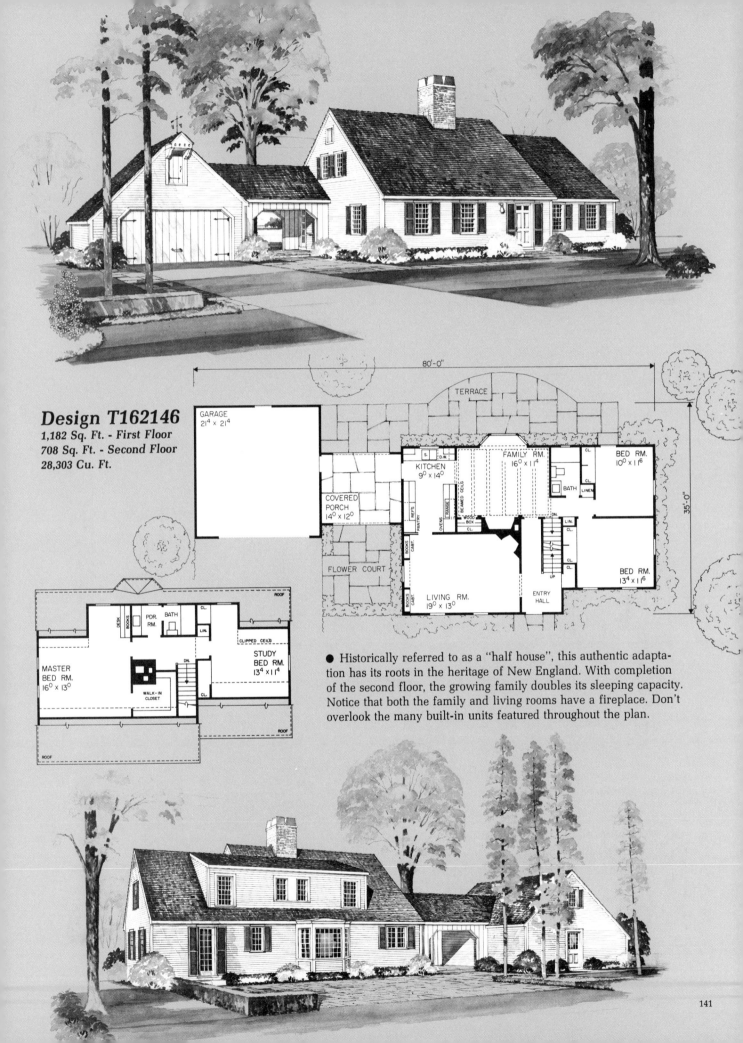

Design T162146

1,182 Sq. Ft. - First Floor
708 Sq. Ft. - Second Floor
28,303 Cu. Ft.

GARAGE
21⁴ x 21⁴

COVERED
PORCH
14⁰ x 12⁰

FLOWER COURT

TERRACE

80'-0"

35'-0"

KITCHEN
9⁰ x 14⁰

FAMILY RM.
16⁰ x 11⁴

BED RM.
10⁰ x 11⁶

BATH

LINEN

PANTRY

BEAMED CEIL'G

WOOD BOX

OVENS

RANGE

BOOKS CAB'T.

CL.

CL.

CL.

LIN.

CL.

DN.

UP

LIVING RM.
19⁰ x 13⁰

ENTRY HALL

BED RM.
13⁴ x 11⁶

BOOKS CAB'T.

MASTER
BED RM.
16⁰ x 13⁰

DESK

BOOKS

PDR. RM.

BATH

CL.

LIN.

CLIPPED CEIL'G

STUDY
BED RM.
13⁴ x 11⁴

WALK-IN CLOSET

DN.

CL.

ROOF

ROOF

ROOF

● Historically referred to as a "half house", this authentic adaptation has its roots in the heritage of New England. With completion of the second floor, the growing family doubles its sleeping capacity. Notice that both the family and living rooms have a fireplace. Don't overlook the many built-in units featured throughout the plan.

Design T162596
1,489 Sq. Ft. - First Floor
982 Sq. Ft. - Second Floor; 38,800 Cu. Ft.

● Captivating as a New England village! From the weathervane atop the garage to the roofed side entry and paned windows, this home is perfectly detailed.

Design T162559
1,388 Sq. Ft. - First Floor
809 Sq. Ft. - Second Floor; 36,400 Cu. Ft.

● Imagine, a 26 foot living room with fireplace, a quiet study with built-in bookshelves and excellent dining facilities. Within such an appealing exterior, too.

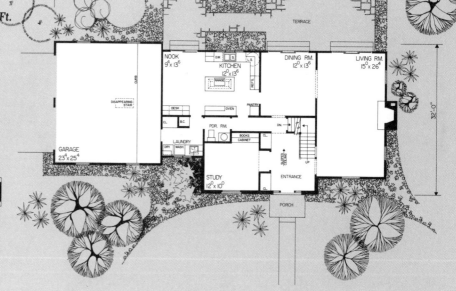

Design T162563
1,500 Sq. Ft. - First Floor
690 Sq. Ft. - Second Floor; 38,243 Cu. Ft.

● You'll have all kinds of fun deciding just how your family will function in this dramatically expanded half-house. There is lots of attic storage, too. Observe three-car garage.

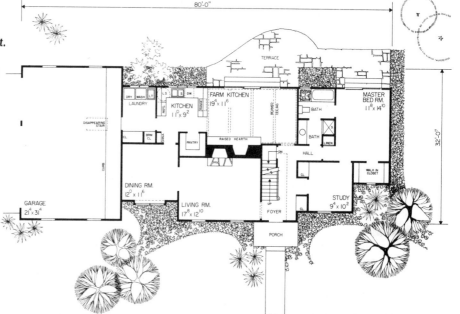

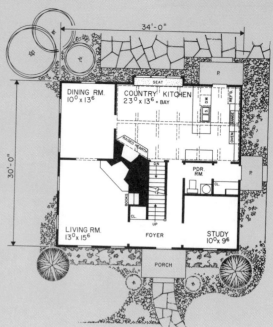

Design T162661 1,020 Sq. Ft. - First Floor
777 Sq. Ft. - Second Floor; 30,745 Cu. Ft.

● Any other starter house or retirement home couldn't have more charm than this design. Its compact frame houses a very livable plan. An outstanding feature of the first floor is the large country kitchen. Its fine attractions include a beamed ceiling, raised hearth fireplace, built-in window seat and a door leading to the outdoors.

Design T162655 893 Sq. Ft. - First Floor
652 Sq. Ft. - Second Floor; 22,555 Cu. Ft.

● Wonderful things can be en-closed in small packages. This is the case for this one-and-a-half story design. The total square footage is a mere 1,545 square feet yet its features are many, indeed. Its exterior ap-peal is very eye-pleasing with horizontal lines and two second story dormers. Livability will be

enjoyed in this plan. The front study is ideal for a quiet escape. Nearby is a powder room also convenient to the kitchen and breakfast room. Two bedrooms and two full baths are located on the second floor.

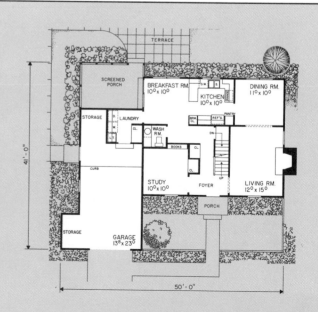

144

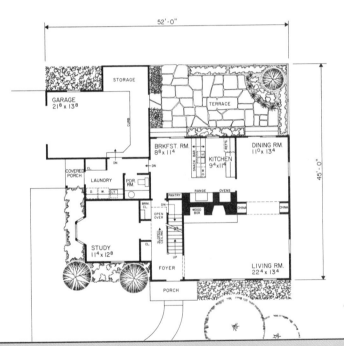

Design T162658 1,218 Sq. Ft. - First Floor
764 Sq. Ft. - Second Floor; 29,690 Cu. Ft.

● Traditional charm of yesteryear is exemplified delightfully in this modest sized one-and-a-half story home. The garage has been conveniently tucked away in the rear of the house which makes this design ideal for a corner lot. Interior livability has been planned for efficient living.

Design T162684 1,600 Sq. Ft. - First Floor
1,498 Sq. Ft. - Second Floor; 47,395 Cu. Ft.

● Highlighting this plan is the spacious, country kitchen. Its features are many, indeed. Also worth a special note is the second floor studio/office. It is accessible by way of a staircase in the back of the plan. Just imagine the many uses for this area. There is a great deal of livability in this plan. Don't miss the three fireplaces or the first floor laundry.

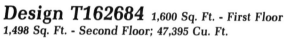

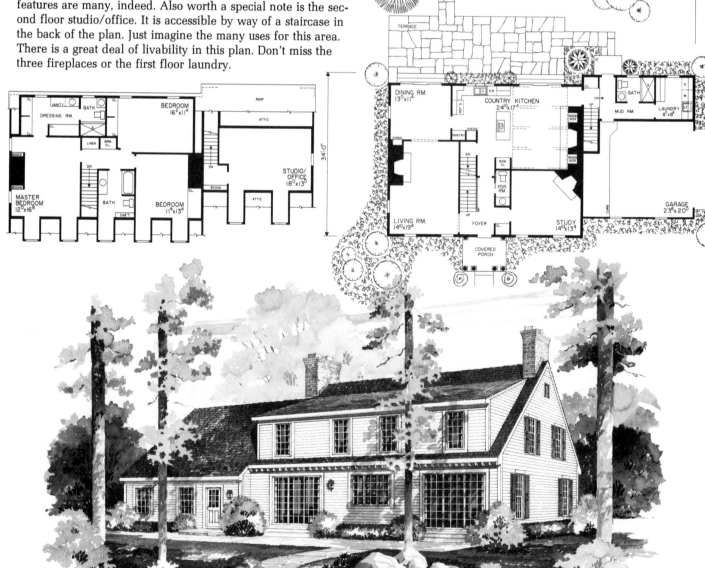

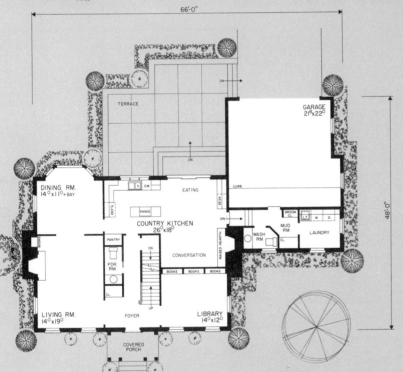

Design T162688 1,588 Sq. Ft. - First Floor
1,101 Sq. Ft. - Second Floor; 44,021 Cu. Ft.

● Here are two floors of excellent livability. Start at the country kitchen. It will be the center for family activities. It has an island, desk, raised hearth fireplace, conversation area and sliding glass doors to the terrace. Adjacent to this area is the washroom and laundry. Quieter areas are available in the living room and library. Three bedrooms are housed on the second floor.

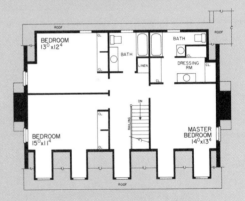

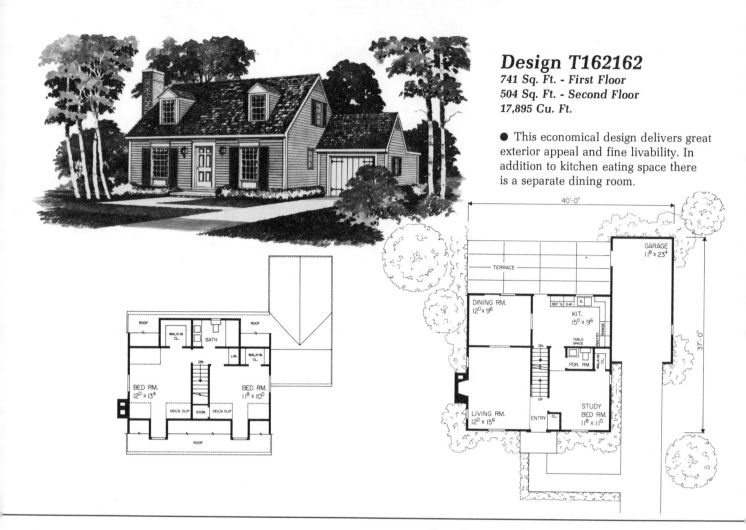

Design T162162
741 Sq. Ft. - First Floor
504 Sq. Ft. - Second Floor
17,895 Cu. Ft.

● This economical design delivers great exterior appeal and fine livability. In addition to kitchen eating space there is a separate dining room.

Design T161241 1,064 Sq. Ft. - First Floor
898 Sq. Ft. - Second Floor; 24,723 Cu. Ft.

● You don't need a mansion to live graciously. What you do need is a practical floor plan which takes into consideration the varied activities of the busy family. This story-and-a-half design will not require a large piece of property. Its living potential is tremendous.

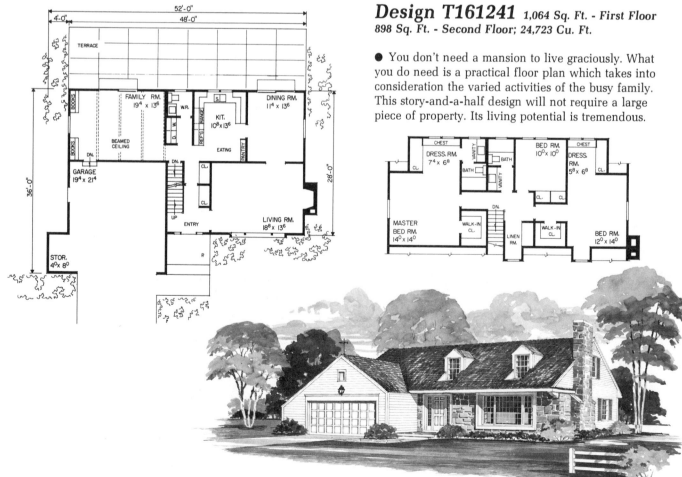

Design T162887 1,338 Sq. Ft. - First Floor; 661 Sq. Ft. - Second Floor; 36,307 Cu. Ft.

● This attractive, contemporary one-and-a-half story will be the envy of many. First, examine the efficient kitchen. Not only does it offer a snack bar for those quick meals but also a large dining room. Notice the adjacent dining porch. The laundry and garage access are also adjacent to the kitchen.

An exciting feature is the gathering room with fireplace. The first floor also offers a study with a wet bar and sliding glass doors that open to a private porch. This will make those quiet times cherishable. Adjacent to the study is a full bath followed by a bedroom. Upstairs a large master bedroom suite oc-

cupies the entire floor. It features a bath with an oversized tub and shower, a large walk-in closet with built-ins and an open lounge with fireplace. Both the lounge and master bedroom, along with the gathering room, have sloped ceilings. Develop the lower level for additional space.

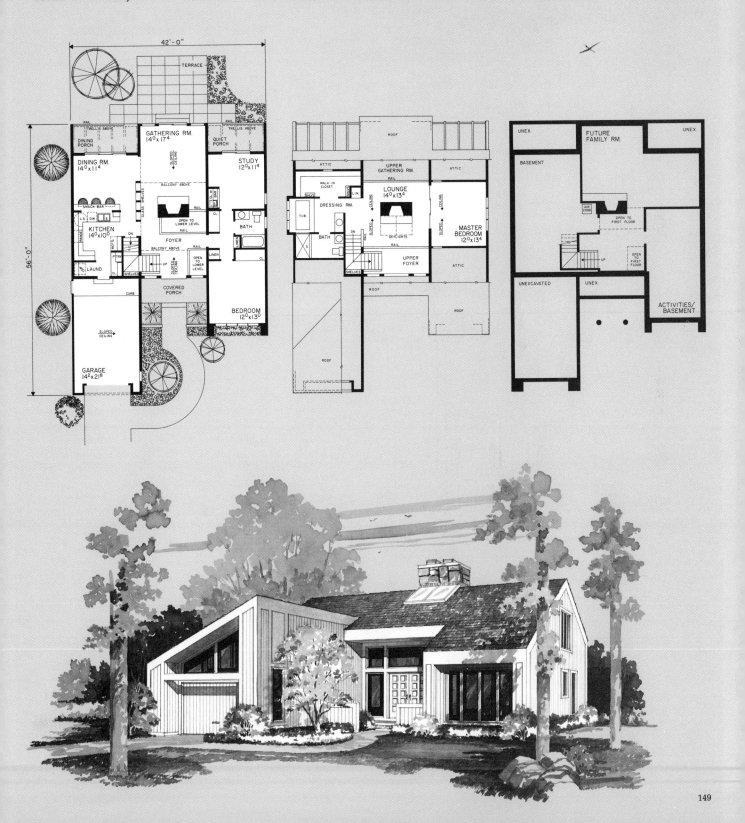

149

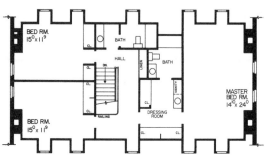

BED RM. 15⁰ x 11⁹

BATH

MASTER BED RM. 14⁴ x 12⁸

CL.

BATH

HALL

DN.

LINEN

CL.

CL.

WALK IN CLOSET

LINEN

RAILING

BED RM. 15⁰ x 11⁹

BED RM. 14¹⁰ x 11⁰

CL. CL.

BED RM. 15⁰ x 11⁹

BATH

CL.

HALL

LINEN

BATH

DN.

CL.

VANITY

CL.

MASTER BED RM. 14¹⁰ x 24⁰

RAILING

DRESSING ROOM

BED RM. 15⁰ x 11⁹

CL. CL.

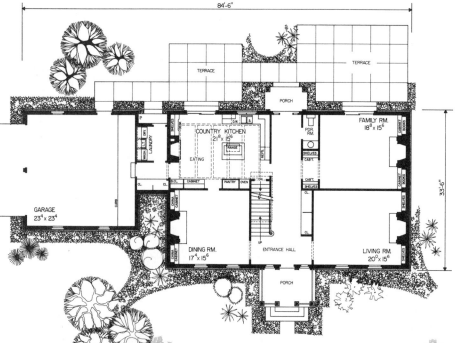

84'-6"

TERRACE

TERRACE

PORCH

P

SHELVES

D.W.

S.

FAMILY RM. 18⁸ x 15⁶

CABINET

LAUNDRY

COUNTRY KITCHEN 21⁸ x 15⁶

PDR. RM.

CABINET

BOOKS

33'-6"

RANGE

REFG.

EATING

SHELVES

CAB'T.

GARAGE 23⁴ x 23⁴

CL.

B.CL.

CABINET

PANTRY

OVEN

DN.

CAB'T.

CHINA CABINET

SHELVES

CABINET BOOKS

CL.

UP

DINING RM. 17⁴ x 15⁶

ENTRANCE HALL

LIVING RM. 20⁰ x 15⁶

CHINA CABINET

SHELVES

PORCH

Design T162638
1,836 Sq. Ft. - First Floor
1,323 Sq. Ft. - Second Floor
57,923 Cu. Ft.

● The brick facade of this two-story represents the mid-18th-Century design concept. Examine its fine exterior. It has a steeply pitched roof which is broken by two large chimneys at each end and by pedimented dormers. Inside Georgian details lend elegance. Turned balusters and a curved banister ornament the formal staircase. Blueprints include details for both three and four bedroom options.

Design T162396
1,616 Sq. Ft. - First Floor; 993 Sq. Ft. - Second Floor; 30,583 Cu. Ft.

● Another picturesque facade right from the pages of our Colonial heritage. The authentic features are many. Note the centered front door with its flanking shutters, the evenly spaced dormers, and the centered chimney. The window detailing, the horizontal siding and the carriage lamps are pleasing highlights. Inside, there is exceptional livability. Observe the spacious living areas, the flexible dining facilities, the fine bedroom and bath potential. Don't miss the stairs to area over the garage.

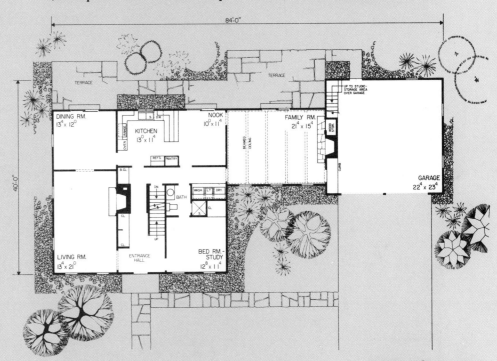

Design T162718 1,941 Sq. Ft. - First Floor
791 Sq. Ft. - Second Floor; 49,895 Cu. Ft.

● You and your family will love the new living patterns you'll experience in this story-and-a-half home. The front entry hall features an impressive open staircase to the upstairs and basement. Adjacent is the master bedroom which has a compartmented bath with both tub and stall shower. The spacious dressing room steps down into a unique, sunken conversation pit.

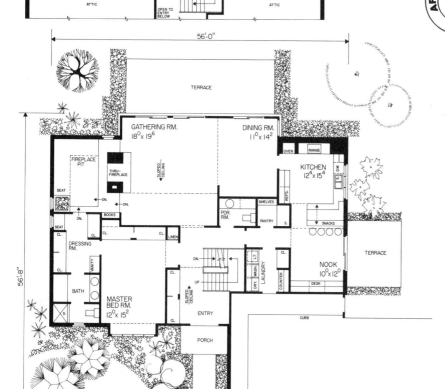

Design T162174

1,506 Sq. Ft. - First Floor
1,156 Sq. Ft. - Second Floor
37,360 Cu. Ft.

● Your building budget could
hardly buy more charm, or
greater livability. The appeal
of the exterior is wrapped up
in a myriad of design features.
They include: the interesting
roof lines; the effective use of
brick and horizontal siding; the
delightful window treatment;
the covered front porch; the
chimney and dove-cote
detailing. The livability of the
interior is represented by a
long list of convenient living
features. There is a formal
area consisting of a living room
with fireplace and dining
room. The family room has a
raised hearth fireplace, wood
box and beamed ceiling. Also
on the first floor is a kitchen,
laundry and bedroom with
adjacent bath. Three bedrooms,
lounge and two baths upstairs
plus plenty of closets and bulk
storage over garage. Don't overlook the sliding glass doors,
the breakfast area and the
basement. An excellent plan.

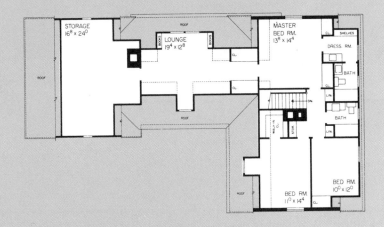

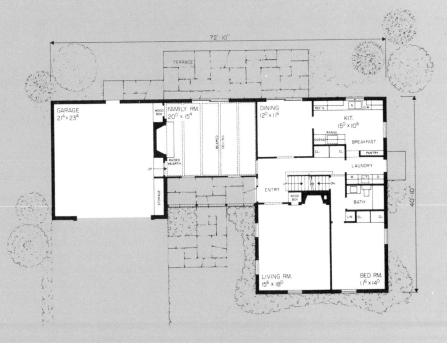

Design T162488 1,113 Sq. Ft. - First Floor
543 Sq. Ft. - Second Floor; 36,055 Cu. Ft.

● A cozy cottage for the young at heart! Whether called upon to serve the young, active family as a leisure-time retreat at the lake, or the retired couple as a quiet haven in later years, this charming design will perform well. As a year round second home, the upstairs with its two sizable bedrooms, full bath and lounge area, looking down into the gathering room below, will ideally accommodate the younger generation.

CUSTOMIZABLE
Custom Alterations? See page 320 for customizing this plan to your specifications.

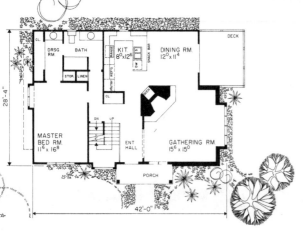

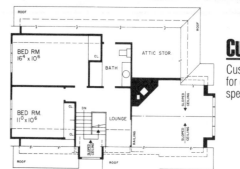

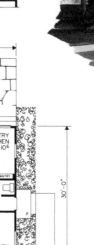

Design T162852 919 Sq. Ft. - First Floor
535 Sq. Ft. - Second Floor; 24,450 Cu. Ft.

● Compact enough for even the smallest lot, this cozy design provides comfortable living space for a small family. At the heart of the plan is a spacious country kitchen. It features a cooking island - snack bar and a dining area that opens to a house-wide rear terrace. The nearby dining room also opens to the terrace. At the front of the plan is the living room, warmed by a fireplace. Across the centered foyer is a cozy study. Two second floor bedrooms are serviced by two baths. Note the first floor powder room and storage closet located next to the side entrance. This home will be a delight.

THE TWO-STORY HOUSE:
A Level Above in Cost-Efficiency

PLAN T162774

For generations Americans have "gone upstairs to bed." This comfortable living pattern, which emanated from the early Colonial period, continues today in economical and thoroughly livable designs. The omnipresent two-story represents not only the best return per construction dollar spent but also a budget-smart residence option in the long-run.

The "stacked livability" features of the two-story house rival other designs in allowing frugality of construction and operating costs. The full two-story creates a doubling of livable square footage without incurring the additional roof or foundation costs required for a similar size one-story.

Another construction advantage is the ease with which plumbing and heating/cooling systems can be installed. Having two stories means shorter wiring and ductwork runs. Also, single-stack plumbing for toilet facilities is possible when upstairs bathrooms are located above those of the first floor.

Before the days of central heating, the two-story chimney often served two or more fireplaces. The rooms on each floor relied upon the fireplace for warmth and comfort. While today the fireplace is no longer a heating necessity, it is a popular amenity and a common and cost-saving practice continues to be the utilization of a single chimney for the first and second floor fireplaces.

Two-story houses also make the most effectual use of building sites. This is a significant economic factor when deciding between a one- or two-story house. The exterior dimensions of a two-story can be much smaller than those

continued on next page

Design T162774

1,370 Sq. Ft. - First Floor
969 Sq. Ft. - Second Floor
38,305 Cu. Ft.

● Another Farmhouse adaptation with all the most up-to-date features expected in a new home. Beginning with the formal areas, this design offers pleasures for the entire family. There is the quiet corner living room which has an opening to the sizable dining room. This room will enjoy plenty of natural light from the delightful bay window overlooking the rear yard. It is also conveniently located with the efficient U-shaped kitchen just a step away. The kitchen features many built-ins with pass-thru to the beamed ceiling breakfast room. Sliding glass doors to the terrace are fine attractions in both the sunken family room and breakfast room. The service entrance to the garage is flanked by a clothes closet and a large, walk-in pantry. There is a secondary entrance through the laundry room. Recreational activities and hobbies can be pursued in the basement area. Four bedrooms, two baths upstairs.

CUSTOMIZABLE

Custom Alterations? See page 320 for customizing this plan to your specifications.

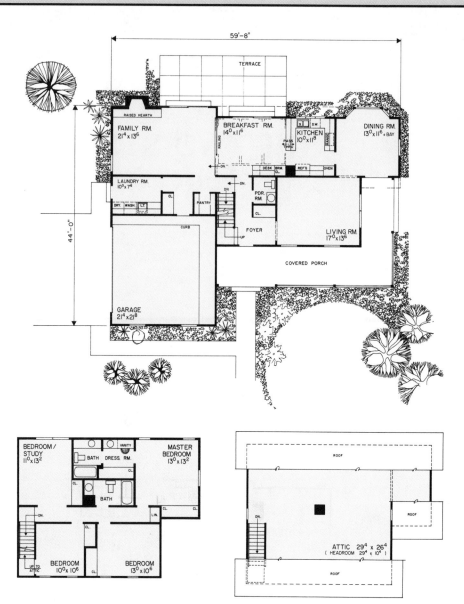

of a one-story house with the same square footage. Because of this, a smaller and consequently less expensive site can be purchased. Narrow, or modest-sized sites are used to full advantage when two-story units are built upon them. With today's inflated land prices, utilizing a smaller, less expensive lot allows the direction of more money to the actual construction of a larger home. Hence, the popularity of the two-story house as attested by the numerous subdivisions throughout the United States.

Like one-story structures, two-story houses can be in-line, L-shaped, U-shaped, or even angular. Two-stories can also be part one-story. And sometimes it is sensible to add only a one-story wing for a family or living room. Winged two-story houses, like Design T162242 on page 192, provide a spacious low-cost alternative.

While the rectangular two-story configuration is the most economical to build for the amount of livable square footage it delivers, there are other popular shapes that can be wisely utilized. Consider, for example, the L-shaped two-story with a front-projecting garage. This plan fits on a smaller site than if the garage were appended to the side of the main house structure.

Two-story houses become even more affordable when attic space is completed. This can also be the case when the basement is developed into bonus recreational, hobby, and storage areas.

Elegant features which can complement the two-story design include grand full-height foyers and sweeping staircases. And, for those who like a more open feeling, such amenities as second-story bridges, interior balconies, and lounges fill the bill.

With a sloping site, the basement can often be exposed and windows and door-walls installed to allow for the creation of light, airy living areas. This can turn a two-story house into a three-story house in a most cost-effective manner. See Design T162511 on page 278.

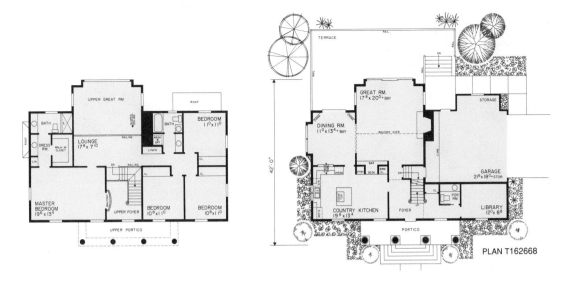

PLAN T162668

By stacking a full second story atop the first, living space is virtually doubled without doubling the cost. A second-story lounge is afforded a dramatic view of the great room

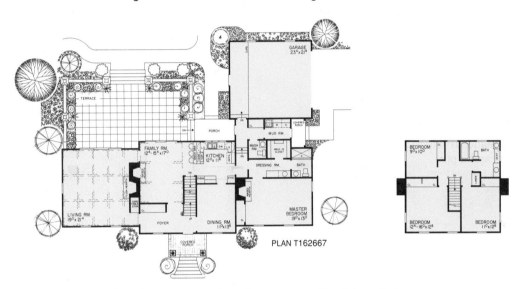

PLAN T162667

Complementary one-story wings are proportionately perfect and keep the master bedroom suite and elegant living room segregated from heavy traffic areas.

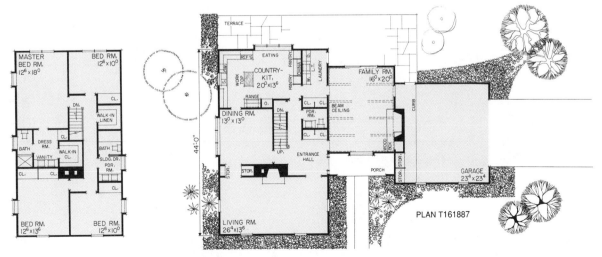

PLAN T161887

With the one-story extensions of a family room and a garage, the overall plan is expanded and enhanced. An otherwise ordinary roof plane becomes more pleasing.

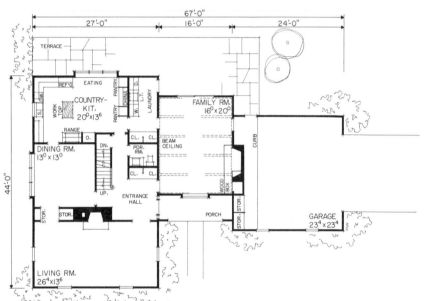

Design T161887
1,518 Sq. Ft. - First Floor
1,144 Sq. Ft. - Second Floor
40,108 Cu. Ft.

● This Gambrel roof Colonial is steeped in history. And well it should be, for its pleasing proportions are a delight to the eye. The various roof planes, the window treatment, and the rambling nature of the entire house revive a picture of rural New England. The covered porch protects the front door which opens into a spacious entrance hall. Traffic then flows in an orderly fashion to the end living room, the separate dining room, the cozy family room, and to the spacious country-kitchen. There is a first floor laundry, plenty of coat closets, and a handy powder room. Two fireplaces enliven the decor of the living areas. Upstairs there is an exceptional master bedroom layout, and abundant storage. Note the walk-in closets.

Design T162320 1,856 Sq. Ft. - First Floor; 1,171 Sq. Ft. - Second Floor; 46,699 Cu. Ft.

● A charming Colonial adaptation with a Gambrel roof front exterior and a Salt Box rear. The focal point of family activities will be the spacious family kitchen with its beamed ceiling and fireplace. Blueprints include details for both three and four bedroom options. In addition to the family kitchen, note the family room with beamed ceiling and fireplace. Don't miss the study with built-in bookshelves and cabinets.

Design T162733 1,177 Sq. Ft. - First Floor; 1,003 Sq. Ft. - Second Floor; 32,040 Cu. Ft.

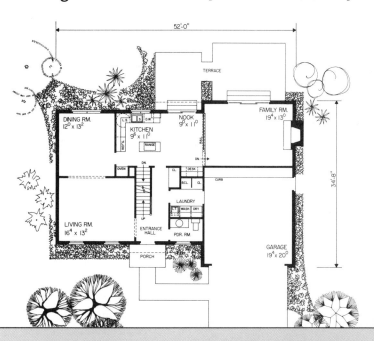

● This is definitely a four bedroom Colonial with charm galore. The kitchen features an island range and other built-ins. All will enjoy the sunken family room with fireplace, which has sliding glass doors leading to the terrace. Also a basement for recreational activities with laundry remaining on first floor for extra convenience.

● The appeal of this Colonial home will be virtually everlasting. It will improve with age and service the growing family well. Imagine your family living here. There are four bedrooms, 2½ baths, plus plenty of first floor living space.

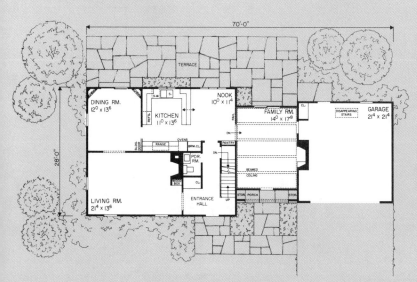

Design T162211
1,214 Sq. Ft. - First Floor
1,146 Sq. Ft. - Second Floor; 32,752 Cu. Ft.

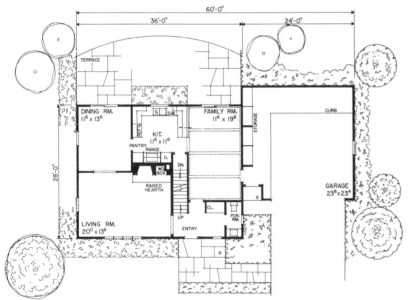

● A Garrison type adaptation that projects all the romance of yesteryear. The narrow horizontal siding, the wide corner boards, the window detailing, the overhanging second floor and the massive, centered chimney help set this home apart.

Design T161849 1,008 Sq. Ft. - First Floor
1,080 Sq. Ft. - Second Floor; 31,153 Cu. Ft.

Design T162654

1,152 Sq. Ft. - First Floor
844 Sq. Ft. - Second Floor; 31,845 Cu. Ft.

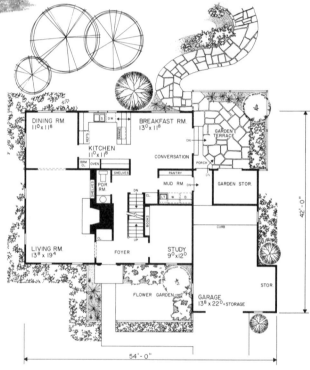

● This is certainly an authentic traditional salt-box. It features a symmetrical design with a center fireplace, a wide, paneled doorway and multi-paned, double-hung windows. Tucked behind the one-car garage is a garden shed which provides work and storage space. The breakfast room features French doors which open onto a flagstone terrace. The U-shaped kitchen has built-in counters which make efficient use of space. The upstairs plan houses three bedrooms.

Design T162659

1,023 Sq. Ft. - First Floor; 1,008 Sq. Ft. - Second Floor
476 Sq. Ft. - Third Floor; 31,510 Cu. Ft

● The facade of this three-storied, pitch-roofed house has a symmetrical placement of windows and a restrained but elegant central entrance. The central hall, or foyer, expands midway through the house to a family kitchen. Off the foyer are two rooms, a living room with fireplace and a study. The windowed third floor attic can be used as a study and studio. Three bedrooms are housed on the second floor.

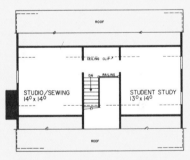

Design T162524 994 Sq. Ft. - First Floor
994 Sq. Ft. - Second Floor; 32,937 Cu. Ft.

● This small two-story with a modest investment will result in an impressive exterior and an outstanding interior. It also will provide exceptional livability. Your list of features will be long and surely impressive.

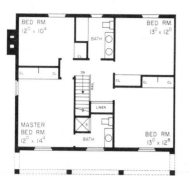

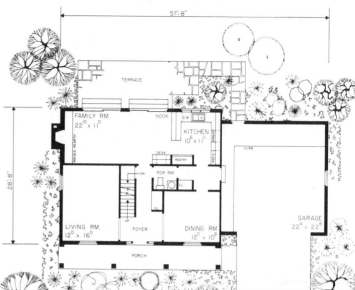

Design T161369 950 Sq. Ft. - First Floor
950 Sq. Ft. - Second Floor; 27,550 Cu. Ft.

● The influence of the Colonial South is delightfully apparent in this gracious, yet modestly designed, home. The stately columns of the front porch set the stage for a memorable visit. Interior livability is outstanding. There is a large L-shaped living/dining area with a centered fireplace. This area will be enjoyed by friends and family members on any given occasion.

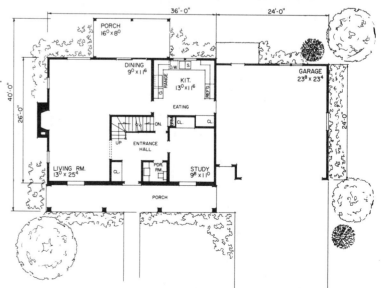

Design T162627 845 Sq. Ft. - First Floor
896 Sq. Ft. - Second Floor; 28,685 Cu. Ft.

● This charming, economically built, home with its stately two-story porch columns is reminiscent of the South. The efficient interior features bonus space over the garage and in the third-floor attic which may be developed into another livable room. The U-shaped kitchen is conveniently located to serve the nook and the dining room with ease.

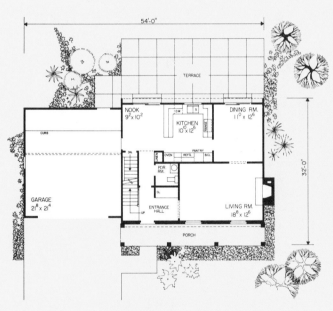

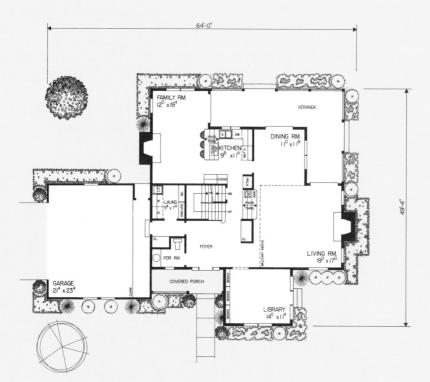

MASTER BEDROOM 12⁰ x 19⁴

SEAT · VANITY · SEAT

DRESSING RM.

CL.

SLOPED CEILING

SHLVS.

WALK-IN CLOSET

CL.

BATH

LINEN

DN.

RAILING

BALCONY

UPPER LIVING RM.

SLOPED CEILING

BEDROOM 10⁰ x 11⁰

BATH

CL.

SLOPED CEILING

BEDROOM 14⁰ x 12⁴

64'-0"

FAMILY RM. 12⁰ x 19⁴

VERANDA

KITCHEN 9⁵ x 11⁴

DINING RM. 11⁰ x 11⁸

OVEN

LAUND. 5⁸ x 7⁰

DN.

UP

SHELVES

PTRY.

FOYER

PDR. RM.

BALCONY ABOVE

LIVING RM. 19⁰ x 17⁰

49'-4"

GARAGE 21⁴ x 23⁴

COVERED PORCH

LIBRARY 14⁰ x 11⁴

Design T162972
1,526 Sq. Ft. - First Floor
1,091 Sq. Ft. - Second Floor
53,930 Cu. Ft.

● The spacious foyer of this Victorian welcomes one to a practical and efficient interior. While the exterior captures all of the nostaglia of yesteryears, the interior reflects what is new in contemporary floor planning. Traffic patterns are orderly and flexible. Zoning is outstanding. The formal living and dining area is located to one side of the plan. Both rooms function well together and have access to the covered veranda. Spaciousness is the byword with that glorious two-story sloping ceiling and the open planning between the two rooms. The more active informal area of the plan includes the fine U-shaped kitchen which opens to the big family room. Here, again, the veranda plays a part. Double French doors access it from the family room while the kitchen looks out upon it. Just inside the entrance from the garage is the laundry, a coat closet with the powder room a few steps away. The library will enjoy its full measure of privacy. Note its access to the front yard. Upstairs, the three bedroom sleeping zone with a fireplace.

Design T162974
911 Sq. Ft. - First Floor; 861 Sq. Ft. - Second Floor
33,160 Cu. Ft.

● Victorian houses are well known for their orientation on narrow building sites. And when this occurs nothing is lost to captivating exterior styling. This house is but 38 feet wide. Its narrow width belies the tremendous amount of livability found inside. And, of course, the ubiquitous porch/veranda contributes mightily to style as well as livability. The efficient, U-shape kitchen is flanked by the informal breakfast room and formal dining room. The rear living area is spacious and functions in an exciting manner with the outdoor areas. Bonus recreational, hobby and storage space is offered by the basement and the attic.

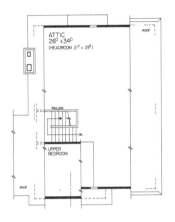

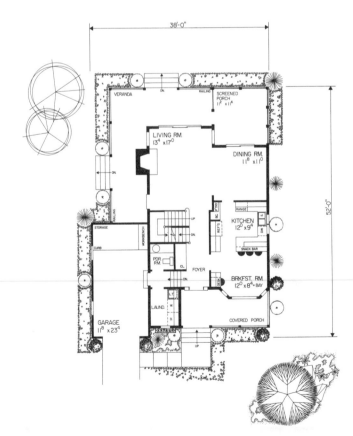

Design T162539
1,450 Sq. Ft. - First Floor
1,167 Sq. Ft. - Second Floor; 46,738 Cu. Ft.

● This appealingly proportioned Gambrel exudes an aura of coziness. The beauty of the main part of the house is delightfully symmetrical and is enhanced by the attached garage and laundry room. The center entrance routes traffic directly to all major zones of the house.

● This Gambrel roofed design has its roots in the early history of New England. While its exterior is decidedly and purposely dated, the interior of this design reflects an impressive 20th Century floor plan. All of the elements are present to guarantee outstanding living patterns for the large, active family of today.

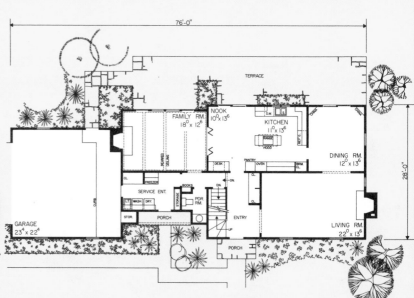

Design T162531
1,353 Sq. Ft. - First Floor
1,208 Sq. Ft. - Second Floor; 33,225 Cu. Ft.

BED RM.
13^8 x 10^0

CL.
CL. CL. CL.
LIN.
BATH

DN.
CL. CL.
WALK IN CL.
VANITY
BATH
S.

MASTER BED RM.
13^8 x 20^0

BED RM.
12^8 x 14^6

BED RM.
12^8 x 10^0

BED RM.
12^8 x 10^0

CL.
CL.
CL. CL. CL. CL.
LINEN
BATH
VANITY
STORAGE

DN.
LIN.
S.
UP

MASTER BED RM.
13^4 x 18^0

BATH
VANITY
CL.

BED RM.
12^8 x 12^4

Design T161142 1,525 Sq. Ft. - First Floor
952 Sq. Ft. - Second Floor (1,053 Sq. Ft. - Four Bedroom Option); 32,980 Cu. Ft.

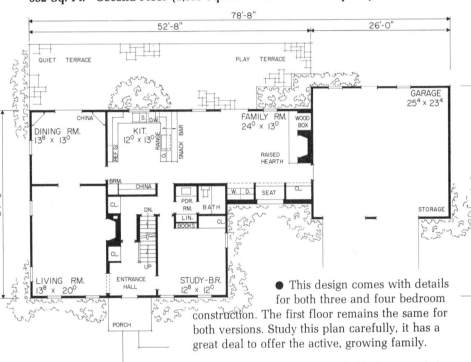

78'-8"

52'-8"   26'-0"

QUIET   TERRACE   PLAY   TERRACE

GARAGE
25^4 x 23^4

DINING RM.
13^8 x 13^0

CHINA

KIT.
12^0 x 13^0

REFG.

S. D.W.
RANGE

SNACK BAR

FAMILY RM.
24^0 x 13^0

WOOD BOX

RAISED HEARTH

34'-0"

38'-0"

BRM.
CHINA
CL.
PDR. RM.
LIN.
BATH
BOOKS
DN.
CL.
W. D.
SEAT
CL.
STORAGE

LIVING RM.
13^8 x 20^0

ENTRANCE HALL
UP

STUDY-B.R.
12^8 x 12^0

PORCH

● This design comes with details for both three and four bedroom construction. The first floor remains the same for both versions. Study this plan carefully, it has a great deal to offer the active, growing family.

Design T162667 1,827 Sq. Ft. - First Floor
697 Sq. Ft. - Second Floor; 46,290 Cu. Ft.

● Two one-story wings flank the two-story center section of this design which echoes the architectural forms of 18th-Century Tidewater Virginia. The left wing is a huge living room; the right, the master bedroom suite, service area and garage. Kitchen, dining room and family room are centrally located with the three bedrooms above. Study both plans and envision your family occupying them.

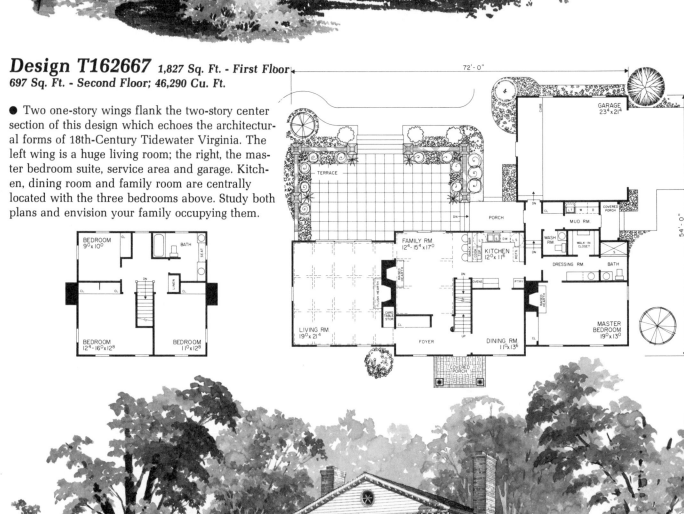

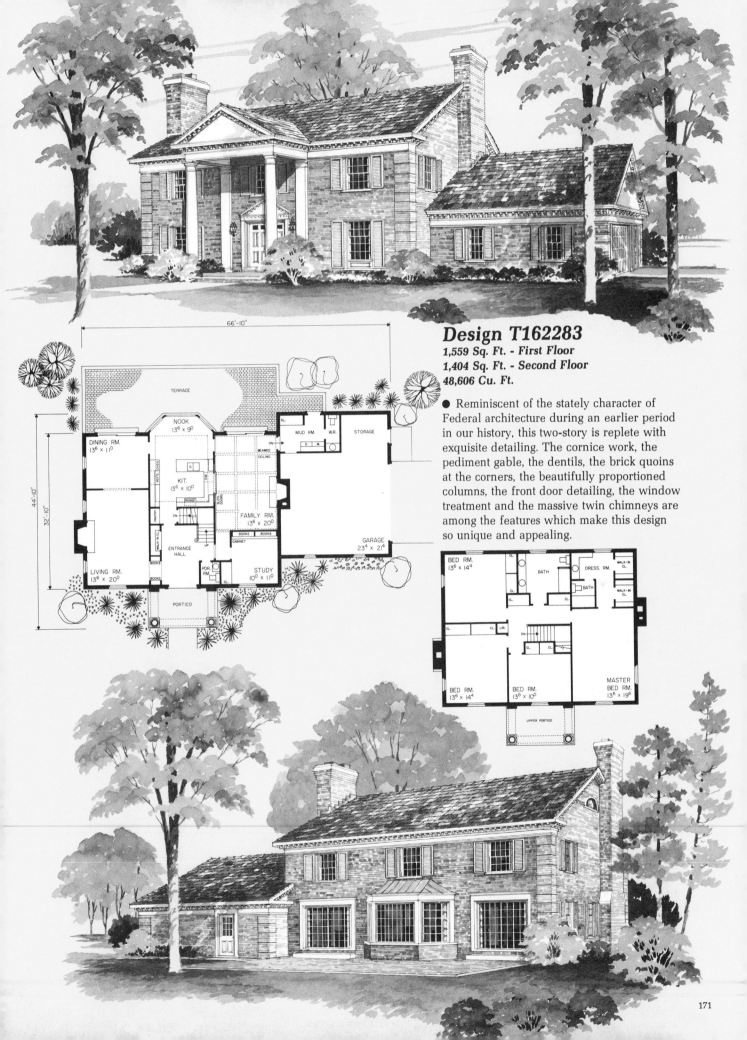

Design T162283

1,559 Sq. Ft. - First Floor
1,404 Sq. Ft. - Second Floor
48,606 Cu. Ft.

● Reminiscent of the stately character of Federal architecture during an earlier period in our history, this two-story is replete with exquisite detailing. The cornice work, the pediment gable, the dentils, the brick quoins at the corners, the beautifully proportioned columns, the front door detailing, the window treatment and the massive twin chimneys are among the features which make this design so unique and appealing.

66'-10"
44'-10"
32'-10"

TERRACE

NOOK
13⁶ x 9⁰

DINING RM.
13⁶ x 11⁰

MUD RM. W.R. STORAGE

D. W.

KIT.
13⁶ x 10⁰

BEAMED CEILING

RANGE

FAMILY RM.
13⁶ x 20⁰

GARAGE
23⁴ x 21⁴

PANTRY

WALK-IN CL.

ENTRANCE HALL

UP

BOOKS CABINET BOOKS

LIVING RM.
13⁶ x 20⁰

BOOKS BOOKS

PDR. RM.

STUDY
10⁰ x 11⁰

PORTICO

BED RM.
13⁶ x 14⁴

CL. BATH DRESS. RM. WALK-IN CL.

CL.

BATH

WALK-IN CL.

CL. LIN.

DN.

BED RM.
13⁶ x 14⁴

BED RM.
13⁶ x 10⁰

MASTER BED RM.
13⁶ x 19⁶

UPPER PORTICO

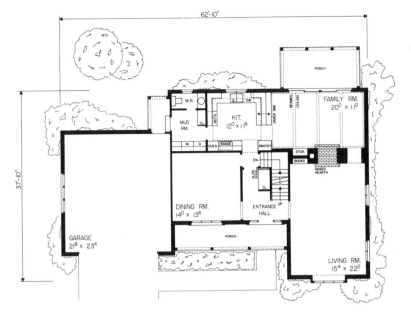

Design T162276 1,273 Sq. Ft. - First Floor
1,323 Sq. Ft. - Second Floor; 40,450 Cu. Ft.

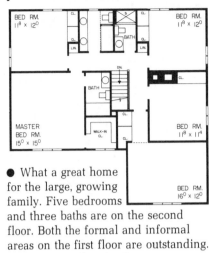

● What a great home for the large, growing family. Five bedrooms and three baths are on the second floor. Both the formal and informal areas on the first floor are outstanding.

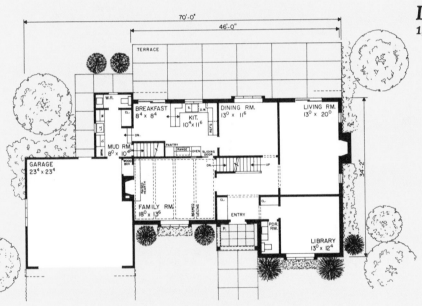

Design T162141 1,490 Sq. Ft. - First Floor
1,474 Sq. Ft. - Second Floor; 50,711 Cu. Ft.

● Imagine, six bedrooms on the second floor. The first floor houses the living areas: family room, living room, dining areas plus a library.

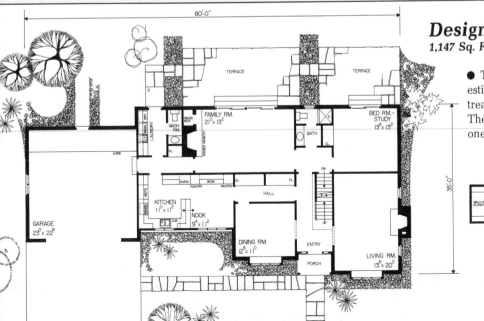

Design T162577 1,718 Sq. Ft. - First Floor
1,147 Sq. Ft. - Second Floor; 42,843 Cu. Ft.

● The exterior of this Tudor has interesting roof planes, delightful window treatment and recessed front entrance. The master suite with sitting room is one of the highlights of the interior.

173

Design T162729

1,590 Sq. Ft. - First Floor
756 Sq. Ft. - Second Floor
39,310 Cu. Ft.

● Entering this home will surely be a pleasure through the sheltered walk-way to the double front doors. And the pleasure and beauty does not stop there. The entry hall and sunken gathering room are open to the upstairs for added dimension.

There's even a built-in seat in the entry area. The kitchen-nook area is very efficient with its many built-ins and the adjacent laundry room. There is a fine indoor-outdoor living relationship in this design. Note the private terrace off the luxurious

master bedroom suite, a living terrace accessible from the gathering room, dining room and nook plus the balcony off the upstairs bedroom. Upstairs there is a total of two bedrooms, each having its own private bath and plenty of closets.

Design T162379 1,525 Sq. Ft. - First Floor; 748 Sq. Ft. - Second Floor; 26,000 Cu. Ft.

● A house that has "everything" may very well look just like this design. Its exterior is well-proportioned and impressive. Inside the inviting double front doors there are features galore. The living room and family room level are sunken. Separating these two rooms is a dramatic thru fireplace. A built-in bar, planter and beamed ceiling highlight the family room. Nearby is a full bath and a study which could be utilized as a fourth bedroom. The fine functioning kitchen has a pass-thru to the snack bar in the breakfast nook. The adjacent dining room overlooks the living room and has sliding doors to the covered porch. Upstairs three bedrooms, two baths and an outdoor balcony. Blueprints for this design include optional basement details.

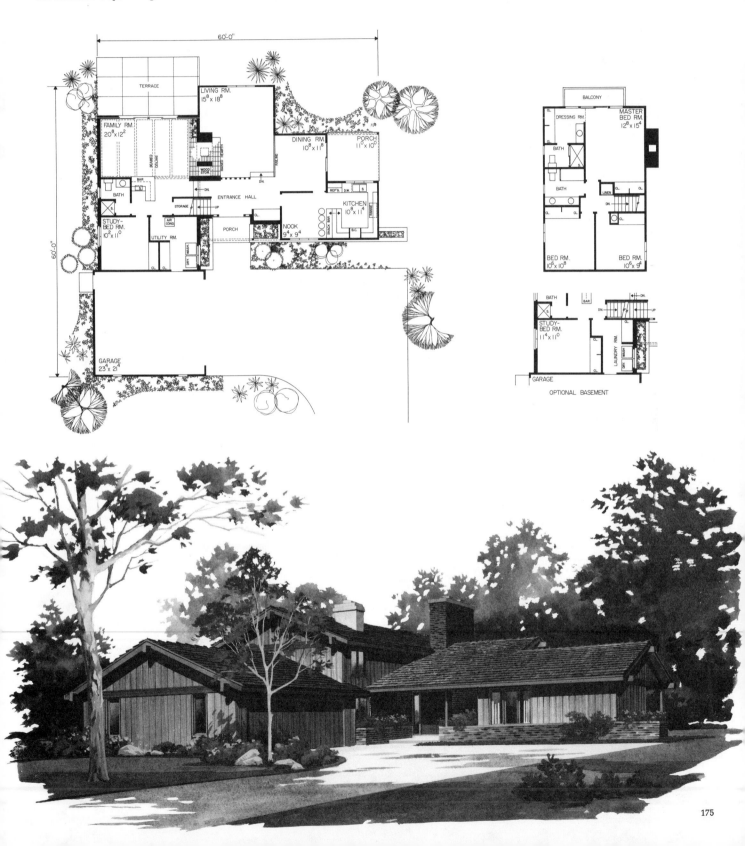

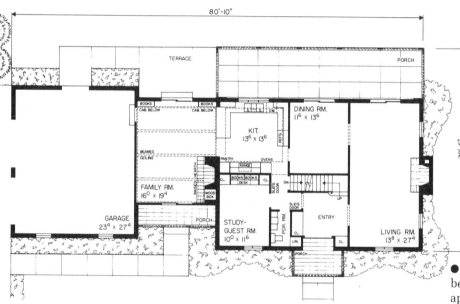

80'-10"

38'-5"

TERRACE

PORCH

BOOKS | BOOKS
CAB. BELOW | CAB. BELOW

DINING RM.
11⁶ x 13⁶

KIT.
13⁶ x 13⁶

BEAMED
CEILING

PANTRY | OVENS
RANGE

FAMILY RM.
16⁰ x 19⁴

BOOKS | BOOKS
DESK

RAISED HEARTH

WOOD
BOX

GARAGE
23⁴ x 27⁴

PORCH

STUDY-
GUEST RM.
10⁰ x 11⁶

PDR. RM.

LIN.

SLID'G
DOOR

SLID'G
DOOR

DN

UP

ENTRY

LIVING RM.
13⁸ x 27⁴

PORCH

BED RM.
13⁶ x 13⁶

DRESS. RM.

CL. | CL.

BATH

MASTER
BED RM.
17⁰ x 13⁶

CL. | CL. | CL.

DN | UP

HALL

BED RM.
10⁰ x 11²

LINEN | LIN.

BATH | PDR. RM.

CL.

CL.

BED RM.
13⁰ x 13⁶

Design T162222

1,485 Sq. Ft. - First Floor
1,175 Sq. Ft. - Second Floor
45,500 Cu. Ft.

● Gracious, formal living could hardly find a better backdrop than this two-story French adaptation. The exterior is truly exquisite. Inside, living patterns will be most enjoyable.

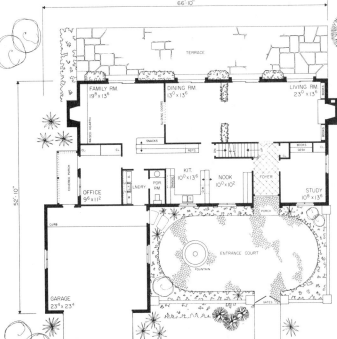

Design T162326
1,674 Sq. Ft. - First Floor
1,107 Sq. Ft. - Second Floor
53,250 Cu. Ft.

● If your family enjoys the view of the backyard, then this is the design for you. The main rooms, family, dining and living, are all in the back of the plan, each having sliding glass doors to the terrace. They are away from the confusion of the work center, yet easily accessible. A study and separate office are also available. Four bedrooms are on the second floor. Be sure to note all of the features in the master bedroom suite.

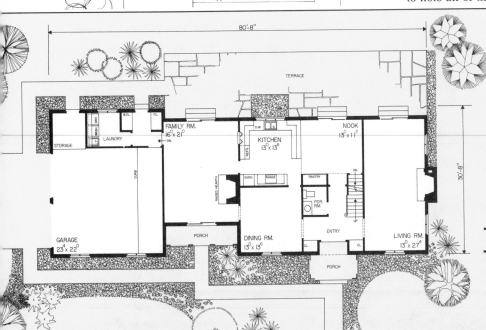

Design T162564
1,706 Sq. Ft. - First Floor
1,166 Sq. Ft. - Second Floor
48,640 Cu. Ft.

● French tone! Here's a home with Old World charm! But liveable in the American style. Formal and informal areas each have a fireplace. Three (optional four) bedrooms upstairs.

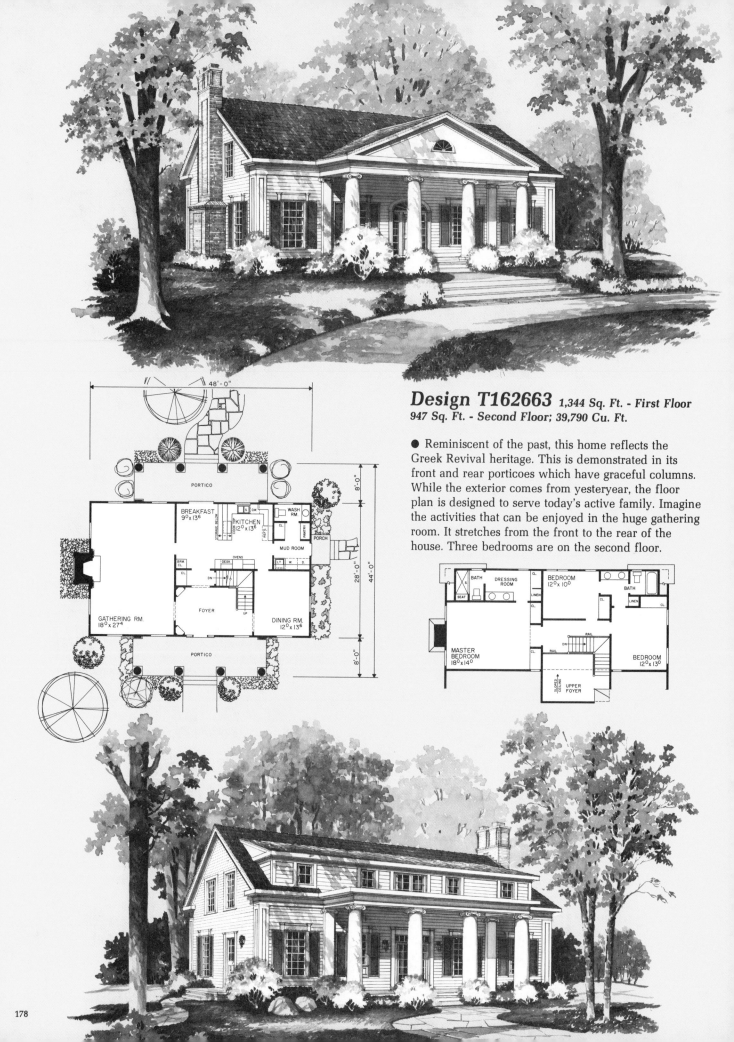

Design T162663 1,344 Sq. Ft. - First Floor
947 Sq. Ft. - Second Floor; 39,790 Cu. Ft.

● Reminiscent of the past, this home reflects the Greek Revival heritage. This is demonstrated in its front and rear porticoes which have graceful columns. While the exterior comes from yesteryear, the floor plan is designed to serve today's active family. Imagine the activities that can be enjoyed in the huge gathering room. It stretches from the front to the rear of the house. Three bedrooms are on the second floor.

Design T162668 1,206 Sq. Ft. - First Floor
1,254 Sq. Ft. - Second Floor; 47,915 Cu. Ft.

● This elegant exterior houses a very livable plan. Every bit of space has been put to good use. The front country kitchen is a good place to begin. It is efficiently planned with its island cook top, built-ins and pass-thru to the dining room. The large great room will be the center of all family activities. Quiet times can be enjoyed in the front library. Study the second floor sleeping areas.

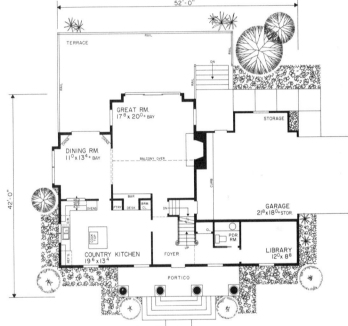

Design T162800

999 Sq. Ft. - First Floor
997 Sq. Ft. - Second Floor; 31,390 Cu. Ft.

● Attractively detailed bay windows are in both the formal dining room and the family room of this design. The beauty and warmth of a fireplace will be enjoyed from the formal living room. Two bedrooms, bath and master bedroom with adjoining nursery/study are on the second floor.

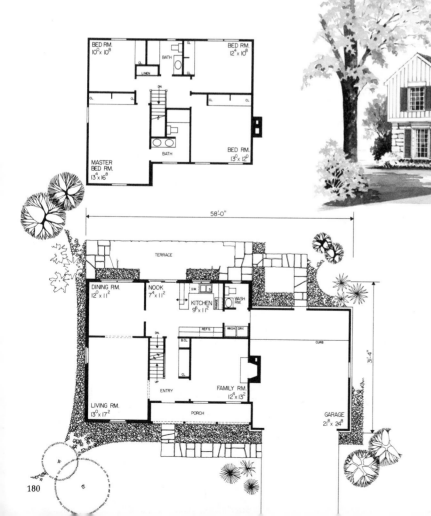

Design T162585

990 Sq. Ft. - First Floor
1,011 Sq. Ft. - Second Floor; 30,230 Cu. Ft.

● This is a version of a front porch type house. The exterior is highlighted with seven large paned-glass windows and pillars. Note that the second floor overhangs in the front to extend the size of the master bedroom. After entering through the front door one can either go directly to the formal area of the living room and dining room or to the informal area which is the front family room with fireplace. No matter which direction you choose, satisfaction will be found.

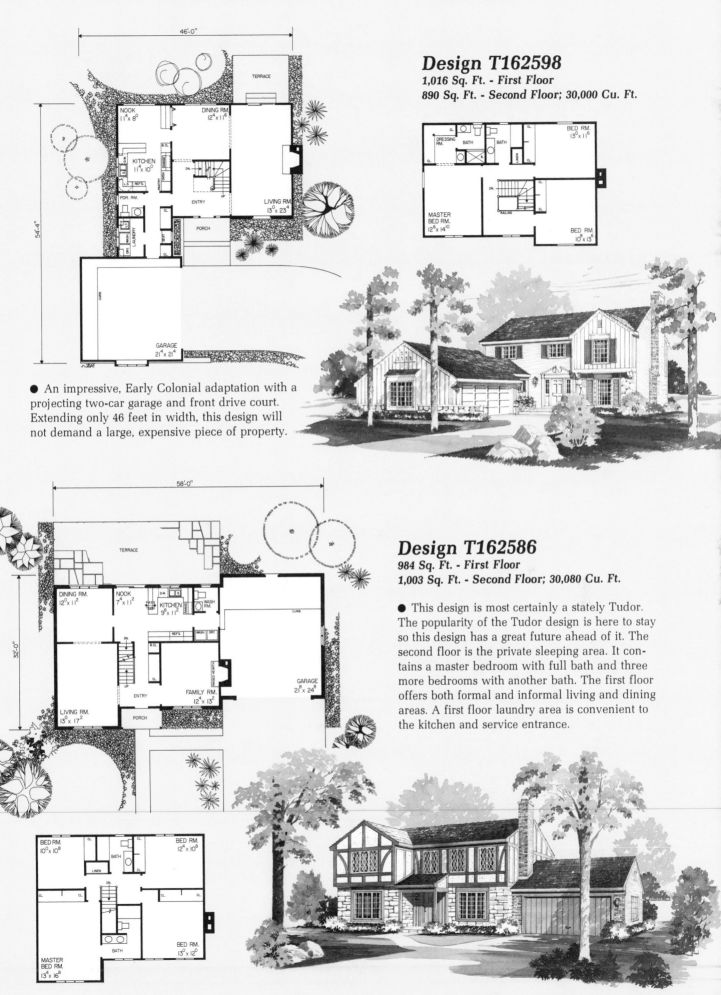

Design T162598
1,016 Sq. Ft. - First Floor
890 Sq. Ft. - Second Floor; 30,000 Cu. Ft.

First Floor:

- NOOK 11⁴ x 8⁰
- DINING RM. 12⁴ x 11⁶
- TERRACE
- KITCHEN 11⁴ x 10
- LIVING RM. 13⁰ x 23⁴
- PDR. RM.
- ENTRY
- PORCH
- LAUNDRY
- GARAGE 21⁴ x 21⁴
- 46'-0"
- 54'-4"

Second Floor:

- DRESSING RM.
- BATH
- BATH
- BED RM. 13⁰ x 11⁶
- MASTER BED RM. 12⁶ x 14¹⁰
- BED RM. 10⁸ x 13⁶
- RAILING

● An impressive, Early Colonial adaptation with a projecting two-car garage and front drive court. Extending only 46 feet in width, this design will not demand a large, expensive piece of property.

Design T162586
984 Sq. Ft. - First Floor
1,003 Sq. Ft. - Second Floor; 30,080 Cu. Ft.

First Floor:

- 58'-0"
- TERRACE
- DINING RM. 12⁰ x 11²
- NOOK 7⁴ x 11²
- KITCHEN 9⁶ x 11²
- WASH RM.
- 32'-0"
- ENTRY
- FAMILY RM. 12⁴ x 13²
- GARAGE 21⁸ x 24⁸
- LIVING RM. 13⁰ x 17²
- PORCH

Second Floor:

- BED RM. 10⁰ x 10⁸
- BED RM. 12⁴ x 10⁸
- BATH
- LINEN
- MASTER BED RM. 13⁴ x 16⁸
- BATH
- BED RM. 13⁰ x 12⁰

● This design is most certainly a stately Tudor. The popularity of the Tudor design is here to stay so this design has a great future ahead of it. The second floor is the private sleeping area. It contains a master bedroom with full bath and three more bedrooms with another bath. The first floor offers both formal and informal living and dining areas. A first floor laundry area is convenient to the kitchen and service entrance.

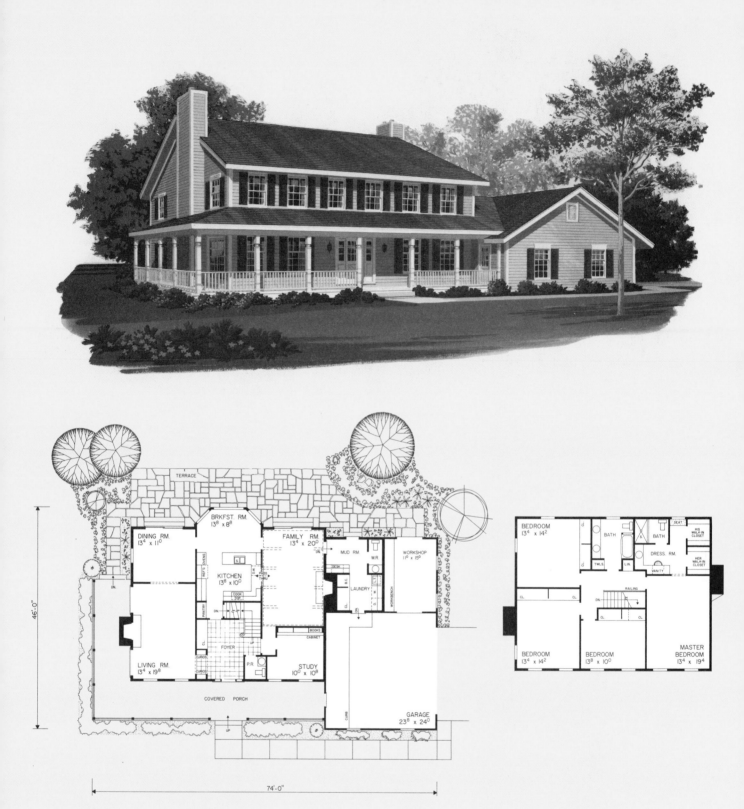

Design T162946 1,590 Sq. Ft. - First Floor; 1,344 Sq. Ft. - Second Floor; 41,498 Cu. Ft.

● Here's a traditional design that's made for down-home hospitality, the pleasures of casual conversation, and the good grace of pleasant company. The star attractions are the large covered porch and terrace, perfectly relaxing gathering points for family and friends. Inside, though, the design is truly a hard worker; separate living room and family room, each with its own fireplace; formal dining room; large kitchen and breakfast area with bay windows; separate study; workshop with plenty of room to maneuver; mud room; and four bedrooms up, including a master suite. Not to be overlooked are the curio niches, the powder room, the built-in bookshelves, the kitchen pass-thru, the pantry, the planning desk, the workbench, and the stairs to the basement.

Design T162865

1,703 Sq. Ft. - First Floor
1,044 Sq. Ft. - Second Floor
47,179 Cu. Ft.

● This comfortable farmhouse with post-rail, covered wrap-around porch is charming, indeed! Fine proportioning and zoning is evident on both floors. Three bedrooms are isolated upstairs to allow privacy and quiet. Two bedrooms enjoy their own window seats, as traditional dormers pierce the roof line. A study downstairs could double as a fourth bedroom. Downstairs one also finds a front living room with its own fireplace and a large back family room with it own fireplace. A formal dining room is positioned in front just off the foyer. A modern kitchen features pass-thru to a breakfast room. A mud room is positioned just off the double garage and adjacent to the kitchen. This traditional design offers plenty of modern comfort for contemporary families.

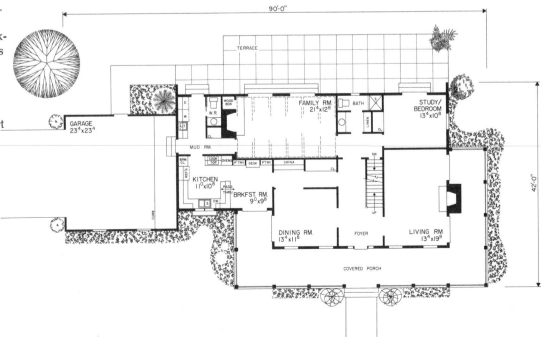

Design T162535
986 Sq. Ft. - First Floor
1,436 Sq. Ft. - Second Floor; 35,835 Cu. Ft.

● What a great package this is! An enchanting Colonial exterior and an exceptional amount of interior livability. Utilizing the space over the garage results in a fifth bedroom with bath.

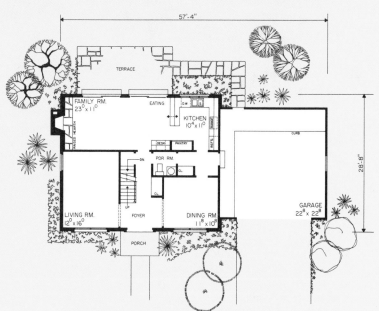

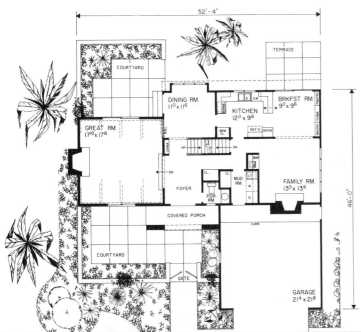

Design T162801 1,172 Sq. Ft. - First Floor
884 Sq. Ft. - Second Floor; 32,510 Cu. Ft.

● Built-ins in the breakfast room for china and pantry goods are certainly features to be mentioned up-front. A second china cabinet is located adjacent to the formal dining room. The great room will be just that. It is sunken two steps, has a beamed ceiling, the beauty of a fireplace and two sets of sliding glass doors to a front and rear courtyard.

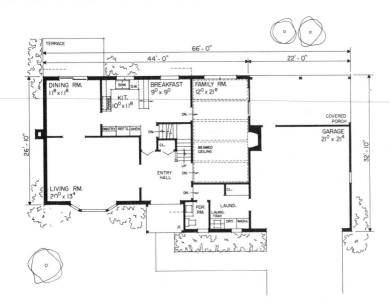

Design T161972
1,286 Sq. Ft. - First Floor
960 Sq. Ft. - Second Floor; 30,739 Cu. Ft.

● What an appealingly different type of two-story home! It is one whose grace and charm project an aura of welcome. The large entry hall routes traffic efficiently to all areas. Don't miss the covered porch.

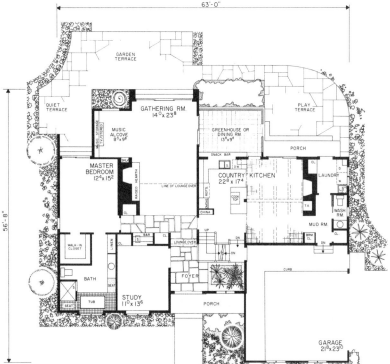

Design T162883 1,919 Sq. Ft. - First Floor
895 Sq. Ft. - Second Floor; 46,489 Cu. Ft.

● A country-style home is part of America's fascination with the rural past. This home's emphasis of the traditional home is in its gambrel roof, dormers and fanlight windows. Having a traditional exterior from the street view, this home has window

walls and a greenhouse, which opens the house to the outdoors in a thoroughly contemporary manner. The interior meets the requirements of today's active family. Like the country houses of the past, it has a gathering room for family get-togethers or entertaining. The adjacent two-story greenhouse doubles as the dining room. There is a pass-thru snack bar to the country kitchen here. This country kitchen just might be the heart of the house with its two areas - work zone and sitting room. There are four bedrooms on the two floors - the master bedroom suite on the first floor; three more on the second floor. A lounge, overlooking the gathering room and front foyer, is also on the second floor.

Design T162826
1,112 Sq. Ft. - First Floor
881 Sq. Ft. - Second Floor; 32,770 Cu. Ft.

ALTERNATE KITCHEN / DINING RM. /
BREAKFAST RM. FLOOR PLAN

● This is an outstanding example of the type of informal, traditional-style architecture that has captured the modern imagination. The interior plan houses all the features that people want most - a spacious gathering room, formal and informal dining areas, efficient, U-shaped kitchen, master bedroom, two children's bedrooms, second-floor lounge, entrance court and rear terrace and deck. Study all areas of this plan carefully.

Design T162518
1,630 Sq. Ft. - First Floor
1,260 Sq. Ft. - Second Floor
43,968 Cu. Ft.

● For those who have a predilection for the Spanish influence in their architecture. Outdoor oriented, each of the major living areas on the first floor have direct access to the terraces. Traffic patterns are excellent.

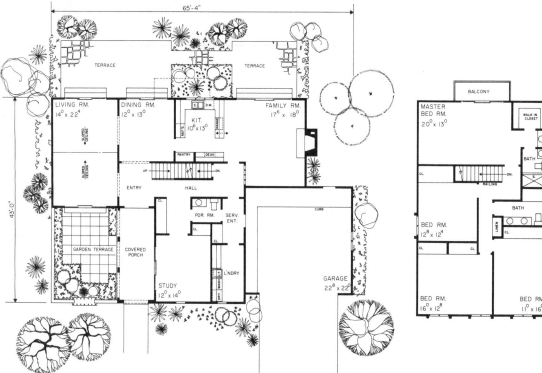

Design T162390 1,368 Sq. Ft. - First Floor
1,428 Sq. Ft. - Second Floor; 37,734 Cu. Ft.

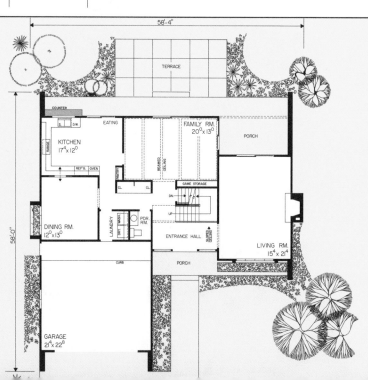

● If yours is a large family and you like the architecture of the Far West, don't look further. Particularly if you envision building on a modest sized lot. Projecting the garage to the front contributes to the drama of this two-story. Its stucco exterior is beautifully enhanced by the clay tiles of the varying roof surfaces.

Design T162517
1,767 Sq. Ft. - First Floor
1,094 Sq. Ft. - Second Floor
50,256 Cu. Ft.

● Wherever built - north, east, south, or west - this home will surely command all the attention it deserves. And little wonder with such a well-designed exterior and such an outstanding interior. List your favorite features.

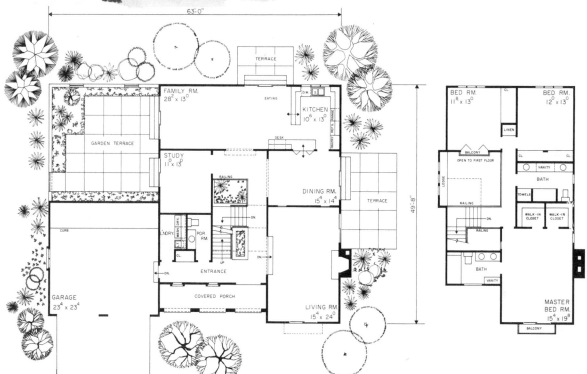

72' - 0"

TERRACE

COVERED PORCH

DINING RM.
13⁸ x 12⁰

COVERED PORCH

PORCH

SEAT

SEWING

MUD RM.

LAUNDRY

WASH RM.

STUDY
12⁸ x 14⁴

PDR. RM.

COOK TOP

COUNTRY KITCHEN
16⁰ x 29⁰

BEAMED CEILING

STORAGE

GARAGE
20⁸ x 22⁰ + STORAGE

46' - 0"

LIVING RM.
18⁰ x 14⁴

FOYER

UP

COVERED PORCH

Design T162680

1,707 Sq. Ft. - First Floor
1,439 Sq. Ft. - Second Floor; 53,865 Cu. Ft.

ROOF

ROOF

BEDROOM
13⁰ x 12⁰

BATH

BATH

DRESS'G RM.

WALK-IN CLOSET

LINEN

OPEN

LINEN

BEDROOM
16⁰ x 12⁰

DN

ATTIC ACCESS

ATTIC ACCESS

ATTIC ACCESS

ATTIC ACCESS

BATH

MASTER BEDROOM
16⁰ x 16⁰

BEDROOM
16⁰ x 12⁰

ATTIC

ROOF

● This Early American, Dutch Colonial not only has charm, but offers many fine features. The foyer allows easy access to all rooms on the first floor - excellent livability. Note the large country kitchen with beamed ceiling, fireplace and island cook top. A large, formal dining room and powder room are only a few steps away. A fireplace also will be found in the study and living room. The service area, mud room, wash room and laundry are tucked near the garage. Two bedrooms, full bath and master bedroom suite will be found on the second floor. A fourth bedroom and bath are accessible through the master bedroom or stairs in the service entrance.

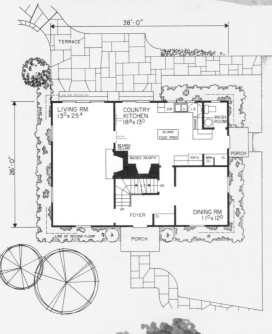

Design T162666 *988 Sq. Ft. - First Floor*
1,147 Sq. Ft. - Second Floor; 35,490 Cu. Ft.

● A spacious country-kitchen highlights the interior of this two-story. Its features include an island work center, fireplace, beamed ceiling and sliding glass doors leading to the rear terrace. A wash room and a side door are only steps away. A second fireplace is in the large living room. It, too, has sliding glass doors in the rear.

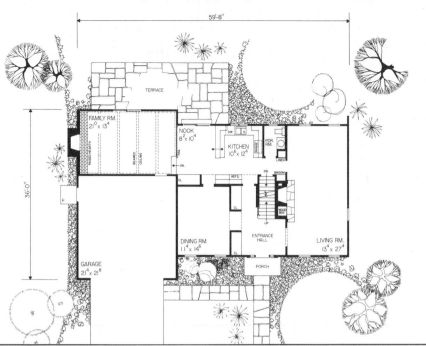

Design T162623
1,368 Sq. Ft. - First Floor
1,046 Sq. Ft. - Second Floor; 35,130 Cu. Ft.

● Take note of this four bedroom Salt Box design. Enter through the large entrance hall to enjoy this home. Imagine a living room 13 x 27 feet. Plus a family room. Both having a fireplace. Also, sliding glass doors in both the family room and nook leading to the rear terrace.

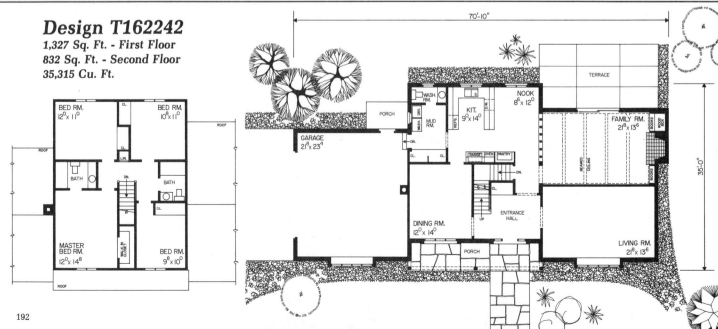

Design T162242
1,327 Sq. Ft. - First Floor
832 Sq. Ft. - Second Floor
35,315 Cu. Ft.

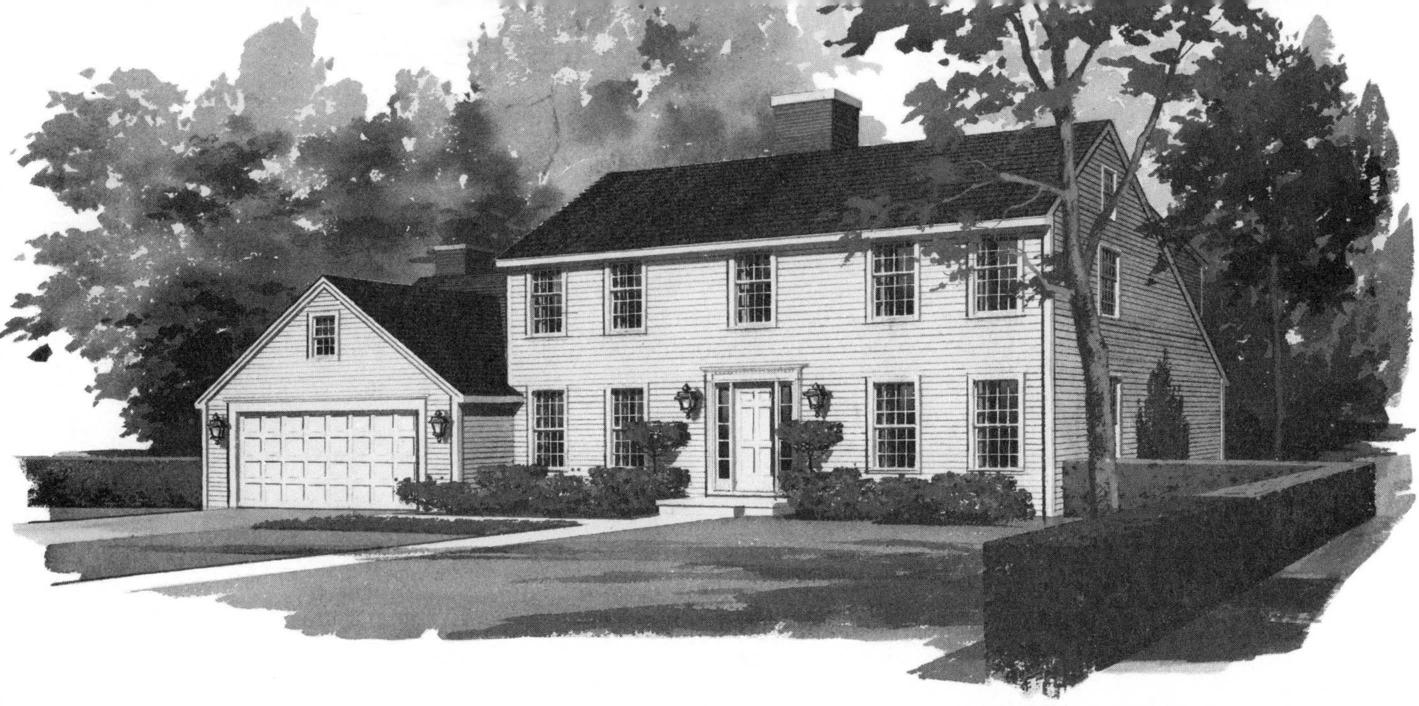

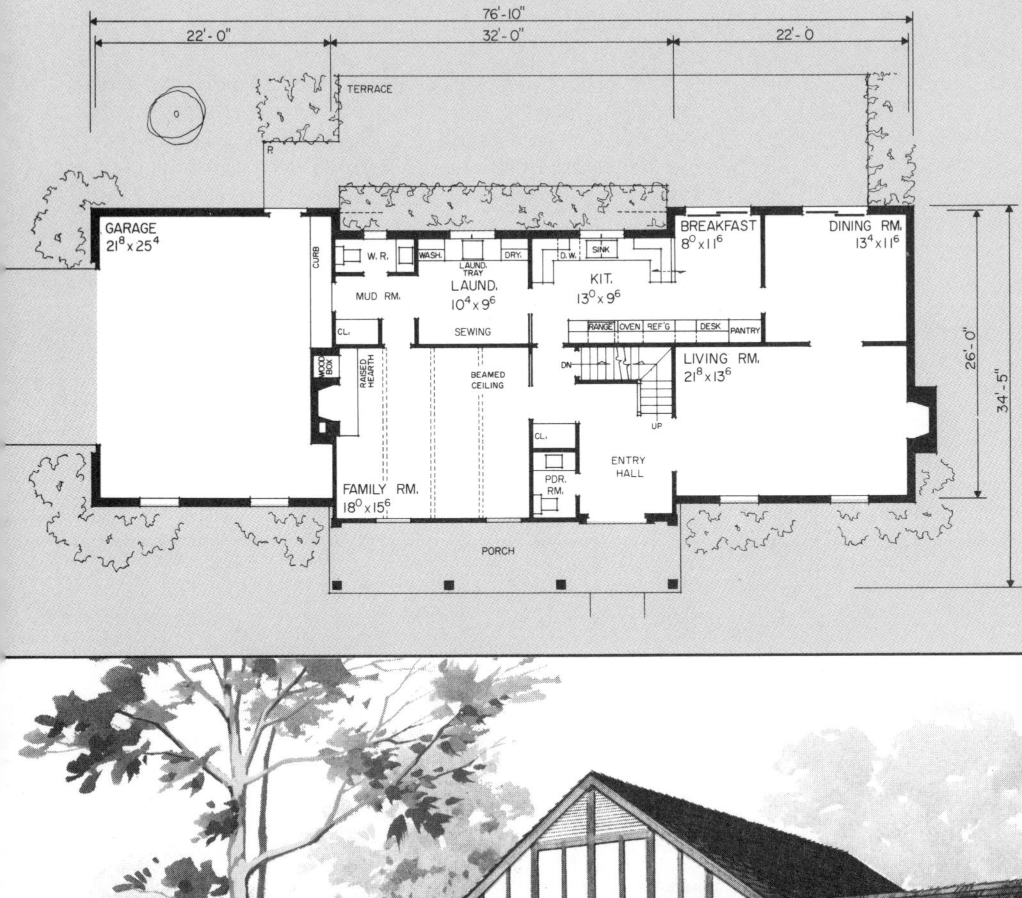

76'-10"
22'-0"
32'-0"
22'-0
TERRACE
GARAGE
$21^8 x 25^4$
CURB
W.R.
WASH.
LAUND. TRAY
DRY.
D.W.
SINK
BREAKFAST
$8^0 x 11^6$
DINING RM.
$13^4 x 11^6$
MUD RM.
LAUND.
$10^4 x 9^6$
KIT.
$13^0 x 9^6$
CL.
SEWING
RANGE
OVEN
REF'G.
DESK
PANTRY
WOOD BOX
RAISED HEARTH
BEAMED CEILING
DN
LIVING RM.
$21^8 x 13^6$
UP
CL.
PDR. RM.
ENTRY HALL
FAMILY RM.
$18^0 x 15^6$
PORCH
26'-0"
34'-5"

Design T161954

1,448 Sq. Ft. - First Floor

896 Sq. Ft. - Second Floor

38,096 Cu. Ft.

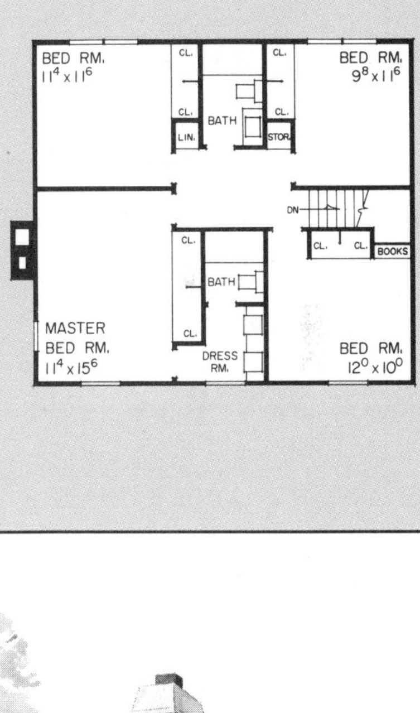

BED RM.
$11^4 x 11^6$
CL.
CL.
BED RM.
$9^8 x 11^6$
CL.
BATH
CL.
LIN.
STOR.
DN
CL.
CL.
CL.
BOOKS
BATH
CL.
MASTER BED RM.
$11^4 x 15^6$
DRESS RM.
BED RM.
$12^0 x 10^0$

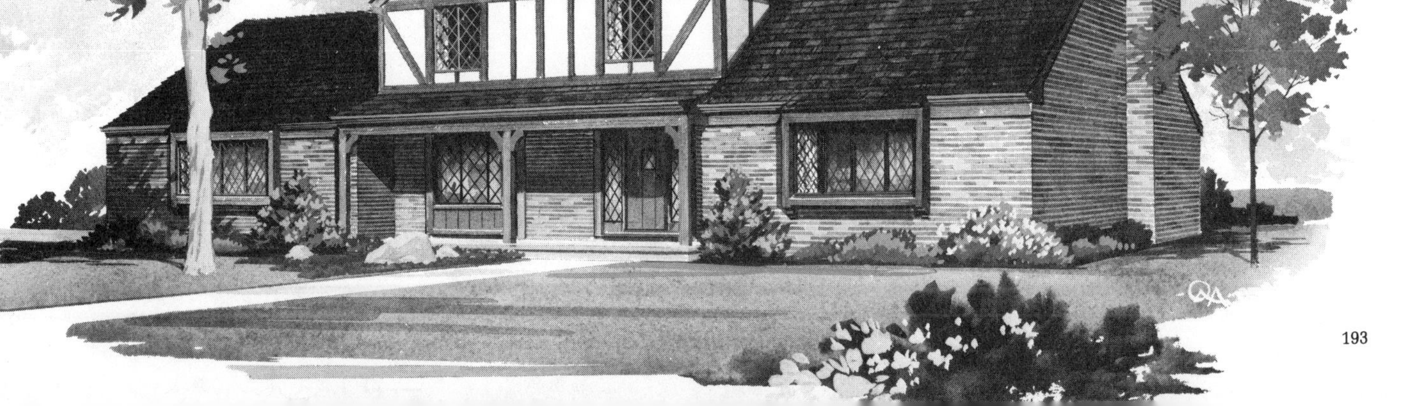

Design T162530 1,616 Sq. Ft. - First Floor
997 Sq. Ft. - Second Floor; 41,925 Cu. Ft.

● This exciting contemporary has dramatic roof lines and appealing glass areas. The interior planning is, indeed, unique. Study this plan carefully and consider how your family would function in it. The sunken gathering room is a delightful area with its dramatic raised hearth fireplace and planter, and access to two terraces. The spaciousness of the dining/family room will make entertaining a memorable occasion.

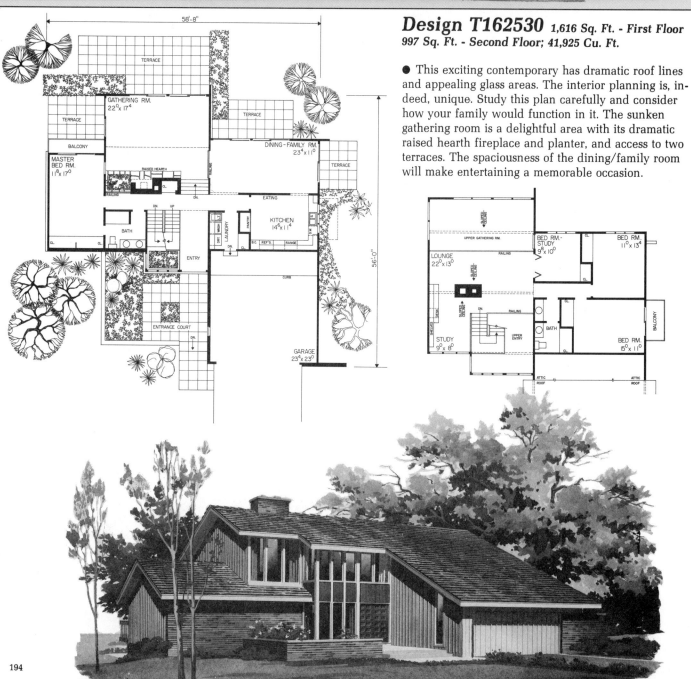

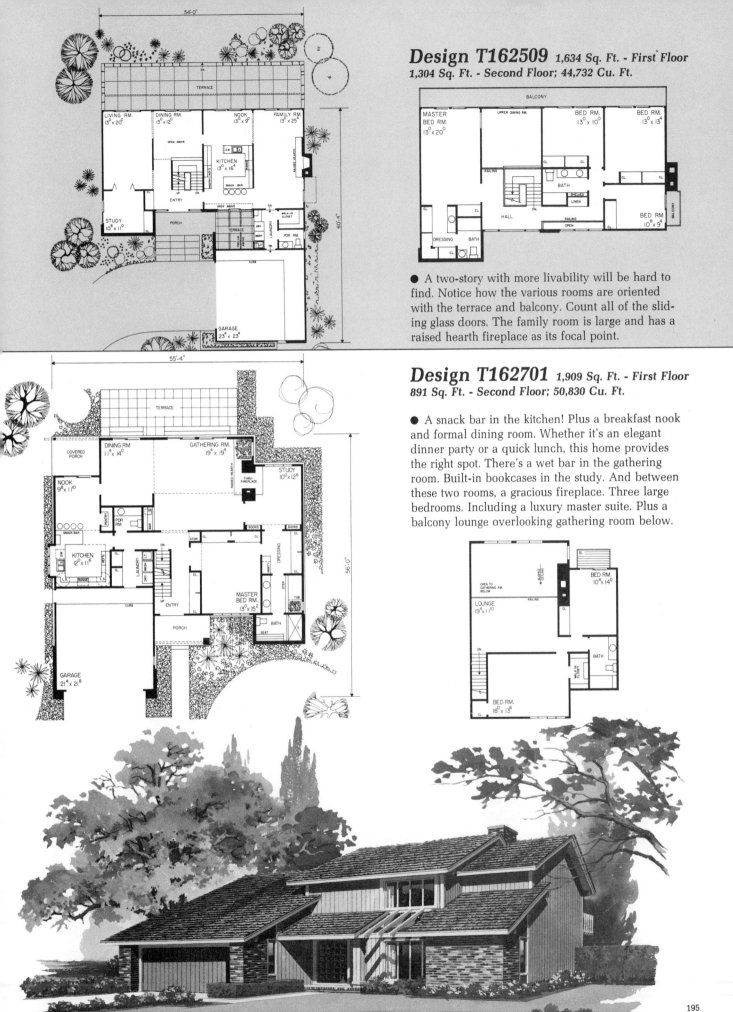

Design T162509 1,634 Sq. Ft. - First Floor
1,304 Sq. Ft. - Second Floor; 44,732 Cu. Ft.

● A two-story with more livability will be hard to find. Notice how the various rooms are oriented with the terrace and balcony. Count all of the sliding glass doors. The family room is large and has a raised hearth fireplace as its focal point.

Design T162701 1,909 Sq. Ft. - First Floor
891 Sq. Ft. - Second Floor; 50,830 Cu. Ft.

● A snack bar in the kitchen! Plus a breakfast nook and formal dining room. Whether it's an elegant dinner party or a quick lunch, this home provides the right spot. There's a wet bar in the gathering room. Built-in bookcases in the study. And between these two rooms, a gracious fireplace. Three large bedrooms. Including a luxury master suite. Plus a balcony lounge overlooking gathering room below.

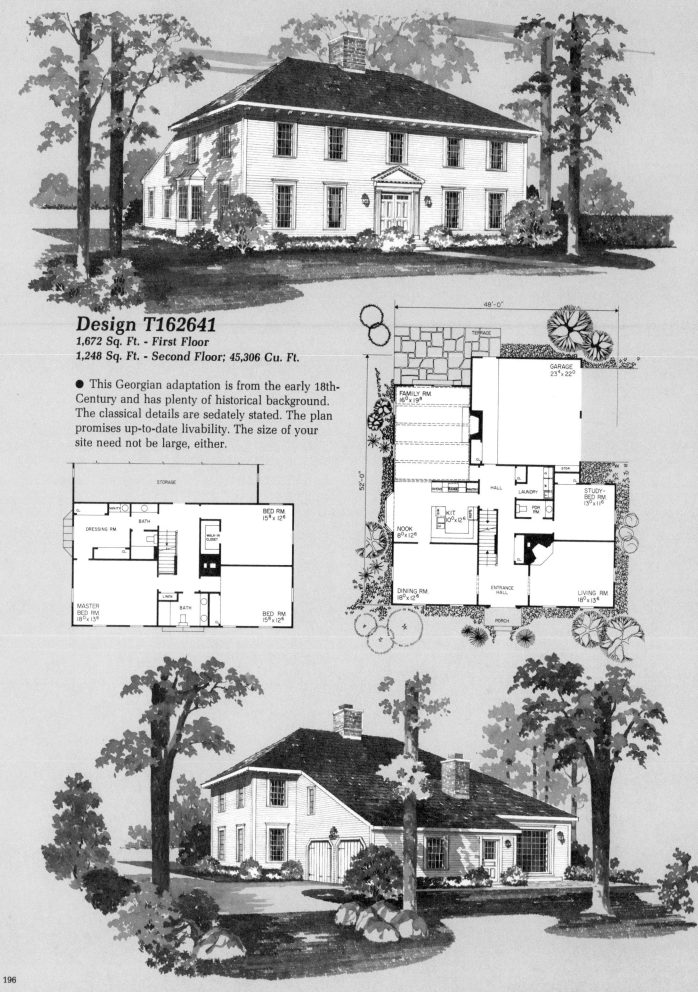

Design T162641

1,672 Sq. Ft. - First Floor
1,248 Sq. Ft. - Second Floor; 45,306 Cu. Ft.

● This Georgian adaptation is from the early 18th-Century and has plenty of historical background. The classical details are sedately stated. The plan promises up-to-date livability. The size of your site need not be large, either.

STORAGE

CL.
VANITY
DRESSING RM.
BATH
WALK-IN CLOSET
CL.
BED RM.
15⁸ x 12⁶

MASTER BED RM
18⁰ x 13⁶
LINEN
BATH
CL.
BED RM.
15⁸ x 12⁶

48'-0"

TERRACE
FAMILY RM.
16⁰ x 19⁸
GARAGE
23⁴ x 22⁰
CL.
STOR.
52'-0"
OVENS RANGE PANTRY
HALL
LAUNDRY
CL.
STUDY-BED RM.
13⁰ x 11⁶
KIT.
10⁰ x 12⁶
PDR. RM.
NOOK
8⁰ x 12⁶
CL.
DINING RM.
18⁰ x 12⁶
ENTRANCE HALL
LIVING RM.
18⁰ x 13⁶
PORCH

Design T162633
1,338 Sq. Ft. - First Floor
1,200 Sq. Ft. - Second Floor
506 Sq. Ft. - Third Floor
44,525 Cu. Ft.

● This is certainly a pleasing Georgian. Its facade features a front porch with a roof supported by 12'' diameter wooden columns. The garage wing has a sheltered service entry and brick facing which complements the design. Sliding glass doors link the terrace and family room, providing an indoor/outdoor area for entertaining as pictured in the rear elevation. The floor plan has been designed to serve the family efficiently. The stairway in the foyer leads to four second-floor bedrooms. The third floor is windowed and can be used as a studio and study.

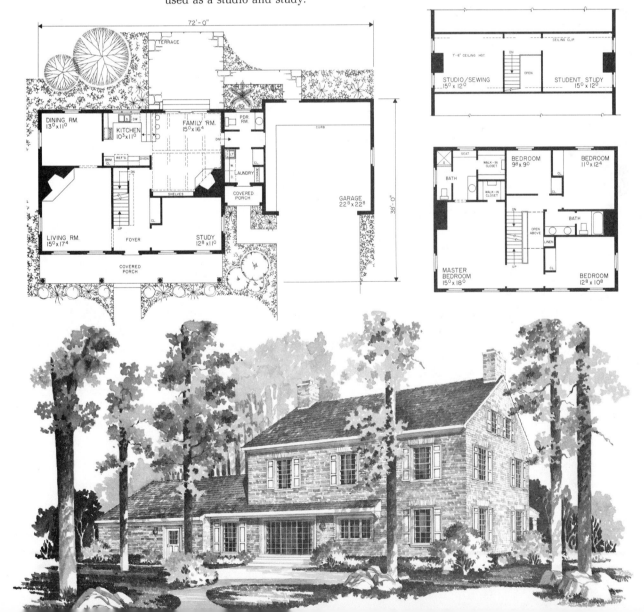

Design T162107

1,020 Sq. Ft. - First Floor
720 Sq. Ft. - Second Floor
25,245 Cu. Ft.

● There is no reason why it must take a fortune to build a Southern Colonial adaptation. This handsome exterior houses a plan under 2,000 square feet.

Design T162128

1,152 Sq. Ft. - First Floor
896 Sq. Ft. - Second Floor
30,707 Cu. Ft.

● This English Tudor adaptation is but another example of just how stylish a modest sized home can be. Inside, is a great plan packed with features.

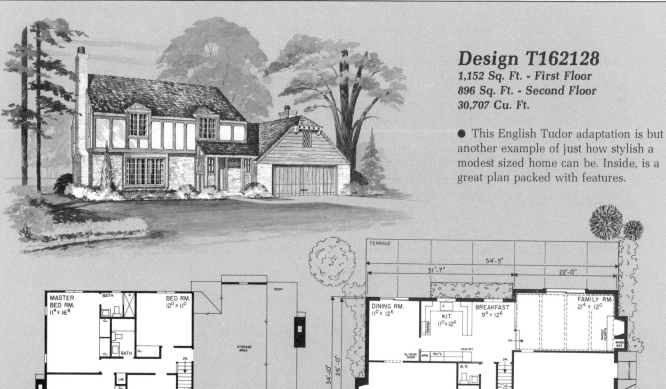

Design T162108

1,188 Sq. Ft. - First Floor
720 Sq. Ft. - Second Floor
27,394 Cu. Ft.

● An interesting version of the two-story idea. Living wing effectively balances garage wing. Don't miss the formal living room and informal family room.

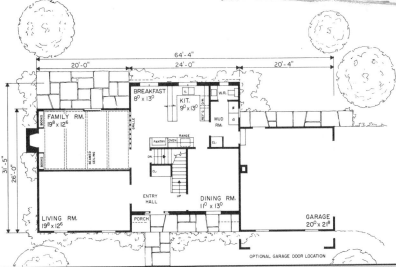

Design T161986

896 Sq. Ft. - First Floor
1,148 Sq. Ft. - Second Floor
28,840 Cu. Ft.

● This Colonial roof design will be distinctive wherever situated - far in the country, or on a busy thoroughfare. The upstairs family room is unique.

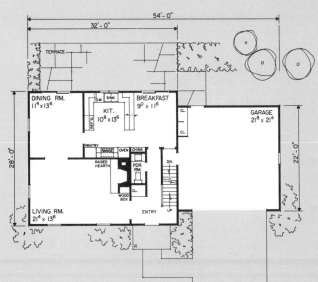

199

Design T162646 1,274 Sq. Ft. - First Floor
1,322 Sq. Ft. - Second Floor; 42,425 Cu. Ft.

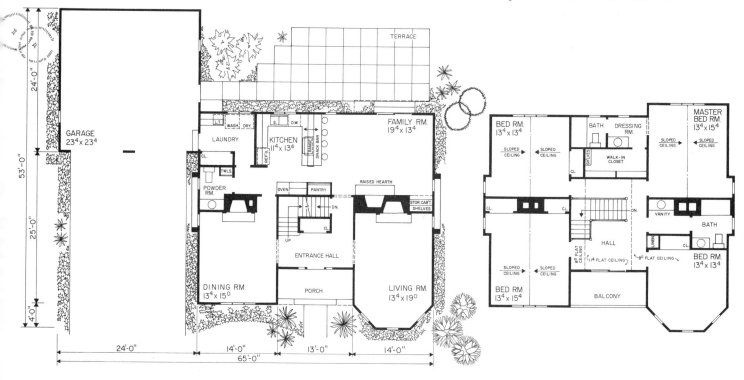

● This refreshing exterior may be referred to as neo-Victorian. The vertical lines, steep roofs and variety of gables remind one of the old Victorian houses of yesteryear. Of particular interest is the large outdoor balcony which provides a shelter for the re-cessed front door. The balcony is ac-cessible to the second floor hall through sliding glass doors. Inside, there is an efficiently working floor plan that is delightfully spacious. In addition to the fireplaces, serving the informal family room and the formal living room, there is even one for the big formal dining room. Upstairs there are four big bedrooms, three of which have sloped ceilings. Don't miss the laundry, the powder room, the snack bar, and the built-in storage. This house has a basement for recreation.

Design T162973
1,269 Sq. Ft. - First Floor
1,227 Sq. Ft. - Second Floor; 48,540 Cu. Ft.

● A most popular feature of the Victorian house has always been its covered porches. These finely detailed outdoor living spaces may be found on the front, the side, the rear or even in all three locations at once. The two designs on these two pages show just that. In addition to being an appealing exterior design feature, covered porches have their practical side, too. They provide wonderful indoor-outdoor living relationships. Imagine, sheltered outdoor living facilities for the various formal and informal living and dining areas of the plan. This home has a myriad of features to cater to the living requirements of the growing, active family.

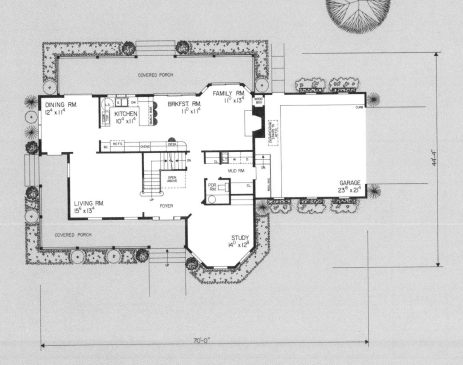

Design T162637

1,308 Sq. Ft. - First Floor
1,063 Sq. Ft. - Second Floor; 34,129 Cu. Ft.

● A generous, centered entrance hall routes traff
efficiently to all areas. And what wonderfully spa
cious areas they are. Note living, dining, sleeping
and bath facilities. Don't miss first floor laundry.

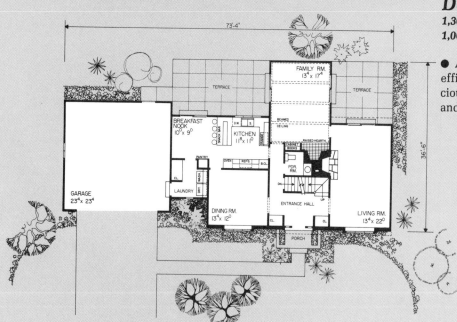

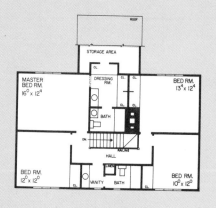

Design T162732

1,071 Sq. Ft. - First Floor
1,022 Sq. Ft. - Second Floor; 34,210 Cu. Ft.

● The two-story front entry hall will be dramatic indeed. Note
the efficient kitchen adjacent to informal family room, formal
dining room. Upstairs, three big bedrooms and two baths.

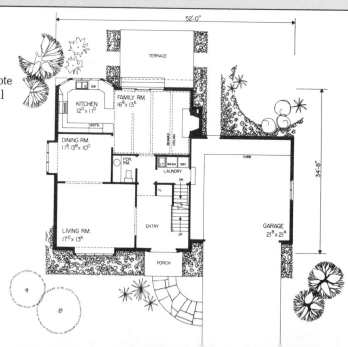

202

Design T162618
1,269 Sq. Ft. - First Floor
1,064 Sq. Ft. - Second Floor; 33,079 Cu. Ft.

● This four bedroom Tudor design is the object of an outstanding investment for a lifetime of proud ownership and fine, family living facilities. Note that the family room is sunken and it, along with the nook, has sliding glass doors to the terrace.

Design T162907 1,546 Sq. Ft. - First Floor; 1,144 Sq. Ft. - Second Floor; 40,750 Cu. Ft.

● This traditional L-shaped farmhouse is charming, indeed, with gambrel roof, dormer windows, and covered porch supported by slender columns and side rails. A spacious country kitchen with a bay provides a cozy gathering place for family and friends, as well as convenient place for food preparation with its central work island and size. There's a formal dining room also adjacent to the kitchen. A rear family room features its own fireplace, as does a large living room in the front. All four bedrooms are isolated upstairs, away from other household activity and noise. Included is a larger master bedroom suite with its own bath, dressing room, and abundant closet space. This is a comfortable home for the modern family who can appreciate the tradition and charm of the past.

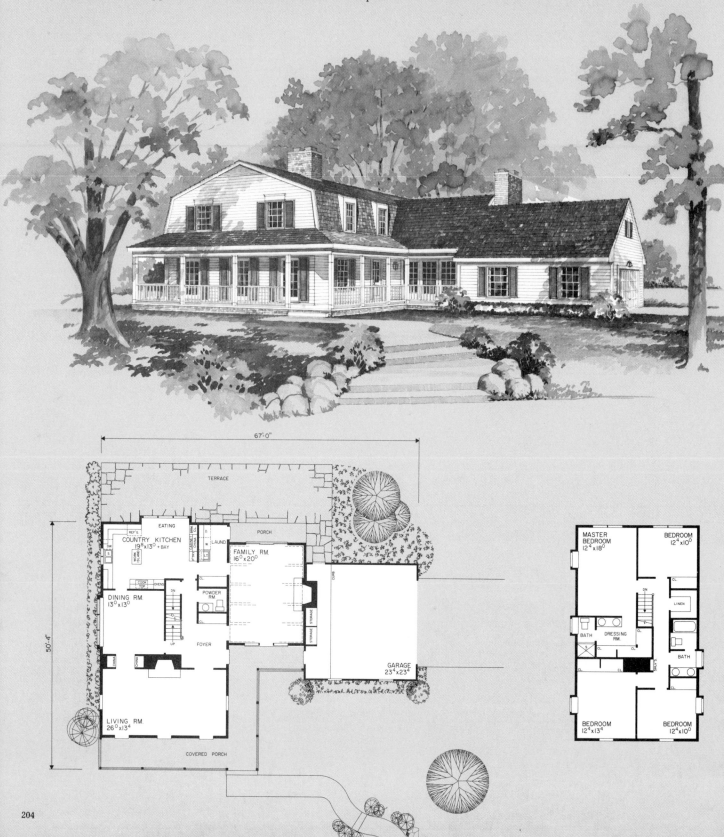

Second Floor Plan (labels):

BEDROOM 12⁰ x 13⁴ → $12^0 \times 13^4$

BATH

BEDROOM $12^8 \times 10^0$

ROOF

ATTIC

CL

DN

LINEN

BRM. CL

DRESSING RM.

BEDROOM $14^0 \times 10^8$

ROOF

MASTER BEDROOM $18^0 \times 13^4$

WALK-IN CLOSET

BATH

ROOF

First Floor Plan (labels):

70'-0"

34'-0"

TERRACE

DINING RM. $12^0 \times 13^4$

KITCHEN $11^0 \times 13^4$

REF'S

LS DW S

BRKFST RM. $9^8 \times 11^0$

LAUNDRY / SEWING $14^8 \times 8^0$

L W D

FREEZER SEWING

DISAPPEARING STAIRS

CURB

BRM CL OVENS COOK TOP STOR

PDR. RM.

PANTRY

DN

FAMILY RM. $14^0 \times 17^0$ + BAY

BOOKS CL

LIVING RM. $18^0 \times 13^4$

FOYER

UP

GARAGE $21^4 \times 21^4$

COVERED PORCH

Design T162908
1,427 Sq. Ft. - First Floor
1,153 Sq. Ft. - Second Floor
38,309 Cu. Ft.

● This Early American farm-house offers plenty of modern comfort with its covered front porch with pillars and rails, double chimneys, building attachment, and four upstairs bedrooms. The first floor attachment includes a family room with bay window. It leads from the main house to a two-car garage. The family room certainly is central focus of this fine design, with its own fireplace and rear entrance to a laundry and sewing room behind the garage. Disappearing stairs in the building attachment lead to one bedroom over the garage. The upstairs also is accessible from stairs just off the front foyer. Included is a master bedroom suite. Downstairs one finds a modern kitchen with breakfast room, dining room, and front living room.

CUSTOMIZABLE

Custom Alterations? See page 320 for customizing this plan to your specifications.

Design T162538

1,503 Sq. Ft. - First Floor
1,095 Sq. Ft. - Second Floor; 44,321 Cu. Ft.

● This Salt Box is charming, indeed. The livability it has to offer to the large and growing family is great. The entry is spacious and is open to the second floor balcony. For living areas, there is the study in addition to the living and family rooms.

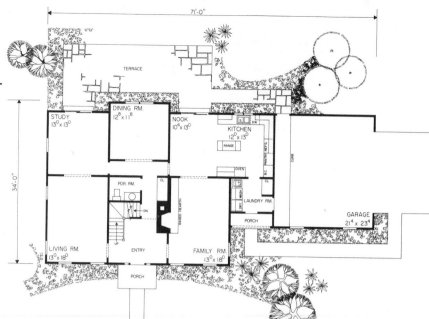

Design T162188

1,440 Sq. Ft. - First Floor
1,280 Sq. Ft. - Second Floor; 40,924 Cu. Ft.

● This design is characteristic of early America and its presence will create an atmosphere of that time in our heritage. However, it will be right at home wherever located. Along with exterior charm, this design has outstanding livability to offer its occupants.

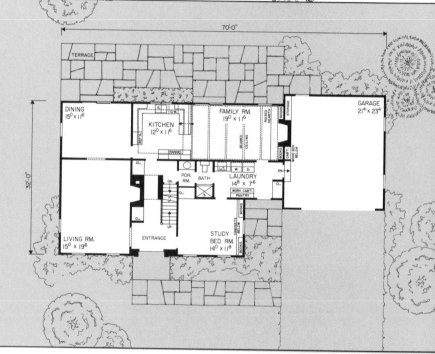

Design T162253

1,503 Sq. Ft. - First Floor
1,291 Sq. Ft. - Second Floor; 44,260 Cu. Ft.

● The overhanging second floor sets the character of this Early American design. Study the features, both inside and out.

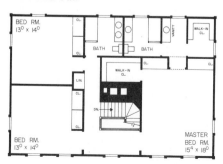

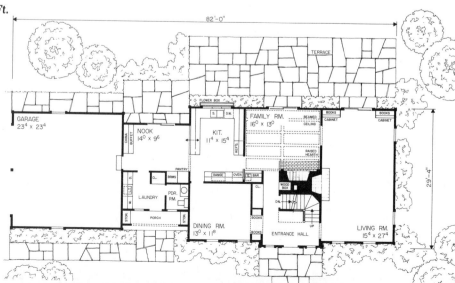

52'-0"

DECK

COVERED TERRACE

SKYLIGHT ABOVE

DINING RM. 12⁰x12¹⁰

KITCHEN 11⁰x11⁶

BRKFST. RM. 10⁰x16⁰

GATHERING RM. 17⁶x15⁰

RAISED HEARTH

SLOPED CEILING

DN

BAR

WALK-IN CLOSET

BRM. CL.

REF'S.

OVEN

PANTRY

CONVERSATION AREA

SEAT

48'-0"

UP DN

CL.

LAUND.

W

D

STUDY 11⁰x11⁸

QUIET TERRACE

SLOPED CEILING

DN

UP

FOYER

PDR. RM.

CURB

PORCH

COURT

GARAGE 21⁰x21⁶

STOR.

STOR.

Design T162823
1,370 Sq. Ft. - First Floor
927 Sq. Ft. - Second Floor
34,860 Cu. Ft.

MASTER BEDROOM 12⁰x14⁸

NURSERY / SITTING RM. 10⁸x7⁸

BEDROOM 10⁰x13⁶

CL.

LINEN

RAILING

WALK-IN CLOSET

OPEN

DN

RAILING

CL.

VANITY

BATH

S

BATH

BEDROOM 10⁰x11²

ATTIC

● The street view of this contemporary design features a small courtyard entrance as well as a private terrace off the study. Inside the livability will be outstanding. This design features spacious first floor activity areas that flow smoothly into each other. In the gathering room a raised hearth fireplace creates a dramatic focal point. An adjacent covered terrace, featuring a skylight, is ideal for outdoor dining and could be screened in later for an additional room.

Design T162905 *1,342 Sq. Ft. - First Floor; 619 Sq. Ft. - Second Floor; 33,655 Cu. Ft.*

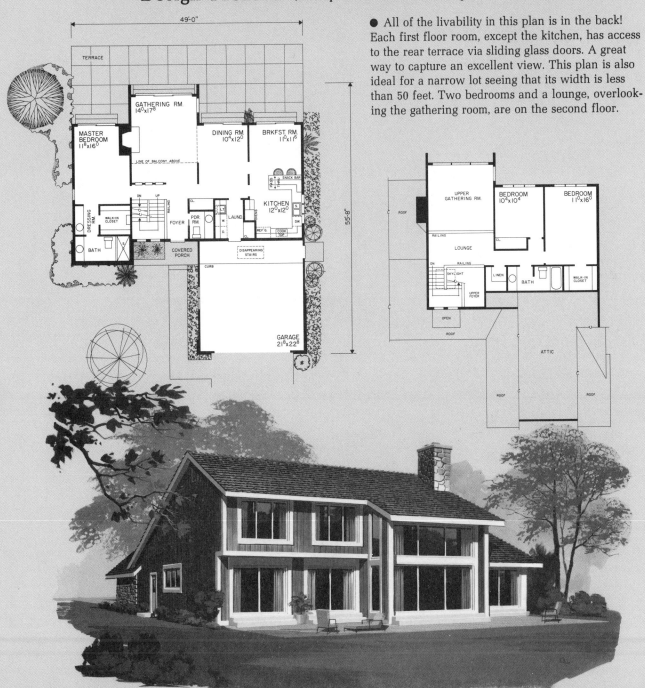

● All of the livability in this plan is in the back! Each first floor room, except the kitchen, has access to the rear terrace via sliding glass doors. A great way to capture an excellent view. This plan is also ideal for a narrow lot seeing that its width is less than 50 feet. Two bedrooms and a lounge, overlooking the gathering room, are on the second floor.

Design T162731

1,039 Sq. Ft. - First Floor
973 Sq. Ft. - Second Floor; 29,740 Cu. Ft.

● The multi-paned windows with shutters of this two-story highlight the exterior delightfully. Inside the livability is ideal. Formal and informal areas are sure to serve your family with ease.

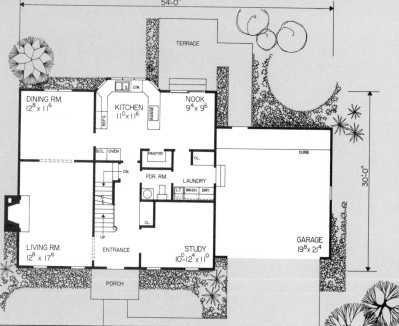

CUSTOMIZABLE

Custom Alterations? See page 320 for customizing this plan to your specifications.

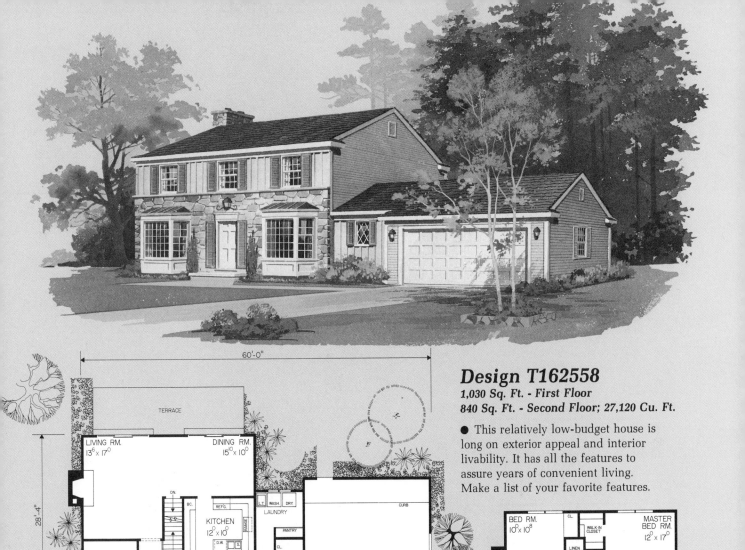

Design T162558

1,030 Sq. Ft. - First Floor
840 Sq. Ft. - Second Floor; 27,120 Cu. Ft.

● This relatively low-budget house is long on exterior appeal and interior livability. It has all the features to assure years of convenient living. Make a list of your favorite features.

60'-0"

28'-4"

TERRACE

LIVING RM.
13^6 x 17^0

DINING RM.
15^0 x 10^0

DN.
B.C.

REF'G.
RANGE

KITCHEN
12^0 x 10^0

D.W.

SNACK BAR

UP

DN.

LT. WASH DRY
LAUNDRY

PANTRY

CL.

CURB

STUDY
9^0 x 10^0

ENTRY

CL.

NOOK
9^0 x 7^0

WASH RM.

GARAGE
21^4 x 21^4

PORCH

BED RM.
10^0 x 10^8

CL.

WALK IN CLOSET

LINEN

MASTER BED RM.
12^0 x 17^0

BATH

DN.

RAILING

WALK IN CLOSET

BATH

BOOKS DESK

BED RM.
17^0 x 1^0

CL.

Design T162622

624 Sq. Ft. - First Floor
624 Sq. Ft. - Second Floor; 19,864 Cu. Ft.

● Appealing design can envelope little packages, too. Here is a charming, Early Colonial adaptation with an attached two-car garage to serve the young family with a modest building budget.

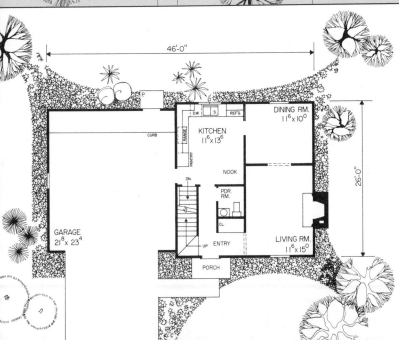

46'-0"

26'-0"

P

D.W.
S.
REF'G.
RANGE

KITCHEN
11^6 x 13^6

DINING RM.
11^6 x 10^0

PANTRY

CURB

NOOK

DN.

PDR. RM.

CL.

UP

ENTRY

GARAGE
21^8 x 23^4

LIVING RM.
11^6 x 15^0

PORCH

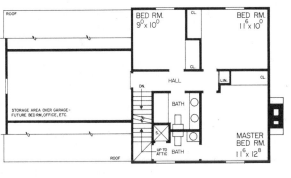

ROOF

BED RM.
9^0 x 10^0

CL.

BED RM.
11^6 x 10^0

CL.

HALL

LIN.

CL.

DN.

STORAGE AREA OVER GARAGE - FUTURE BED RM, OFFICE, ETC

BATH

BATH

UP TO ATTIC

ROOF

MASTER BED RM.
11^6 x 12^8

211

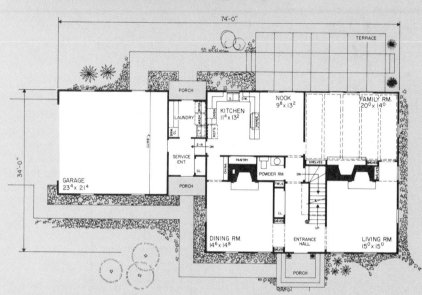

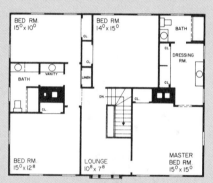

● Here is a New England Georgian adaptation with an elevated doorway highlighted by pilasters and a pediment. It gives way to a second-story Palladian window, capped in turn by a pediment projecting from the hipped roof. The interior is decidely up-to-date with even an upstairs lounge.

Design T162639 1,556 Sq. Ft. - First Floor; 1,428 Sq. Ft. - Second Floor; 46,115 Cu. Ft.

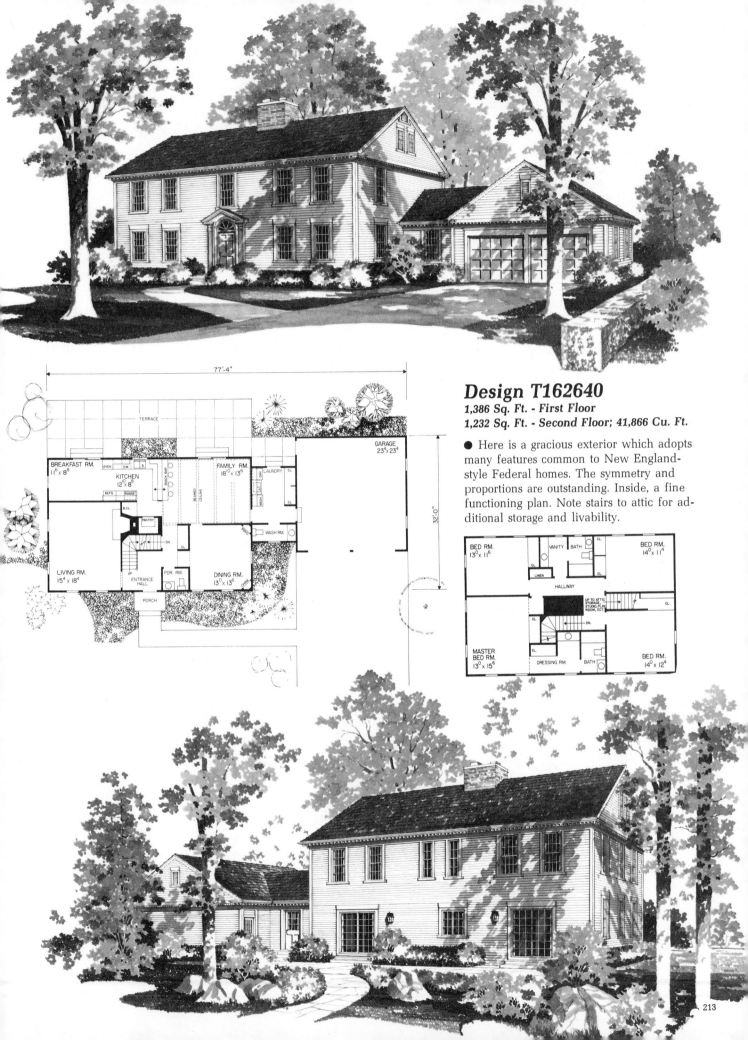

Design T162640

1,386 Sq. Ft. - First Floor
1,232 Sq. Ft. - Second Floor; 41,866 Cu. Ft.

● Here is a gracious exterior which adopts many features common to New England-style Federal homes. The symmetry and proportions are outstanding. Inside, a fine functioning plan. Note stairs to attic for additional storage and livability.

77'-4"

32'-0"

TERRACE

GARAGE
23⁴ x 23⁴

BREAKFAST RM.
11⁶ x 8⁸

KITCHEN
12⁰ x 8⁸

FAMILY RM.
18¹⁰ x 13⁶

LAUNDRY

OVEN   D.W.

SNACK BAR

BEAMED CEILING

REF'G.   RANGE

B. CL.

PANTRY

WASH RM.

LIVING RM.
15⁴ x 18⁴

UP

ENTRANCE HALL

DN.

PDR. RM.

DINING RM.
13⁰ x 13⁶

PORCH

BED RM.
13⁰ x 11⁶

VANITY   BATH

BED RM.
14⁰ x 11⁴

LINEN

HALLWAY

UP TO ATTIC STORAGE, STUDIO, PLAY ROOM, ECT.

DN.

MASTER BED RM.
13⁰ x 15⁶

DRESSING RM.

BATH

BED RM.
14⁰ x 12⁴

Design T162365
1,194 Sq. Ft. - First Floor
802 Sq. Ft. - Second Floor
24,693 Cu. Ft.

● This unadorned contemporary has an appeal all its own. The wide overhanging roof, the box bay window and the horizontal siding are features which set the character. A welcomed change of pace to any neighborhood will be the two-story middle section flanked by the projecting one-story wings. Inside, there is livability galore.

CUSTOMIZABLE

Custom Alterations? See page 320 for customizing this plan to your specifications.

Design T162711
975 Sq. Ft. - First Floor
1,024 Sq. Ft. - Second Floor; 31,380 Cu. Ft.

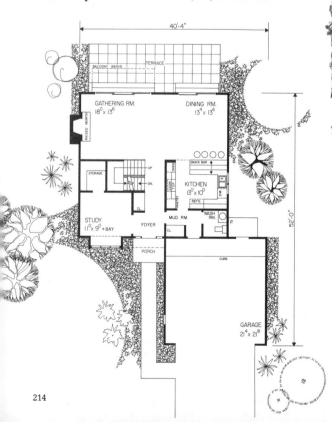

● Special features! A complete master suite with a private balcony plus two more bedrooms and a bath upstairs. The first floor has a study with a storage closet. A convenient snack bar between kitchen and dining room. The kitchen offers many built-in appliances. Plus a gathering room and dining room that measures 31 feet wide. Note the sliding glass doors and fireplace in gathering room.

214

Design T162748

1,232 Sq. Ft. - First Floor
720 Sq. Ft. - Second Floor
27,550 Cu. Ft.

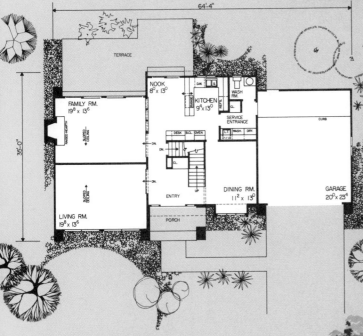

● This four bedroom contemporary definitely will have appeal for the entire family. The work center of U-shaped kitchen-nook with its built-in desk, adjacent laundry/wash room and service entrance will be very efficient for the busy household activities. The living and family rooms of identical size are both sunken one step and both have sloped ceiling. Other features of the family room are the raised hearth fireplace and the sliding glass doors to the rear terrace.

Design T161879

1,008 Sq. Ft. - First Floor
1,008 Sq. Ft. - Second Floor
27,518 Cu. Ft.

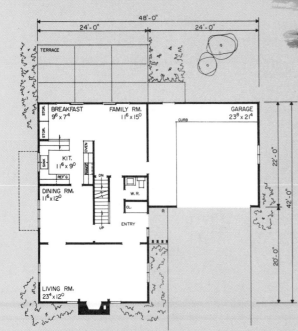

● An engaging contemporary two-story which will be most economical to build. Thus, the return on your construction dollar in the way of livability will be weighted in your favor. Consider; four bedrooms - three for the kids and one for the parents; one main bath with vanity for the younger set, one private bath and dressing room for Mr. and Mrs., and an extra powder room downstairs for the convenience of everyone; two distinct eating areas - the informal breakfast room and the formal dining room and more.

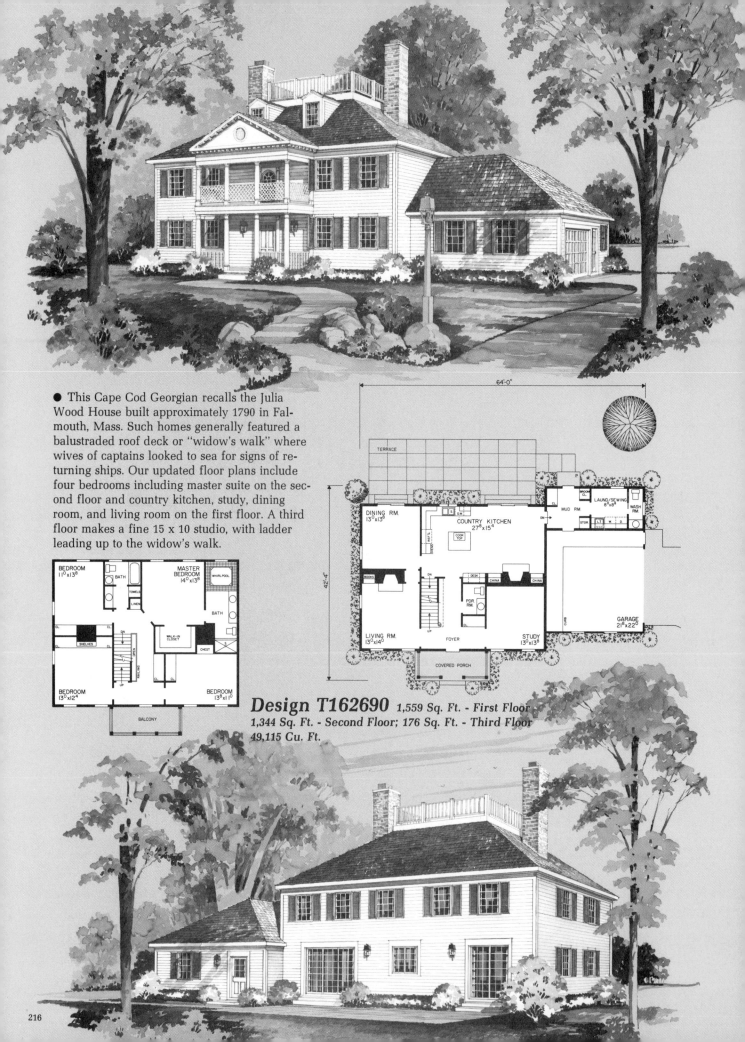

● This Cape Cod Georgian recalls the Julia Wood House built approximately 1790 in Falmouth, Mass. Such homes generally featured a balustraded roof deck or "widow's walk" where wives of captains looked to sea for signs of returning ships. Our updated floor plans include four bedrooms including master suite on the second floor and country kitchen, study, dining room, and living room on the first floor. A third floor makes a fine 15 x 10 studio, with ladder leading up to the widow's walk.

Design T162690 1,559 Sq. Ft. - First Floor
1,344 Sq. Ft. - Second Floor; 176 Sq. Ft. - Third Floor
49,115 Cu. Ft.

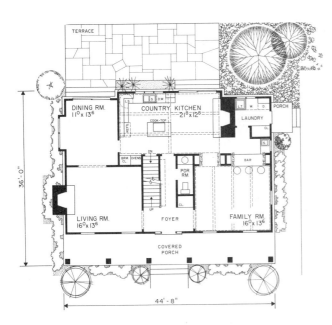

TERRACE

DINING RM.
11⁰ x 13⁶

COUNTRY KITCHEN
21⁸ x 12⁸
COOK-TOP

LAUNDRY

PORCH

BRM OVENS

PDR. RM.

BAR

36' - 0"

LIVING RM.
16⁰ x 13⁶

FOYER

UP

DN

CL

FAMILY RM.
16⁰ x 13⁶

COVERED PORCH

44' - 8"

● The exterior of this full two-story is highlighted by the covered porch and balcony. Many enjoyable hours will be spent at these outdoor areas. The interior is highlighted by a spacious country kitchen. Be sure to notice its island cook-top, fireplace and the beamed ceiling. A built-in bar is in the family room.

BEDROOM
11⁰ x 12⁴

BEDROOM
12⁰ x 10⁰

WALK-IN CLOSET

BATH

DRESSING RM.

LINEN

DN

BEDROOM
16⁰ x 12⁴

BATH

MASTER BEDROOM
16⁰ x 13⁶

COVERED BALCONY

Design T162664
1,308 Sq. Ft. - First Floor
1,262 Sq. Ft. - Second Floor; 49,215 Cu. Ft.

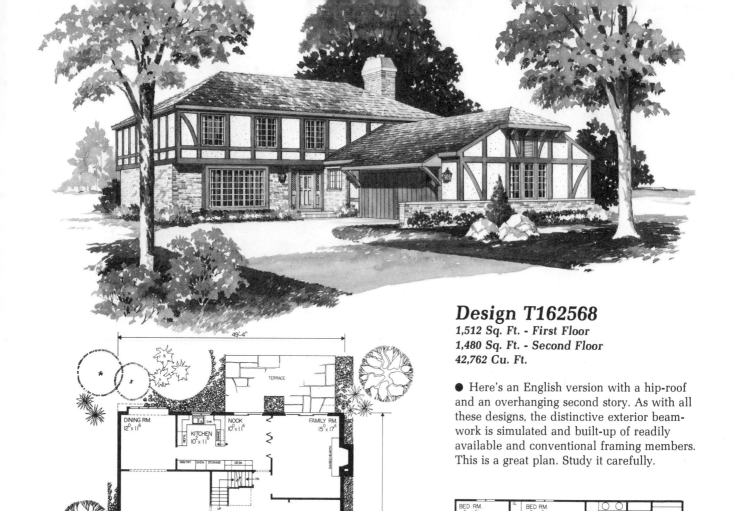

Design T162568

1,512 Sq. Ft. - First Floor
1,480 Sq. Ft. - Second Floor
42,762 Cu. Ft.

● Here's an English version with a hip-roof and an overhanging second story. As with all these designs, the distinctive exterior beam-work is simulated and built-up of readily available and conventional framing members. This is a great plan. Study it carefully.

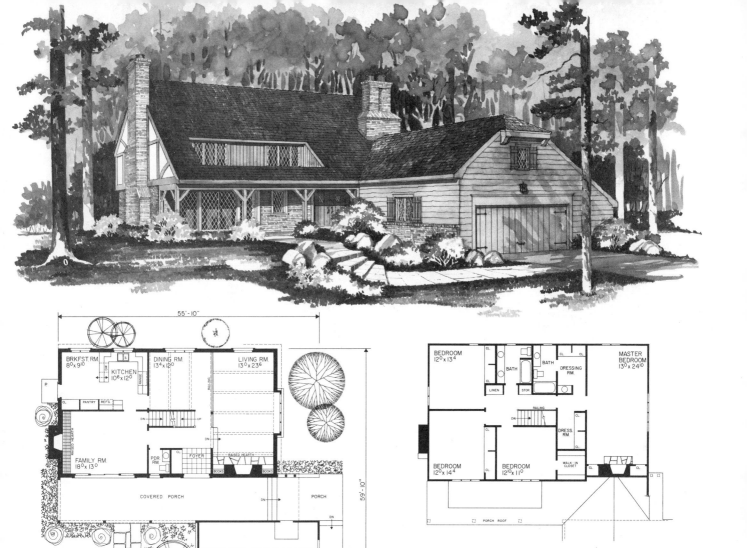

Design T162324 *1,256 Sq. Ft. - First Floor*
1,351 Sq. Ft. - Second Floor; 37,603 Cu. Ft.

● Dramatic, indeed! Both the interior and the exterior of these three Tudor designs deserve mention. Study each of them closely. The design featured here has a simple rectangular plan which will be relatively economical to build. This design is ideal for a corner lot.

● The fine proportion and architectural detailing of this stately Tudor give it a distinctive character all its own. Study the floor plan. It has an outstanding number of features.

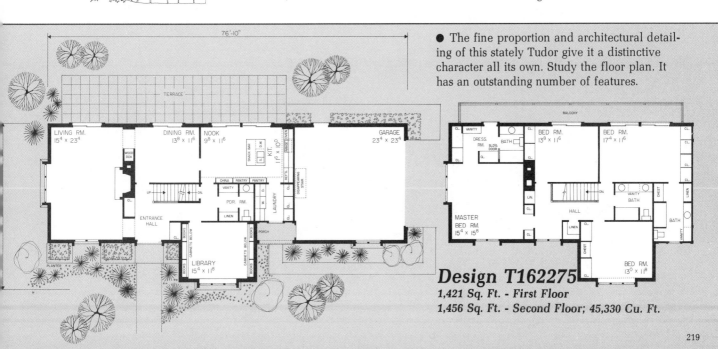

Design T162275
1,421 Sq. Ft. - First Floor
1,456 Sq. Ft. - Second Floor; 45,330 Cu. Ft.

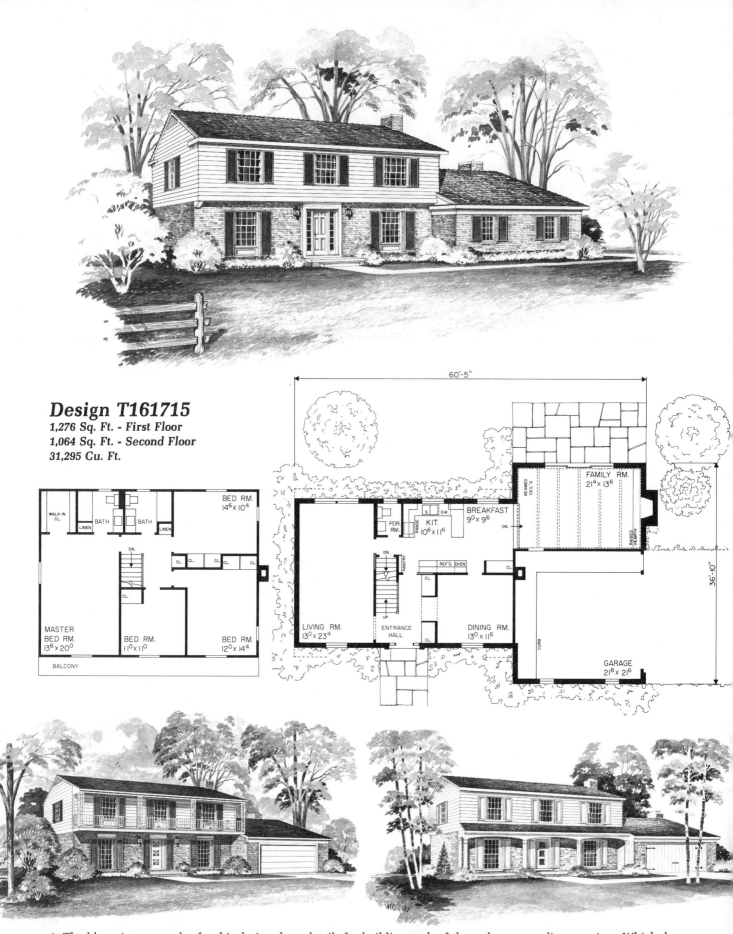

Design T161715

1,276 Sq. Ft. - First Floor
1,064 Sq. Ft. - Second Floor
31,295 Cu. Ft.

Second Floor Plan:

WALK-IN CL.
BATH · LINEN · BATH · LINEN
BED RM. 14⁶ x 10⁴
DN.
CL. · CL. · CL. · CL.
CL.
MASTER BED RM. 13⁶ x 20⁰
BED RM. 11⁰ x 11⁰
BED RM. 12⁰ x 14⁴
BALCONY

First Floor Plan:

60'-5"
36'-10"

FAMILY RM. 21⁴ x 13⁶
BEAMED CEIL'G
RAISED HEARTH
PDR. RM.
RANGE · KIT. 10⁶ x 11⁶
S. · D.W.
BREAKFAST 9⁰ x 9⁶
DN.
PANTRY
REF'G. · OVEN
CL.
LIVING RM. 13⁰ x 23⁴
UP · DN.
ENTRANCE HALL
CL.
DINING RM. 13⁰ x 11⁶
CL.
CURB
GARAGE 21⁸ x 21⁶

● The blueprints you order for this design show details for building each of these three appealing exteriors. Which do you like best? Whatever your choice, the interior will provide the growing family with all the facilities for fine living. The living room has views of both the front and rear yards and is exceptionally large. Informal family activities will be enjoyed in the rear family room which features a fireplace and sliding glass doors.

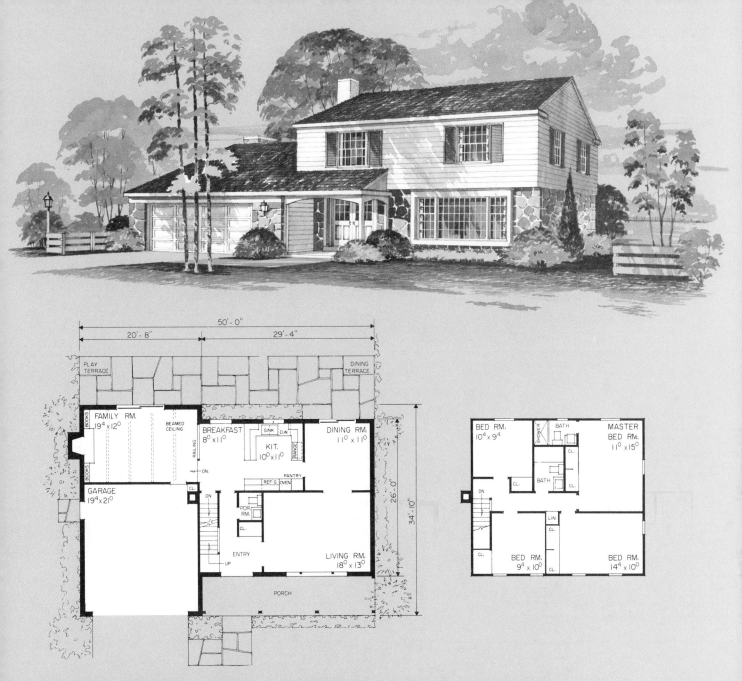

Design T161957 1,042 Sq. Ft. - First Floor; 780 Sq. Ft. - Second Floor; 24,982 Cu. Ft.

● When you order your blueprints for this design you will receive details for the construction of each of the three charming exteriors pictured above. Whichever the exterior you finally decide to build, the floor plan will be essentially the same except the location of the windows. This will be a fine home for the growing family. It will serve well for many years. There are four bedrooms and two full baths (one with a stall shower) upstairs.

Design T161914

1,470 Sq. Ft. - First Floor
888 Sq. Ft. - Second Floor
30,354 Cu. Ft.

● What an interesting facade for passers-by to enjoy. Here, the delightful configuration of the Gambrel roof is fully visible from the road. The interior has all the features to help assure living convenience at its best. What are your favorite features?

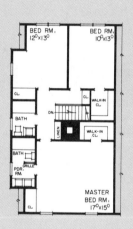

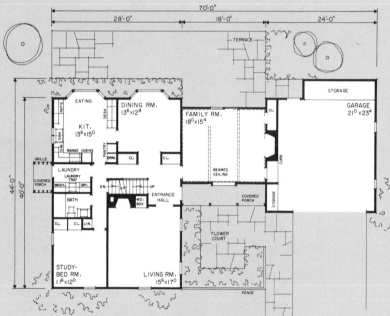

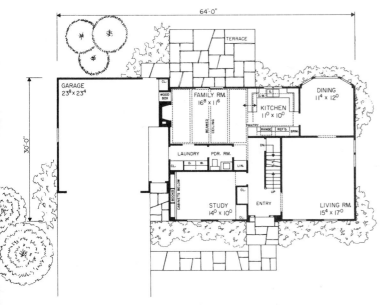

Design T162189
1,134 Sq. Ft. - First Floor
1,063 Sq. Ft. - Second Floor; 31,734 Cu. Ft.

● Imagine this Colonial adaptation on your new building site! The recessed entrances add an extra measure of appeal. While each family member will probably have his own favorite set of highlights, all will surely agree that the living patterns will be just great.

Design T162131
1,214 Sq. Ft. - First Floor
1,097 Sq. Ft. - Second Floor
28,070 Cu. Ft.

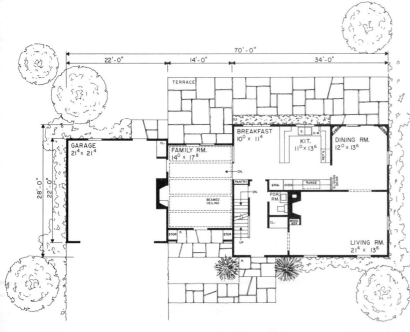

Design T162713 1,830 Sq. Ft. - First Floor
1,056 Sq. Ft. - Second Floor; 41,370 Cu. Ft.

● This home with its Gambrel roof and paned windows is sure to be a pleasure for the entire family. Along with the outside, the inside is a delight. The spacious family room creates an inviting atmosphere with sliding glass doors to the terrace, beamed ceilings and a raised-hearth fireplace that includes a built-in wood box. A spectacular kitchen, too. Presenting an island counter/range as well as a built-in oven, desk and storage pantry. A sunny breakfast nook, too, also with sliding glass doors leading to the terrace. Note the size of the formal dining room and the fireplace in the living room. A first floor study/bedroom with a private terrace. Upstairs, there is the master suite and two more bedrooms and a bath.

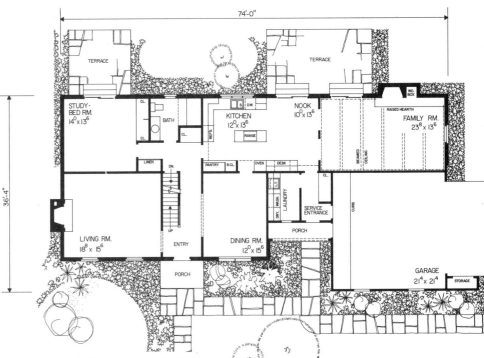

PLAN OF ATTACK

Here's some basic training to help you find the right design. Step by step:

- Define what you need and want in a house.
- List ways in which you plan to use space, both inside and out. Note approximate room sizes.
- Pinpoint the housing type and style you're after. Pay attention to how the design matches the site you have.
- Arrange interior and exterior spaces. Keep in mind proper zoning, circulation, and indoor-outdoor relationships.
- Make sure doors and windows are properly placed—to provide the best views, to move traffic logically, and to capture sunlight.

Source: *"New House Planning & Idea Book,"* Brick House Publishing Co.

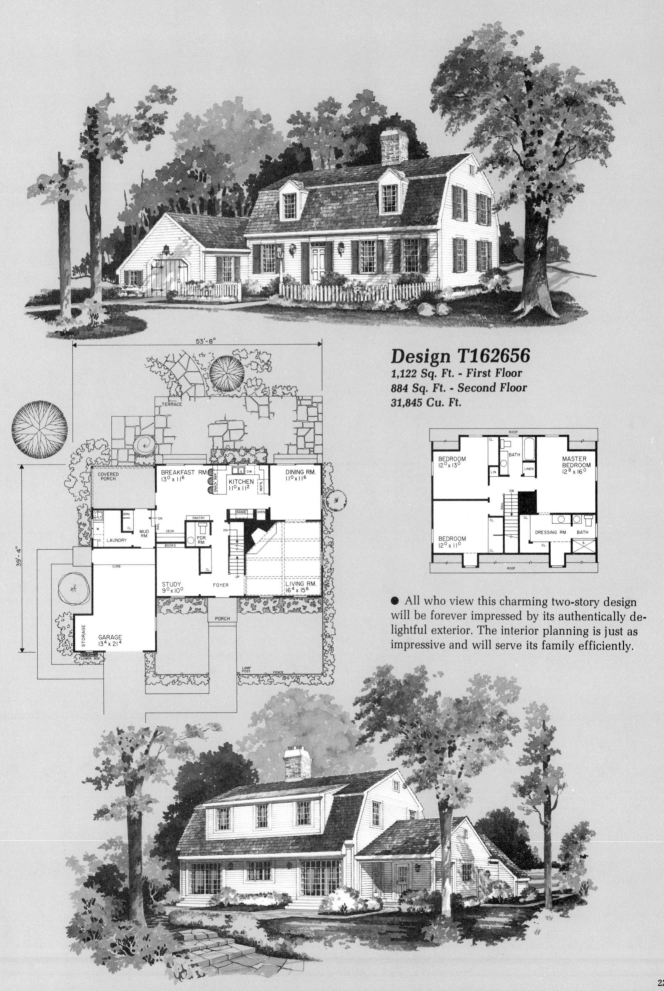

Design T162656

1,122 Sq. Ft. - First Floor
884 Sq. Ft. - Second Floor
31,845 Cu. Ft.

TERRACE

53'-8"

COVERED PORCH

BREAKFAST RM.
13⁰ x 11⁶

KITCHEN
11⁰ x 11²

DINING RM.
11⁰ x 11⁶

MUD RM.

LAUNDRY

PANTRY

DESK

BOOKS

PDR. RM.

RANGE   OVEN

39'-4"

CURB

STUDY
9⁰ x 10⁰

FOYER

LIVING RM.
16⁴ x 15⁶

STORAGE

GARAGE
13⁴ x 21⁴

PORCH

FLOWER BOX

LAMP POST   FENCE

BEDROOM
12⁰ x 13⁰

ROOF

BATH

LIN

LINEN

MASTER BEDROOM
12⁸ x 16⁰

DN

CL

CL

BEDROOM
12⁰ x 11⁰

DRESSING RM.

BATH

CL

CL

ROOF

● All who view this charming two-story design will be forever impressed by its authentically delightful exterior. The interior planning is just as impressive and will serve its family efficiently.

Design T162176

1,485 Sq. Ft. - First Floor
1,175 Sq. Ft. - Second Floor
41,646 Cu. Ft.

● This Georgian adaptation will serve your family well. It will be the soundest investment you'll make in your lifetime and provide your family with wonderful living.

Design T162139
1,581 Sq. Ft. - First Floor
991 Sq. Ft. - Second Floor
36,757 Cu. Ft.

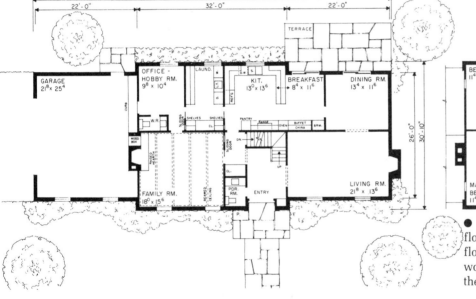

● Four bedrooms are on the second floor of this two-story design. The first floor has all of the living areas and work center. Note the convenience of the powder room at the entry.

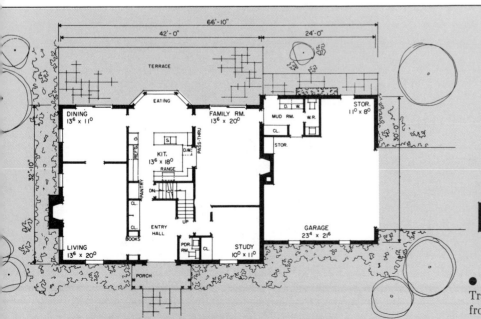

Design T161767
1,510 Sq. Ft. - First Floor
1,406 Sq. Ft. - Second Floor
42,070 Cu. Ft.

● An impressive Georgian adaptation. Traffic flows conveniently to all areas from the spacious center entry hall.

227

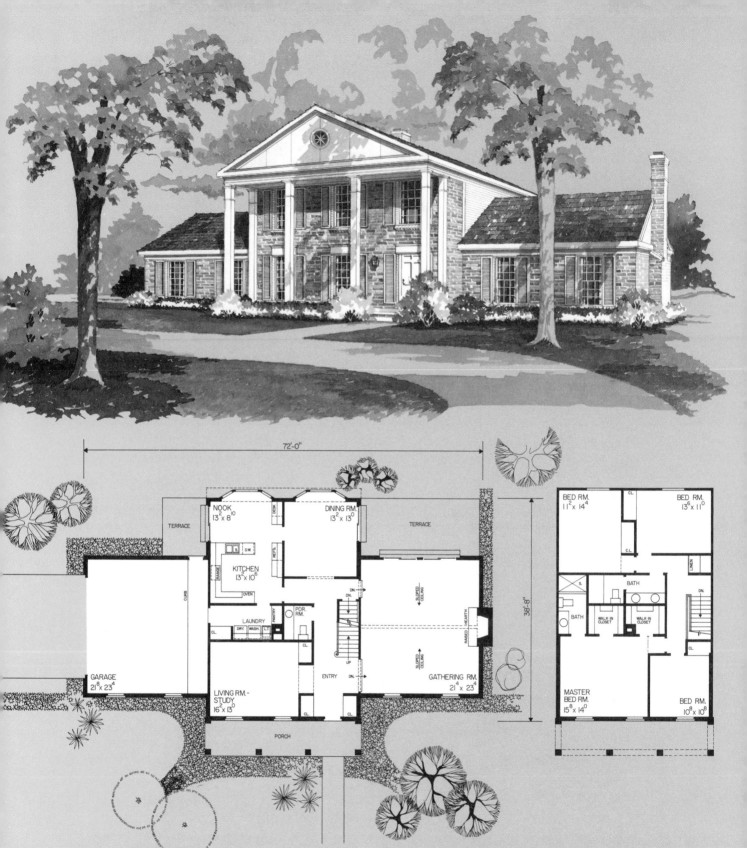

Design T162700 *1,640 Sq. Ft. - First Floor; 1,129 Sq. Ft. - Second Floor; 42,200 Cu. Ft.*

● Southern Colonial grace! And much more. An elegant gathering room, more than 21' by 23' large. . . with sloped ceilings and a raised-hearth fireplace. Plus two sets of sliding glass doors that open onto the terrace. Correctly appointed formal rooms! A living room with full length paned windows. And a formal dining room that features a large bay window. Plus a contemporary kitchen. A separate dining nook that includes another bay window. Charming and sunny! Around the corner, a first floor laundry offers more modern conveniences. Four large bedrooms! Including a master suite with two walk-in closets and private bath. This home offers all the conveniences that make life easy! And its eminently suited to a family with traditional tastes. List your favorite features.

BED RM.
13⁴ x 14⁴

BATH

DRESSING RM.

WALK-IN CLOSET

BATH

WALK IN CLOSET

DN

BED RM.
13⁶ x 14⁴

BED RM.
13⁶ x 10²

MASTER BED RM.
13⁶ x 19⁸

Design T162610 1,505 Sq. Ft. - First Floor
1,344 Sq. Ft. - Second Floor; 45,028 Cu. Ft.

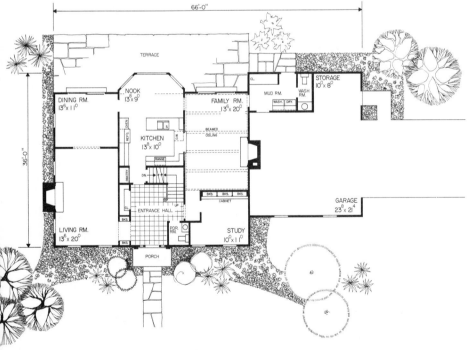

66'-0"

36'-0"

TERRACE

NOOK
13⁸ x 9⁰

DINING RM.
13⁶ x 11⁰

KITCHEN
13⁸ x 10⁰

BEAMED CEILING

RANGE

FAMILY RM.
13⁶ x 20⁰

MUD RM.

WASH RM.

STORAGE
10⁰ x 8⁰

WASH DRY

BKS. BKS. BKS.

CABINET

GARAGE
23⁸ x 21⁴

ENTRANCE HALL

LIVING RM.
13⁶ x 20⁰

PDR. RM.

STUDY
10⁰ x 11⁰

PORCH

HOW TO LEND YOURSELF A HAND

AFFORDABILITY
$
TIP

Building by yourself? You'll have to persuade a lender. Here are four tips:

- Reduce your debt. Pay off large credit-card balances, and postpone large installment purchases.
- Invest a substantial amount of your own money in the project. Some experts say the more you leverage a deal, the better, but if you're doing most of the work yourself, many lenders prefer to see a big commitment on your part. To lenders, "commitment" means money.
- Prove that you've got a track record in construction. A resumé that shows prior building experience improves your chances.
- Prepare a professional-looking loan package. This should include plans, a detailed cost breakdown, a construction schedule, a preliminary title report, and a detailed personal financial statement.

Source: *"A Salute to the Owner-Builder,"* Practical Homeowner *magazine.*

● This full two-story traditional will be worthy of note wherever built. It strongly recalls images of a New England of yesteryear. And well it might; for the window treatment is delightful. The front entrance detail is inviting. The narrow horizontal siding and the corner boards are appealing as are the two massive chimneys. The center entrance hall is large with a handy powder room nearby. The study has built-in bookshelves and offers a full measure of privacy. The interior kitchen has a pass-thru to the family room and enjoys all that natural light from the bay window of the nook. A beamed ceiling, fireplace and sliding glass doors are features of the family room. The mud room highlights a closet, laundry equipment and an extra wash room. Study the upstairs with those four bedrooms, two baths and plenty of closets. An excellent arrangement for all.

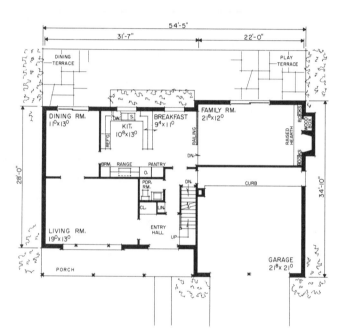

Design T161868
1,190 Sq. Ft. - First Floor
1,300 Sq. Ft. - Second Floor
32,327 Cu. Ft.

● A five bedroom Farmhouse adaptation that is truly a home for family living. The big family room will be everyone's favorite area. Note the master bedroom suite located over the garage.

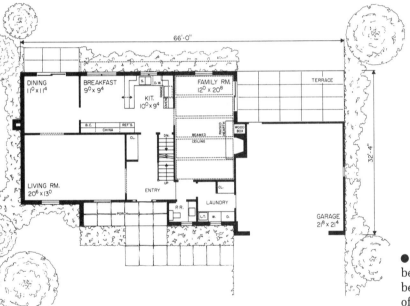

Design T161285
1,202 Sq. Ft. - First Floor
896 Sq. Ft. - Second Floor
27,385 Cu. Ft.

● Laundry, extra powder room, two full baths, four bedrooms, separate dining room, breakfast room and beamed ceiling family room are among the features of this two-story traditional design.

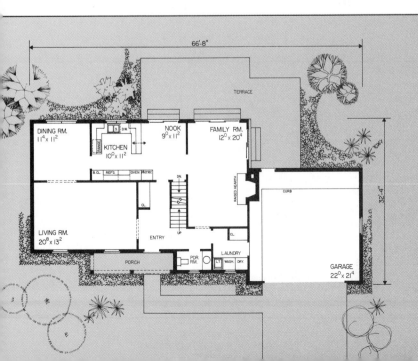

Design T162752
1,209 Sq. Ft. - First Floor
960 Sq. Ft. - Second Floor; 34,725 Cu. Ft.

● This impressive two-story home is sure to catch the eye of even the most casual of on-lookers. The extended one-story wings add great appeal to the exterior. The covered porch with pillars also is a charming feature.

Design T162309 1,719 Sq. Ft. - First Floor; 456 Sq. Ft. - Second Floor; 31,073 Cu. Ft.

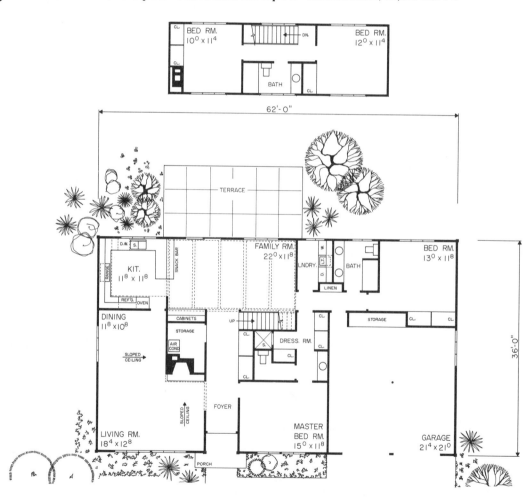

● Here's proof that the simple rectangle (which is relatively economical to build, naturally) can, when properly planned, result in unique living patterns. The exterior can be exceedingly appealing, too. Study the floor plan carefully. The efficiency of the kitchen could hardly be improved upon. It is strategically located to serve the formal dining room, the family room and even the rear terrace. The sleeping facilities are arranged in a most interesting manner. The master bedroom with its attached bath and dressing room will enjoy a full measure of privacy on the first floor. A second bedroom is also on this floor and has a full bath nearby. Upstairs there are two more bedrooms and a bath. Don't miss the laundry, the snack bar, the beamed ceiling or the sliding glass doors.

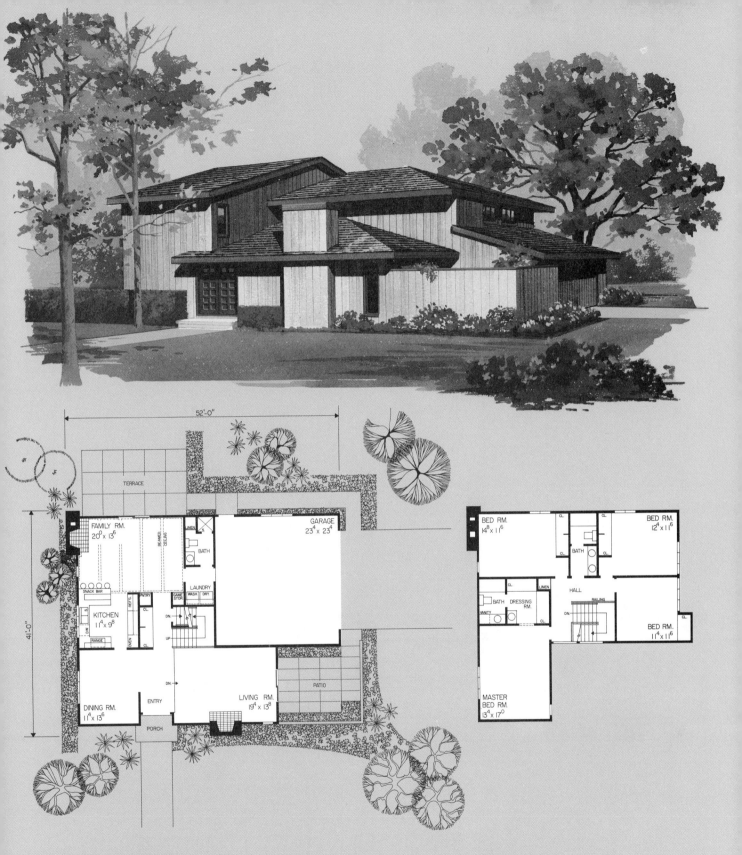

Design T162602 1,154 Sq. Ft. - First Floor; 1,120 Sq. Ft. - Second Floor; 30,370 Cu. Ft.

● Varying roof planes, wide overhangs, interestingly shaped blank wall areas and patterned double front doors provide the distinguishing characteristics of this refreshing, contemporary two-story design. The extension of the front wall results in an enclosed, private outdoor patio area accesssible from the living room. Inside the compact plan there is a fine feeling of spaciousness. The living area features open planning. The U-shaped kitchen is but a step or two from the dining room and the family room. There is a snack bar, laundry area, full bath with stall shower, pantry and game storage, and two fireplaces located on the first floor. Upstairs, four good-sized bedrooms, two baths, a dressing room and plenty of closets.

Design T161719
864 Sq. Ft. - First Floor
896 Sq. Ft. - Second Floor
26,024 Cu. Ft.

● What an appealing low-cost Colonial adaptation. Most of the livability features generally found in the largest of homes are present to cater to family needs. Both formal and informal living patterns will be served adequately in the living and family rooms.

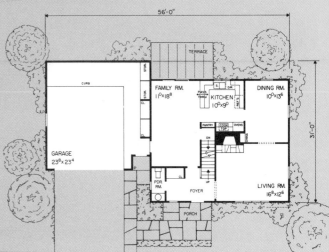

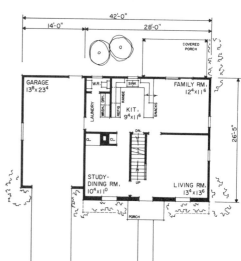

Design T161913
740 Sq. Ft. - First Floor
728 Sq. Ft. - Second Floor
20,860 Cu. Ft.

● With or without a basement this will be a great low-cost two-story home for the large family. Note first floor laundry and wash room.

Design T161368
728 Sq. Ft. - First Floor
728 Sq. Ft. - Second Floor
20,020 Cu. Ft.

● Similar in plan to T161913 on the opposing page, this home features an entirely different exterior. Which do you prefer? Note covered rear porches.

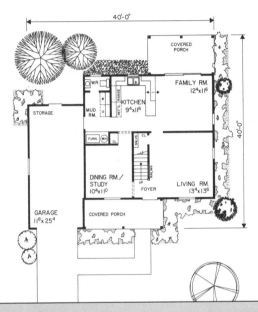

OPTIONAL BASEMENT

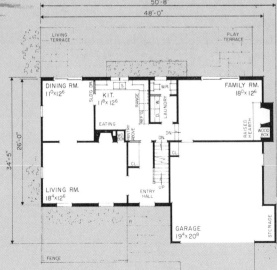

Design T161856
1,023 Sq. Ft. - First Floor
784 Sq. Ft. - Second Floor
25,570 Cu. Ft.

● Small house with big house features and livability. Some of the features are two full baths and extra storage upstairs; laundry, wash room and two fireplaces each with a wood box on the first floor. Two sets of sliding glass doors leading to the terrace.

235

Design T162964

1,441 Sq. Ft. - First Floor
621 Sq. Ft. - Second Floor
42,581 Cu. Ft.

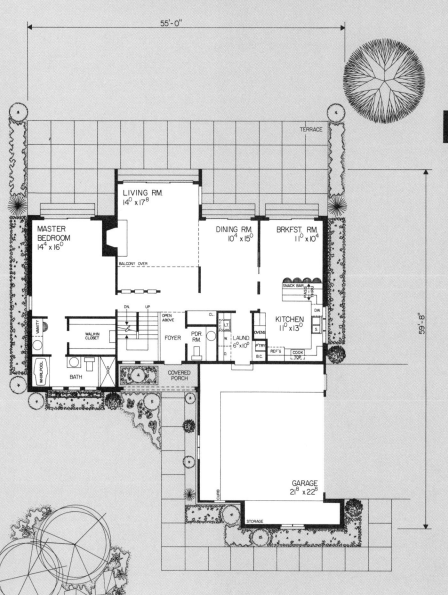

● Tudor houses have their own unique exterior design features. They include: gable roofs, simulated beam work, stucco and brick surfaces, diamond-lite windows, muntins, panelled doors, varying roof planes and hefty cornices. This outstanding two-story features a first floor master bedroom, plus two more with lounge upstairs. The living room is dramatically spacious. It has a two-story sloping ceiling which permits it to look upward to the lounge. Large glass areas across the rear further enhance the bright, cheerful atmosphere of this area as well as the bedroom, dining and breakfast rooms. The open staircase to the upstairs has plenty of natural light as does the stairway to the basement recreation area.

CUSTOMIZABLE

Custom Alterations? See page 320 for customizing this plan to your specifications.

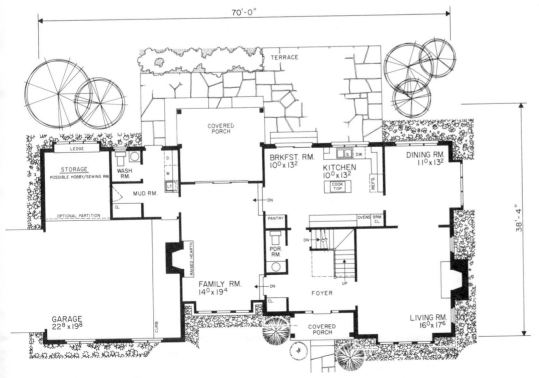

Design T162855

1,372 Sq. Ft. - First Floor
1,245 Sq. Ft. - Second Floor
44,495 Cu. Ft.

● This elegant Tudor house is perfect for the family who wants to move-up in living area, style and luxury. As you enter this home you will find a large living room with a fireplace on your right. Adjacent, the formal dining room has easy access to both the living room and the kitchen. The kitchen/breakfast room has an open plan and access to the rear terrace. Sunken a few steps, the spacious family room is highlighted with a fireplace and access to the rear, covered porch. Note the optional planning of the garage storage area. Plan this area according to the needs of your family. Upstairs, your family will enjoy three bedrooms and a full bath, along with a spacious master bedroom suite. Truly a house that will bring many years of pleasure to your family.

Design T162223

1,266 Sq. Ft. - First Floor
1,232 Sq. Ft. - Second Floor; 34,286 Cu. Ft.

●The appealing double front doors of this home open wide to fine livability. The spacious entrance hall is flanked by the formal, end living room and the all-purpose, beamed ceiling family room. Both rooms have a commanding fireplace. The U-shaped kitchen overlooks the rear yard and is but a step, or two, from the breakfast nook and the formal dining room.

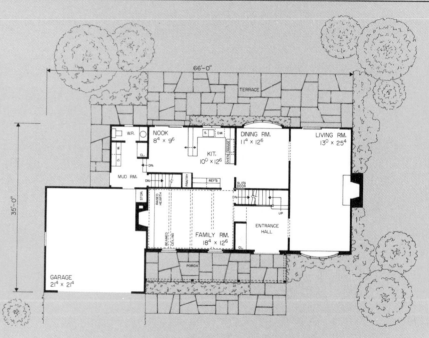

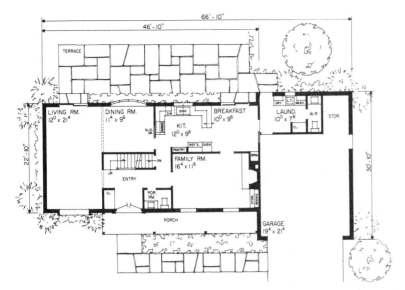

Design T161933

1,184 Sq. Ft. - First Floor
884 Sq. Ft. - Second Floor; 27,976 Cu. Ft.

● Here is an attractive Farmhouse adaptation with just loads of livability. The center entrance routes traffic efficiently to all areas of the plan. Note the spacious end living room and its adjacent formal dining room. A great family room, kitchen, laundry and two wash rooms are also on the first floor.

Design T161996

1,056 Sq. Ft. - First Floor
1,040 Sq. Ft. - Second Floor; 29,071 Cu. Ft.

● This Farmhouse adaptation has a delightful mixture of natural stone and narrow, horizontal siding. The covered front porch extends across the entire front providing protection for the large windows and the double front doors. The center entry hall dispatches traffic most effectively. The room relationships are outstanding.

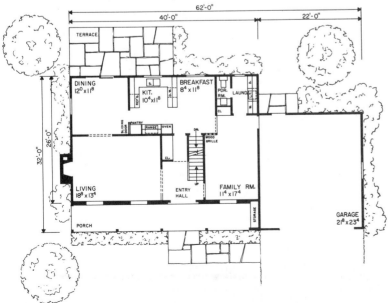

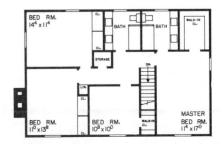

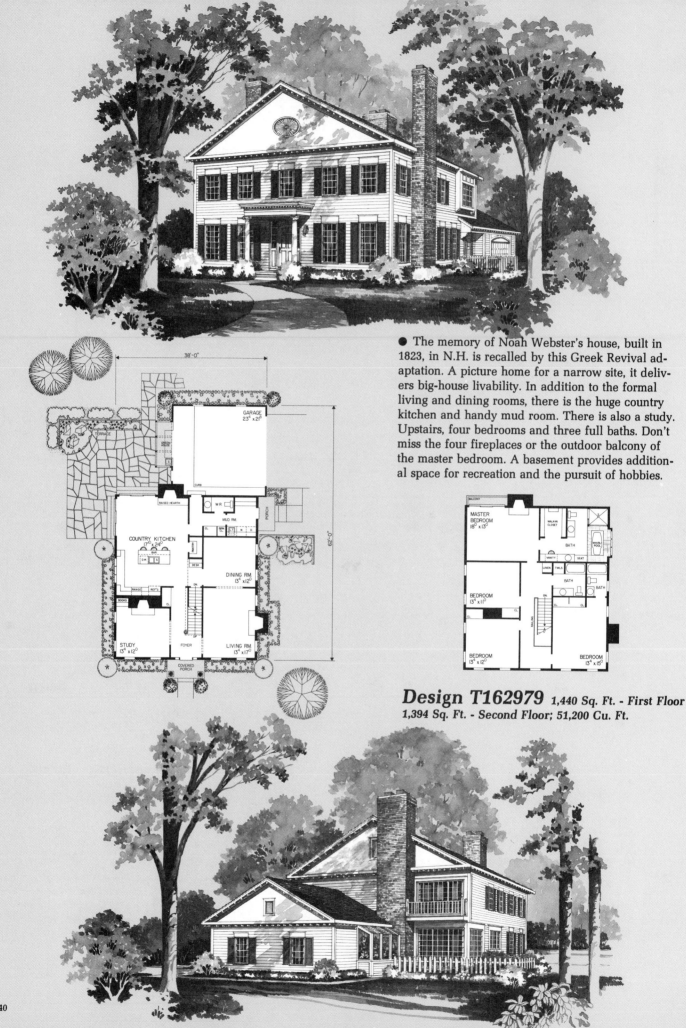

● The memory of Noah Webster's house, built in 1823, in N.H. is recalled by this Greek Revival adaptation. A picture home for a narrow site, it delivers big-house livability. In addition to the formal living and dining rooms, there is the huge country kitchen and handy mud room. There is also a study. Upstairs, four bedrooms and three full baths. Don't miss the four fireplaces or the outdoor balcony of the master bedroom. A basement provides additional space for recreation and the pursuit of hobbies.

Design T162979 1,440 Sq. Ft. - First Floor
1,394 Sq. Ft. - Second Floor; 51,200 Cu. Ft.

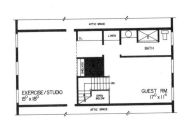

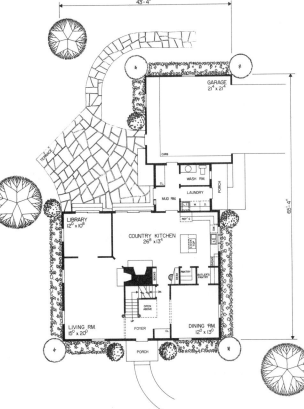

Design T162978 1,451 Sq. Ft. - First Floor
1,268 Sq. Ft. - Second Floor; 746 Sq. Ft. - Third Floor
38,665 Cu. Ft.

● The Nathaniel Hawthorne house in Salem, Mass. was the inspiration for this New England gambrel-roofed design. It was orignally constructed around 1730. This 20th Century version offers a heap of living potential. The family's favorite spot will be in front of the fireplace in the spacious country kitchen. However, there are other places to retire to such as the formal living room, the adjacent library, the bedrooms, or the areas on the third floor. The full basement offers the potential for the development of additional recreational space. Don't overlook the mud room strategically located with access from the garage and both yards.

Design T161275

1,314 Sq. Ft. - First Floor
1,080 Sq. Ft. - Second Floor; 33,656 Cu. Ft.

● Of French origin, the characteristic feature of this two story design is its Mansard roof. Also, enhancing the formality of its exterior are the beautifully proportioned windows, the recessed front entrance with double doors, the two stately chimneys and the attached two-car garage. The wonderfully efficient floor plan highlights a large end-living room with centered fireplace and a separate dining room.

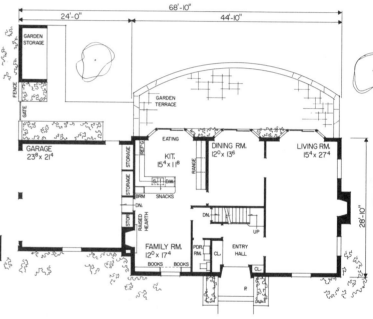

Design T161951
1,346 Sq. Ft. - First Floor
1,114 Sq. Ft. - Second Floor; 39,034 Cu. Ft.

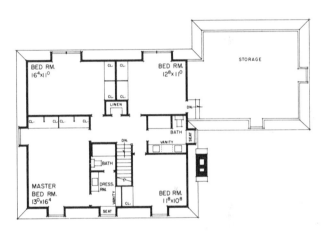

● This is surely a marvelous French home with its Mansard roof. It is equipped with all the necessary features including a large living room, dining room with access to the terrace, efficient kitchen and more.

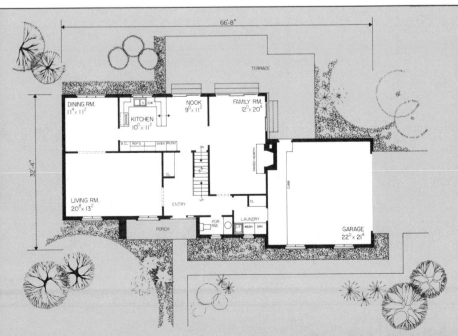

Design T162750
1,209 Sq. Ft. - First Floor
965 Sq. Ft. - Second Floor; 32,025 Cu. Ft.

● This four bedroom Mansard roof design is impressive, indeed. The covered front porch leads the way to an efficient floor plan. Includes a basement.

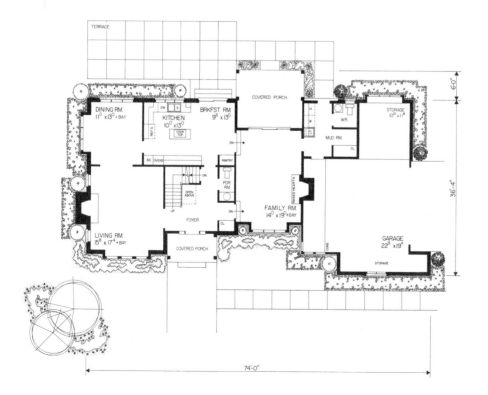

Design T162960

1,372 Sq. Ft. - First Floor
1,245 Sq. Ft. - Second Floor
44,557 Cu. Ft.

● The swooping roof of the projecting front gable results in a sheltered entrance to the foyer of this unique design. It would be difficult to imagine more appealing roof lines than this Tudor has to offer. Roof, exterior wall, and window treatment all blend together to present a harmonious facade. The two chimneys with their massive caps add their appeal, too. Once inside your guests will be impressed again. They will delight to find two such large living areas - one for formal and another for informal living. They will enthuse further over the eating facilities - a formal dining room and an informal breakfast room. The L-shaped kitchen will be a charm in which to work. It has an island cooking station, plenty of cupboard and counter space and a pantry nearby. The homemaker will love the strategic location of the mud room. It is just inside the entrance from the garage and is directly accessible from the rear yard. The covered porch is a nice feature. And don't miss the two fireplaces - one with a raised hearth. Upstairs there are four bedrooms, two baths and good storage facilities.

Design T162959

1,003 Sq. Ft. - First Floor
1,056 Sq. Ft. - Second Floor; 32,891 Cu. Ft.

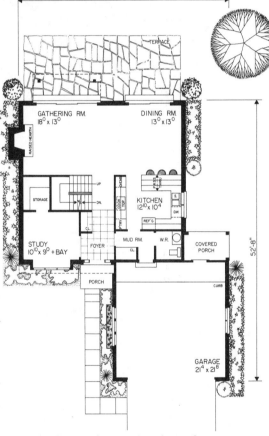

KNOW YOUR RIGHTS ON SITES

If you're thinking about buying a lot from a developer, it'll pay to know what the federal government stipulates. Typically, companies offering 100 or more unimproved lots for sale or lease are required to register with the U.S. Department of Housing and Urban Development. Each developer must file a report containing detailed information about the property, a document that you're free to inspect and, if you like, copy at a cost of 10 cents per page. Among others, here are some of the items a property report has to include:

- A copy of the corporate charter and financial statement.
- Information about the land, including a title policy or attorney's title opinion and copies of deeds and mortgages.
- Information on local ordinances, health regulations, etc.
- Information about facilities available in the area, such as schools, hospitals, and transportation systems.
- Information about availability of utilities and water, as well as plans for sewage disposal.
- Plans for the property, including information on roads, streets, and recreational facilities.

Source: "Buying Lots from Developers," U.S. Department of Housing and Urban Development.

● Here the stateliness of Tudor styling is captured in a design suited for a narrow building site. This relatively low-budget two-story delivers all the livability found in many much larger homes. Imagine, a 31 foot living-dining area that stretches across the entire rear of the house and functions with the big terrace. Then, there is the efficient U-shaped kitchen with built-in cooking facilities and a pass-thru to the snack bar. Just inside the entrance from the garage is the mud room with its adjacent wash room. Enhancing first floor livability is the study with its big walk-in closet. An open staircase leads to the basement recreation area. Upstairs, three bedrooms, two baths and an outdoor balcony.

Design T161278

1,336 Sq. Ft. - First Floor
1,080 Sq. Ft. - Second Floor
34,304 Cu. Ft.

● This inviting Early American design will be outstanding in any area. Note the uniqueness of the front covered porch entry to the family room.

Design T161179 1,378 Sq. Ft. - First Floor; 1,040 Sq. Ft. - Second Floor; 35,022 Cu. Ft.

● Loads of livability. This home could be called upon to serve as a five bedroom design. It would function admirably.

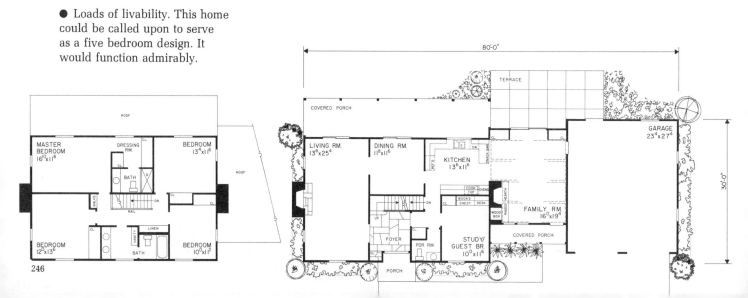

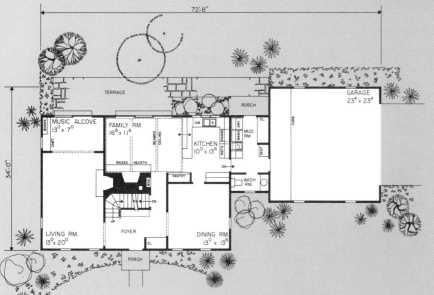

72'-8"

34'-0"

TERRACE

MUSIC ALCOVE
13⁰ x 7⁰

FAMILY RM.
16⁸ x 11⁶

BEAMED CEILING

KITCHEN
10⁰ x 13⁶

PORCH

GARAGE
23⁴ x 23⁴

CURB

RAISED HEARTH

PANTRY

MUD RM.

WASH RM.

LIVING RM.
13⁰ x 20⁰

FOYER

DINING RM.
13⁰ x 13⁶

PORCH

Design T162521

1,272 Sq. Ft. - First Floor
1,139 Sq. Ft. - Second Floor
37,262 Cu. Ft.

● Here is a house to remind one of the weather beaten facades of Nantucket. The active family plan is as up-to-date as tomorrow.

BATH

DRESSING RM.

BED RM.
13⁰ x 11⁶

VANITY

DRESSING RM.

BATH

DRESS RM.

MASTER BED RM.
13⁰ x 18⁰

HALL

RAILING

BED RM.
13⁰ x 15⁶

LINEN   SEAT   LINEN

Design T162118

908 Sq. Ft. - First Floor
866 Sq. Ft. - Second Floor
24,429 Cu. Ft.

● The cedar shakes would make this Farmhouse adaptation at home on Cape Cod. Wherever built, whatever the exterior material, there's plenty of livability.

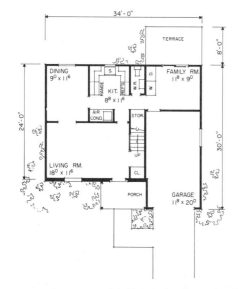

Design T161354

644 Sq. Ft. - First Floor
572 Sq. Ft. - Second Floor
11,490 Cu. Ft.

● Livability galore for that 50 foot building site. The homemaker will enjoy the U-shaped work center with the extra wash room, laundry equipment nearby.

Design T161361

965 Sq. Ft. - First Floor
740 Sq. Ft. - Second Floor
23,346 Cu. Ft.

● All the elements are present in this design for fine family living. Three bedrooms, 2½ baths, family room, dining room and even a first floor laundry.

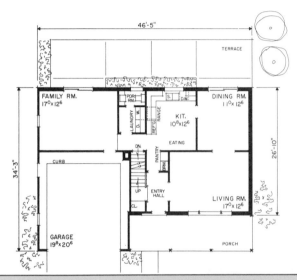

Design T161723

888 Sq. Ft. - First Floor
970 Sq. Ft. - Second Floor
19,089 Cu. Ft.

● You'll not need a large parcel of property to accommodate this home. Neither will you need too large a building budget. Note fourth bedroom.

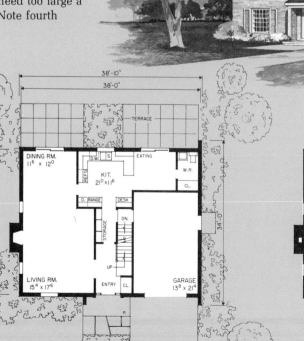

Expandable Cape Ann Cottage

Design T162983 776 Sq. Ft. - First Floor (Basic Plan)
1,072 Sq. Ft. - First Floor (Expanded Plan); 652 Sq. Ft. - Second Floor (Both Plans)
24,650 Cu. Ft. Basic Plan; 27,865 Cu. Ft. Expanded Plan

● This charming gambrel-roofed Colonial cottage is reminiscent of the simple houses built and occupied by seafarers on Cape Ann, Mass. in the 17th and 18th Centuries. However, this adaptation offers a new twist. It is designed to expand as your need and/or budget grows. Of course, building the expanded version first will deliver the bonus livability promised by the formal dining room and quiet study, plus the convenience of the attached garage.

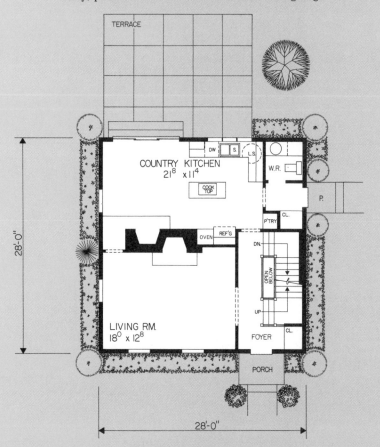

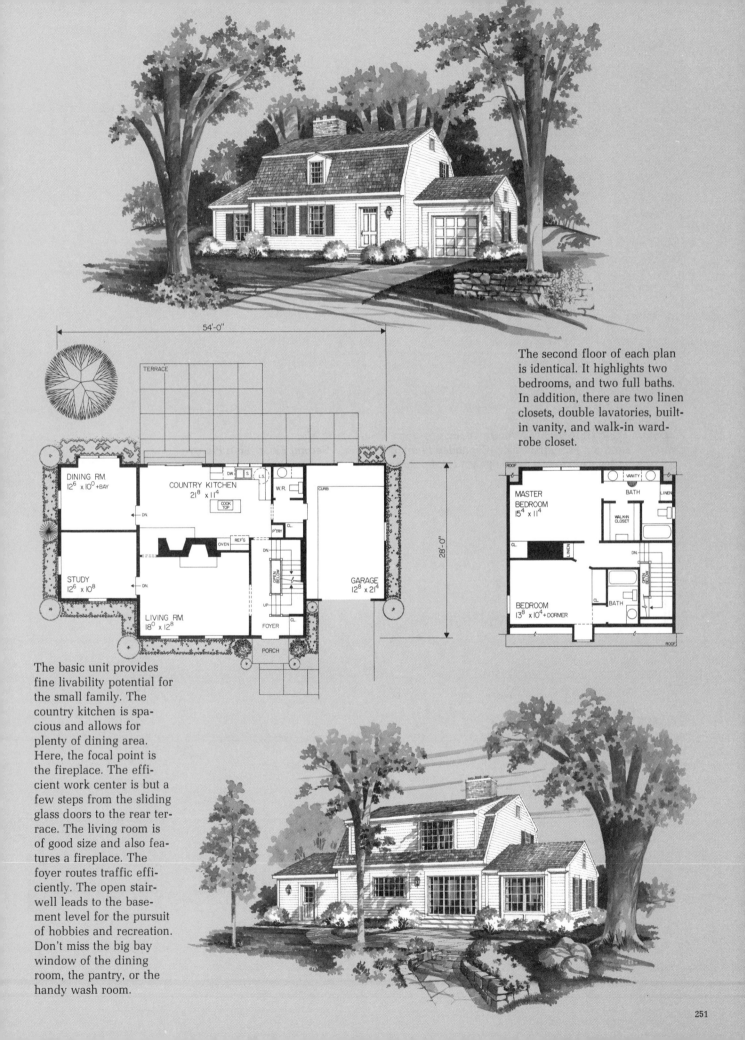

54'-0"

TERRACE

DINING RM.
12^6 x 10^0 +BAY

COUNTRY KITCHEN
21^8 x 11^4

DW. S.

W.R.

CURB

COOK TOP

DN.

P'TRY CL.

OVEN REF'G

DN.

OPEN BELOW

STUDY
12^6 x 10^8

GARAGE
12^8 x 21^4

28'-0"

UP

LIVING RM.
18^0 x 12^8

FOYER

CL.

PORCH

The second floor of each plan is identical. It highlights two bedrooms, and two full baths. In addition, there are two linen closets, double lavatories, built-in vanity, and walk-in wardrobe closet.

ROOF

VANITY

MASTER BEDROOM
15^4 x 11^4

BATH

LINEN

WALK-IN CLOSET

CL.

LINEN

DN.

OPEN BELOW

BEDROOM
13^8 x 10^4 +DORMER

CL.

BATH

ROOF

The basic unit provides fine livability potential for the small family. The country kitchen is spacious and allows for plenty of dining area. Here, the focal point is the fireplace. The efficient work center is but a few steps from the sliding glass doors to the rear terrace. The living room is of good size and also features a fireplace. The foyer routes traffic efficiently. The open stairwell leads to the basement level for the pursuit of hobbies and recreation. Don't miss the big bay window of the dining room, the pantry, or the handy wash room.

Design T162540

1,306 Sq. Ft. - First Floor
1,360 Sq. Ft. - Second Floor; 40,890 Cu. Ft.

● This efficient Colonial abounds in features. A spacious entry flanked by living areas. A kitchen flanked by eating areas. Upstairs, four bedrooms including a sitting room in the master suite.

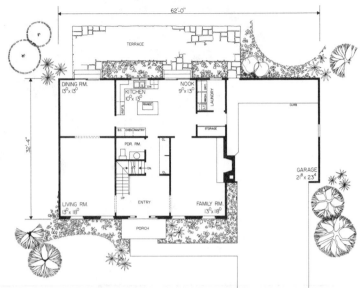

Design T162799

1,196 Sq. Ft. - First Floor
780 Sq. Ft. - Second Floor; 35,080 Cu. Ft.

● This two-story traditional design's facade with its narrow clapboards, punctuated by tall multi-paned windows, appears deceptively expansive. Yet the entire length of the house, including the garage, is 66 feet.

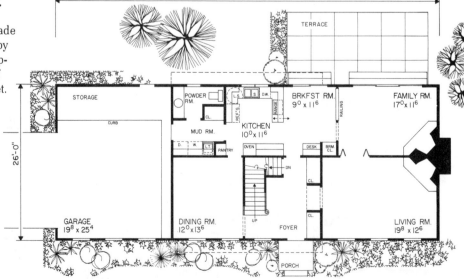

Design T162870
900 Sq. Ft. - First Floor
467 Sq. Ft. - Second Floor Left Suite
493 Sq. Ft. - Second Floor Right Suite; 35,970 Cu. Ft.

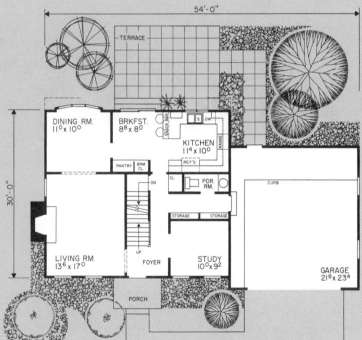

● This Colonial home was designed to provide comfortable living space for two families. The first floor is the common living area, with all of the necessary living areas; the second floor has two two-bedroom-one-bath suites. Built-ins are featured in the smaller bedroom.

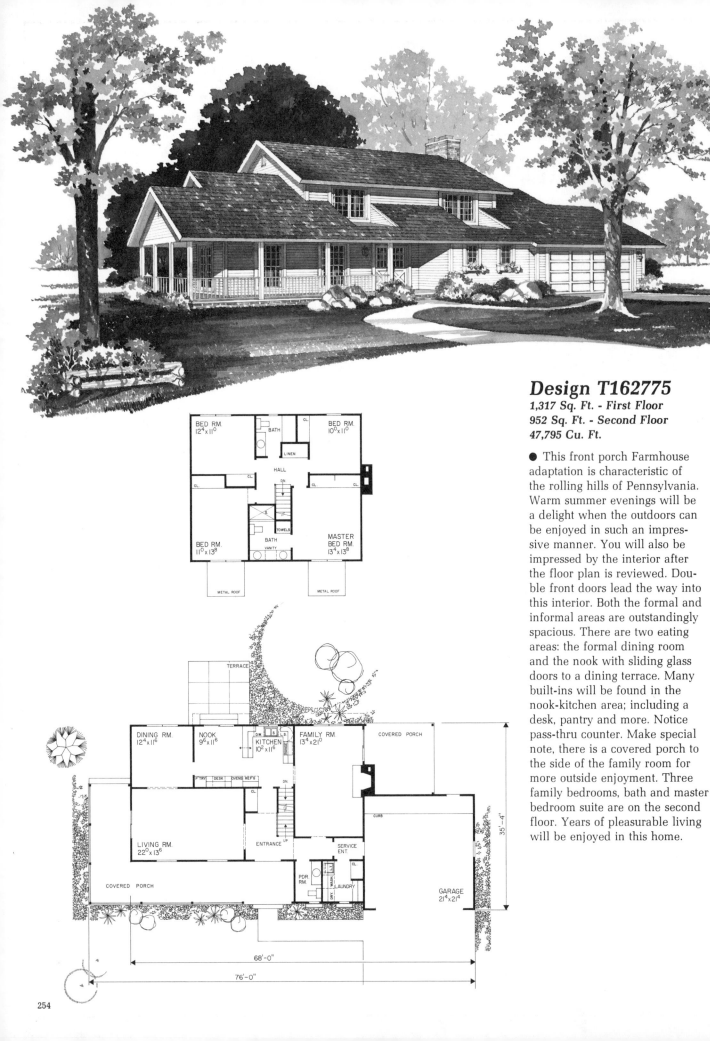

Design T162775

1,317 Sq. Ft. - First Floor
952 Sq. Ft. - Second Floor
47,795 Cu. Ft.

● This front porch Farmhouse adaptation is characteristic of the rolling hills of Pennsylvania. Warm summer evenings will be a delight when the outdoors can be enjoyed in such an impressive manner. You will also be impressed by the interior after the floor plan is reviewed. Double front doors lead the way into this interior. Both the formal and informal areas are outstandingly spacious. There are two eating areas: the formal dining room and the nook with sliding glass doors to a dining terrace. Many built-ins will be found in the nook-kitchen area; including a desk, pantry and more. Notice pass-thru counter. Make special note, there is a covered porch to the side of the family room for more outside enjoyment. Three family bedrooms, bath and master bedroom suite are on the second floor. Years of pleasurable living will be enjoyed in this home.

THE MULTI-LEVEL HOUSE:
Economical Options on Any Level

PLAN T162624

Versatility of form is the key to multi-level houses. Among their many faces are the split-level, bi-level, and hillside house. Each of these types shares a common feature — complete livability achieved by the "stacking" of living areas or zones. Like 1½- and two-story structures, such stacking minimizes site size requirements, the size of the roof area, and the expanse of the foundation.

The split-level house may have its living levels arranged in several ways. The most common are the side-to-side split and the front-to-back split (see examples). The levels are usually identified as the main living level, the upper sleeping level, and the lower recreation level. When a fourth level is added — generally the basement — the structure is often called a quad-level.

The bi-level (also referred to as a split-foyer) is characterized by a central foyer, or entry hall, from which two flights of stairs originate. Usually one flight of several steps leads to the living level; the other with a similar number of steps leads to the sleeping level, most often located above the lower living level. Variations of the popular split-foyer house may have these levels reversed.

The hillside house is designed to take advantage of a sloping building site. It may take the form of a one- or two-story structure with an exposed lower level.

Because of their unique structure, multi-levels often incorporate a garage into the main area of the house. This design not only achieves convenience but results in lower initial expense — such houses can be con-

continued on next page

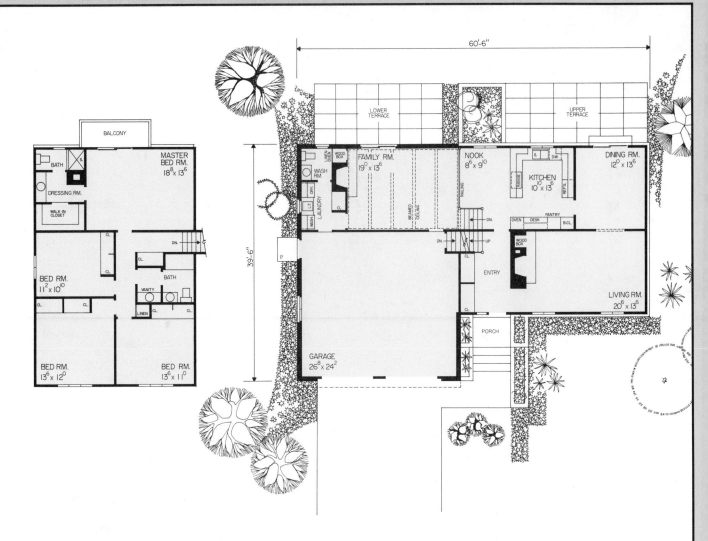

Design T162624

904 Sq. Ft. - Main Level; 1,120 Sq. Ft - Upper Level
404 Sq. Ft. - Lower Level; 39,885 Cu. Ft.

● This is tri-level living at its best. The exterior is that of the most popular Tudor styling. A facade which will hold its own for many a year to come. Livability will be achieved to its maximum on the four (including basement) levels. The occupants of the master bedroom can enjoy the outdoors on their private balcony. Additional outdoor enjoyment can be gained on the two terraces. That family room is more than 19' x 13' and includes a beamed ceiling and fireplace with wood box. Its formal companion, the living room, is similar in size and also will have the added warmth of a fireplace.

structed on smaller, less costly sites.

However, the main cost-effective aspect of the split-level is that it features a lower level which is raised above ground, easily accommodating living areas. Such amenities as large window walls and sliding glass doors with access to patios and terraces are often found in such a design. It is also not uncommon to find bedrooms on the lower level as in Design T162773 on page 289.

Another cost savings is realized in areas where sloping or uneven sites are found. Considered "problem sites" or, at least, less desirable sites, they may be available for sale at prices far below those of flatter sites. Building an appropriate multi-level on a bargain

lot may make an otherwise unaffordable house within range even though engineering costs may be a bit more expensive than with a flat site. And building on such sites will often result in a most striking and unique finished product.

While each of these three types of multi-levels adapt well to sloping sites, the split-level and the bi-level can also be effectively utilized on flat sites, making the multi-level one of the most popular styles for any region of the country. It is also the perfect design for both interior and exterior balconies and overlooks, and lends itself quite well to taking advantage of a view from all angles. For cost-effective housing with a variety of options, the multi-level is a wise choice.

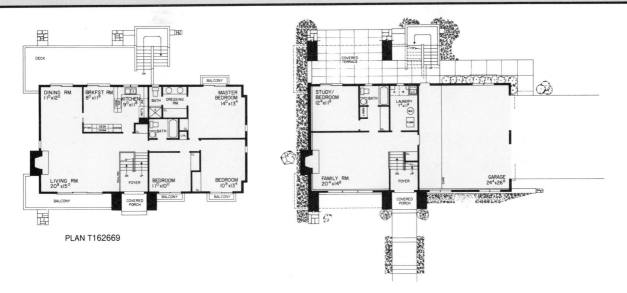

PLAN T162669

The split-foyer design puts less-formal living on a level of its own. Covered terraces and sunny upper level decks are often the result.

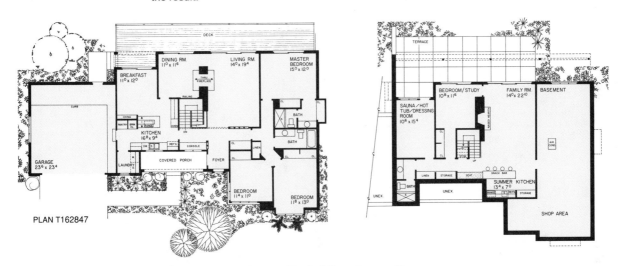

PLAN T162847

A sloping site is easily tamed by building a home with an exposed lower level. Notice the sense of privacy achieved by the lower level patio.

PLAN T162786

A separation of living and dining rooms from the more casual family room, on a lower level, creates functional and formal spaces. Bedrooms, all on the upper level, are completely private.

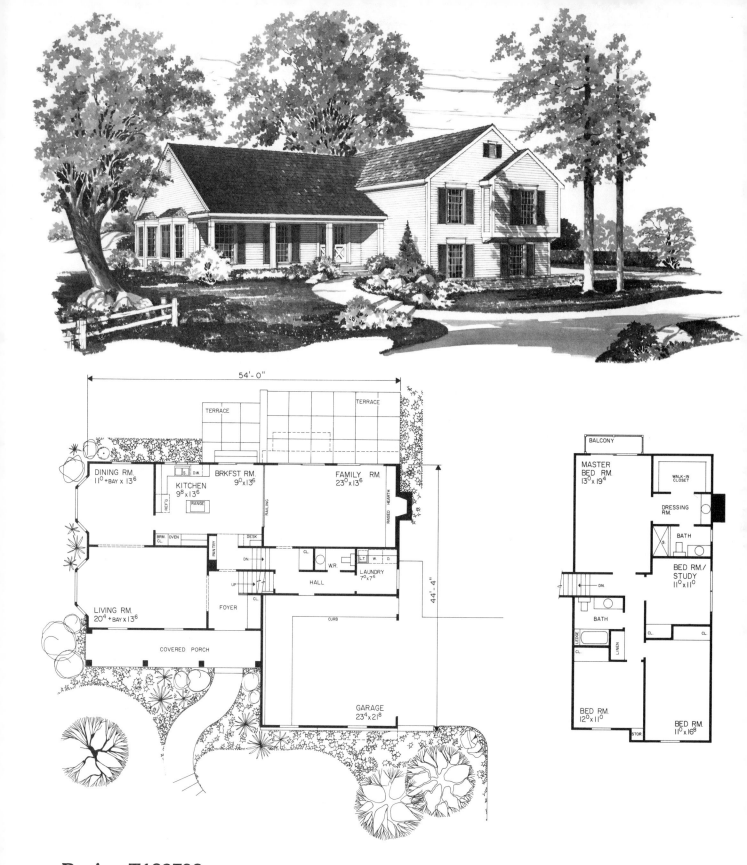

Design T162786 *871 Sq. Ft. - Main Level; 1,132 Sq. Ft. - Upper Level; 528 Sq. Ft. - Lower Level; 44,000 Cu. Ft.*

● A bay window in each the formal living room and dining room. A great interior and exterior design feature to attract attention to this tri-level home. The exterior also is enhanced by a covered front porch to further the Colonial charm. The interior livability is outstanding, too. An abundance of built-ins in the kitchen create an efficient work center. Features include an island range, pantry, broom closet, desk and breakfast room with sliding glass doors to the rear terrace. The lower level houses the informal family room, wash room and laundry. Further access is available to the outdoors by the family room to the terrace and laundry room to the side yard.

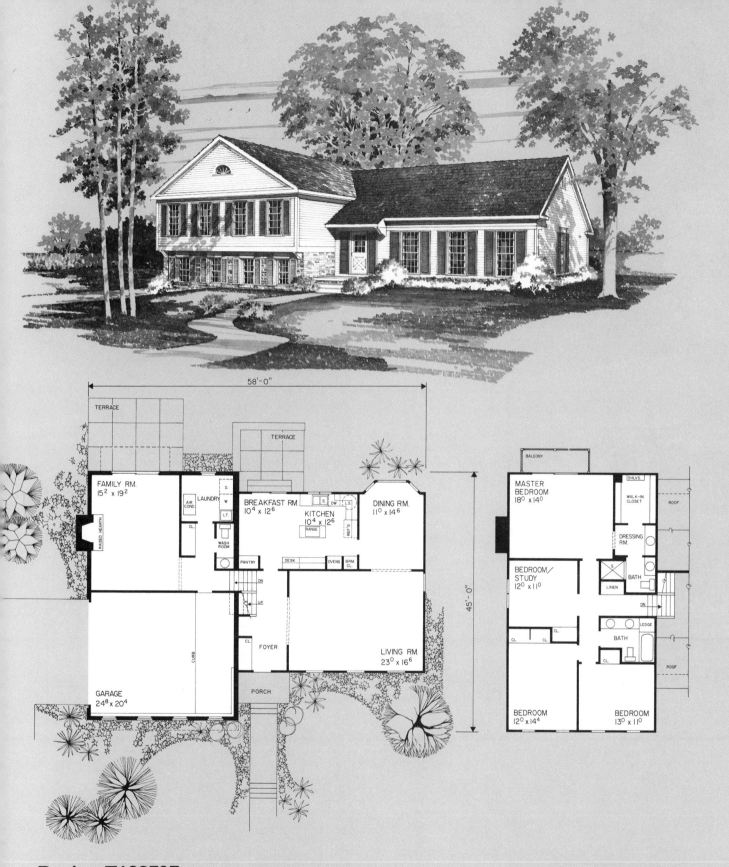

Design T162787
976 Sq. Ft. - Main Level; 1,118 Sq. Ft. - Upper Level; 524 Sq. Ft. - Lower Level; 36,110 Cu. Ft.

● Three level living! Main, upper and lower levels to serve you and your family with great ease. Start from the bottom and work your way up. Family room with raised hearth fireplace, laundry and wash room on the lower level. Formal living and dining rooms, kitchen and breakfast room on the main level. Stop and take note at the efficiency of the kitchen with its many outstanding extras. The upper level houses the three bedrooms, study (or fourth bedroom if you prefer) and two baths. This design has really stacked up its livability to serve its occupants to their best advantage. This design has great interior livability and exterior charm.

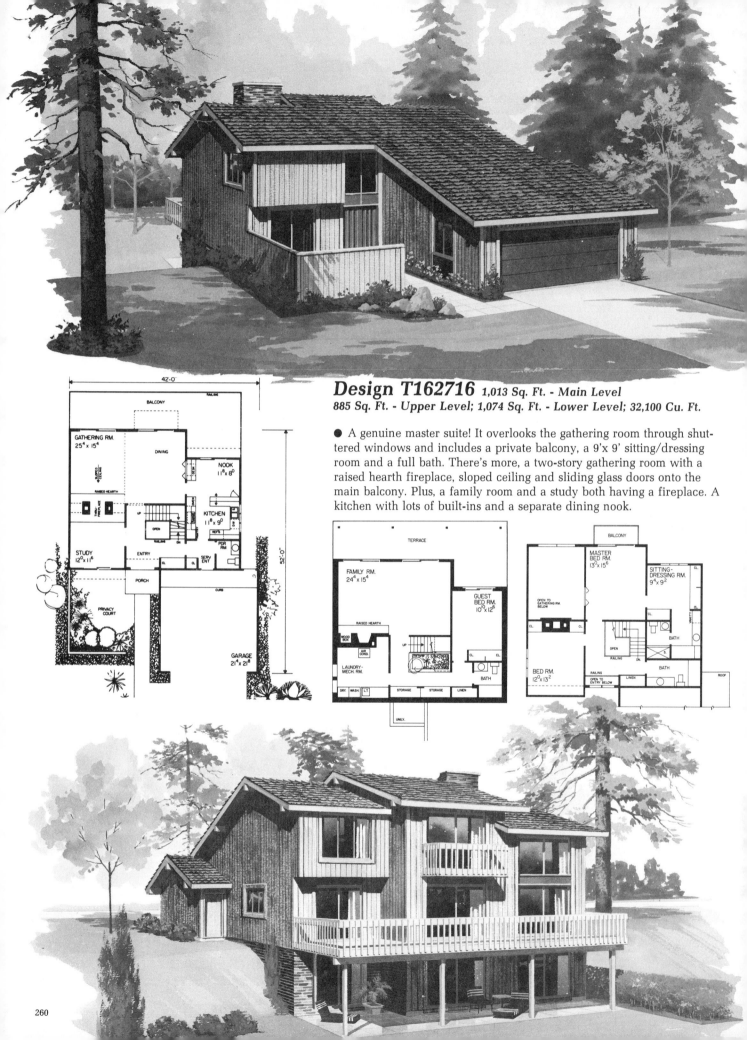

Design T162716 1,013 Sq. Ft. - Main Level
885 Sq. Ft. - Upper Level; 1,074 Sq. Ft. - Lower Level; 32,100 Cu. Ft.

● A genuine master suite! It overlooks the gathering room through shuttered windows and includes a private balcony, a 9'x 9' sitting/dressing room and a full bath. There's more, a two-story gathering room with a raised hearth fireplace, sloped ceiling and sliding glass doors onto the main balcony. Plus, a family room and a study both having a fireplace. A kitchen with lots of built-ins and a separate dining nook.

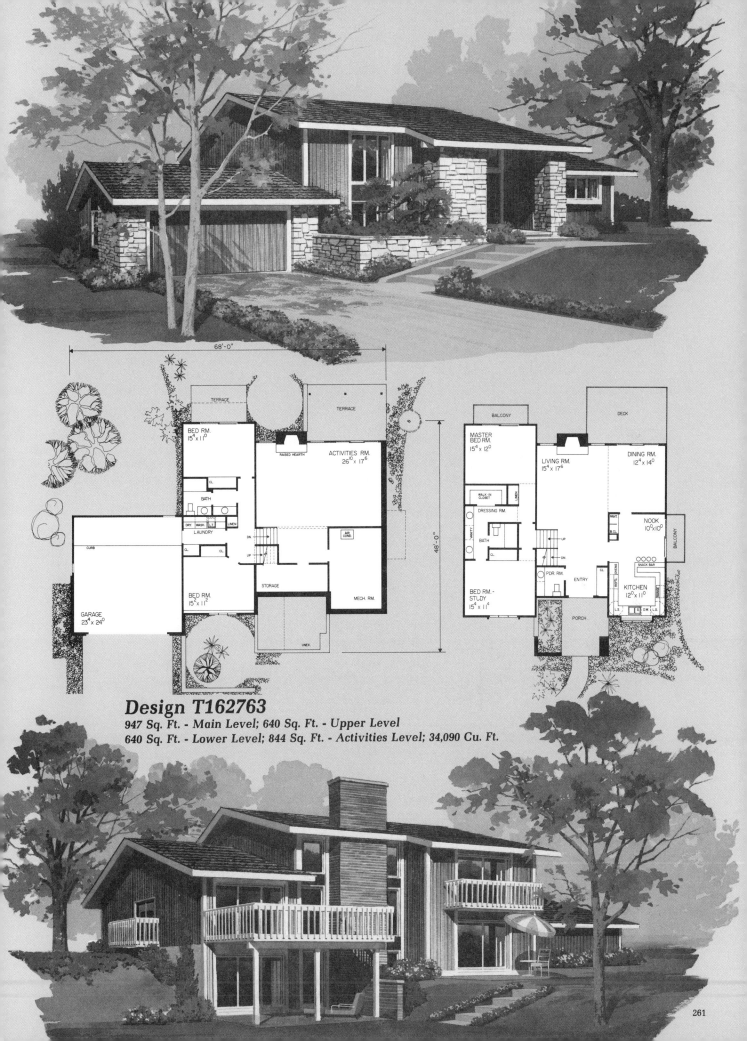

Design T162763

947 Sq. Ft. - Main Level; 640 Sq. Ft. - Upper Level
640 Sq. Ft. - Lower Level; 844 Sq. Ft. - Activities Level; 34,090 Cu. Ft.

68'-0"

48'-0"

BED RM.
15⁴ x 11⁰

ACTIVITIES RM.
26¹⁰ x 17⁶

TERRACE

TERRACE

RAISED HEARTH

CL

BATH

DRY. WASH. LINEN

LAUNDRY

DN.

UP

AIR COND.

CURB

CL CL

STORAGE

MECH. RM.

GARAGE
23⁴ x 24⁰

BED RM.
15² x 11²

UNEX.

BALCONY

DECK

MASTER BED RM.
15⁴ x 12⁰

LIVING RM.
15⁴ x 17⁶

DINING RM.
12⁴ x 14⁰

WALK-IN CLOSET

LINEN

DRESSING RM.

VANITY

BATH

CL

UP

DN.

PANT.

B. CL.

NOOK
10⁰ x 10⁰

BALCONY

SNACK BAR

REFR.

KITCHEN
12⁰ x 11⁰

POR. RM.

ENTRY

CL

BED RM. - STUDY
15⁴ x 11⁴

PORCH

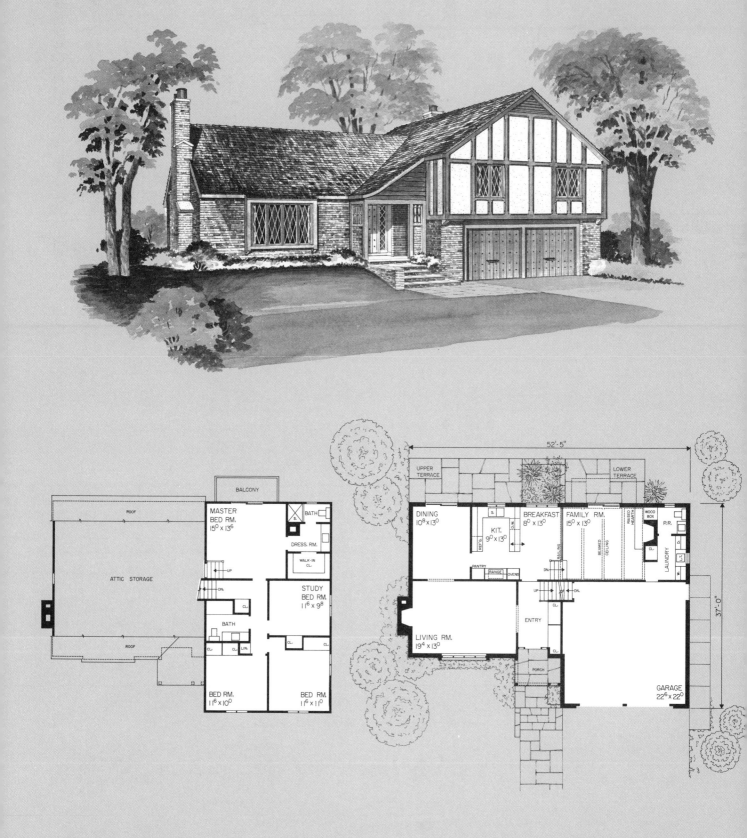

Design T162171 *795 Sq. Ft. - Main Level; 912 Sq. Ft. - Upper Level; 335 Sq. Ft. - Lower Level; 33,243 Cu. Ft.*

● This English Tudor split-level adaptation has much to recommend it. Perhaps, its most significant feature is that it can be built economically on a relatively small site. The width of the house is just over 52 feet. But its size does not inhibit it's livability features. There are many fine qualities: Observe the living room fireplace in addition to that in the family room with a wood box. Don't miss the balcony off the master bedroom. Also, worthy of note is the short flight of stairs leading to the huge attic storage area. For the development of even more space there is the basement below the main level. Access to this area is directly from the two-car garage. The breakfast room with its railing looks down into the lower level family room. Also it has a pass-thru to the kitchen.

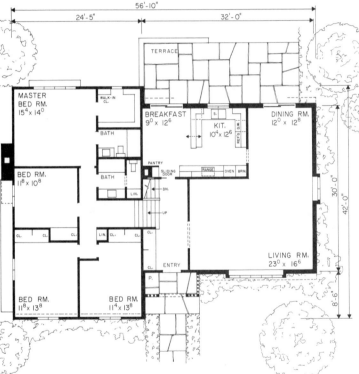

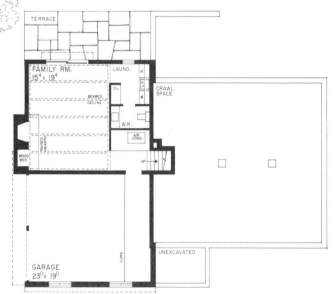

Design T162137

987 Sq. Ft. - Main Level
1,043 Sq. Ft. - Upper Level
463 Sq. Ft. - Lower Level
29,382 Cu. Ft.

● Tudor design adapts to split level living. The result is a unique charm for all to remember. As for the livability, the happy occupants of this tri-level home will experience wonderful living patterns. A covered porch protects and adds charm to the front entry. The center hall routes traffic conveniently to the spacious formal living and dining area; the informal breakfast room and kitchen zone; the upper level bedrooms; the lower level all-purpose family room. Contributing to fine living are such highlights as 2½ baths, walk-in closet, four bedrooms, sliding glass doors, pass-thru from kitchen to breakfast room, beamed ceiling, raised hearth fireplace, separate laundry and an attached two-car garage. Note the two terraces.

THAT'S THE SIZE OF IT

How big is big? Here are the dimensions, in feet, for key rooms.

ROOM	SMALL	AVERAGE	LARGE
Living room	12x18	16x20	22x28
Dining room	10x12	12x15	15x18
Kitchen	5x10	10x16	12x20
Bedroom	10x10	12x12	14x16
Bathroom	5x7	7x9	9x12

Source: "Home Planners' Guide to Residential Design," McGraw-Hill Inc.

Design T161850
1,456 Sq. Ft. - Upper Level
728 Sq. Ft. - Lower Level
23,850 Cu. Ft.

● This attractive, traditional bi-level house will surely prove to be an outstanding investment. While it is a perfect rectangle - which leads to economical construction - it has a full measure of eye-appeal. Setting the character of the exterior is the effective window treatment, plus the unique design of the recessed front entrance.

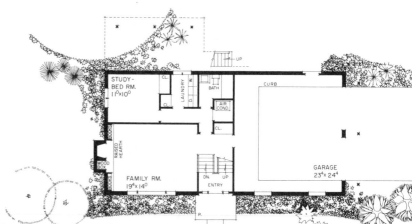

Design T162885   1,922 Sq. Ft. - Main Level
492 Sq. Ft. - Lower Level, 34,640 Cu. Ft.

● Vertical wood siding and fieldstone merge nicely on the exterior of this home. This contemporary bi-level will prove to be very livable.

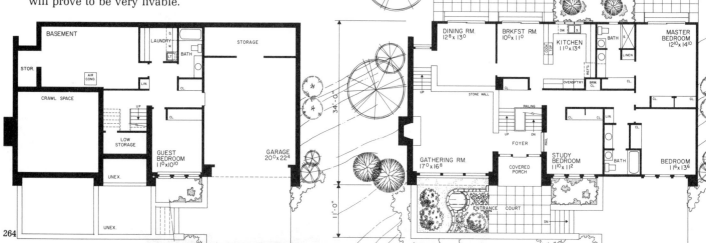

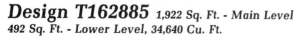

264

Design T161220

1,456 Sq. Ft. - Upper Level
862 Sq. Ft. - Lower Level
22,563 Cu. Ft.

● This fresh, contemporary exterior sets the stage for exceptional livability. Measuring only 52 across the front, this bi-level home offers the large family outstanding features. Whether called upon to function as a four or five bedroom home, there is plenty of space in which to move around.

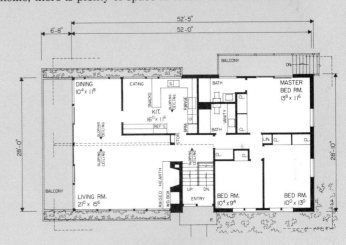

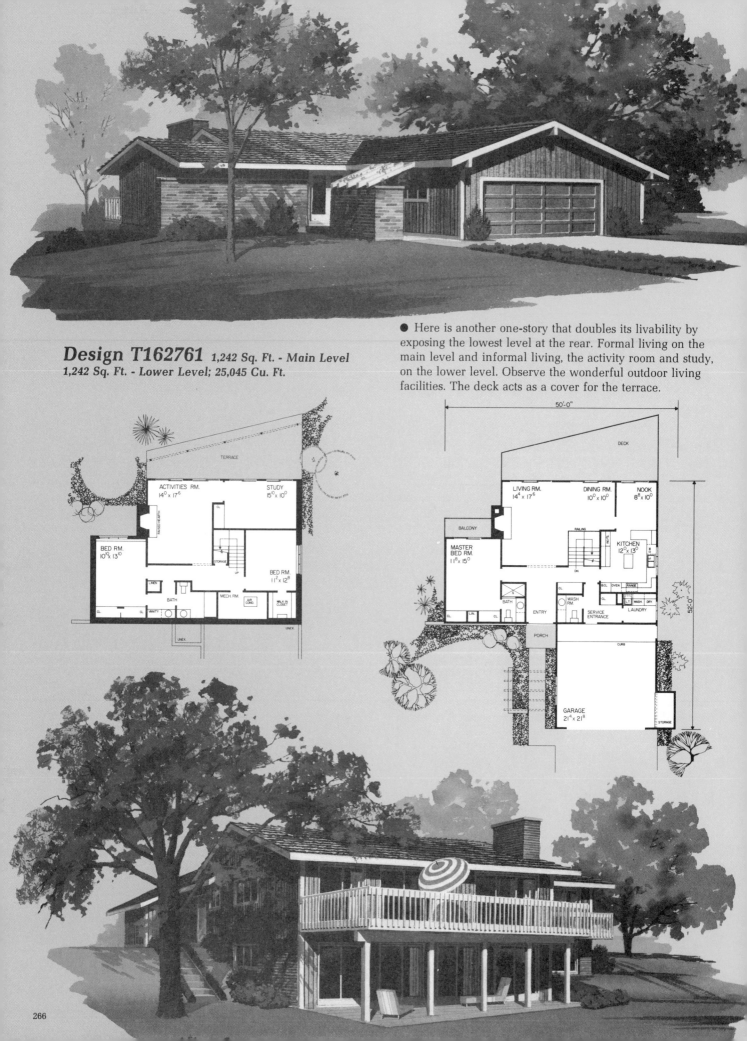

Design T162761 1,242 Sq. Ft. - Main Level
1,242 Sq. Ft. - Lower Level; 25,045 Cu. Ft.

● Here is another one-story that doubles its livability by exposing the lowest level at the rear. Formal living on the main level and informal living, the activity room and study, on the lower level. Observe the wonderful outdoor living facilities. The deck acts as a cover for the terrace.

TERRACE

ACTIVITIES RM.
14⁰ x 17⁶

STUDY
15⁰ x 10⁰

BED RM.
10⁰ x 13⁰

BED RM.
11² x 12⁸

LINEN

BATH

MECH. RM.

AIR. COND.

WALK IN CLOSET

STORAGE

UP

CL

CL

CL

VANITY

UNEX.

UNEX.

RAISED HEARTH

50'-0"

DECK

LIVING RM.
14⁴ x 17⁶

DINING RM.
10⁰ x 10⁰

NOOK
8⁸ x 10⁰

BALCONY

MASTER BED RM.
11⁸ x 15⁰

KITCHEN
12⁰ x 13⁰

RAILING

REF'G.

DN.

BATH

LIN.

CL

CL

WASH RM.

CL

ENTRY

B.CL.

OVEN

RANGE

CL

LT

WASH

DRY.

SERVICE ENTRANCE

LAUNDRY

PORCH

CURB

GARAGE
21⁴ x 21⁸

STORAGE

52'-0"

266

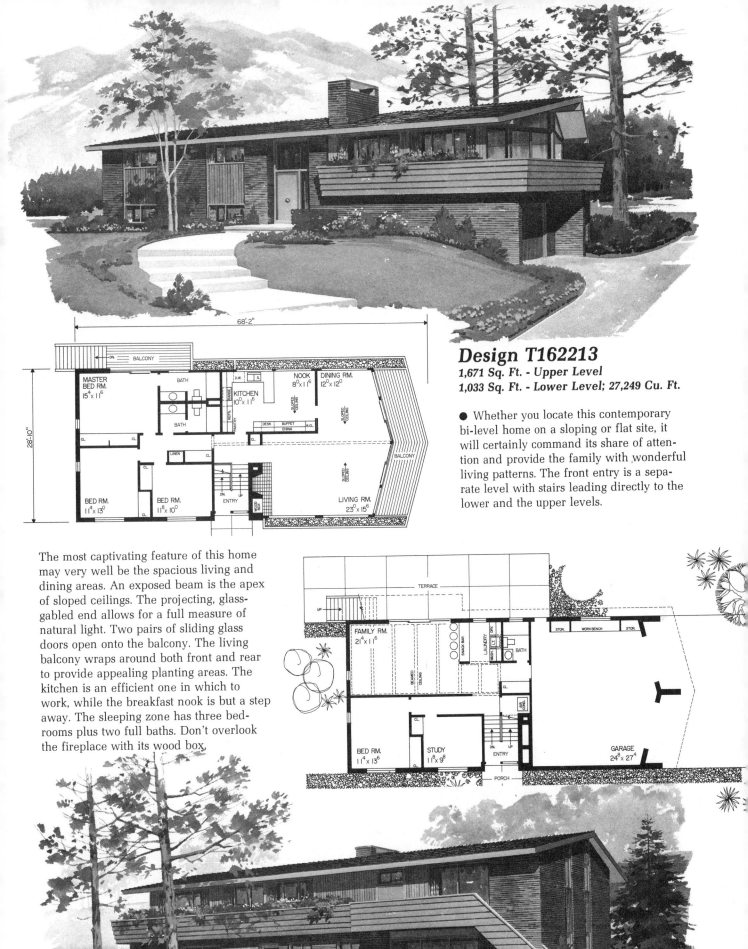

68'-2"

28'-10"

BALCONY

MASTER BED RM. 15'4 x 11'6

BATH

BATH

KITCHEN 10'0 x 11'6

NOOK 8'0 x 11'6

DINING RM. 12'0 x 12'0

DESK BUFFET CHINA

SLOPED CEILING

SLOPED CEILING

BALCONY

CL.

CL.

LINEN

CL.

CL.

BED RM. 11'4 x 13'0

BED RM. 11'8 x 10'0

ENTRY

WOOD BOX

SLOPED CEILING

LIVING RM. 23'0 x 15'6

Design T162213

1,671 Sq. Ft. - Upper Level
1,033 Sq. Ft. - Lower Level; 27,249 Cu. Ft.

● Whether you locate this contemporary bi-level home on a sloping or flat site, it will certainly command its share of attention and provide the family with wonderful living patterns. The front entry is a separate level with stairs leading directly to the lower and the upper levels.

The most captivating feature of this home may very well be the spacious living and dining areas. An exposed beam is the apex of sloped ceilings. The projecting, glass-gabled end allows for a full measure of natural light. Two pairs of sliding glass doors open onto the balcony. The living balcony wraps around both front and rear to provide appealing planting areas. The kitchen is an efficient one in which to work, while the breakfast nook is but a step away. The sleeping zone has three bedrooms plus two full baths. Don't overlook the fireplace with its wood box.

TERRACE

UP

FAMILY RM. 21'4 x 11'6

BEAMED CEILING

SNACK BAR

LAUNDRY

BATH

STOR.

WORK BENCH

STOR.

CL.

BED RM. 11'4 x 13'6

STUDY 11'8 x 9'8

ENTRY

UP

AIR COND.

GARAGE 24'8 x 27'4

PORCH

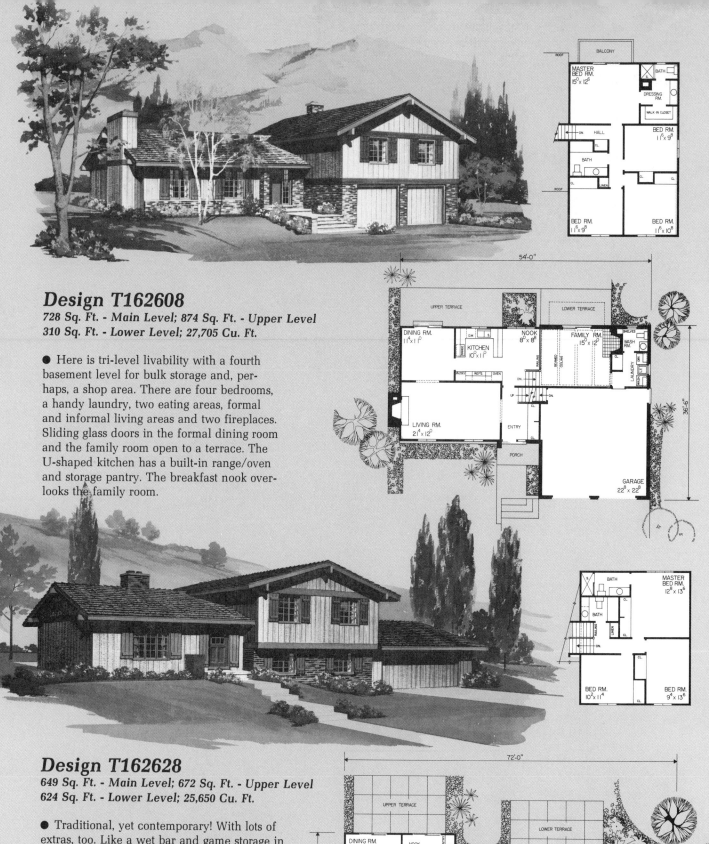

Design T162608
**728 Sq. Ft. - Main Level; 874 Sq. Ft. - Upper Level
310 Sq. Ft. - Lower Level; 27,705 Cu. Ft.**

● Here is tri-level livability with a fourth
basement level for bulk storage and, perhaps, a shop area. There are four bedrooms,
a handy laundry, two eating areas, formal
and informal living areas and two fireplaces.
Sliding glass doors in the formal dining room
and the family room open to a terrace. The
U-shaped kitchen has a built-in range/oven
and storage pantry. The breakfast nook overlooks the family room.

Design T162628
**649 Sq. Ft. - Main Level; 672 Sq. Ft. - Upper Level
624 Sq. Ft. - Lower Level; 25,650 Cu. Ft.**

● Traditional, yet contemporary! With lots of
extras, too. Like a wet bar and game storage in
the family room. A beamed ceiling, too, and a
sliding glass door onto the terrace. In short, a
family room designed to make your life easy
and enjoyable. There's more. A living room
with a traditionally styled fireplace and built-
in bookshelves. And a dining room with a sliding glass door that opens to a second terrace.
Here's the appropriate setting for those times
when you want a touch of elegance.

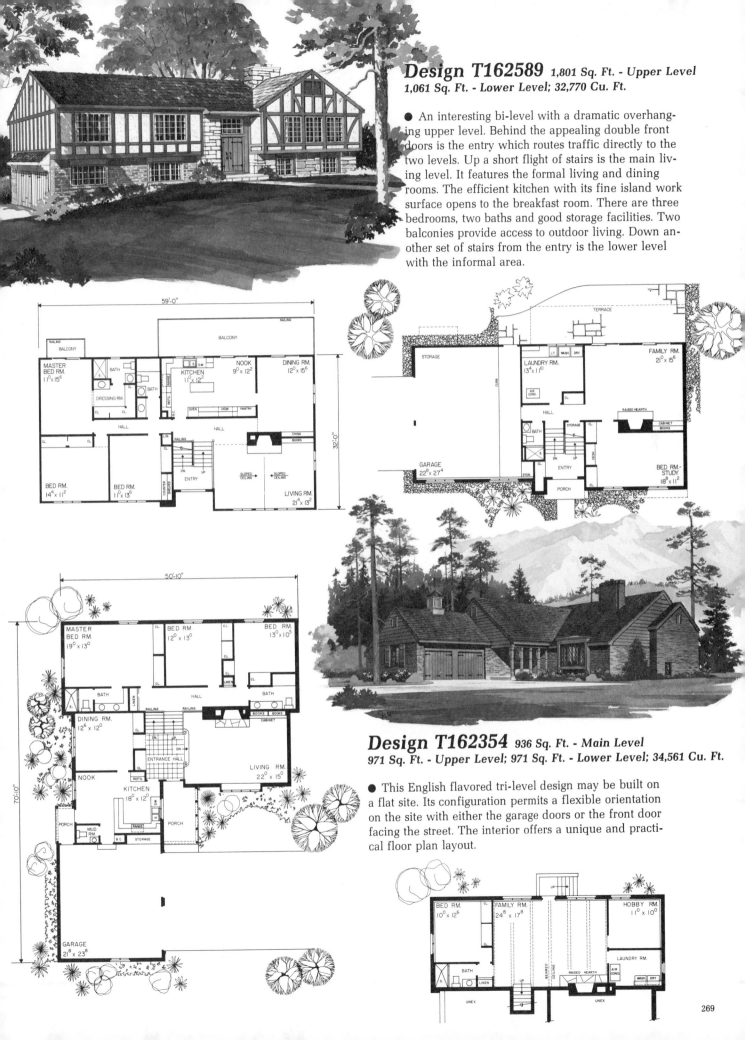

Design T162589
**1,801 Sq. Ft. - Upper Level
1,061 Sq. Ft. - Lower Level; 32,770 Cu. Ft.**

● An interesting bi-level with a dramatic overhanging upper level. Behind the appealing double front doors is the entry which routes traffic directly to the two levels. Up a short flight of stairs is the main living level. It features the formal living and dining rooms. The efficient kitchen with its fine island work surface opens to the breakfast room. There are three bedrooms, two baths and good storage facilities. Two balconies provide access to outdoor living. Down another set of stairs from the entry is the lower level with the informal area.

Design T162354
**936 Sq. Ft. - Main Level
971 Sq. Ft. - Upper Level; 971 Sq. Ft. - Lower Level; 34,561 Cu. Ft.**

● This English flavored tri-level design may be built on a flat site. Its configuration permits a flexible orientation on the site with either the garage doors or the front door facing the street. The interior offers a unique and practical floor plan layout.

Design T161977

896 Sq. Ft. - Main Level; 884 Sq. Ft. - Upper Level
896 Sq. Ft. - Lower Level; 36,718 Cu. Ft.

● This split-level with its impressive two-story center portion flanked by a projecting living wing on one side and a two-car garage on the other side, still maintains that very desirable ground-hugging quality. Built entirely of frame with narrow horizontal siding (brick veneer could be substituted), this home will sparkle with a New England flavor. Upon passing through the double front doors, you'll be impressed by an orderly flow of traffic. You'll go up to the sleeping zone; down to the hobby/recreation level; straight ahead to the kitchen and breakfast room; left to the quiet living room. Noteworthy are the extra baths, bedrooms and beamed ceiling family room with fireplace on lower level.

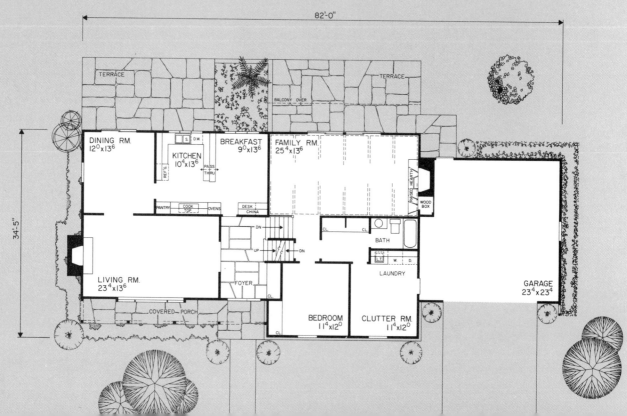

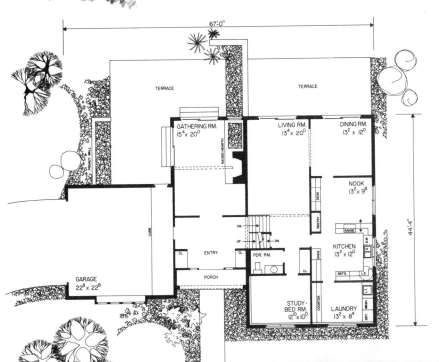

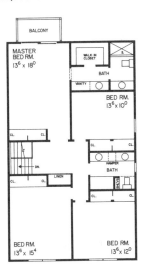

Design T162727

506 Sq. Ft. - Entry Level
1,288 Sq. Ft. - Upper Level
1,241 Sq. Ft. - Lower Level
38,590 Cu. Ft.

● Tri-level living at its glorious best. This Colonial facade is picturesque, indeed. The double front doors with their flanking side panels of glass are protected by the overhanging roof. The overhang of the upper level is an appealing detail and adds extra footage. Noteworthy is the size of the four bedrooms, the various storage facilities and the master bedroom balcony. Observe how the entry hall is utilized to receive traffic from both garage and front entrance. The gathering room has a dramatic planter/fireplace wall and functions through two sets of sliding glass doors with the big, L-shaped, upper terrace. The lower, main living level is wonderfully planned. Don't miss the extra bedroom, or study, located on the lower level, with a nearby powder room.

NEVER BUY A SITE UNSEEN

When you've landed the site you want—and before you buy it—get answers to lots of questions, including:

● How large will the development become? What zoning controls are in place?
● What are the provisions for sewer and water service? For garbage and trash collection?
● Are all of the promised facilities and utilities in the contract?
● Will there be access roads or streets to your property, and how will they be surfaced? How much will they cost?
● Will you have clear title to the property?
● Will you receive a deed upon purchase?

Source: "Buying Lots from Developers," U.S. Department of Housing and Urban Development.

271

Design T162546 1,143 Sq. Ft. - Main Level; 746 Sq. Ft. - Upper Level
1,143 Sq. Ft. - Lower Level; 31,128 Cu. Ft.

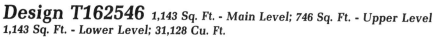

42'-4"

BALCONY

GATHERING RM.
29² x 13⁴

BALCONY

DINING

SNACK BAR   STORAGE

BED RM.-
STUDY
11⁸ x 17⁰

BALCONY

KITCHEN
12⁰ x 12⁰

RANGE   REF'S.

ENTRY

BATH

SEAT

52'-4"

OPEN TRELLIS

CARPORT
15' x 22'

STOR.
6² x 9⁴

TERRACE

LOUNGE
28⁸ x 13⁴

BALCONY

SLEEPING LOFT
19⁸ x 13⁴

RAILING

AIR COND.

UP

OPEN TO
GATHERING RM. BELOW

CL.   CL.   CL.   LIN.

DN.

ACTIVITIES
14⁹ x 15⁴

STORAGE

BATH

LAUNDRY
11⁶ x 18⁴

LT   WASH.   DRY.

BED RM.
14⁸ x 13²

RAILING

TOWELS

BATH

ENTRY BELOW

Design T162770
1,182 Sq. Ft. - Main Level
998 Sq. Ft. - Upper Level
25,830 Cu. Ft.

● If you are looking for a home with loads of livability, then consider these two-story contemporary homes which have an exposed lower level.

42'-0"

RAILING

DECK

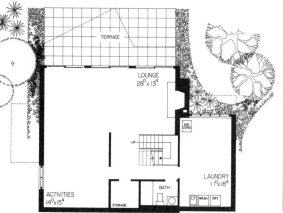

KIT.
8⁰ x 11⁶

REF'S.

RANGE

SNACK BAR

OVENS

PANTRY   DESK

FLUE

NOOK
11⁴ x 11⁶

GATHERING RM.
19² x 13⁴

RAISED HEARTH

FIRE PLACE

BOOKS

BALCONY

37'-4"

DN.

DINING RM.
12⁰ x 15⁶

CL.   CL.

ENTRY

PDR. RM.

STORAGE

LIBRARY
13¹⁰ x 12⁴

PORCH

WALK-IN CLOSET

BED RM.
14⁴ x 10⁰

OPEN TO
GATHERING RM.
BELOW

BATH

SLOPED CEILING

FLUE   CL.

DN.

LINEN

RAIL

BOOKS

RAIL

SLOPED CEILING

BALCONY

BED RM.
12⁰ x 13²

CL.   CL.

DRESSING RM.

VANITY

MASTER
BED RM.
13¹⁰ x 12⁴

BATH

BASEMENT

AIR COND.

STOR.

MECH. RM.

CL.

UP

LAUNDRY

DRY.   WASH.   LT.

CURB

STORAGE

GARAGE
19⁴ - 23⁸ x 26⁴

Design T162548 1,109 Sq. Ft. - Main Level; 739 Sq. Ft. - Upper Level
869 Sq. Ft. - Lower Level; 31,370 Cu. Ft.

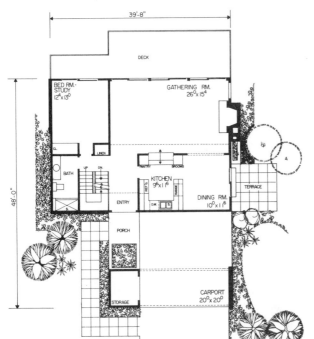

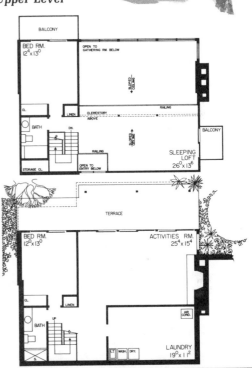

Design T162844 1,882 Sq. Ft. - Upper Level
1,168 Sq. Ft. - Lower Level; 37,860 Cu. Ft.

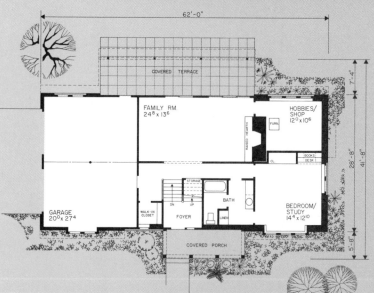

62'-0"

COVERED TERRACE

FAMILY RM.
24⁸ x 13⁶

HOBBIES/
SHOP
12⁰ x 10⁶

FURN

BOOKS
DESK

CL

STORAGE

DN

UP

BATH

BEDROOM/
STUDY
14⁴ x 12¹⁰

GARAGE
20⁰ x 27⁴

WALK-IN
CLOSET

FOYER

LINEN

COVERED PORCH

7'-4"

28'-8"

41'-8"

5'-8"

DECK

BEDROOM
12⁰ x 14⁴

BREAKFAST
12⁰ x 13⁶

KITCHEN
10⁰ x 13⁶

DINING RM.
11⁰ x 13⁶

LIVING RM.
13⁰ x 19⁰ + BAY

OPEN
THRU

OVEN PNTRY

CL

CL

LINEN

BEDROOM
12⁰ x 12⁰

BATH

BRM
CL

LAUNDRY

DN

UP

FOYER

CL

WALK-IN
CLOSET

BATH

MASTER
BEDROOM
16⁰ x 12⁰

COVERED PORCH

● Bi-level living will be enjoyed to the fullest in this Tudor design. The split-foyer type design will be very efficient for the active family. Three bedrooms are on the upper level, a fourth on the lower level.

Design T162843

1,861 Sq. Ft. - Upper Level
1,181 Sq. Ft. - Lower Level; 32,485 Cu. Ft.

● Bi-level living will be enjoyed to its fullest in this Spanish styled design. There is a lot of room for the various family activities. Informal living will take place on the lower level in the family room and lounge. The formal living and dining rooms, sharing a thru-fire-place, are located on the upper level.

Design T161308 496 Sq. Ft. - Main Level
572 Sq. Ft. - Upper Level; 537 Sq. Ft. - Lower Level; 16,024 Cu. Ft.

Design T161717
556 Sq. Ft. - Main Level
642 Sq. Ft. - Upper Level
596 Sq. Ft. - Lower Level; 17,975 Cu. Ft.

● A relatively small split-level that will return loads of livability for the building dollar. Certainly your building budget will purchase a well designed home. One that will be hard to beat for exterior appeal.

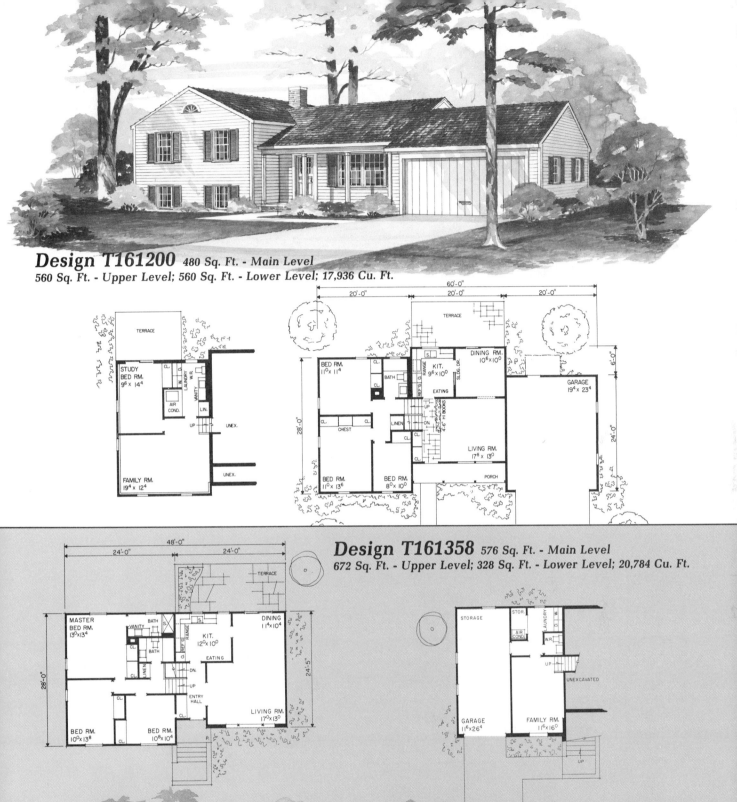

Design T161200 480 Sq. Ft. - Main Level
560 Sq. Ft. - Upper Level; 560 Sq. Ft. - Lower Level; 17,936 Cu. Ft.

TERRACE

STUDY
BED RM.
9^6 x 14^4

CL.

LAUNDRY
W.R.
VANITY

AIR
COND.

LIN.

UP

UNEX.

FAMILY RM.
19^4 x 12^4

UNEX.

60'-0"
20'-0" / 20'-0" / 20'-0"

TERRACE

BED RM.
11^0 x 11^4

CL.
CL.
BATH

CHEST
CL.
CL.

CL.

S
RANGE
REF'G
KIT.
9^6 x 10^0

DINING RM.
10^6 x 10^0

SLDG. DR.

EATING

UP
DN.
LINEN
4-6 HI BOOKS

CL.

6'-0"

GARAGE
19^4 x 23^4

24'-0"

LIVING RM.
17^6 x 13^0

28'-0"

BED RM.
11^0 x 13^6

BED RM.
8^0 x 10^0

PORCH

Design T161358 576 Sq. Ft. - Main Level
672 Sq. Ft. - Upper Level; 328 Sq. Ft. - Lower Level; 20,784 Cu. Ft.

48'-0"
24'-0" / 24'-0"

TERRACE

MASTER
BED RM.
13^0 x 13^4

VANITY
BATH

BATH

CL.

S
RANGE
REF'G
KIT.
12^0 x 10^0

DINING
11^4 x 10^4

LINEN

CL.

DN.

UP

EATING

24'-5"

28'-0"

BED RM.
10^0 x 13^8

CL.

BED RM.
10^8 x 10^4

ENTRY
HALL

LIVING RM.
17^0 x 13^0

STORAGE

STOR.

AIR
COND.

LAUNDRY
W.R.

UP

UNEXCAVATED

GARAGE
11^6 x 26^4

FAMILY RM.
11^6 x 16^0

UP

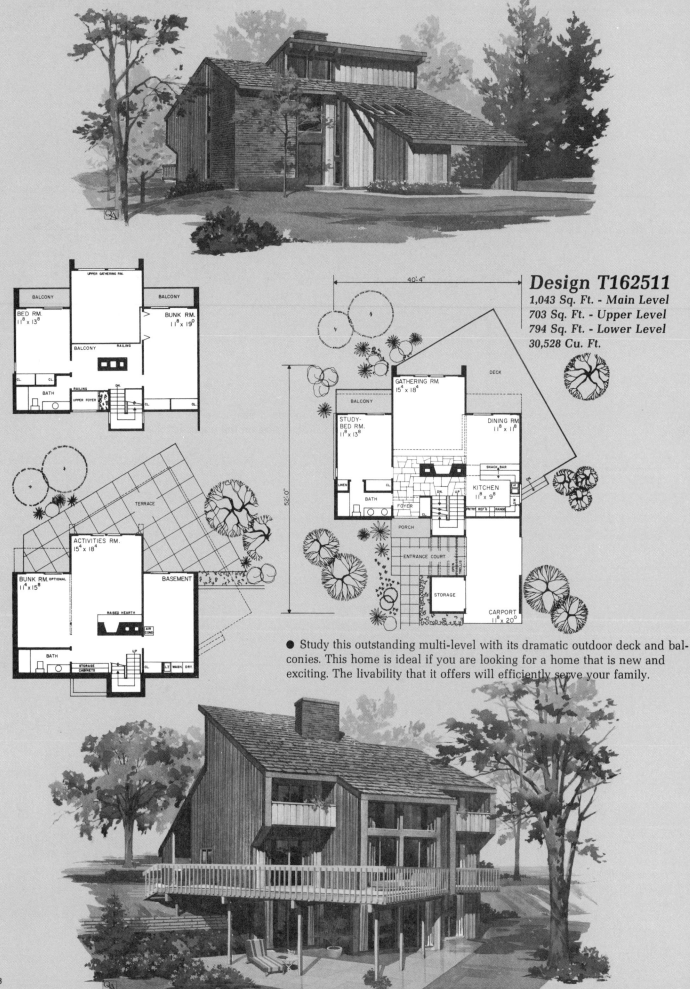

UPPER GATHERING RM.

BALCONY

BALCONY

BED RM.
11⁸ x 13⁸

BUNK RM.
11⁸ x 19⁰

BALCONY   RAILING

CL.   CL.

BATH

RAILING

UPPER FOYER   DN.

CL.   CL.

Design T162511

1,043 Sq. Ft. - Main Level
703 Sq. Ft. - Upper Level
794 Sq. Ft. - Lower Level
30,528 Cu. Ft.

40'-4"

52'-0"

DECK

GATHERING RM.
15⁴ x 18⁴

BALCONY

STUDY-
BED RM.
11⁸ x 13⁸

DINING RM.
11⁸ x 11⁸

SNACK BAR

KITCHEN
11⁸ x 9⁸

LINEN   CL.

BATH   DN.   UP

FOYER   ENTRY REF'G RANGE

CL.

PORCH

ENTRANCE COURT

STORAGE

CARPORT
11⁸ x 20⁰

TERRACE

ACTIVITIES RM.
15⁴ x 18⁴

BUNK RM. OPTIONAL
11⁴ x 15⁸

BASEMENT

RAISED HEARTH

AIR
COND.

BATH

UP

STORAGE
CABINETS

CL.   L.T. WASH. DRY.

● Study this outstanding multi-level with its dramatic outdoor deck and balconies. This home is ideal if you are looking for a home that is new and exciting. The livability that it offers will efficiently serve your family.

Design T162937 1,096 Sq. Ft. - Main Level
1,104 Sq. Ft. - Lower Level; 1,115 Sq. Ft. - Upper Level; 38,440 Cu. Ft.

● This contemporary multi-level home features an extended rear balcony that covers a rear patio, plus a master bedroom suite, complete with whirlpool and raised-hearth pass-thru. Two other bedrooms and a second bath are on the upper level.

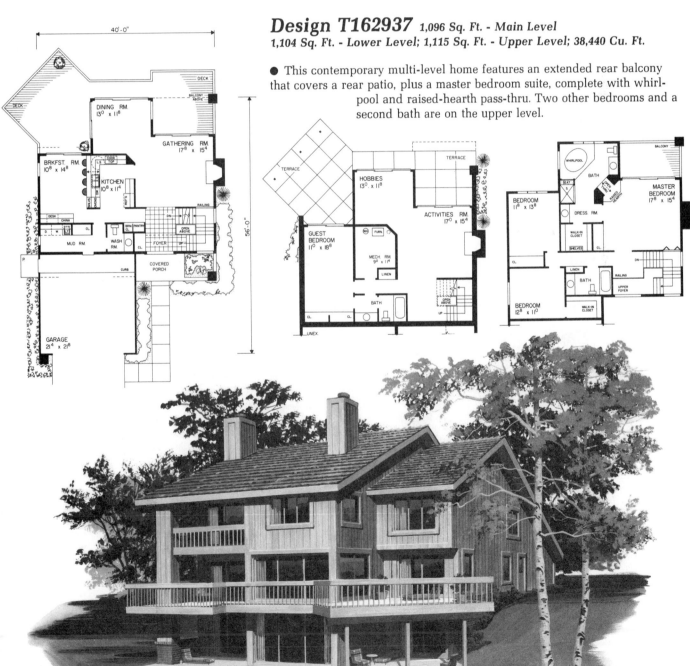

Design T162334

1,694 Sq. Ft. - Upper Level
1,020 Sq. Ft. - Lower Level; 34,259 Cu. Ft.

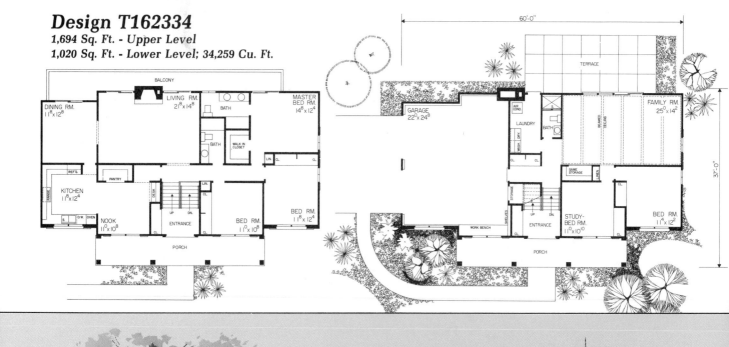

Design T162788

1,795 Sq. Ft. - Upper Level
866 Sq. Ft. - Lower Level; 34,230 Cu. Ft.

Design T161842 1,747 Sq. Ft. - Upper Level; 937 Sq. Ft. - Lower Level; 27,212 Cu. Ft.

Lower Level floor plan labels:

- UP
- COVERED TERRACE
- WORK SHOP STORAGE
- FAMILY RM. 31⁸x13⁰
- CURB
- STORAGEWALL
- RAISED HEARTH
- STOR.
- AIR COND.
- CL.
- GARAGE 27⁴x27⁴
- DN.
- UP
- ENTRY
- W.R.
- W
- D
- LAUNDRY
- STOR
- STOR
- STUDY-BED RM. 11⁴x11⁴
- P.

Upper Level floor plan labels:

- 60'-10"
- RAILING
- DN.
- DECK
- BALCONY
- GLASS GABLE
- MASTER BED RM. 15⁴x13⁶
- CL.
- CL.
- DRESS. RM.
- VANITY
- BATH
- VANITY
- BATH
- LIVING RM. 20⁰x13⁰
- SLOPED CEIL'G
- SLOPED CEIL'G
- DINING RM. 11⁸x13⁶
- 3' HI CHINA
- SLOPED CEIL'G
- RAISED HEARTH
- 7' HI WALL
- GLASS GABLE
- 28'-10"
- SLOPED CEIL'G
- BAR-B-Q
- PANTRY
- REF'S.
- LIN.
- CL.
- BED RM. 11⁸x13⁶
- BED RM. 10⁸x10⁰
- CL.
- DN.
- UP
- CL.
- 7' HI CHINA
- ENTRY
- BREAKFAST 12⁸x11⁶
- SNACKS
- RANGE
- DESK
- KIT. 11⁰x13⁶
- P.

281

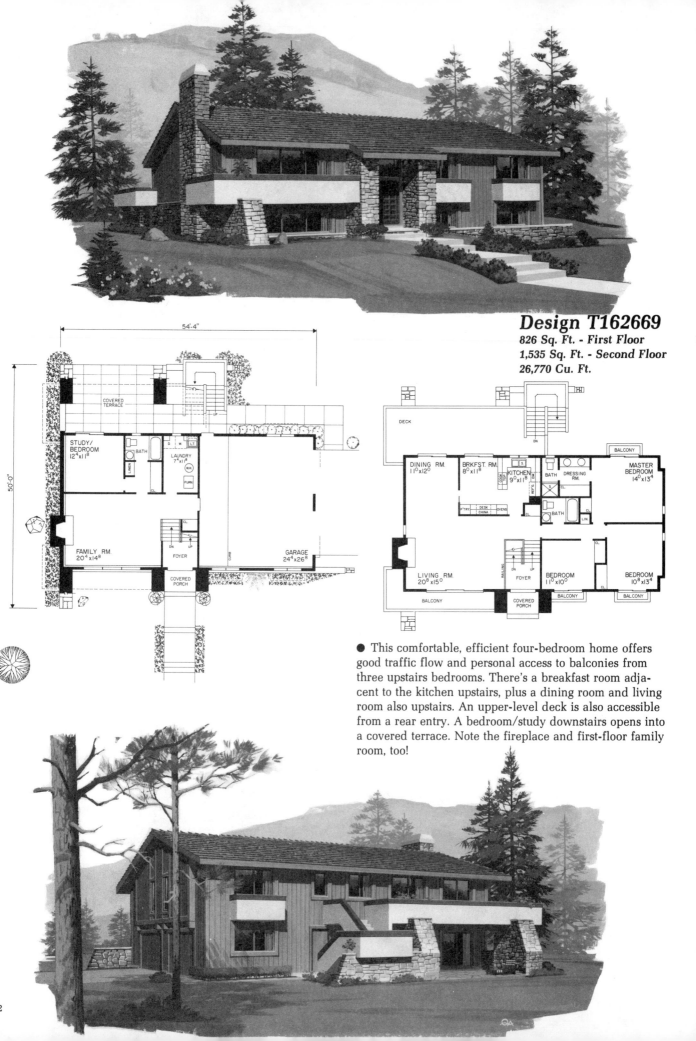

Design T162669

826 Sq. Ft. - First Floor
1,535 Sq. Ft. - Second Floor
26,770 Cu. Ft.

● This comfortable, efficient four-bedroom home offers good traffic flow and personal access to balconies from three upstairs bedrooms. There's a breakfast room adjacent to the kitchen upstairs, plus a dining room and living room also upstairs. An upper-level deck is also accessible from a rear entry. A bedroom/study downstairs opens into a covered terrace. Note the fireplace and first-floor family room, too!

Design T162842

6 Sq. Ft. - Entrance Level; 1,040 Sq. Ft. - Upper Level
22 Sq. Ft. - Lower Level; 25,630 Cu. Ft.

BALCONY

MASTER BEDROOM 12⁸ x 15⁰

BEDROOM 11⁰ x 11⁶

BEDROOM 14⁸ x 11⁶

CL.

CL.

LIN.

CL.

CL.

SHLVS

BATH

DN

OPEN

WALK-IN CLOSET

BATH

BEDROOM 11⁴ x 9²

● This narrow, 42 foot width, house can be built on a narrow lot to cut down overall costs. Yet its dramatic appeal surely is worth a million. The projecting front garage creates a pleasing curved drive. One enters this house through the covered porch to the entrance level foyer. At this point the stairs lead down to the living area consisting of formal living room, family room, kitchen and dining area then up the stairs to the four bedroom-two bath sleeping area. The indoor-outdoor living relationship at the rear is outstanding.

42'-0"

TERRACE

FAMILY RM. 12⁰ x 11⁶

DINING RM. 11⁰ x 11⁶

LIVING RM. 14⁰ x 22¹⁰

THRU FIREPLACE

SNACK BAR

PANTRY

STOR.

AIR COND.

RANGE

KITCHEN 12⁰ x 11⁴

PDR. RM.

REF.

UP

DN

58'-4"

COVERED PORCH

FOYER

CL.

LAUNDRY

DN

W

D

CURB

GARAGE 27⁴ x 20⁸

SLOPED CEILING

Design T162361 257 Sq. Ft. - Entry Level; 575 Sq. Ft. - Main Level; 896 Sq. Ft. - Upper Level
304 Sq. Ft. - Lower Level; 23,500 Cu. Ft.

Design T161324 682 Sq. Ft. - Main Level; 672 Sq. Ft. - Upper Level; 656 Sq. Ft. - Lower Level; 24,208 Cu. Ft.

Design T161292 640 Sq. Ft. - Main Level; 672 Sq. Ft. - Upper Level; 646 Sq. Ft. - Lower Level; 20,537 Cu. Ft.

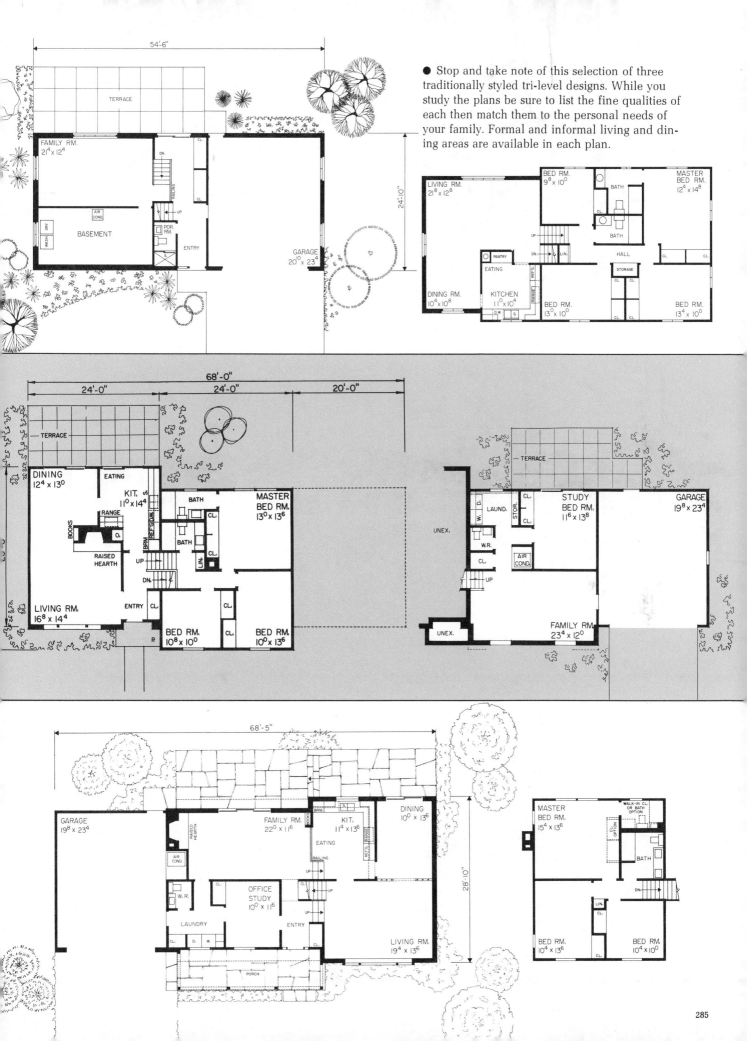

● Stop and take note of this selection of three traditionally styled tri-level designs. While you study the plans be sure to list the fine qualities of each then match them to the personal needs of your family. Formal and informal living and dining areas are available in each plan.

Plan 1 (top):

54'-6"
24'-10"

TERRACE

FAMILY RM.
21⁴ x 12⁴

AIR COND.
DRY
WASH
BASEMENT

DN
UP
RAILING
CL.
CL.
PDR. RM.
ENTRY

GARAGE
20¹⁰ x 23⁴

LIVING RM.
21⁸ x 12⁸

BED RM.
9⁸ x 10⁰

BATH

MASTER BED RM.
12⁴ x 14⁸

UP
DN
LIN.
REF'G.
PANTRY
EATING

HALL
STORAGE
CL.
CL.

DINING RM.
10⁴ x 10⁸

KITCHEN
11⁰ x 10⁴

D.W.
S.

BED RM.
13⁰ x 10⁰

CL.
CL.

BED RM.
13⁴ x 10⁰

Plan 2 (middle):

68'-0"
24'-0"
24'-0"
20'-0"

TERRACE

DINING
12⁴ x 13⁰
EATING

KIT.
11⁰ x 14⁴
RANGE
BOOKS
RAISED HEARTH

REF'G.
D.W.
BRM.

BATH
CL.
MASTER BED RM.
13⁰ x 13⁶
BATH
LIN.

UP
DN
ENTRY
CL.

LIVING RM.
16⁸ x 14⁴

BED RM.
10⁸ x 10⁰

CL.
CL.

BED RM.
10⁰ x 13⁶

TERRACE

W. D.
LAUND.
STOR.
CL.
CL.

STUDY BED RM.
11⁶ x 13⁸

GARAGE
19⁸ x 23⁴

UNEX.
W.R.
CL.
AIR COND.

UP

UNEX.

FAMILY RM.
23⁴ x 12⁰

Plan 3 (bottom):

68'-5"
28'-10"

GARAGE
19⁸ x 23⁴

RAISED HEARTH
AIR COND.
W.R.

FAMILY RM.
22⁰ x 11⁶
EATING
RAILING

KIT.
11⁴ x 13⁶
REF'G.
RANGE
BRM.

DINING
10⁰ x 13⁶

OFFICE STUDY
10⁰ x 11⁶

UP
UP
CL.
CL.

LAUNDRY
D.
W.
CL.
ENTRY
CL.

PORCH

LIVING RM.
19⁴ x 13⁶

MASTER BED RM.
15⁴ x 13⁶

WALK-IN CL. OR BATH OPTION

CLON OPTION

BATH

DN
LIN.
CL.

BED RM.
10⁴ x 13⁶

BED RM.
10⁴ x 10⁰

285

Design T161974 1,680 Sq. Ft. - Main Level; 1,344 Sq. Ft. - Lower Level; 34,186 Cu. Ft.

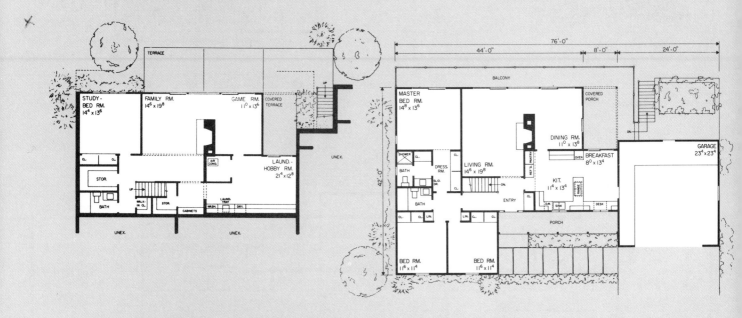

● You would never guess from looking at the front of this traditional design that it possessed such a strikingly different rear. From the front, you would guess that all of its livability is on one floor. Yet, just imagine the tremendous amount of livability that is added to the plan as a result of exposing the lower level - 1,344 square feet of it. Living in this hillside house will mean fun. Obviously, the most popular spot will be the balcony. Then again, maybe it could be the terrace adjacent to the family room. Both the terrace and the balcony have a covered area to provide protection against unfavorable weather. The interior of the plan also will serve the family with ease.

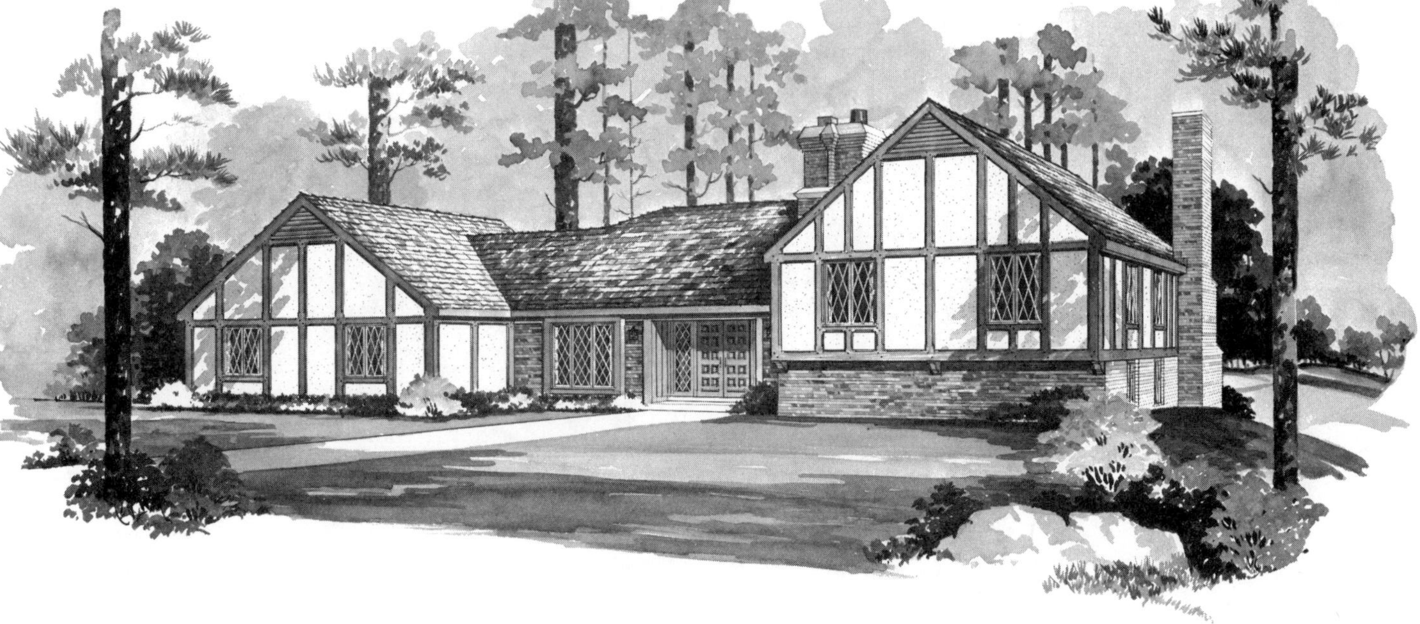

Design T162218

889 Sq. Ft. - Main Level; 960 Sq. Ft. - Upper Level
936 Sq. Ft. - Lower Level; 33,865 Cu. Ft.

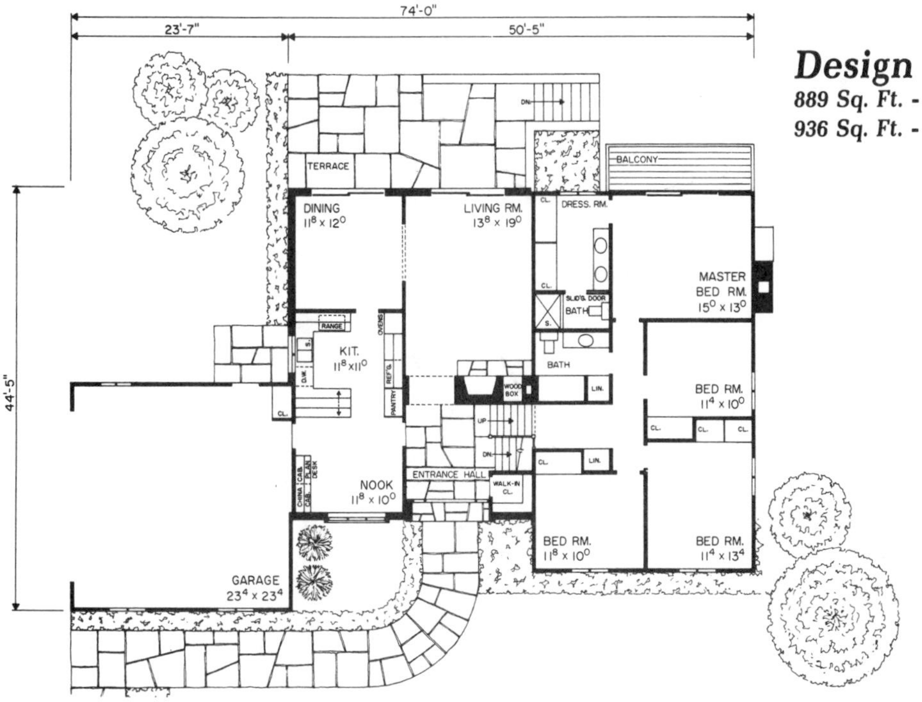

74'-0"
23'-7"
50'-5"
44'-5"
TERRACE
BALCONY
DN
DINING
11⁸ x 12⁰
LIVING RM.
13⁸ x 19⁰
DRESS. RM.
MASTER
BED RM.
15⁰ x 13⁰
KIT.
11⁸ x 11⁰
RANGE
OVENS
PANTRY
BATH
BED RM.
11⁴ x 10⁰
WOOD BOX
LIN.
UP
DN
ENTRANCE HALL
WALK-IN CL.
NOOK
11⁸ x 10⁰
DESK
GARAGE
23⁴ x 23⁴
BED RM.
11⁸ x 10⁰
BED RM.
11⁴ x 13⁴

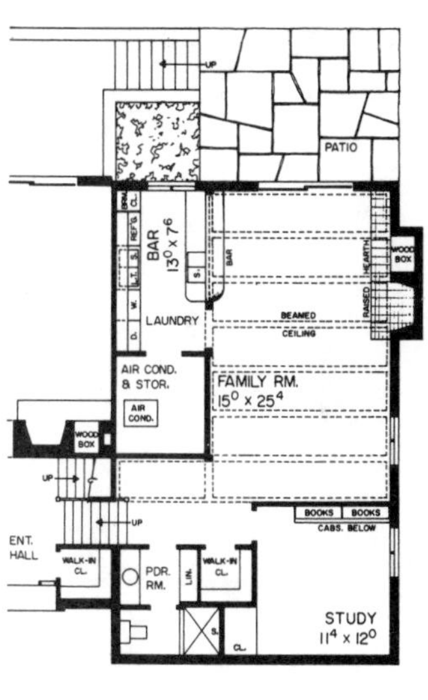

UP
PATIO
BAR
13⁰ x 7⁶
LAUNDRY
BEAMED CEILING
HEARTH
WOOD BOX
AIR COND. & STOR.
FAMILY RM.
15⁰ x 25⁴
WOOD BOX
ENT. HALL
BOOKS
BOOKS
CABS. BELOW
WALK-IN CL.
PDR. RM.
LIN.
WALK-IN CL.
STUDY
11⁴ x 12⁰

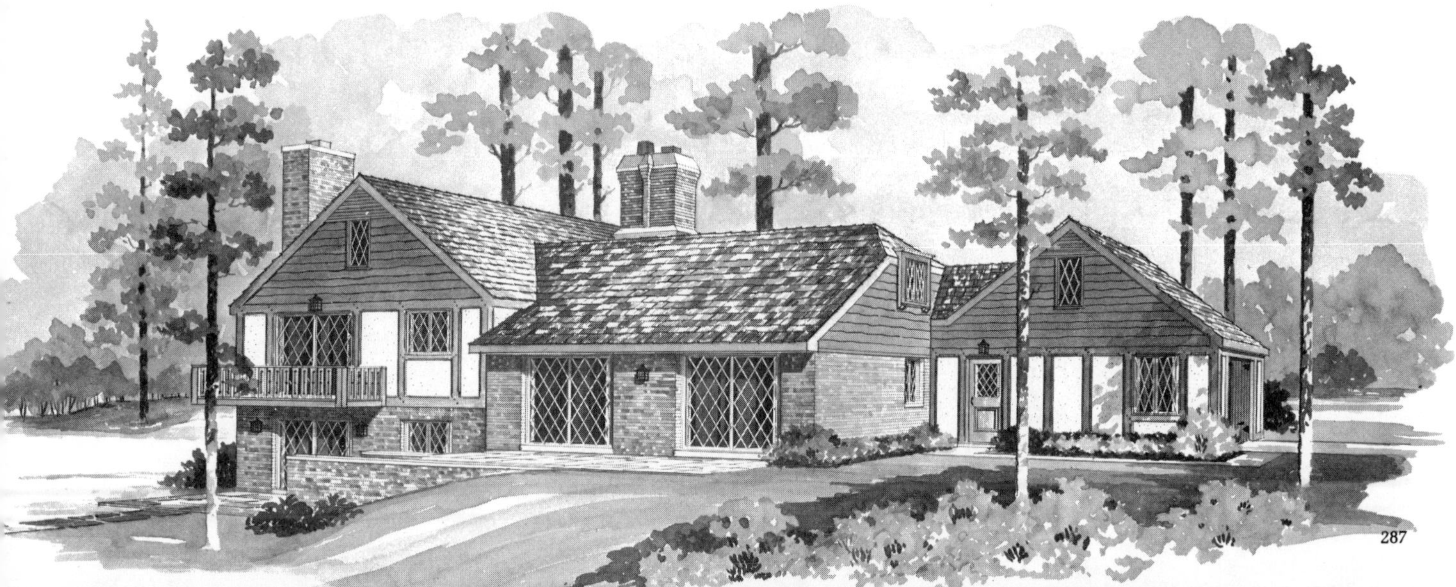

Design T162758

1,143 Sq. Ft. - Main Level
792 Sq. Ft. - Upper Level
770 Sq. Ft. - Lower Level
43,085 Cu. Ft.

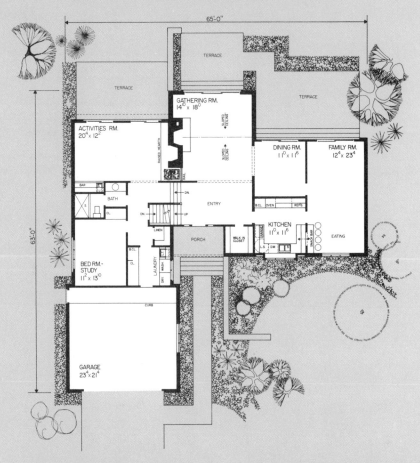

● An outstanding Tudor with three levels of exceptional livability, plus a basement. A careful study of the exterior reveals many delightful architectural details which give this home a character of its own. Notice the appealing recessed front entrance. Observe the overhanging roof with the exposed rafters. Don't miss the window treatment, the use of stucco and simulated beams, the masses of brick and the stylish chimney. Inside, the living potential is unsurpassed. Imagine, there are three living areas - the gathering, family and activities rooms. Having a snack bar, informal eating area and dining room, eating patterns can be flexible. In addition to the three bedrooms, two-bath upper level, there is a fourth bedroom with adjacent bath on the lower level.

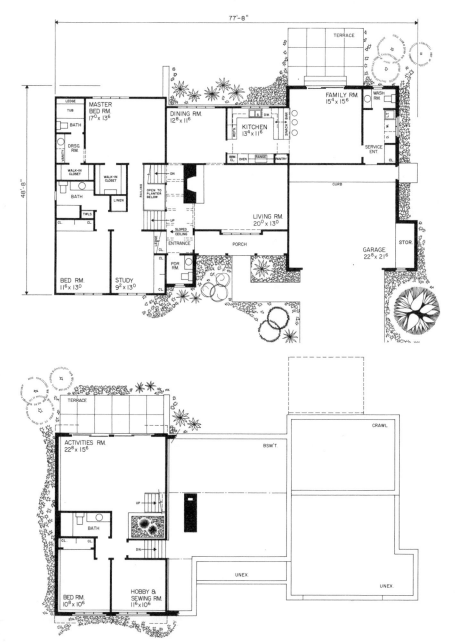

Design T162773

1,157 Sq. Ft. - Main Level
950 Sq. Ft. - Upper Level
912 Sq. Ft. - Lower Level
44,354 Cu. Ft.

● Here is another exquisitely styled Tudor tri-level designed to serve its happy occupants for many years. The contrasting use of material surely makes the exterior eye-catching. Another outstanding feature will be the covered front porch. A delightful way to enter this home. Many fine features also will be found inside this design. Formal living and dining room, U-shaped kitchen with snack bar and family room find themselves located on the main level. Two of the three bedrooms are on the upper level with two baths. Activities room, third bedroom and hobby/ sewing room are on the lower level. Notice the built-in planter on the lower level which is visible from the other two levels. A powder room and a wash room both are on the main level. A study is on the upper level which is a great place for a quiet retreat. The basement will be convenient for the storage of any bulk items.

Design T161882

800 Sq. Ft. - Main Level
864 Sq. Ft. - Upper Level
344 Sq. Ft. - Lower Level
28,600 Cu. Ft.

● Four level livability. And what livability it will be! This home will be most economical to build. As the house begins to take form you'll appreciate even more all the livable space you and your family will enjoy. List features that appeal to you.

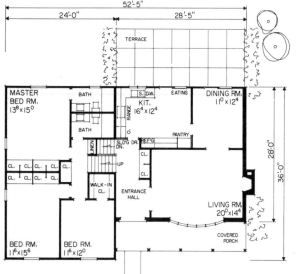

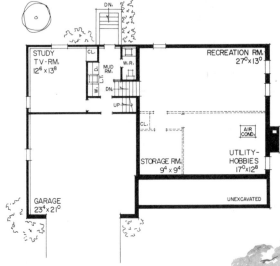

Design T161981

784 Sq. Ft. - Main Level
912 Sq. Ft. - Upper Level
336 Sq. Ft. - Lower Level
26,618 Cu. Ft.

● This four bedroom design is ideal for those who have a restricted building budget or a relatively narrow building site. A fireplace is featured in both the formal living room and the beamed ceilinged family room.

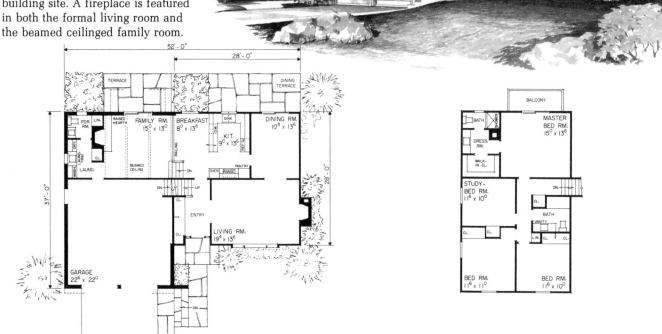

Design T162125

728 Sq. Ft. - Main Level
672 Sq. Ft. - Upper Level
656 Sq. Ft. - Lower Level
28,315 Cu. Ft.

● This four level traditional home has a long list of features to recommend it. Inside, the livability is outstanding for such a modest home. There are such highlights as the fireplace, the laundry and the sliding glass doors.

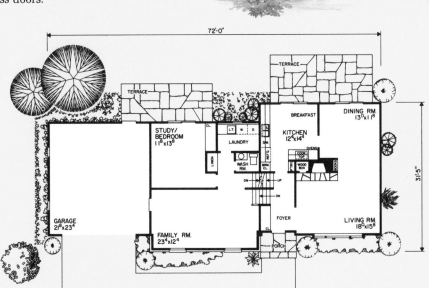

Design T161770

636 Sq. Ft. - Main Level
672 Sq. Ft. - Upper Level
528 Sq. Ft. - Lower Level
19,980 Cu. Ft.

● Charming? It certainly is. And with good reason, too. This delightfully proportioned split level is highlighted by fine window treatment, interesting roof lines, an attractive use of materials and an inviting front entrance.

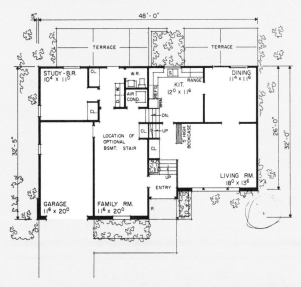

● This multi-level design will be ideal on a sloping site, both in the front and the rear of the house. The contemporary exterior is made up of vertical wood siding. The sloping roofline adds to the exterior appeal and creates a sloped ceiling in the formal living and dining rooms. An attractive bay window highlights the living room as will sliding glass doors in the dining room. The U-shaped kitchen and breakfast room also are located on this main level. The lower level houses the family room, wash room, laundry and access to the two-car garage. All of the sleeping facilities will be found on the upper level: three bedrooms and an exceptional master bedroom suite. Note two fireplaces, island range, two leveled terraces, covered porch, two balconies, etc.

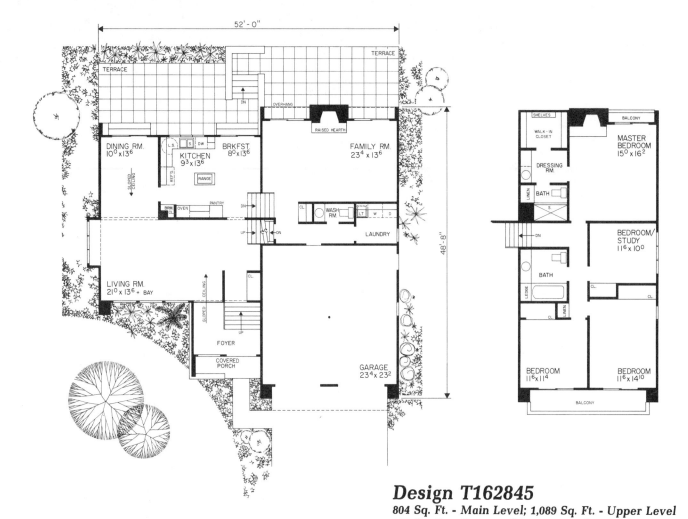

Design T162845
804 Sq. Ft. - Main Level; 1,089 Sq. Ft. - Upper Level
619 Sq. Ft. - Foyer and Lower Level; 36,030 Cu. Ft.

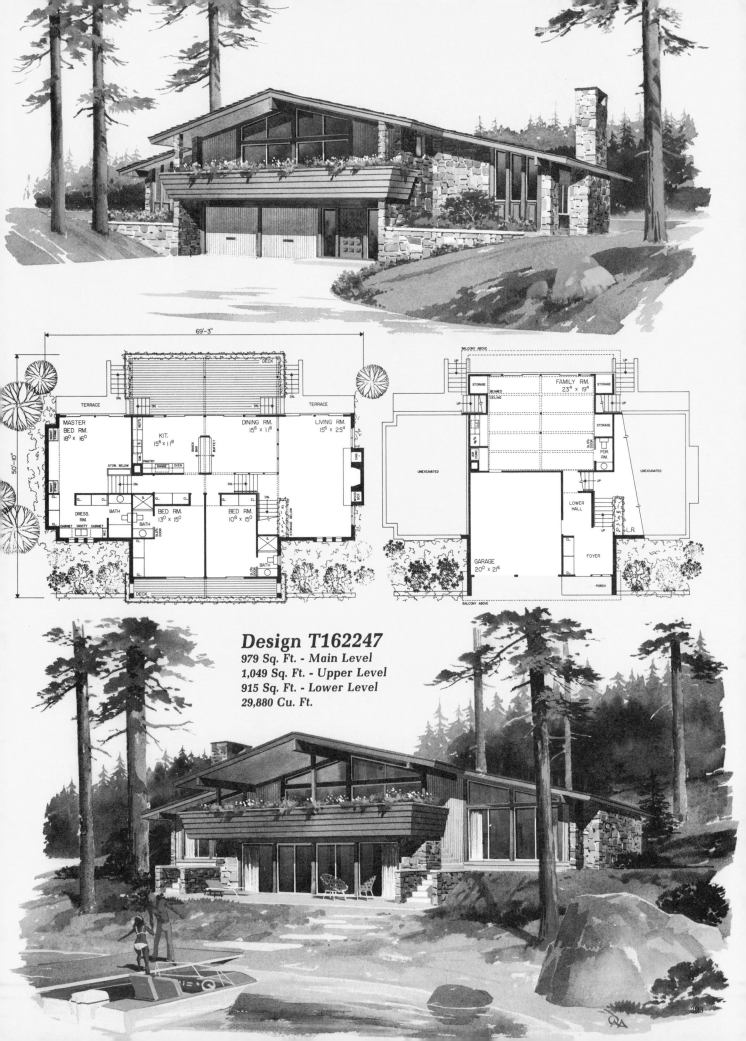

Design T162247
979 Sq. Ft. - Main Level
1,049 Sq. Ft. - Upper Level
915 Sq. Ft. - Lower Level
29,880 Cu. Ft.

69'-3"

50'-10"

TERRACE

DECK

DN.

MASTER
BED RM.
18⁰ x 16⁰

KIT.
15⁶ x 11⁸

DINING RM.
15⁶ x 11⁸

LIVING RM.
15⁶ x 25⁴

SNACK
BAR

BUFFET

RANGE OVEN

PANTRY

STOR. BELOW

STORAGE BELOW

DRESS.
RM.

BATH

BED RM.
13⁰ x 15⁰

BED RM.
10⁸ x 15⁰

CABINET VANITY CABINET

CL.

CL.

CL.

CL.

BATH

BATH

DN.

DN.

DN.

WOOD
BOX

DECK

BALCONY ABOVE

UP

UP

STORAGE

BEAMED
CEILING

FAMILY RM.
23⁴ x 19⁴

STORAGE

STORAGE

W/D

AIR
COND.

SLD'G.
DOOR

PDR.
RM.

UNEXCAVATED

UNEXCAVATED

UP

LOWER
HALL

UP

L.R.

GARAGE
20⁰ x 21⁶

CL.

FOYER

CL.

PORCH

BALCONY ABOVE

293

Design T162847 1,874 Sq. Ft. - Main Level
1,131 Sq. Ft. - Lower Level; 44,305 Cu. Ft.

● This is an exquisitely styled Tudor, hillside design, ready to serve its happy occupants for many years. The contrasting use of material surely makes the exterior eye-catching.

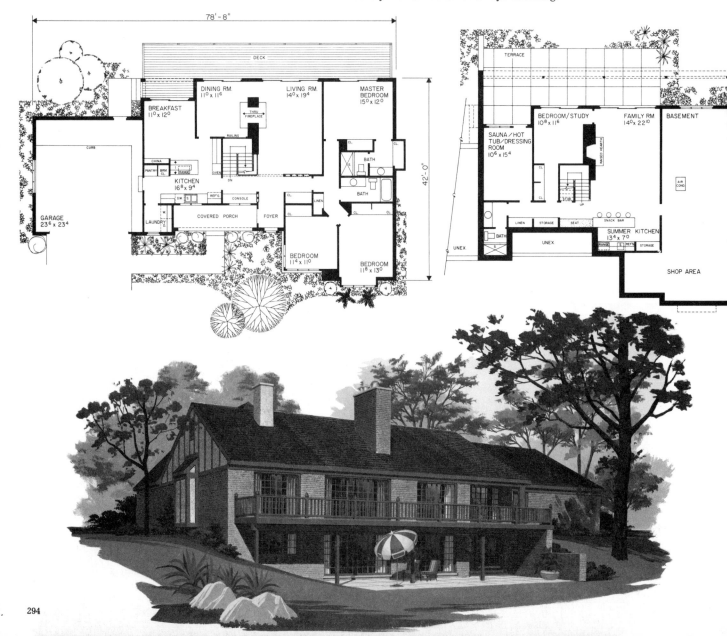

Design T162769 1,898 Sq. Ft. - Main Level
1,134 Sq. Ft. - Lower Level; 41,910 Cu. Ft.

● This traditional hillside design has fine architectural styling. It possesses all of the qualities that a great design should have to serve its occupants fully.

Main Level Floor Plan:

70'-8"

- DECK
- LIVING RM. 15⁰ x 20⁴
- DINING RM. 11⁶ x 12⁴
- NOOK 10⁰ x 10⁸
- LT. WASH. DRY.
- LAUNDRY
- DESK
- PANTRY
- OVEN
- RANGE
- SERV. ENT.
- SLOPED CEILING
- RAILING
- KITCHEN 13⁰ x 9⁸
- REFR.
- WASH RM.
- CURB
- GARAGE 23⁴ x 23⁴
- DW
- DN
- ENTRY
- PORCH
- BED RM.- SITTING RM. 11⁶ x 12⁰
- CL. CL.
- BATH
- VANITY
- WALK IN CLOSET
- BATH
- BED RM. 11⁶ x 14⁰
- MASTER BED RM. 15⁶ x 13⁰

54'-4"

Lower Level Floor Plan:

- TERRACE
- FAMILY RM. 14¹⁰ x 25⁴
- STUDY - BED RM. 11⁶ x 12⁰
- GUEST BED RM. 15⁰ x 11⁶
- RAISED HEARTH
- STOR.
- UP
- CL.
- BATH
- LINEN
- UNEX.
- AIR COND.
- BASEMENT

Design T161378 1,040 Sq. Ft. - Upper Level
1,040 Sq. Ft. - Lower Level; 19,624 Cu. Ft.

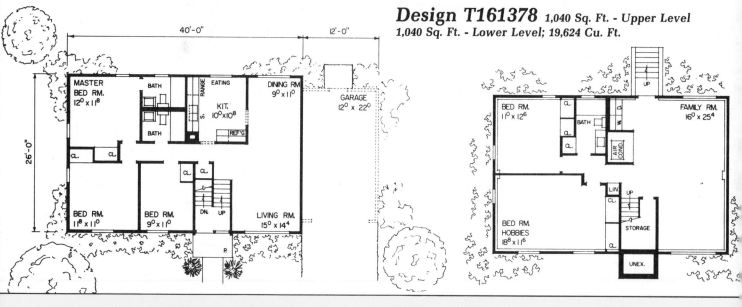

Design T161310 1,040 Sq. Ft. - Upper Level
694 Sq. Ft. - Lower Level; 17,755 Cu. Ft.

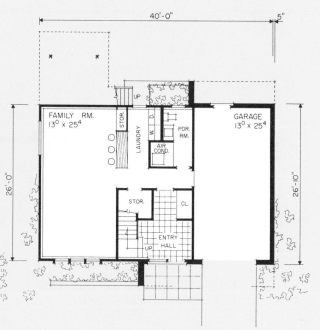

Design T161778
1,344 Sq. Ft. - Upper Level
768 Sq. Ft. - Lower Level; 22,266 Cu. Ft.

COVERED TERRACE   OPEN TERRACE

UP

STUDY - B.R.
11^0 x 12^6

BATH

LAUNDRY

AIR COND.

CL.

LIN.

W D

S.

STOR.

CL.

GARAGE
18^8 x 25^4

CL.

UP   DN.
ENTRY

FAMILY RM.
21^0 x 12^6

UP

48'-0"

DECK
20^0 x 10^0

DN.

DINING RM.
10^0 x 11^8

EATING

RANGE

KIT.
13^4 x 11^6

SINK

O D.W.

PANTRY

REF'G

BATH

S.

BATH

LIN.

CL.

MASTER
BED RM.
13^4 x 11^6

CL.   CL.   CL.

28'-0"

LIVING RM.
19^4 x 15^6

BOOKS

CL.   CL.

UP   DN.
ENTRY

BED RM.
11^0 x 10^0

BED RM.
10^0 x 13^0

UP

297

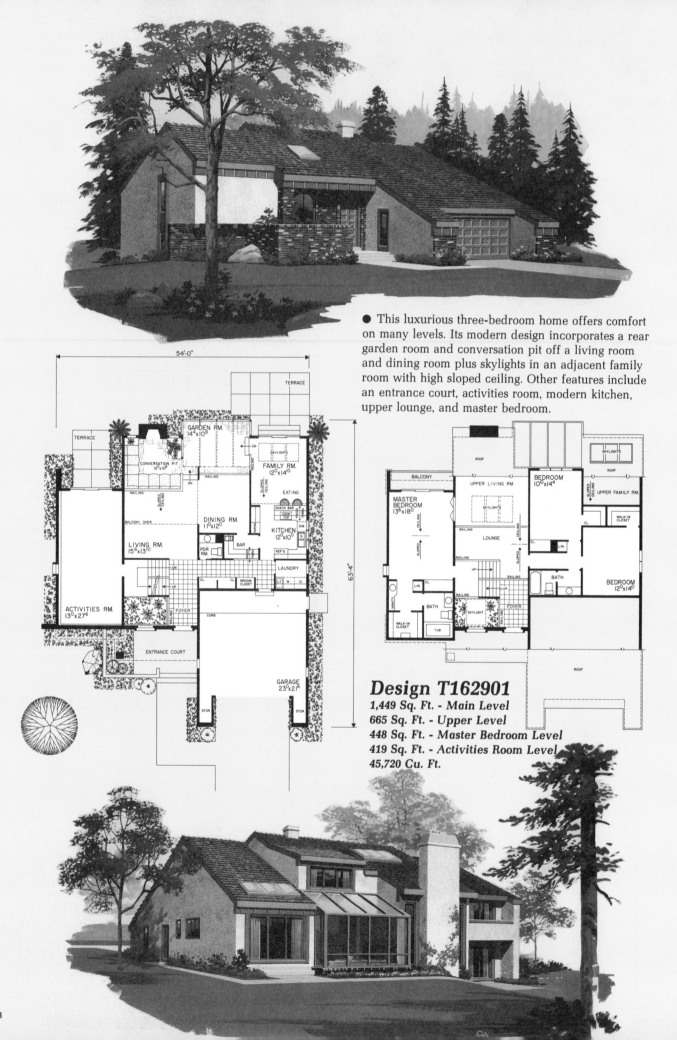

● This luxurious three-bedroom home offers comfort on many levels. Its modern design incorporates a rear garden room and conversation pit off a living room and dining room plus skylights in an adjacent family room with high sloped ceiling. Other features include an entrance court, activities room, modern kitchen, upper lounge, and master bedroom.

Design T162901

1,449 Sq. Ft. - Main Level
665 Sq. Ft. - Upper Level
448 Sq. Ft. - Master Bedroom Level
419 Sq. Ft. - Activities Room Level
45,720 Cu. Ft.

Design T162841 1,044 Sq. Ft. - Main Level
753 Sq. Ft. - Lower Level
851 Sq. Ft. - Upper Level; 30,785 Cu. Ft.

● This spacious tri-level with traditional stone exterior offers excellent comfort and zoning for the modern family. The rear opens to balconies and a deck that creates a covered patio below. A main floor gathering room is continued above with an upper gathering room. The lower level offers an activities room with raised hearth, in addition to an optional bunk room with bath. A modern kitchen on main level features a handy snack bar, in addition to a dining room. A study on main level could become an optional bedroom. The master bedroom is located on the upper level, along with a rectangular bunk room with its own balcony.

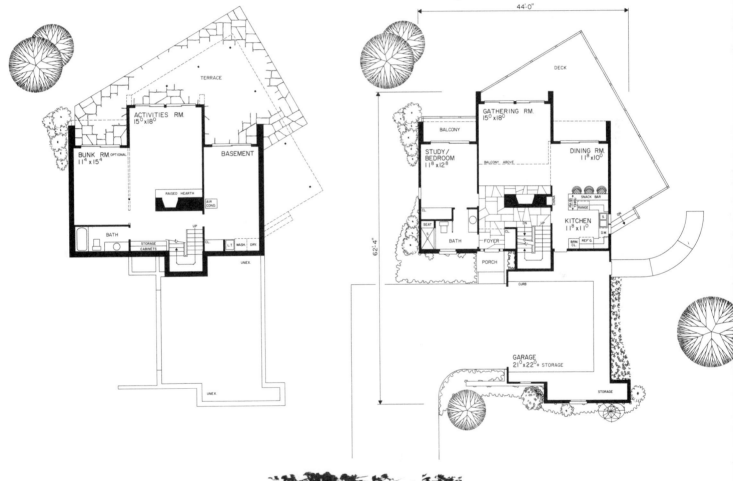

TERRACE

ACTIVITIES RM.
15⁰ x 18⁰

BASEMENT

BUNK RM. OPTIONAL
11⁴ x 15⁴

RAISED HEARTH

AIR COND.

BATH

STORAGE CABINETS

UP

L.T. WASH. DRY.

CL.

UNEX.

UNEX.

44'-0"

DECK

GATHERING RM.
15⁰ x 18⁰

BALCONY

STUDY / BEDROOM
11⁸ x 12⁸

BALCONY ABOVE

DINING RM.
11⁸ x 10⁰

SNACK BAR

RANGE

KITCHEN
11⁸ x 11⁰

S.

DW

62'-4"

CL.

SEAT

DN

UP

BATH

FOYER

BRM. CL.

REF'G.

PORCH

CURB

GARAGE
21⁰ x 22⁰ + STORAGE

STORAGE

BALCONY

UPPER GATHERING RM.

BALCONY

BEDROOM
11⁸ x 12⁸

RAILING

BUNK RM.
11⁸ x 18⁸

LOUNGE
15⁰ x 6⁰

LINEN

CL.

RAILING

RAILING

BATH

SEAT

DN

UPPER FOYER

CL.

CL.

Design T161112

686 Sq. Ft. - Main Level; 672 Sq. Ft. - Upper Level
336 Sq. Ft. - Lower Level; 19,132 Cu. Ft.

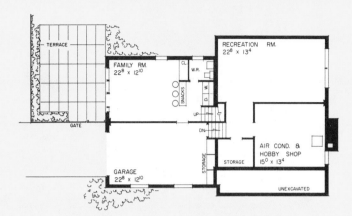

● Traditional tri-level living is guaranteed from this three bedroom design. Three floors of outstanding livability with a fourth level serving as additional recreational space or just use it for storage.

Design T161353

484 Sq. Ft. - Main Level; 624 Sq. Ft. - Upper Level
300 Sq. Ft. - Lower Level; 13,909 Cu. Ft.

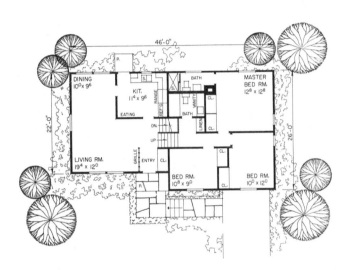

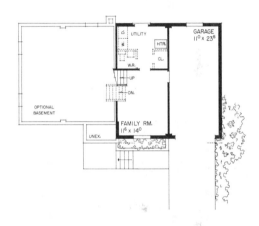

● This three bedroom contemporary is zoned for efficiency without a bit of wasted space. Note the two back-to-back baths, the separate dining room and the kitchen eating area. The lower level has a family room and the utility room.

Design T161386

880 Sq. Ft. - Upper Level
596 Sq. Ft. - Lower Level; 14,043 Cu. Ft.

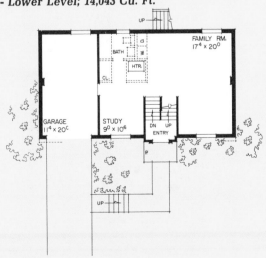

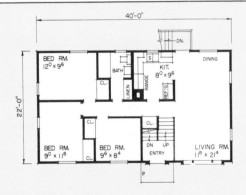

● This design features traditional exterior styling with a split foyer bi-level living interior. Owners of a bi-level design achieve a great amount of livability from an economical plan without sacrificing any of the fine qualities of a much larger and more expensive plan.

301

Design T162894
1,490 Sq. Ft. - Main Level
1,357 Sq. Ft. - Lower Level; 38,450 Cu. Ft.

● Contemporary, bi-level living will be enjoyed by all members of the family. Upon entering the foyer, complimented by skylights, stairs will lead you to the upper and lower levels. Up a few steps, you will find yourself in the large gathering room. The fireplace, sloped ceiling and the size of this room will make this a favorite spot. To the left is a study/bedroom with a full bath and walk-in closet. Notice the efficient kitchen and breakfast room with nearby wet bar. The lower level houses two bedrooms and a bath to one side; and a master bedroom suite to the other. Centered is a large activity room with raised-hearth fireplace. It will be enjoyed by all. Note - all of the rear rooms on both levels have easy access to the outdoors for excellent indoor-outdoor livability.

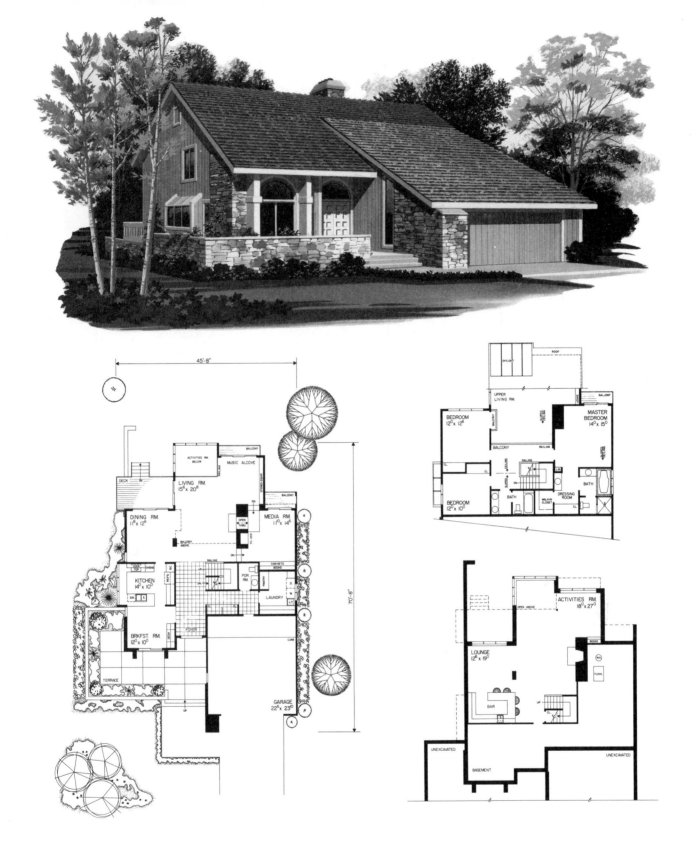

Design T162944 1,545 Sq. Ft. - Main Level; 977 Sq. Ft - Upper Level; 933 Sq. Ft. - Lower Level; 48,845 Cu. Ft.

● This eye-catching contemporary features three stacked levels of livability. And what livability it will truly be! The main level has a fine U-shaped kitchen which is flanked by the informal breakfast room and formal dining room. The living room will be dramatic, indeed. Its sloping ceiling extends through the upper level. It overlooks the lower level activities room and has wonderfully expansive window areas for full enjoyment of surrounding vistas. A two-way fireplace can be viewed from dining, living and media rooms. A sizable deck and two cozy balconies provide for flexible outdoor living. Don't miss the music alcove with its wall for stereo equipment. Upstairs, the balcony overlooks the living room. It serves as the connecting link for the three bedrooms. The lower level offers more cheerful livability with the huge activities room plus lounge area. Note bar, fireplace.

Design T161935 904 Sq. Ft. - Main Level; 864 Sq. Ft. - Upper Level; 840 Sq. Ft. - Lower Level; 26,745 Cu. Ft.

● If there was ever a design that looked a part of the ground it was built on, this particular multi-level looks just that. This design will adapt equally well to a flat or sloping site. There would be no question about the family's ability to adapt to what the interior has to offer. Everything is present to satisfy the family's desire to "live a little". Features include: a covered porch, balcony, two fire-places, extra study, family room with a beamed ceiling, complete laundry and a basement level for added recreational and storage space. Blueprints include non-basement details.

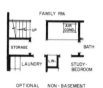

OPTIONAL NON-BASEMENT

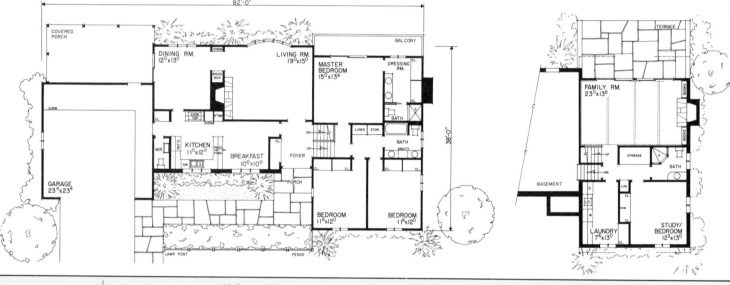

Design T162291 942 Sq. Ft. - Main Level
1,101 Sq. Ft. - Upper Level; 534 Sq. Ft. - Lower Level
40,932 Cu. Ft.

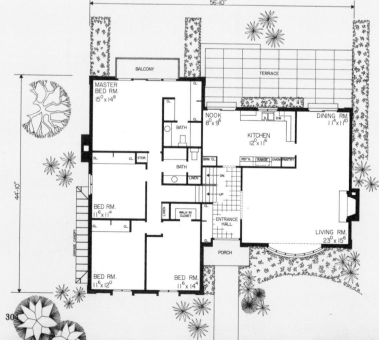

Design T161930 *947 Sq. Ft. - Main Level; 768 Sq. Ft. - Upper Level; 740 Sq. Ft. - Lower Level; 25,906 Cu. Ft.*

● The warmth of this inspiring Colonial adaptation of the split-level idea is not restricted to the exterior. Its homey charm is readily apparent upon stepping through the double front doors. The sunken living room and the beamed ceiling family room with its raised hearth fireplace will be cozy, indeed. The kitchen, powder room and closet, just inside the door from the garage, will be three added conveniences of this design that you should not overlook. There are three bedrooms on the upper level, while there is a fourth to be found on the lower level. Don't miss the big laundry and extra wash room.

Design T162143 *832 Sq. Ft. - Main Level; 864 Sq. Ft. - Upper Level; 864 Sq. Ft. - Lower Level; 27,473 Cu. Ft.*

● Here the Spanish Southwest comes to life in the form of an enchanting multi-level home. There is much to rave about. The architectural detailing is delightful, indeed. The entrance courtyard, the twin balconies and the roof treatment are particular-ly noteworthy. Functioning at the rear of the house are the covered patio and the balcony with its lower patio. Well zoned, the upper level has three bedrooms and two baths; the main level has its formal living and dining rooms to the rear and kitchen area looking onto the courtyard; the lower level features the family room, study and laundry. Be sure to notice the extra wash room and the third full bath. There are two fireplaces each with a raised hearth. A dramatic house wherever built!

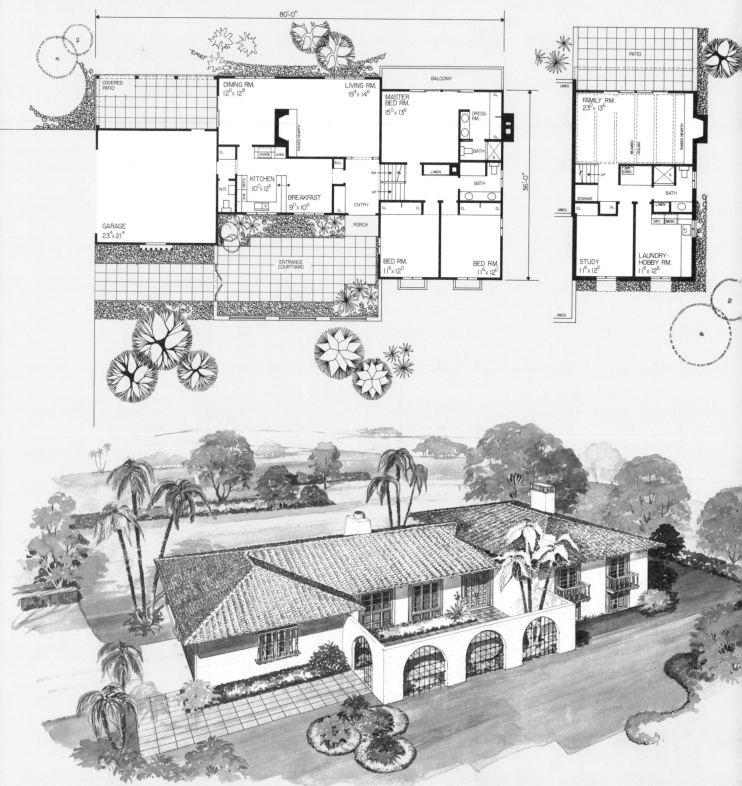

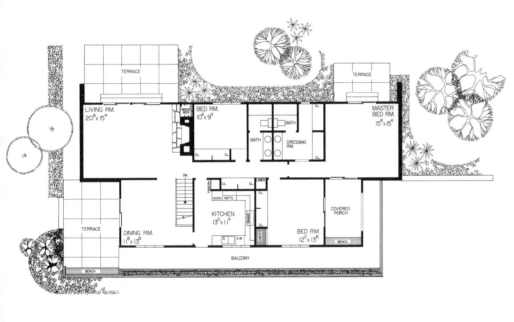

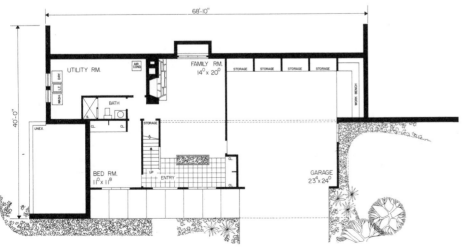

Design T162601
1,724 Sq. Ft. - Upper Level
986 Sq. Ft. - Lower Level
28,240 Cu. Ft.

● Surely it would be difficult to improve upon the refreshing appeal of this contemporary bi-level design. Built into a sloping site, its lower level has direct grade access at the rear. With four bedrooms and three full baths, the large family will be well-served. Each of the living areas has a fireplace. The family dining room is but a step or two from the side terrace for convenient, outdoor dining. The kitchen is handy to the balcony for ease of caring for those potted plants. Worthy of particular note, is the covered porch which functions with two of the upper level bedrooms. Don't miss the oversized garage with all those storage facilities and the work bench. While the blueprints call for an exterior of stone and stucco, you may wish to substitute your own choice of materials.

Design T162868

1,203 Sq. Ft. - Upper Level
1,317 Sq. Ft. - Lower Level; 29,595 Cu. Ft.

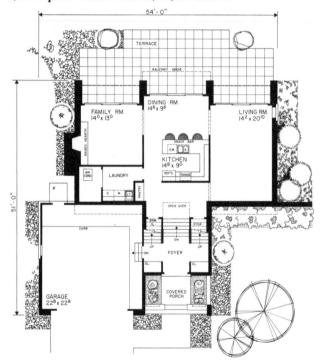

Common Living Areas – Sleeping Privacy

● Two couples sharing the expense of a house has got to be ideal and, of course, economical. The occupants of this house could do just that. The lower level, housing the kitchen, dining room, family and living rooms and the laundry facilities, is the common area to be shared by both couples. Centrally located, the kitchen and dining room act as a space divider to the living and family rooms so both couples can enjoy privacy.

Separate stairways lead to the upper level from the skylit foyer. Each private area has two bedrooms, a dressing room and a full bath. Individual entrances can be locked for additional privacy. Sliding glass doors are in each of the rear rooms on both levels so the outdoors can be enjoyed to its fullest.

Design T162827 1,618 Sq. Ft. - Upper Level
1,458 Sq. Ft. - Lower Level; 41,370 Cu. Ft.

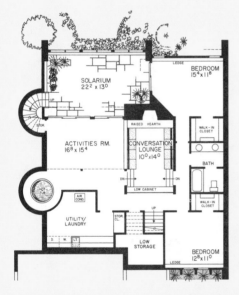

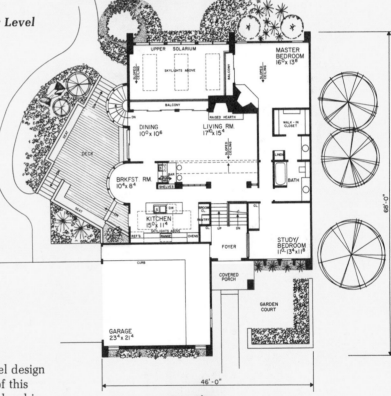

● The towering, two-story solarium in this bi-level design is its key to energy savings. Study the efficiency of this floor plan. The conversation lounge on the lower level is a unique focal point.

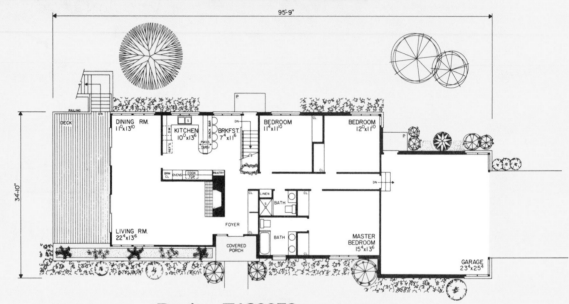

Design T162272

1,731 Sq. Ft. - Main Level
672 Sq. Ft. - Lower Level; 27,802 Cu. Ft.

● Certainly not a huge house. But one, nevertheless, that is long on livability and one that surely will be fun to live in. With its wide-overhanging hip roof, this unadorned facade is the picture of simplicity. As such, it has a quiet appeal all its own. The living-dining area is one of the focal points of the plan. It is wonderfully spacious. The large glass areas and the accessibility, through sliding glass doors, of the outdoor balcony are fine features. For recreation, there is the lower level area which opens onto a large terrace covered by the balcony above.

Design T162725

1,212 Sq. Ft. - Main Level
996 Sq. Ft. - Lower Level
25,120 Cu. Ft.

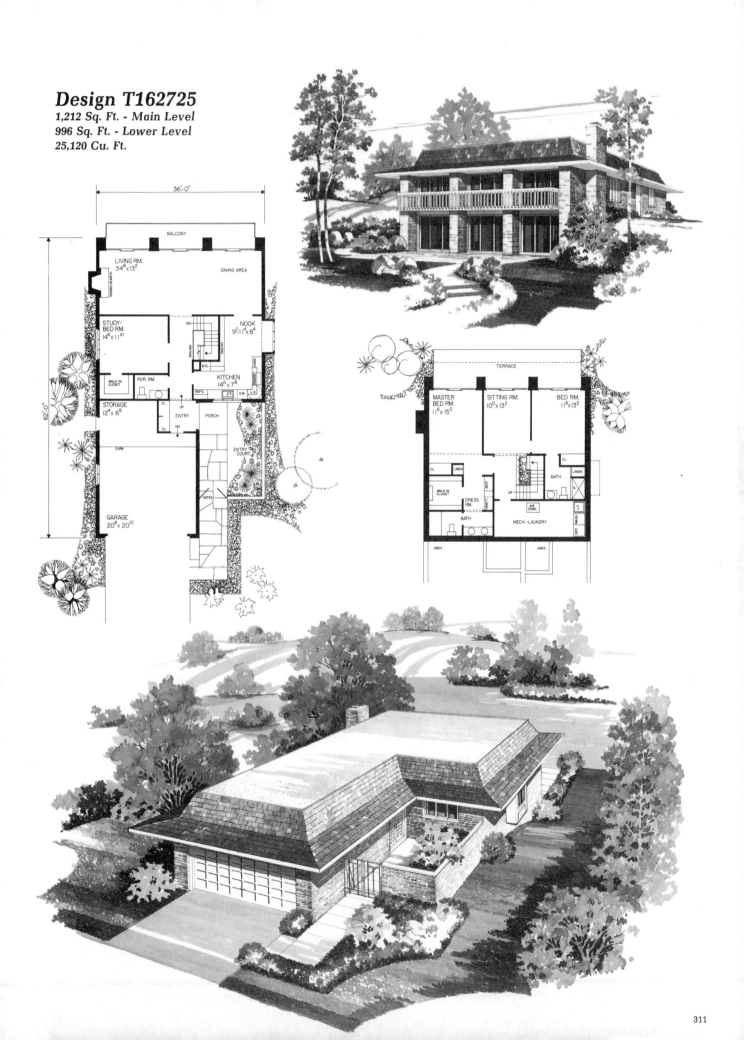

Main Level floor plan:

36'-0"

62'-0"

BALCONY

LIVING RM.
34⁸ x 13²

DINING AREA

RAISED HEARTH

STUDY-
BED RM.
14⁶ x 11¹⁰

DN.

RAILING

PANTRY

NOOK
9⁰ x 11⁴ x 8⁴

OVEN

RANGE

B.CL.

WALK IN
CLOSET

PDR. RM.

REF.

KITCHEN
14⁶ x 7⁸

STORAGE
12⁴ x 6⁸

CL.

UP

ENTRY

PORCH

CL.

DN.

CURB

ENTRY
COURT

GARAGE
20⁸ x 20¹⁰

GATES

Lower Level floor plan:

TERRACE

MASTER
BED RM.
11⁶ x 15⁰

SITTING RM.
10⁰ x 13²

BED RM.
11⁶ x 13²

CL.

LINEN

CL.

LINEN

BATH

WALK IN
CLOSET

SEAT

UP

DRESS.
RM.

VANITY

AIR
COND.

BATH

MECH.-LAUNDRY

DRY.

WASH.

L.T.

UNEX.

UNEX.

311

When You're Ready to Order . . .

Let Us Show You Our Blueprint Package.

Building a home? Planning a home? Our Blueprint Package contains nearly everything you need to get the job done right, whether you're working on your own or with help from an architect, designer, builder or subcontractors. Each Blueprint Package is the result of many hours of work by licensed architects or professional designers.

QUALITY

Hundreds of hours of painstaking effort have gone into the development of your blueprint set. Each home has been quality-checked by professionals to insure accuracy and buildability.

VALUE

Because we sell in volume, you can buy professional-quality blueprints at a fraction of their development cost. With Home Planners, your dream home design costs only a few hundred dollars, not the thousands of dollars that custom architects charge.

SERVICE

Once you've chosen your favorite home plan, we stand ready to serve you with knowledgeable sales people and prompt, efficient service. We ship most orders within 48 hours of receipt and stand behind every set of blueprints we sell.

SATISFACTION

We have been in business since 1946 and have shipped over 2.5 million blueprints to home builders just like you. Nearly 50 years of service and hundreds of thousands of satisfied customers are your guarantee that Home Planners can do the job for you.

ORDER TOLL FREE
1-800-521-6797

After you've studied our Blueprint Package and Important Extras on the following pages, simply mail the accompanying order form on page 317 or call Toll Free on our Blueprint Hotline: 1-800-521-6797. We're ready and eager to serve you.

Each set of blueprints is an interrelated collection of floor plans, interior and exterior elevations, dimensions, cross-sections, diagrams and notations showing precisely how your house is to be constructed.

Here's what you get:

Frontal Sheet
This artist's sketch of the exterior of the house, done in realistic perspective, gives you an idea of how the house will look when built and landscaped. Large ink-line floor plans show all levels of the house and provide a quick overview of your new home's livability, as well as a handy reference for studying furniture placement.

Foundation Plan
Drawn to 1/4-inch scale, this sheet shows the complete foundation layout including support

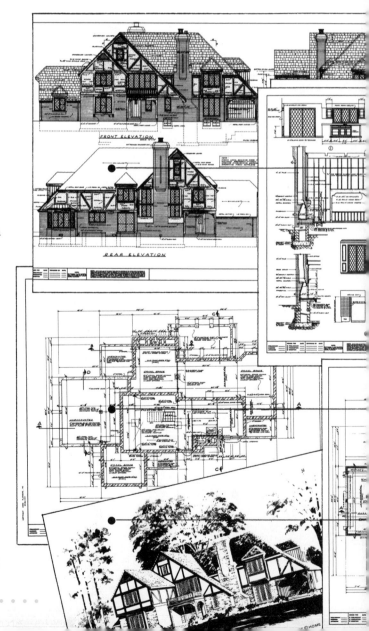

walls, excavated and unexcavated areas, if any, and foundation notes. If slab construction rather than basement, the plan shows footings and details for a monolithic slab. This page, or another in the set, also includes a sample plot plan for locating your house on a building site.

Detailed Floor Plans

Complete in 1/4-inch scale, these plans show the layout of each floor of the house. All rooms and interior spaces are carefully dimensioned and keys are provided for cross-section details given later in the plans. The positions of all electrical outlets and switches are clearly shown.

House Cross-Sections

Large-scale views, normally drawn at 3/8-inch equals 1 foot, show sections or cut-aways of the foundation, interior walls, exterior walls,

floors, stairways and roof details. Additional cross-sections are given to show important changes in floor, ceiling or roof heights or the relationship of one level to another. Extremely valuable for construction, these sections show exactly how the various parts of the house fit together.

Interior Elevations

These large-scale drawings show the design and placement of kitchen and bathroom cabinets, laundry areas, fireplaces, bookcases and other built-ins. Little "extras," such as mantelpiece and wainscoting drawings, plus moulding sections, provide details that give your home that custom touch.

Exterior Elevations

Drawings in 1/4-inch scale show the front, rear and sides of your house and give necessary notes on exterior materials and finishes. Particular attention is given to cornice detail, brick and stone accents or other finish items that make your home distinctive.

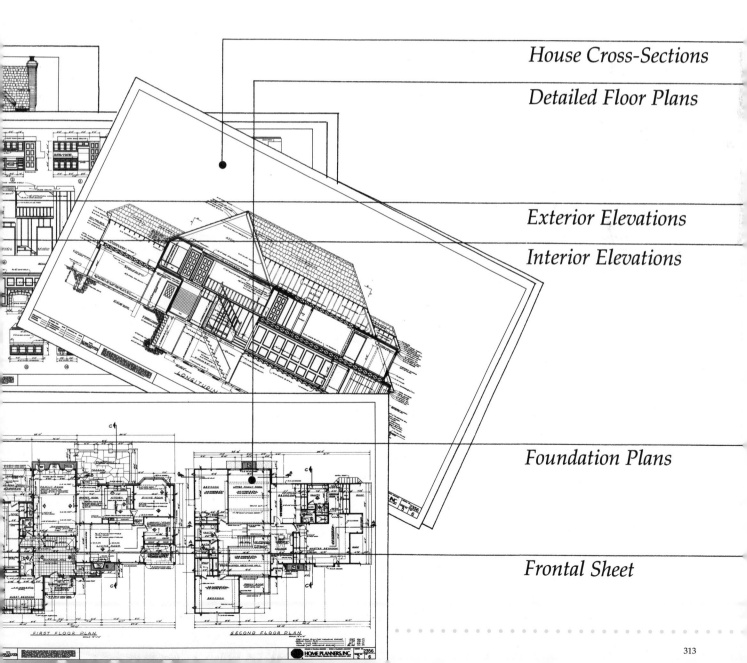

House Cross-Sections

Detailed Floor Plans

Exterior Elevations

Interior Elevations

Foundation Plans

Frontal Sheet

Important Extras To Do The Job Right!

Introducing six important planning and construction aids developed by our professionals to help you succeed in your home-building project.

To Order, Call Toll Free 1-800-521-6797

To add these important extras to your Blueprint Package, simply indicate your choices on the order form on page 317 — or call us Toll Free 1-800-521-6797 and we'll tell you more about these exciting products.

MATERIALS LIST

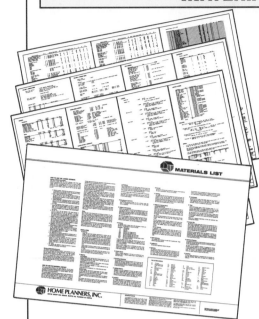

For many of the designs in our portfolio, we offer a customized materials take-off that is invaluable in planning and estimating the cost of your new home. This comprehensive list outlines the quantity, type and size of material needed to build your house (with the exception of mechanical system items). Included are:

- framing lumber
- roofing and sheet metal
- windows and doors
- exterior sheathing material and trim
- masonry, veneer and fireplace materials
- tile and flooring materials
- kitchen and bath cabinetry
- interior sheathing and trim
- rough and finish hardware
- many more items

(Note: Because of differing local codes, building methods, and availability of materials, our Materials Lists do not include mechanical materials. To obtain necessary take-offs and recommendations, consult heating, plumbing and electrical contractors. Materials Lists are not sold separately from the Blueprint Package.)

This handy list helps you or your builder cost out materials and serves as a ready reference sheet when you're compiling bids. It also provides a cross-check against the materials specified by your builder and helps coordinate the substitution of items you may need to meet local codes.

SPECIFICATION OUTLINE

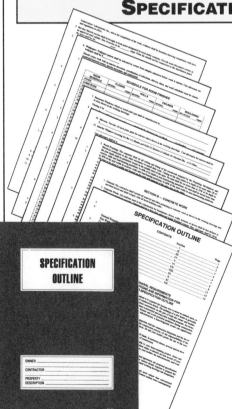

This valuable 16-page document is critical to building your house correctly. Designed to be filled in by you or your builder, this booklet lists 166 stages or items crucial to the building process.

For the layman, it provides a comprehensive review of the construction process and helps in making the specific choices of materials, models and processes. For the builder, it serves as a guide to preparing a building quotation and forms the basis for the construction program.

Designed primarily as a reference for the homeowner, this Specification Outline can become a legally binding document. Once it is filled out and agreed upon by owner and builder, it becomes a complete Project Specification.

When combined with the blueprints, a signed contract and schedule, the Specification Outline becomes a legal document and record for the building of your home. Many home builders find it useful to order two of these outlines—one as a worksheet in formulating the specifications and another to be carefully completed as a legal document.

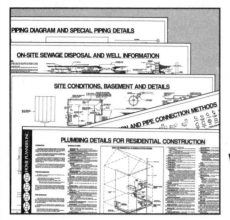
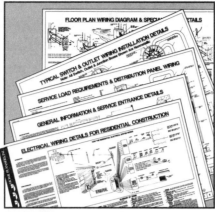

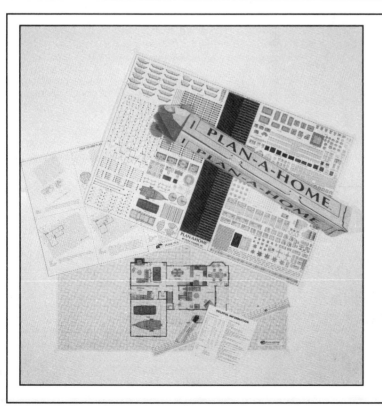

Price Schedule & Plans Index

These pages contain all the information you need to price your blueprints. In general the larger and more complicated the house, the more it costs to design and thus the higher the price we must charge for the blueprints. Remember, how-ever, that these prices are far less than you would normally pay for the services of a licensed architect or professional designer. By ordering our blueprints you are potentially saving enough money to afford a larger house, or to add those "extra" amenities.

To use the index below, refer to the design number listed in numerical order (a helpful page reference is also given). Note the price index letter and refer to the House Blueprint Price Schedule at right for the cost of one, four or eight sets of blueprints or the cost of a reproducible sepia. Additional prices are shown for identical and reverse blueprint sets, as well as a very useful Materials List for the plans.

House Blueprint Price Schedule
(Prices effective through December 31, 1992)

	1-set Study Package	4-set Building Package	8-set Building Package	1-set Reproducible Sepias
Schedule A	$180	$240	$300	$360
Schedule B	$210	$270	$330	$420
Schedule C	$240	$300	$360	$480
Schedule D	$270	$330	$390	$540

Additional Identical Blueprints in same order .....$40 per set
Reverse Blueprints (mirror image) ....$40 per set
Specification Outlines ....$5 each
Materials Lists...$35

To Order: Fill in and send the Order Form on page 317 — or call us **Toll Free 1-800-521-6797.**

316

Before You Order . . .

Before completing the coupon at right or calling us on our Toll-Free Blueprint Hotline, you may be interested to learn more about our service and products. Here's some information you will find helpful.

Quick Turnaround

We process and ship every blueprint order from our office within 48 hours. On most orders, we do even better. Normally, if we receive your order by 5 p.m. Eastern Time, we'll process it the same day and ship it the following day. Because of this quick turn-around, we won't send a formal notice acknowledging receipt of your order.

Our Exchange Policy

Since blueprints are printed in response to your order, we cannot honor requests for refunds. However, we will exchange your entire first order for an equal number of blueprints at a price of $20.00 for the first set and $10.00 for each additional set, plus the difference in cost if exchanging for a design in a higher price bracket. (Sepias are not exchangeable.) All sets from the first order must be returned before the exchange can take place. Please add $7.00 for postage and handling via UPS regular service; $10.00 via UPS 2nd Day Air.

About Reverse Blueprints (Mirror Image)

If you want to build in reverse of the plan as shown, we will include an extra set of reversed blueprints for an additional fee of $40. Although lettering and dimensions appear backward, reverses will be a useful visual aid if you decide to flop the plan.

Modifying or Customizing Our Plans

Many of our plans are customizable through our Home Customizer™ service (see page 320 for details), however if you need to make minor modifications to plans that are not customizable, these can normally be accomplished by your builder without the need for expensive blueprint modifications. However, if you decide to revise the plans significantly, we strongly suggest that you order our reproducible sepias and consult a licensed architect or professional designer to help you redraw the plans to your particular needs.

Architectural and Engineering Seals

Some cities and states are now requiring that a licensed architect or engineer review and "seal" your blueprints prior to construction. This is often due to local or regional concerns over energy consumption, safety codes, seismic ratings, etc. For this reason, you may find it necessary to consult with a local professional to have your plans reviewed. This can be accomplished with minimum delays and for a nominal fee.

Compliance with Local Codes and Regulations

At the time of creation, our plans are drawn to specifications published by Building Officials Code Administrators (BOCA), the Southern Standard Building Code, or the Uniform Building Code and are designed to meet or exceed national building standards.

Some states, counties and municipalities have their own codes, zoning requirements and building regulations. Before starting construction, consult with local building authorities and make sure you comply with all local ordinances and codes, including obtaining any necessary permits or inspections as building progresses. In some cases, minor modifications to your plans by your builder, local architect or designer may be required to meet local conditions and requirements.

Foundation and Exterior Wall Changes

Most of our plans are drawn with either a full or partial basement foundation. Depending upon your specific climate or regional building practices, you may wish to convert this basement to a slab or crawlspace. If your plan is customizable, we'll be happy to make this change for you. If not, most professional contractors and builders can easily adapt your plans to alternate foundation types. Likewise, most can easily convert 2x4 wall construction to 2x6, or vice versa. If you need more guidance on these conversions, our handy Construction Detail Sheets, shown on page 315, describe how such conversions can be made.

How Many Blueprints Do You Need?

A single set of blueprints is sufficient to study a home in greater detail. However, if you are planning to obtain cost estimates from a contractor or subcontractors — or if you are planning to build immediately — you will need more sets. Because additional sets are cheaper when ordered in quantity with the original order, make sure you order enough blueprints to satisfy all requirements. The following checklist will help you determine how many you need:

_____ Owner

_____ Builder (generally requires at least three sets; one as a legal document, one to use during inspections, and at least one to give to subcontractors)

_____ Local Building Department (often requires two sets)

_____ Mortgage Lender (usually one set for a conventional loan; three sets for FHA or VA loans)

_____ TOTAL NUMBER OF SETS

Canadian Customers: Order plans Toll-Free 1-800-848-2550. Or complete the order form at right, and mail with your check indicating U.S. funds to Home Planners, Inc., 3275 W. Ina Road, Suite 110, Tucson, Arizona 85741.

HOME ORDER FORM

HOME PLANNERS, INC., 3275 WEST INA ROAD SUITE 110, TUCSON, ARIZONA 85741

THE BASIC BLUEPRINT PACKAGE

Rush me the following (please refer to the Plans Index and Price Schedule in this section):

_____ Set(s) of blueprints for plan number(s) _____. $_____

_____ Set(s) of sepias for plan number(s) _____. $_____

_____ Additional identical blueprints in same order @ $40.00 per set. $_____

_____ Reverse blueprints @ $40.00 per set. $_____

_____ Home Customizer™ Kit(s) for Plan(s)_____ @ $19.95 per kit. $_____

IMPORTANT EXTRAS

Rush me the following:

_____ Materials List @ $35.00 $_____

_____ Specification Outlines @ $5.00 each. $_____

_____ Detail Sets @ $14.95 each; any two for $22.95; all three for $29.95 (save $14.90). $_____

❏ Plumbing ❏ Electrical ❏ Construction
(These helpful details provide general construction advice and are not specific to any single plan.)

_____ Plan-A-Home® @ $29.95 each. $_____

SUB-TOTAL $_____

SALES TAX (Arizona residents add 5% sales tax; Michigan residents add 4% sales tax.) $_____

POSTAGE AND HANDLING	1-3 sets	4 or more sets	
UPS DELIVERY (Requires street address - No P.O. Boxes)			
•UPS Regular Service Allow 4-5 days delivery	❏ $5.00	❏ $7.00	$_____
•UPS 2nd Day Air Allow 2-3 days delivery	❏ $7.00	❏ $10.00	$_____
•UPS Next Day Air Allow 1-2 days delivery	❏ $16.50	❏ $20.00	$_____
POST OFFICE DELIVERY If no street address available. Allow 4-5 days delivery	❏ $7.00	❏ $10.00	$_____
OVERSEAS AIR MAIL DELIVERY Note: All delivery times are from date Blueprint Package is shipped.	❏ $30.00	❏ $50.00	$_____
	❏ Send COD		

TOTAL (Sub-total, tax, and postage) $_____

YOUR ADDRESS (please print)

Name _____

Street _____

City _____ State _____ Zip _____

Daytime telephone number (_____)_____

FOR CREDIT CARD ORDERS ONLY

Please fill in the information below:

Credit card number _____

Exp. Date: Month/Year _____

Check one ❏ Visa ❏ MasterCard ❏ Discover Card

Signature _____

Order Form Key   Please check appropriate box:

TB16BP   ❏ Licensed Builder-Contractor
                  ❏ Home Owner

 ORDER TOLL FREE 1-800-521-6797

Additional Plans Books

THE DESIGN CATEGORY SERIES

1.

ONE-STORY HOMES
A collection of 470 homes to suit a range of budgets in one-story living. All popular styles, including Cape Cod, Southwestern, Tudor and French. **384 pages. $8.95 ($10.95 Canada)**

2.

TWO-STORY HOMES
478 plans for all budgets in a wealth of styles: Tudors, Saltboxes, Farmhouses, Victorians, Georgians, Contemporaries and more. **416 pages. $8.95 ($10.95 Canada)**

3.

MULTI-LEVEL AND HILL-SIDE HOMES 312 distinctive styles for both flat and sloping sites. Includes exposed lower levels, open staircases, balconies, decks and terraces. **320 pages. $6.95 ($8.95 Canada)**

4.

VACATION AND SECOND HOMES 258 ideal plans for a favorite vacation spot or perfect retirement or starter home. Includes cottages, chalets, and 1-, 1½-, 2-, and multi-levels. **256 pages. $5.95 ($7.50 Canada)**

THE EXTERIOR STYLE SERIES

9.

330 EARLY AMERICAN HOME PLANS A heartwarming collection of the best in Early American architecture. Traces the style from Colonial structures to popular traditional versions. Includes a history of different styles. **304 pages. $9.95 ($11.95 Canada)**

10.

335 CONTEMPORARY HOME PLANS Required reading for anyone interested in the clean-lined elegance of Contemporary design. Features plans of all sizes and types, as well as a history of this style. **304 pages. $9.95 ($11.95 Canada)**

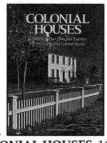

11.

COLONIAL HOUSES 161 history-inspired homes with up-to-date plans are featured along with 2-color interior illustrations and 4-color photographs. Included are many plans developed for *Colonial Homes'* History House Series. **208 pages. $10.95 ($12.95 Canada)**

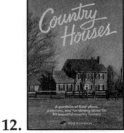

12.

COUNTRY HOUSES Shows off 80 country homes in three eye-catching styles: Cape Cods, Farmhouses and Center-Hall Colonials. Each features an architect's exterior rendering, artist's depiction of a furnished interior room, large floor plans, and planning tips. **208 pages. $10.95 ($12.95 Canada)**

PLAN PORTFOLIOS

MOST POPULAR HOME DESIGNS
Our customers' favorite plans, including one-story, 1½-story, two-story, and multi-level homes in a variety of styles. Designs feature many of today's most popular amenities: lounges, clutter rooms, media rooms and more.

14. 272 pages. $8.95 ($10.95 Canada)

AFFORDABLE HOME PLANS For the prospective home builder with a modest or medium budget. Features 430 one-, 1½-, two-story and multi-level homes in a wealth of styles. Included are cost saving ideas for the budget-conscious.

15. **320 pages. $8.95 ($10.95 Canada)**

LUXURY DREAM HOMES At last, the home you've waited for! A collection of 150 of the best luxury home plans from seven of the most highly regarded designers and architects in the United States. A dream come true for anyone interested in designing, building or remodeling a luxury home.

16. **192 pages. $14.95 ($17.95 Canada)**

NEW FROM HOME PLANNERS

5.

WESTERN HOME PLANS over 215 home plans from Spanish Mission and Monterey to Northwest Chateau and San Francisco Victorian. Historical notes trace the background and geographical incidence of each style. **208 pages. $8.95 ($10.95 Canada)**

6.

DECK PLANNER 25 practical plans and details for decks the do-it-yourselfer can actually build. How-to data and project starters for a variety of decks. Construction details available separately. **112 pages. $7.95 ($9.95 Canada)**

7.

THE HOME LANDSCAPER 55 fabulous front- and backyard plans that even the do-it-yourselfer can master. Complete construction blueprints and regionalized plant lists available for each design. **208 pages. $12.95 ($15.95 Canada)**

8.

BACKYARD LANDSCAPER Sequel to the popular *Home Landscaper*, contains 40 professionally designed plans for backyards to do yourself or contract out. Complete construction blueprints and regionalized plant lists available. **160 pages. $12.95 ($15.95 Canada)**

13.

VICTORIAN DREAM HOMES 160 Victorian and Farmhouse designs by three master designers. Victorian style from Second Empire homes through the Queen Anne and Folk Victorian era. Beautifully drawn renderings accompany the modern floor plans. **192 Pages. $12.95 ($15.95 Canada)**

17.

NEW ENCYCLOPEDIA OF HOME DESIGNS Our best collection of plans is now bigger and better than ever! Over 500 plans organized by architectural category including all types and styles and 269 brand-new plans. The most comprehensive plan book ever. **352 pages. $9.95 ($11.95 Canada)**

Please fill out the coupon below. We will process your order and ship it from our office within 48 hours. Send coupon and check for the total to:

HOME PLANNERS, INC.
3275 West Ina Road, Suite 110, Dept. BK
Tucson, Arizona 85741

THE DESIGN CATEGORY SERIES — A great series of books edited by design type. Complete collection features 1376 pages and 1273 home plans.

1. _____ One-Story Homes @ $8.95 ($10.95 Canada) $ _____
2. _____ Two-Story Homes @ $8.95 ($10.95 Canada) $ _____
3. _____ Multi-Level & Hillside Homes @ $6.95 ($8.95 Canada) $ _____
4. _____ Vacation & Second Homes @ $5.95 ($7.50 Canada) $ _____

NEW FROM HOME PLANNERS

5. _____ Western Home Plans @ $8.95 ($10.95 Canada) $ _____
6. _____ Deck Planner @ $7.95 ($9.95 Canada) $ _____
7. _____ The Home Landscaper @ $12.95 ($15.95 Canada) $ _____
8. _____ The Backyard Landscaper @ $12.95 ($15.95 Canada) $ _____

THE EXTERIOR STYLE SERIES

9. _____ 330 Early American Home Plans @ $9.95 ($11.95 Canada) $ _____
10. _____ 335 Contemporary Home Plans @ $9.95 ($11.95 Canada) $ _____
11. _____ Colonial Houses @ $10.95 ($12.95 Canada) $ _____
12. _____ Country Houses @ $10.95 ($12.95 Canada) $ _____
13. _____ Victorian Dream Homes @ $12.95 ($15.95 Canada) $ _____

PLAN PORTFOLIOS

14. _____ Most Popular Home Designs @ $8.95 ($10.95 Canada) $ _____
15. _____ Affordable Home Plans @ $8.95 ($10.95 Canada) $ _____
16. _____ Luxury Dream Homes @ $14.95 ($17.95 Canada) $ _____
17. _____ New Encyclopedia of Home Designs @ $9.95 ($11.95 Canada) $ _____

Sub-Total $ _____
Arizona residents add 5% sales tax; Michigan residents add 4% sales tax $ _____
ADD Postage and Handling $ 3.00
TOTAL (Please enclose check) $ _____

Name (please print) _____

Address _____

City _____ State _____ Zip _____

CANADIAN CUSTOMERS: Order books Toll-Free 1-800-848-2550. Or, complete the order form above, and mail with your check indicating U.S. funds to: Home Planners, Inc., 3275 W. Ina Road, Suite 110, Tucson, AZ 85741.

TO ORDER BOOKS BY PHONE CALL TOLL FREE 1-800-322-6797

TB16BK

The Home Customizer™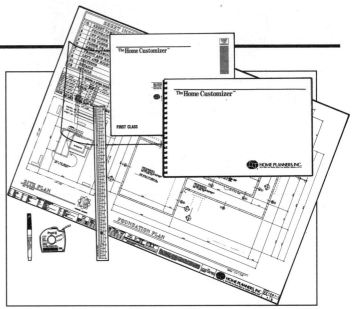

Many of the plans in this book are customizable through our Home Customizer™ service. Look for this symbol 🏠 on the pages of home designs. It indicates that the plan on that page is part of The Home Customizer™ service.

Some changes to customizable plans that can be made include:

- exterior elevation changes
- kitchen and bath modifications
- roof, wall and foundation changes
- room additions
- and much more!

If the plan you have chosen to build is one of our customizable homes, you can easily order the Home Customizer™ kit to start on the path to making your alterations. The kit, priced at only $19.95, may be ordered at the same time you order your blueprint package by calling on our toll-free number or using the order blank on page 319. Or you can wait until you receive your blueprints, spend some time studying them and then order the kit by phone, FAX or mail. If you then decide to proceed with the customizing service, the $19.95 price of the kit will be refunded to you after your customization order is received. The Home Customizer™ kit includes:

- instruction book with examples
- architectural scale
- clear acetate work film
- erasable red marker
- removable correction tape
- ¼" scale furniture cutouts
- 1 set of Customizable Drawings with floor plans and elevations

The service is easy, fast and *affordable*. Because we know and work with our plans and have them available on state-of-the-art computer systems, we can make the changes efficiently at prices much lower than those charged by architectural or drafting services. In addition, you'll be getting custom changes directly from Home Planners—the company whose dedication to excellence and long-standing professional experience are well recognized in the industry.

Call now to learn more about how simple it can be to have the *custom home* you've always wanted.

The Home Customizer™ kit contains everything you'll need to make your home a one of a kind.

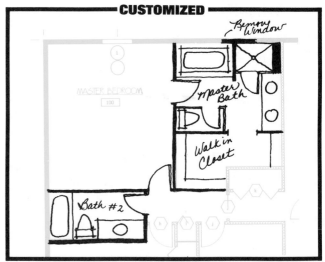

Making interior changes to the floor plan is simple and fun using the tools provided in The Home Customizer™ kit!

Look for this symbol next to Home Planners' designs that are customizable.

CALL TOLL-FREE **1-800-322-6797** EXT. 134

Custom Alterations? For information about how easily this plan can be altered — at rates surprisingly below standard architectural fees — call our Home Customizer Specialist at **1-800-322-6797**.